Managing High Performance Sport

- How can managers design and implement effective high performance programmes in sport?
- What are the key challenges in managing elite athletes, sports people and teams?

This is the first book to provide a comprehensive introduction to management practice, process and policy in elite and high performance sport (HPS). Drawing on real-world case studies of elite sport around the world, the book shows a conceptual framework for studying and analysing HPS and introduces the skills and techniques that managers and administrators will need to develop effective HPS programmes.

The book examines the macro level factors that determine a nation's sporting success, including political, social and cultural elements, and then moves on to unpack the specifics of elite athlete and team management at a micro level. Adopting an integrated, holistic approach throughout, the book highlights best practice in every key area of an HPS programme, including:

- defining performance and success
- organizational structure and leadership
- finance, funding and marketing
- coaching and coach development
- talent identification and development
- competition and events
- training and facilities
- scientific research and sport science support.

The book features contributions from world-leading sport management academics as well as practitioners with experience of managing HPS programmes at world and Olympic level. Each chapter includes a full range of useful features, such as summaries, case studies, review questions and guides to further reading. This is essential reading for all serious students and professionals working in sport management or high performance sport.

Popi Sotiriadou is Senior Lecturer at the Department of Tourism, Hotel and Sport Management, Griffith Business School, Griffith University, Australia.

Veerle De Bosscher is a Professor in and Management, Vrije Universiteit Brussel, Belgium.

Foundations of Sport Management

Series Editors:
David Hassan, University of Ulster at Jordanstown, UK
Allan Edwards, Griffith University, Australia

Foundations of Sport Management is a discipline-defining series of texts on core and cutting-edge topics in sport management. Featuring some of the best known and most influential sport management scholars from around the world, each volume represents an authoritative, engaging and self-contained introduction to a key functional area or issue within contemporary sport management. Packed with useful features to aid teaching and learning, the series aims to bridge the gap between management theory and practice and to encourage critical thinking and reflection among students, academics and practitioners.

Also available in this series

Managing Sport Business: An Introduction
David Hassan and Linda Trenberth

Managing Sport: Social and Cultural Perspectives
David Hassan and Jim Lusted

Managing High Performance Sport
Popi Sotiriadou and Veerle De Bosscher

Managing High Performance Sport

Edited by
Popi Sotiriadou and
Veerle De Bosscher

Routledge
Taylor & Francis Group

LONDON AND NEW YORK

First published 2013
by Routledge
2 Park Square, Milton Park, Abingdon, Oxon OX14 4RN

Simultaneously published in the USA and Canada
by Routledge
711 Third Avenue, New York, NY 10017

Routledge is an imprint of the Taylor & Francis Group, an informa business

British Library Cataloguing in Publication Data
A catalogue record for this book is available from the British Library

Library of Congress Cataloging in Publication Data
Managing high performance sport/edited by Popi Sotiriadou
  and Veerle De Bosscher.
    p. cm.—(Foundations of sport management)
    1. Sports—Management. 2. Sports—Coaching. 3. Sports sciences.
    4. Sports—Physiological aspects. 5. Performance. I. Sotiriadou, Popi.
    II. Bosscher, Veerle de.
    GV713.M3615 2012
    796.06′9—dc23
    2012024066

ISBN: 978-0-415-67195-8 (hbk)
ISBN: 978-0-415-67199-6 (pbk)
ISBN: 978-0-203-13238-8 (ebk)

Typeset in Perpetua and Bell Gothic
by Florence Production Ltd, Stoodleigh, Devon, UK

Contents

CONTENTS

Tables

Figures

FIGURES

Foreword

This book is a milestone. It marks an important point in the evolution of the thinking and the systems that can be applied to the development of sport.

Historically (to my mind at least) sport began as a relatively structured process for activities, or games, to be played in a competitive environment for the purposes of recreation, and perhaps to fulfil the need to be active, maintain fitness, and provide social opportunities for bonding, identification as a group and self-esteem through achievement. The idea of professionalism in sport appeared early – think of the gladiators of Ancient Rome and then the 'champions' of medieval Europe who went from one jousting tournament to another – and inevitably the focus shifted from participation for its own sake to the pursuit of excellence. There was a transition from 'player' to 'player as athlete', and athletes and teams became engaged in regular training for competition, supported by specific training for strength or skill or tactics. The development of full-time coaches became important.

Associated with this was the development of systems of governance of sport, to provide the framework for sport to flourish, and to protect sport from those influences that would see it corrupted or otherwise negatively affected. Ethics, the protection of the rights of the individual, the health and safety of competitors and players, issues around doping and fairness in sport became better described and managed. As sport became more sophisticated it was broadened proactively to include participants from across the community and attention was paid to the disabled, those with long-term medical conditions, and the (so-called) special interest groups – children, the older athlete and (dare I say) women (with questions around exercise and pregnancy, for example, being examined).

There was also the need for experts to provide the services and the support required for excellence in competition – and these experts are now becoming more and more specialized, especially with the recognition of sport as a national enterprise. High performance sport managers, administrators, policymakers, sport scientists and sports physicians, coach development specialists and sports lawyers are all part of the mix in this new sporting environment.

Sport is important to nations for a variety of reasons, and international competitiveness is seen as a mark of prestige and national pride. High performance sport development is about competitiveness and excellence, and underpins this national aspiration.

High performance sport is showcased by professional competitions, and major international events such as the Olympic Games and World Cups. The development of high performance sport from the grassroots to the elite is now a focus for those who want to take sport to its ultimate in terms of excellence and in its capacity to provide opportunities for whole nations.

Hence this book. The editors have assembled a range of authors from around the globe who are all well versed and highly regarded in their areas of expertise. The emphasis is to provide a thoughtful analysis of the various threads of the fabric of high performance and then to present a synthesis of thinking on the applications of these fundamental elements to the development of high performance systems.

The concept of the pathway for athletes runs through the book, and the matrix of services and systems that underpins success is described by way of discussion in the text and by case studies and recommended reading.

The book provides a 'macro' view of high performance and then moves through to 'meso' and 'micro' views to take the reader through a logical series of discussions and provide a framework for thinking on just how development of high performance sport can work.

I am delighted to introduce this book to you. It will sit very nicely on any bookshelf and will be a constant source of reference for the practitioner.

Professor Peter Fricker OAM
MBBS FACSP FRACP (Hon.) FFSEM (UK) (Hon.)
Director, Australian Institute of Sport 2005–2011
Chief Sports Medicine Advisor, Office of the President
Aspire Zone Foundation, Doha, Qatar

Preface

Popi Sotiriadou

Griffith University, Australia

Veerle De Bosscher

Vrije Universiteit Brussel, Belgium

As the discipline of sport management matures, high performance sport management emerges as a swiftly developing branch of knowledge. The high performance industry and sport practitioners are leading the way by adopting practices that recognize the significance of managing high performance sport. Indicative of these practices is also the recognition and establishment of the role of high performance directors on athlete performance. These shifts in industry practices (i.e. hiring high performance directors and placing an emphasis on high performance management practices) have not been matched with an equivalent focus of academic inquiry that would help define the field, distinguish it from other fields and illustrate its significance in empirical ways. Chapter 1, written by Popi Sotiriadou, represents the start of an inquiry into defining the discipline of managing high performance sport and the roles of high performance directors in athlete success.

The book uses the funnel of high performance sport management (HPSM) illustrated in Figure A overleaf. The funnel of HPSM is a conceptual framework for examining, studying or analysing HPSM in this book.

The funnel of HPSM comprises three interrelated components: (a) high performance management of elite sport (Part A of this book); (b) managing high performance athletes (Part B of this book); and (c) issues in the management of high performance sport (Part C of this book). The funnel of HPSM implies that athlete performance (at the lowest part of Figure A) is a factor of all three components. Unquestionably, performances at top-level sports are the result of a combination of the broader environmental and physical circumstances in which people live; the opportunities they are offered to excel through sport systems; the genetic qualities they are born with; and other athlete related issues. Accordingly, the factors that contribute to international sporting success can be classified into three different levels. The macro-level (Part A: High performance management of elite sport), the micro-level (Part B: Managing high performance athletes) and the high-performance environment (Part C: Issues in the management of high performance sport). Factors at each level are systematically considered in the three parts of this book.

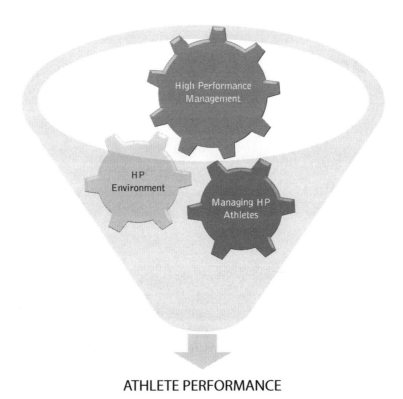

ATHLETE PERFORMANCE

Figure A *The funnel of high performance sport management*

PART A: HIGH PERFORMANCE MANAGEMENT OF ELITE SPORT (CHAPTERS 2–7)

Macro-level factors reflect the different political ideologies, and social and cultural factors that impact the systems, policies and athlete pathways. As described by Barrie Houlihan in Chapter 2, these factors are closely intertwined and affect the operation of national and international organizations at the public, not-for-profit or commercial sectors. The management context of high performance sport is consequently complex. This is also related to the complexity of measuring success or output in elite sport, as demonstrated by Simon Shibli, Veerle De Bosscher, Maarten van Bottenburg and Hans Westerbeek in Chapter 3. The authors illustrate the various layers of performance. They use the Beijing 2008 Olympic Games as a case to describe the different methods of measuring performance output. As not all nations win medals at Olympic Games, the authors propose alternative measures of success, such as season's best performance. Then, in Chapter 4, Veerle De Bosscher, Maarten van Bottenburg and Simon Shibli search for answers to how to best manage sporting success, and conclude that nine pillars of national policies represented in their 'SPLISS' model help explain national sporting successes. The SPLISS model presents a useful tool for the evaluation of effectiveness in other contexts, such as the level of national sport organizations, clubs, regions or even commercial teams. The 'mix and match' of these policy factors, or pillars, varies considerably across nations. This divergence of sport systems is demonstrated in Chapter 5 by Winston Wing Hong To, Peter Smolianov and Darwin Michael Semotiuk, who compare the high performance systems of the USSR and Russia, the United States of America, and Canada. They take the reader on a journey in time that explores what these countries have done to succeed in sport at the elite level.

From exploring the broader environment and policies around high performance sport, Part A of the book continues by offering accounts on high performance management from an organizational level. In Chapter 6, Jo Van Hoecke, Hugo Schoukens and Paul De Knop discuss the principles of effective management and quality management in high performance organizations, such as national sport organizations, professional clubs or youth academies. Following this, in Chapter 7, Lesley Ferkins and Maarten van Bottenburg illustrate how sport organizations, from local clubs to national bodies, government agencies, sport service organizations and professional teams around the world, need to be directed, controlled and regulated. The authors apply governance principles to an elite sport setting and make an important distinction between governance of organizations and governance between organizations.

PART B: MANAGING HIGH PERFORMANCE ATHLETES (CHAPTERS 8–12)

The micro-level is concerned with the qualities of individual athletes and their close environment, such as parents and friends. The management of these individuals is the theme of the second part of this book. In order to manage high performance athletes, high performance directors need first to develop systems and processes that would attract, retain and nurture these athletes. In Chapter 8, Popi Sotiriadou and David Shilbury explain how sport development processes form the backbone of athlete development in high performance sports. The authors present an empirically delivered sport development model – the attraction, retention/transition and nurturing (ARTN) process – and discuss the stakeholders involved in shaping sport development pathways. In Chapter 9 Paul Wylleman, Anke Reints and Paul De Knop stress that high performance requires both talent and a system. They use a holistic approach to describe how athlete success is influenced by various transitions and stages during athletic and academic development. The chapter also offers an understanding on how to use their lifespan model to optimize the chances for smooth transitions, and the continued development of the athlete's elite sport career. Peter Fricker, in Chapter 10, adds to this discussion of athlete transition by an elaborate examination of the nature of sports sciences and sport medicine, and the counselling services that can be provided to athletes and coaches in a high performance environment. Most importantly, Chapter 10 links the roles of the coach to the role of the high performance director and the relationship between service provision and high performance coordination.

The role of coaches and the requirements to be a successful high performance coach receive further attention in Chapter 11. In this chapter, Dave Collins, John Trower and Andrew Cruickshank explain the changes in coaching systems at different stages of athlete or coaching careers. An athlete can only be as successful as his or her own retirement from sports. In support of this proposition, Anke Reints and Paul Wylleman close Part B of this book with Chapter 12 by identifying the factors that facilitate adjustment to post-athletic careers. The authors recognize and discuss the importance and availability of career support services to athletes.

PART C: ISSUES IN THE MANAGEMENT OF HIGH PERFORMANCE SPORT (CHAPTERS 13–15)

High performance sports operate in fast changing and highly volatile environments where athletes and teams are exposed to pressures from media, sponsors, society, coaches, peers and family to mention a few. This environment, as Hans Westerbeek and Allan Hahn explain in Chapter 13, is driven by economic values that lead to the commercialization and globalization of aspects of high performance sports. Chapter 13 presents the main trends, pressures and responses by institutes, government bodies and sport businesses. Also, the authors explain how these developments have led to the emergence of a sub-industry of high performance experts, agents, coaches and consultants. In Chapter 14, Dag Vidar Hanstad and Svein S. Andersen discuss another just as critical issue in high performance sport. They explore the management of a major sport event from the perspective of a participating team. They present a framework to identify risk management issues and to implement risk minimization strategies. In the last chapter of this book and in closing Part C, Jason Mazanov tackles a long-standing concern: the prevention of performance-enhancing substances and uses in sports. Using an innovative approach, the author provides high performance directors with the necessary background to make policy and operational decisions around the role of performance-enhancing drugs in their programmes.

David Lavallee's concluding comments in the Afterword are undoubtedly the pinnacle in this book. After reading this volume, in his review, David notes the potential of this book to have a wide appeal to readers of various backgrounds. More importantly, he foresees the theoretical and practical implications of the content in this book in the ways that knowledge in the field of managing high performance is being shaped. Also, he projects and illustrates (see Figure B on p. 297) the intellectual influences and challenges this book may present to researchers, students and practitioners in managing high performance sport.

Contributing authors

CHAPTER AUTHORS

Svein S. Andersen
Norwegian Business School, Norway
(Chapter 14)

Svein S. Andersen is a professor of organization studies at the Norwegian Business School, BI and adjunct professor at the Centre for Training and Performance, Norwegian School of Sport Sciences. He has been director for the Centre for EU research, University of Oslo, and chair of the Department of Leadership and Organizational Behaviour as well as Dean of studies at the Norwegian Business School. He has a Ph.D. from Stanford University. In recent years his research has focused on leadership and organization in Nordic elite sport.

Maarten van Bottenburg
Utrecht University, Netherlands
(Chapters 3, 4 and 7)

Maarten van Bottenburg studied sociology at the University of Utrecht and Amsterdam in the Netherlands. In 1994 he obtained his Ph.D. in the social sciences with a thesis on the differential popularization of sports. Since 2002, he has been the research director of W.J.H. Mulier Institute, Centre for Research on Sports in Society, a joint venture of the University of Amsterdam, University of Groningen, Tilburg University and Utrecht University. In 2004, he was appointed professor of sociology of sport at Utrecht University and professor of sport business at Fontys University of Applied Sciences. Maarten has published several books and reports in the field of the sociology of sport and sports management.

Dave Collins

University of Central Lancashire, United Kingdom
(Chapter 11)

Following careers in the military, teaching, research and elite sport, Dave now combines performance consultancy with a university professorship. Previously Performance Director of UK Athletics, Dave has worked with over sixty World and Olympic medallists, plus professional performers across a variety of domains. His research interests encompass many aspects of performance promotion, including elite cultures, professional training and expertise, resilience and skill change/refinement.

Andrew Cruickshank

University of Central Lancashire, United Kingdom
(Chapter 11)

After four years' playing experience with Scottish Premier League side Hibernian FC, two as a professional, Andrew began to pursue a career in sport psychology in 2004. He joined UCLan's Institute of Coaching and Performance as a researcher in April 2010, and his current work examines the culture change process in elite team environments. From an applied perspective, Andrew has also held head coach roles in university football and has provided sport psychology consultancy across a range of sports, including the elite levels of motor sport, judo and mountain biking.

Veerle De Bosscher

Vrije Universiteit Brussel, Belgium
(Preface, Chapters 3 and 4; Case studies 4.1, 6.2 and 8.2)

Veerle De Bosscher is professor at the Department of Sports Policy and Management (Faculty of Physical Education) in the Vrije Universiteit Brussel (VUB), Belgium. She researches in the area of sport and elite sport policies, international comparisons, measuring competitiveness and benchmarking of nations, on which she has published several articles and books. She is coordinating an international network of research cooperation in high performance sport, including over fifteen nations, SPLISS: Sports Policy Factors Leading to International Sporting Success, which was also the subject of her Ph.D. Veerle is a board member of the European Association for Sport Management (EASM) and of the Steering Committee of elite sport in Flanders.

Paul De Knop

Vrije Universiteit Brussel, Belgium
(Chapters 4, 6 and 9; Case study 9.3)

Paul De Knop has a Ph.D. in Physical Education at the Faculty of Physical Education of Vrije Universiteit Brussel (VUB), Belgium. He graduated in leisure studies at the same university and earned a Master's degree in Sports Sociology and Sports Management from the University of Leicester (UK). He is a full-time professor at the VUB and was dean of the Faculty of Physical Education.

In October 2008 he was elected as the Rector Magnificus of the VUB.

He was chairman of the board of BLOSO (Flemish sports administrative body) from 1999 to 2006, and has been chairman of the RAGO (Council of the Community Education of Flanders) since 2002 and deputy chief of cabinet to the Flemish minister of Sport since 2004. Furthermore, he is coordinator of a 'Top Level Sport and Studies' programme at the Vrije Universiteit Brussel, and project manager of two sport centres. Teaching includes areas of sport, leisure and physical education from a socio-pedagogical perspective. Research interests are: youth and sport, sport and ethnic minorities, sport and tourism, sport management, quality in sport and sport policy. He has used qualitative research in studies related to:

- ethic and qualitative aspects of youth sport;
- sport for underprivileged youth;
- sport for Islamic minority girls;
- motives of sport tourists;
- benchmark of top-level sport success;
- top-level sport students at the university;
- competencies of sport managers;
- sport policy strategic plans; and
- evaluation of physical education programmes.

Paul De Knop has realized two sport centres as private–public partnership (PPP) projects on the VUB campus, was the architect of the '250 million euro DBFM(O)-sport infrastructure plan' of the Flemish government, is author of a book on PPP, is the project leader of a DBFM(O)-hotel project on campus and has delivered several keynote speeches and recommendations on PPP.

Lesley Ferkins

Deakin University, Australia
(Chapter 7)

Dr Lesley Ferkins is senior lecturer in sport management at Deakin University, Melbourne, Australia. Her area of specialization is the governance of sport organizations, a primary focus of her teaching and research. Lesley has worked closely with the boards of national and state sport organizations in New Zealand and Australia and has held the position of president of the Sport Management Association of Australia and New Zealand (SMAANZ). Prior to joining Deakin University, Lesley was Postgraduate Head and Senior Lecturer within the School of Sport and Recreation at AUT University in Auckland, New Zealand and spent nine years at Unitec New Zealand as Programme Director and Senior Lecturer in the School of Sport. Lesley has presented at numerous conferences around the globe and has published in the world's top sport management journals (*Journal of Sport Management* and *Sport Management Review*).

Peter Fricker

Australian Sports Commission, Australia
(Foreword, Chapter 10)

Dr Fricker is currently Chief Sports Medicine Advisor, Office of the President, Aspire Zone Foundation, in Doha, Qatar. He advises on strategy for sports science, sports medicine, research and technology. From 2005 to 2011 he served as the Director of the Australian Institute of Sport and as Acting Chief Executive Officer of the Australian Sports Commission. He is a Fellow (and Past President) of the Australasian College of Sports Physicians and has been awarded Honorary Fellowships of the Royal Australian College of Physicians and the Faculty of Sport and Exercise Medicine in the United Kingdom. He has a long history of involvement as Medical Officer and Medical Director of Australian Olympic Teams (1988–2004) and Commonwealth Games Teams (1986–2006). He serves on the Australian Olympic Committee Medical Commission and chaired the Medical Commission of the Australian Commonwealth Games Association. He has also served on the Australian Sports Drugs Medical Advisory Committee and Australia's Antidoping Research Panel. He has served appointments as Adjunct Professor to the Australian National University Medical Faculty, to the University of Canberra Faculty of Science and Design and the University of North Carolina at Greensboro Faculty of Medicine. He has written and co-edited three textbooks and a book on lifestyle and health, together with numerous book chapters on sports medicine and sports science. He also serves on a number of editorial boards of international journals and has published a large number of refereed papers on sports injuries, exercise and immunology, and sports medicine related topics generally. He has an interest in genetics and the athlete and has presented at a number of international conferences on this subject. He was awarded the Medal of the Order of Australia in 1993 and the Australian Sports Medal in 2001. He is also a Graduate of the Australian Institute of Company Directors.

Allan Hahn

Australian Institute of Sport, Australia
(Chapter 13; Case study 13.2)

Allan Hahn has recently stepped down as the Chief Scientist of the Australian Institute of Sport (AIS) in Canberra, Australia, where he worked for twenty-seven years. He now holds an honorary Emeritus position at the AIS. Allan is also Professor of Sport Partnerships at the Institute of Sport, Exercise and Active Living (ISEAL), Victoria University, a Professorial Research Fellow at the University of Canberra and the Research Leader for Coaching within the Centre of Excellence for Applied Sport Science Research at the Queensland Academy of Sport.

Dag Vidar Hanstad

Norwegian School of Sport Sciences, Norway
(Chapter 14; Case study 15.2)

Dag Vidar Hanstad is an associate professor in sport management and head of the Department of Social and Cultural Studies at the Norwegian School of Sport Sciences in Oslo. Hanstad was Sports Editor with *Aftenposten*, the biggest newspaper of Norway. His research interests include anti-doping policy, media, elite level sport and volunteerism.

Barrie Houlihan

Loughborough University, United Kingdom
(Chapter 2)

Professor Houlihan has degrees from the Universities of Liverpool and Salford. He taught courses in government and sociology in a secondary school for a year before moving to Millbank College of Commerce where he taught public administration. In 1979 he was appointed as lecturer in public administration at Staffordshire Polytechnic. During his time at Staffordshire University he was Principal Lecturer in Public Policy and later Head of the Division of International Relations and Politics. In 1994 he became Associate Dean of the School of Social Sciences and later Associate Dean of the School of Humanities and Social Sciences. In 1994 he was appointed Chair in Public Policy. Professor Houlihan has chaired, or been a member of, various committees for Sport England, UK Sport and the Centre for Social Justice. He has also undertaken consultancy work for the European Union, the Youth Sport Trust, the Department of Culture, Media and Sport, PEAUK, BAALPE, the Department for Education and Skills, the Council of Europe, the World Anti-Doping Agency, UK Sport, Sport England and Sport Scotland. In 2011 Professor Houlihan was elected a member of the Academy of Social Sciences.

David Lavallee

University of Stirling, United Kingdom
(Afterword)

David Lavallee is Professor and Head of the School of Sport. Prior to his appointment in July, 2011, he was Professor and Head of the Department of Sport and Exercise Sciences at Aberystwyth University from 2007 to 2011 and Professor of Psychology of Sport at Loughborough University.

His academic qualifications include a Master's degree from Harvard University and a Ph.D. from The University of Western Australia.

Jason Mazanov

University of New South Wales, Australia
(Chapter 15)

Dr Jason Mazanov is a Senior Lecturer with the UNSW-Canberra School of Business. Dr Mazanov is keenly interested in the social science of drugs in sport, and in the management of scandal in sport. He is also working to understand the role of performance enhancement in broader society. Dr Mazanov is a founding editor of the journal *Performance Enhancement and Health*.

Anke Reints

Vrije Universiteit Brussel, Belgium
(Chapters 9 and 12; Case study 9.3)

Anke Reints graduated in Psychology with a Ph.D. on the career development and transitions of former elite athletes at the Faculty of Psychology and Educational Sciences at the Vrije Universiteit Brussel. She graduated in 2006 in both Developmental Psychology (Universiteit Utrecht, The Netherlands) and Sport Psychology (Universiteit van Amsterdam, The Netherlands). In 2008 the International Olympic Committee privileged her Ph.D. study with a research grant on the provision of career support services worldwide. Anke has already presented at several international congresses on her research into the career development of elite athletes and on career support services. As a sport psychology consultant, Anke has worked with several talented tennis players in elite sport schools.

Darwin Michael Semotiuk

University of Western Ontario, Canada
(Chapter 5)

Darwin Michael Semotiuk is a Professor of Kinesiology at The University of Western Ontario (Canada). He earned a BPE (1963), MA (1965) at The University of Alberta and completed his Ph.D. at The Ohio State University (1970). He was a five-year stand-out for the football and basketball teams at the University of Alberta and was named male athlete of the year at the University of Alberta in 1967. He played for Canada's national basketball team from 1965 to 1966. Professor Semotiuk has served as co-editor for the *Journal of Comparative Physical Education and Sport* (JCPES), has been the Research Coordinator for the International Society for Comparative Physical Education and Sport (ISCPES) and was the President of ISCPES.

Simon Shibli

Sheffield Hallam University, United Kingdom
(Chapters 3 and 4)

Simon Shibli is Professor of Sport Management at Sheffield Hallam University where he is also the Director of the Sport Industry Research Centre (SIRC). Simon graduated from Loughborough University with a degree in Physical Education, Sports Science and Recreation Management in 1985. He is a qualified management accountant with the Chartered Institute of Management Accountants (CIMA). His research interests are in the fields of economics and finance applied to the sport and leisure industries.

David Shilbury

Deakin University, Australia
(Chapter 8)

Professor David Shilbury is the Foundation Chair in Sport Management and a former Head of the School of Management and Marketing (2002–2007) at Deakin University. Dr Shilbury commenced at Deakin University in 1990, and in 2000 was appointed as Australia's first professor of sport management. He has in excess of ninety publications including nine books and fifty-five refereed publications. Dr Shilbury was the Foundation President of the Sport Management Association of Australia and New Zealand (SMAANZ) from 1995 to 2001, was a member of the Australian Football League Tribunal from 1992 to 2003, a board member of the Confederation of Australian Sport in 2005 and a Trustee to the Bowater Trust from 2002 to 2007. He was editor of *Sport Management Review* from 2002 to 2004, associate editor of the *Journal of Sport Management* in 2011–2012 and is currently the Senior Associate Editor of *JSM*.

Hugo Schoukens

Vrije Universiteit Brussel, Belgium
(Chapter 6; Case study 6.1)

Hugo Schoukens is a Postgraduate in Sports Management from Vlekho Postgraduate School, Belgium, and earned an MBA of Sports Management from the University of Leicester (UK). He is Business Manager of Double PASS, a spin-off company of the Vrije Universiteit Brussel in the field of Quality and Performance Management in Sports.

Peter Smolianov

Salem State University, USA
(Chapter 5)

Peter Smolianov, Associate Professor at Salem State University, USA, went through the USSR system of athlete development and competed for Moscow Dynamo in the modern pentathlon, Moscow University in swimming and fencing, and in the United States for Brigham Young University in fencing. After managing elite athletes in preparation for the Sydney 2000 Olympics, he published and presented on high performance management in the *International Journal of Sport Management*, *Sport Science Bulletin*, and at Sport Management Conferences of Europe, North America, Australia and New Zealand.

Popi Sotiriadou

Griffith University, Australia
(Preface, Chapters 1 and 8; Case study 8.1)

Dr Sotiriadou is a Senior Lecturer and Undergraduate Program Director at Griffith University, Gold Coast, Australia. Popi's research has gained such acceptance that she has been invited to consult the Australian Sports Commission, Cycling Australia and Sarawak (Malaysia) on sport development. She has published her work in refereed journals including the *Journal of Sport Management*, the *International Journal of Sport Policy*, the *International Journal of Sport Management* (IJSM) and the *Sport Management Review*. She is on the editorial board for the IJSM and the *International Journal of Sport Management, Recreation and Tourism*. Popi is the Vice President of the *Sport Management Association of Australia and New Zealand* (SMAANZ).

Winston Wing Hong To

University of Western Ontario, Canada
(Chapter 5)

Winston Wing Hong To is a Doctoral (Ph.D.) student at the University of Western Ontario (Canada). He earned a BA[H] (2008) from the University of Windsor (2008) and an MSpMgt (2010) from Bond University. He has played rugby at university level and currently is an athlete in the sport of surf lifesaving. He has worked with sport organizations such as Lifesaving/Sauvetage Canada, Surf Life Saving Australia, Gold Coast Blaze, and has been a consultant to high performance sport athletes.

John Trower

University of Central Lancashire, United Kingdom
(Chapter 11)

John competed internationally in the javelin event in the late 1970s and early 1980s, until injury shortened his competitive career. John started coaching in 1986 and was the National Event Coach (Juniors) for the javelin in 1987. He coached Steve Backley from 1987 to his retirement after the Athens Olympic Games in 2004. Backley was successful at European, world and Olympic levels, and set two world records in javelin. He has coached other male and female elite javelin throwers and has extensive performance management experience in the other events. Currently he is a performance consultant and is the Elite Coach Mentor for UCLan's PG Dip in Elite Coaching Practice – a high-level coaching programme.

Jo Van Hoecke

Vrije Universiteit Brussel, Belgium
(Chapter 6; Case study 6.1)

Jo Van Hoecke (1972) has a Ph.D. in Physical Education (Sport Management) from the Vrije Universiteit Brussel (Belgium). He is Associate Professor at the Department of Sports Policy and Management of the Vrije Universiteit Brussel and teaches sport management and sport marketing. He is also Business/Product Manager of Double PASS, a spin-off company of the Vrije Universiteit Brussel in the field of Quality and Performance Management in Sports.

Hans Westerbeek

Victoria University, Australia
(Chapters 3 and 13)

Hans Westerbeek is the Director of the Institute of Sport, Exercise and Active Living (ISEAL) at Victoria University (VU) in Melbourne, Australia. He is Professor in Sport Business in VU's School of International Business and he also holds a part-time appointment at the Free University of Brussels (VUB) in Belgium as a Professor in Sport Management. He has also served as the Head of the School of Sport, Tourism and Hospitality Management at La Trobe University. Before migrating to Australia in 1994, he worked as a marketing professional in the Netherlands. He co-founded the European Association for Sport Management (EASM) and was a founding member of the European Union's European Network of Sport Science Institutes. Professor Westerbeek is an active researcher and consultant to a variety of international organizations.

Paul Wylleman

Vrije Universiteit Brussel, Belgium
(Chapters 9 and 12; Case study 9.3)

Paul Wylleman is professor at the Vrije Universiteit Brussel where he teaches sport psychology, mental support provision across the athletic career, psychological aspects of leisure, and human resources management and lifestyle management for elite athletes. He also heads the department 'Topsport and Study' that provides support to elite student-athletes in their combination of an academic and elite athletic career. Paul has more than 110 (peer-reviewed) publications to his name, and has been a keynote speaker at international congresses as well as at meetings of the IOC, EOC and NOCs presenting on the topic of, among others, career and lifestyle management of elite (young) athletes, the quality of sport psychology support service/providers and mental skills of elite athletes and coaches. Related to career and lifestyle management are his co-authored publications 'Career transitions in sport: International perspectives' and 'A developmental perspective on transitions faced by athletes'. Paul initiated and developed the 'Career support services' project that provides career support services for talented, elite and retired Flemish athletes with regard to the combination of study and elite sport and the post-athletic career. Finally, as sport psychology consultant, Paul works with talented and elite athletes at European and World Championships and the Olympic Games (e.g. tennis, figure ice-skating, swimming, judo, soccer).

CASE STUDY AUTHORS

In addition to the chapter authors, the editors would like to acknowledge the following case study authors:

Louise M. Burke (Case study 10.1)
Australian Sports Commission, Australia

Dirk De Clercq (Case study 10.2)
University of Ghent, Belgium

Stephanie De Croock (Case study 6.2)
Vrije Universiteit Brussel, Belgium

Lisa Gowthorp (Case study 9.2)
Australian Sports Commission, Australia

Jeff Greenhill (Case study 6.3)
Queensland Academy of Sport, Australia

Jason Harding (Case study 14.1)
Griffith University, Australia

Bruno Heyndels (Case study 4.1)
Vrije Universiteit Brussel, Belgium

Sue Hooper (Case study 6.3)
Queensland Academy of Sport, Australia

Adam Karg (Case study 7.1)
Deakin University, Australia

Johnny Maeschalck (Case study 15.1)
Van Landuyt & Partners, Belgium

Philippe Malcolm (Case study 10.2)
University of Ghent, Belgium

David Rouffet (Case study 13.1)
Victoria University, Australia

Hebe Schaillée (Case study 8.2)
Vrije Universiteit Brussel, Belgium

Megan Stronach (Case study 12.1)
University of Technology Sydney, Australia

Bill Sweetenham (Case study 5.1)
Gold Coast, Queensland, Australia

Kristel Taelman (Case study 9.1)
Bloso, Belgium

Jasper Truyens (Case study 4.1)
Vrije Universiteit Brussel, Belgium

Key terms and definitions

Athlete development   A process that encompasses the use of sport sciences, sport medicine, talent identification and coaching; requires the contribution of various interested groups in an array of specifically designed strategies and programmes targeted to those athletes that compete nationally and internationally; with the potential to create and regenerate involvement from governments, sponsors, participants, spectators, sports supporters and athletes themselves.

Board composition   How the board of a governing body is comprised with specific acknowledgement of the responsibility to govern on behalf of the members as 'owners'. There are three types of board composition models evident within sport organizations (i.e., representative, hybrid and independent).

Clinical sciences   The clinical sciences include medicine, physiotherapy, soft tissue therapy and massage, psychology and aspects of nutrition and dietetics. The focus is on performance enhancement through optimizing health and fitness.

Comparative HPS model   A research methodology that has a set of ingredients composed by an academic researcher or researchers to compare different HPS systems.

Confidentiality   Confidentiality refers to the protection of privacy of an individual who has provided personal information. Such information must be respected and only passed on to a third party with the written permission of the individual whose privacy is at risk.

Contrasting systems of governance   Refers to the notion that every country has developed its own system for the governance of high performance sport.

Elite athlete   An individual who has represented his or her country in a major international sporting competition (World Championships, Olympic Games).

Governance   A process in which an organization, network of organizations or a society steers itself, allocates resources and exercises control and coordination (Rosenau, 1995; Rhodes, 1996).

High performance   High performance refers to the process and outcomes of athletes and coaches in a daily training environment and in competition at the elite end of the spectrum of sport. Examples include professional sport, Olympic and Paralympic Games and World Championships.

HPS system   The communication or non-communication and organization of stakeholders (such as athletes, coaches, organizations, government) that focuses on HPS within a country.

Hybrid board model   Where there is a mix of elected board members and appointed board members.

Independent board model   Where board members are appointed, usually by an appointments panel, to govern on behalf of the membership at large.

Laissez-faire sport governance system   Refers to a country's system for the governance of high performance sport where there is little government intervention (e.g. the United States).

Member 'ownership'   Refers to individuals or organizations of a non-profit body that are legally recognized as members and, therefore, usually hold the right to direct who governs or governs on their behalf.

National Governing Body (NGB)   In general, we use the term 'National Governing Body' to describe the governing body for a specific sport (similar to federations and National Sport Organizations (NSOs)). The NGBs manage eligibility, rules and championships for their sport. Each NGB sanctions competitions in its country and those competitions follow NGB rules. Typical examples of NGBs include Athletics Canada, the Flemish Gymnastics Federation and the Lawn Tennis Association (also known as British Tennis).

National Olympic Committee (NOC)   The NOC for any given nation is the body recognized by the International Olympic Committee (IOC) to promote Olympism and to ensure that athletes from their nation attend the Olympic Games. Examples could be the Belgium Olympic and Interfederal Committee (BOIC) and the British Olympic Association (BOA).

National sport agencies (NSA)   The national sport agencies act as a leading organization working in partnership with others to promote sport generally or elite sport in particular. They can be governmental, quasi-governmental or non-governmental. For example, in the United Kingdom, UK Sport is the lead body for the development of elite sport. In some nations, for example the Netherlands, the National Olympic Committee and the umbrella organization for sport have merged to form a single body: NOC/NSF (National Olympic Committee/National Sport Federation).

Olympiatoppen   The central organization for elite sports within the Norwegian Olympic and Paralympic Committee and Confederation of Sports (NIF), with an overall responsibility for results in Norwegian elite sports.

Organization or administration   This can be defined as the people (or committees or departments, etc.) who constitute a body for the purpose of administering something, in this case the elite sport policy and development.

Organizational governance   Refers to governance of organizations, also known as corporate governance. These terms encompass the governance issues of steering, accountability and responsibility of a specific organization such as the governance of a local sport club or a national sport organization.

Performance director   In the elite sport climate survey, the performance director is the head of the elite sport department of a National Governing Body (or National Sport Organization/federation, see definition above), who manages elite sport development for a particular sport. Sometimes, when no such person is available (especially in smaller nations or smaller NGBs), it means the person responsible for sport development and elite sport development (e.g. development of the nine pillars) in general within that sport, or a sport technical director. In the overall sport policy inventory, a performance director can also be the head of the national sports agency (see above) that is responsible for elite sport. For example, Peter Keen is the Performance Director at UK Sport, Peter Fricker was the Performance Director at the Australian Institute of Sport.

Representative board model   Where board members are elected from specific member organizations/entities to represent those members.

Risk   The effect of uncertainty on objectives. Uncertainties include events (which may or not happen) and uncertainties caused by a lack of information or ambiguity.

Risk management   A systematic application of management policies, procedures and practices to the tasks of establishing the context, identifying, analysing, evaluating, monitoring and communicating risk. In the event literature the objective of risk management is to control the impact of unforeseen issues or accidents that take place within a project. Risk management is thus a proactive process.

Role and function of the sport board   Process by which the board sets strategic direction and priorities; establishes policies and performance expectations; characterizes and manages risk; and evaluates and monitors an organization's achievements on behalf of its 'owners' and stakeholders (Sport and Recreation New Zealand, 2006).

Sport development   A dynamic process in which stakeholder involvement (inputs) provides the necessary sport development strategies (throughputs) and pathways (outcomes) that facilitate the attraction, retention/transition and nurturing (ARTN) (i.e., sport development processes) of participants.

Sporting event   Events are often divided into categories, such as hallmark/mega events (e.g. Olympic Games), major events (international, national or regional) or local events (e.g. high school state championships). Categories are based on various evaluation criteria, such as volume of visitors, image effects and costs.

Sports science   Sports science is a collective term that covers the activity and application of servicing and research in the scientific disciplines. These include physiology, biomechanics, performance analysis, skill acquisition and decision making, recovery and aspects of strength and conditioning.

State interventionist sport governance system   Refers to a country's system for the governance of high performance sport where there is heavily centralized state intervention (e.g. Poland, China).

Systemic governance   Refers to governance between organizations and is related to the governance of high performance sport in a system, network or configuration of institutions.

Transition   An event or non-event which results in a change in assumptions about oneself and the world and thus requires a corresponding change in one's behavior and relationships (Schlossberg, 1981).

Voluntary sector sport governance system   Refers to a country's system for the governance of high performance sport where there is a combination of state, commercial and voluntary sector involvement (e.g. Australia).

Chapter 1

The roles of high performance directors within national sporting organizations

Popi Sotiriadou
Griffith University

INTRODUCTION

This chapter offers an understanding of the roles of high performance directors and the management processes that allow high performance sport to take place. These processes entail the ways leadership occurs in a high performance environment to ensure positive team and athlete culture, teamwork and success. The chapter is based on the results of a qualitative study on the roles and responsibilities of high performance directors and represents an effort to enhance the performance of leaders and managers in elite sport.

High performance sport is characterized by the effective amalgamation and synergy of elements including financial and managerial support, coaching, sport sciences and sport medicine support, talent identification and athlete pathways, training facilities and equipment, and competitions. Nations are becoming more strategic in the way they produce elite athletes (De Bosscher *et al.*, 2008). Consequently, national sport systems have moved beyond the mere application of sport sciences and coaching as a sole base for elite athlete success. There is a rapid recognition and overwhelming evidence to suggest that the 'new' point of difference and competitive advantage for nations is effective management and governance (e.g. Bayle and Robinson, 2007; Chelladurai, 2007; Ferkins *et al.*, 2005; Hoye, 2007; Hoye and Cuskelly, 2007) of high performance sport and all the processes involved.

Unquestionably, high performance sport and its management is a rapidly expanding profession in many countries around the world. High performance sport management is a billion-dollar industry, and one that continues to grow in size and sophistication. Although the number of athletes represented at this level of performance is marginal compared to the overall population, the number of stakeholders involved with high performance sport (e.g. specializing coaches, team directors, performance managers, administrators, sport agencies, sport organizations, individuals and beneficiaries, sponsors and media, governments and government agencies at all levels, academics and researchers, facility managers, team owners, athlete agents, sports and other scientists) is increasingly expanding to an industry that is becoming largely compound (Sotiriadou and Shilbury, 2009).

That expansion drives the need for a core of full-time experts to provide specialized administrative skills in response to the increasingly commercialized and professionalized high performance sport industry (Jones *et al.*, 2008). A similar trend occurred during the early 1990s when the growing complexity of sport led to an urgent need to upgrade the quality of sports administration through well-trained and educated sport managers (Shilbury and Kellett, 2011). The increased professionalism of sports and sport management practices since the early 1980s led to the introduction of sport management tertiary programs across many countries (Sotiriadou, 2011). Now specialization is taken one step further to introduce modules and courses on high performance sport management and the new generation of graduates is becoming equipped for this trend.

Although the field of sport management has been widely defined, the newly emerged concept of high performance sport management is in its infancy and its characteristics are far from clear. This chapter is the result of a study on high performance sport and high performance directors in an effort to respond to the need to fill this gap in an expanding field. The chapter acts as a vehicle for clarifying the concept of high performance sport management and the roles of high performance directors in elite sport.

STUDY AIMS AND METHODS

From the outset, the field of high performance sport recognized the role of coaching and the power of biomechanics in identifying talented athletes and improving athlete performance. Following the recognition of the role of coaching and biomechanics, other sport sciences, including nutrition, physiotherapy, psychology and more recently performance analysis, data mining and vocational guidance have taken high performance sport and athlete performances to new heights. Some of the influences of sport sciences and sport medicine in the 1960s and beyond resulted in successful talent identification programmes with great results for countries including East Germany and the former Soviet Union. These practices were subsequently adopted by various other countries. Even though coaching, sport sciences and sport medicine, and talent identification and development pathways remain essential for high performance sport, countries are always searching for other competitive advantages. It has now become apparent to countries that the coordination of all facets of high performance sport, from planning a national programme to executing it and reporting on it, is in the hands of high performance directors (or high performance managers). Professionalization demands running sport as business by business-based and experienced professionals. However, the field is still in its infancy. This explains the lack of common ground, definitions and understanding of the high performance director's roles, their profile and their relationships with other high performance stakeholders. This lack of knowledge limits the understanding of the ways high performance directors 'fit' within the high performance system and the extent to which high performance directors can foster athlete success.

In the management and business sector there is strong evidence (e.g. Fletcher and Arnold, 2011; Grude *et al.*, 2002) to suggest that when managers perform well the organization is more likely to be successful in achieving its goals. In fact, Fletcher and Wagstaff (2009) emphasize the importance to better understand organizational influences on athletic performance. More specifically, they concluded, 'the way individuals are led and managed will become an increasingly important factor in determining NSO's (national sporting organizations) success in Olympic competition' (p. 433). It can subsequently be argued that a similar relationship exists between high performance directors and their role in achieving excellence in the sport they manage and the success of athletes. Therefore, the aim of this study was to understand how the performance of directors may influence athlete performance. However, in order to test this assumption, it was deemed essential to take a step back and explore issues around: (a) defining high performance management and (b) identifying the roles and responsibilities of high performance directors. This chapter reports the findings on those two areas.

In view of the rather scant knowledge of high performance management and the role of high performance directors in elite sport, this study was deemed best suited to qualitative methods. Therefore, for the purposes of this inquiry the author collected rich, descriptive data that best allow an explorative approach (Silverman, 2006). Data to inform the aforementioned areas of inquiry were collected from two sources. First, in order to define high performance management and distinguish it from managing high performance, the existing literature was critically reviewed and evaluated. These findings are discussed in this chapter in the section titled 'High performance management and managing high performance athletes'.

Second, in order to profile high performance directors, their roles and their responsibilities for success of athletes/teams, nineteen position description documents from four countries representing a total of thirteen sports were collected and analysed. The four participating countries included Australia, Malaysia, Canada and the United States. Participating sports included Canoeing, Equestrian, Lacrosse, Badminton, Fencing, Biathlon, Squash, Water polo, Weight lifting, Triathlon, Volleyball, Athletics and Touch football. The countries, sports and data were selected based on the online availability of these public documents. In the data information was sought to answer two questions: 'What are the important considerations related to the high performance director role in elite sport?', and 'What qualities do directors require in order to successfully lead sport organizations and athlete to success?'. These results are reported in this chapter in the section titled 'High performance directors' roles and responsibilities'.

Deductive reasoning was used in order to review the extant literature on management, performance, excellence in sport with the purpose of defining high performance management and distinguishing it from managing high performance sport. Deductive reasoning facilitated the appellation of themes and dimensions in the aforementioned areas. Data from the position descriptions were analysed using inductive reasoning to foster innovation (Neuendorf, 2002). More specifically, 'thematic interpretational content analysis' (Gibbs, 2007) was used to analyse the documents. This approach has been previously used in performance leadership and management studies (e.g. Fletcher and Arnold, 2011) and allows the generation of new knowledge through the emergence of themes (Aronson, 1994). After collecting the data, the author extracted raw-data quotations from position descriptions pertaining to high performance directors' roles and detail on their role requirements. The raw themes that emerged after grouping the raw-data were divided into the *higher order themes* before including it into the general dimensions of (a) position summaries and reporting lines and (b) key high performance director roles and responsibilities.

3

HIGH PERFORMANCE MANAGEMENT OF ELITE SPORT (PART A OF THE BOOK) AND MANAGING HIGH PERFORMANCE ATHLETES (PART B OF THE BOOK)

Besides the infancy of the emerging subfield of management called high performance management, the intricacy of defining the area rests on the fact that it is not a single phenomenon. Rather, high performance management is a collection of phenomena that consists of management, performance, measuring management performance and, of course, excellence in high performance sport. In sport, performance management and its measures are often misunderstood and confused with managing performance and excellence. This section makes a distinction between these terms by defining them and pinpointing salient differences.

The purpose of performance management is 'to share understanding about what is to be achieved, to develop the capacity of people and the organization to achieve it, and to provide the support and guidance individuals and teams need to improve their performance' (Thorpe and Holloway, 2008, p. 88). Performance management is the process of identifying, measuring and developing the performance of individuals and teams and aligning performance with the strategic goals of the organization (Aguinis, 2009). Within an organizational context, measurement is the process of quantification (e.g. measures and key performance indicators) and actions that lead to achieving performance (Neely *et al.*, 2005). More specifically, performance measurement is seen as the development of indicators as well as data to describe, to report on and to analyse performance (Marshall *et al.*, 1999). The following section in this chapter and Figure 1.1 illustrate how the roles of high performance directors epitomize the overall understanding of performance management as explained here.

Managing high performance sport is the application of performance management processes to the context of high performance sport in order to obtain and maintain excellence in elite sport. These processes include planning, executing and monitoring the performance of a sports organization or a network of organizations and their athletes or teams. In this context, Fletcher and Arnold's (2011) findings 'highlight the multifaceted nature of orchestrating elite performance involving the development of a vision, the management of operations, the leadership of people, and the creation of a culture' (p. 234). More specifically, in order to sustain the highest levels of performance and excellence in their teams, 'leaders and managers must identify and disseminate their vision, optimize their resources and processes, challenge and support their people, and transform individuals' attitudes and group cohesion' (p. 238). The findings from the analysis of the position descriptions undeniably illustrate that high performance directors are responsible for delivering results in these areas that Fletcher and Arnold (2011) proposed.

Excellence in high performance sport is the label used to represent those performers who constitute the apex of the performance pyramid. The term is 'reserved for sporting performance by those sportsmen and women who constitute the highest levels of achievement in competition' (Lyle, 1997, p. 314). Lyle (1997) stressed that even though excellence in sport has overtones of a 'natural ability' school of thought in performance sport, unorganized activity is not sufficient to generate the conditions for sporting excellence. A sport 'system' is required as a measure of control and direction. A system can be defined as 'a whole, comprising interrelated parts that are intended to accomplish a clearly defined objective' (Lyle, 1997, p. 15) and this set of interrelated parts function as a whole to achieve a common purpose.

In conceptual terms, the management of sports performance can be conceived of as an input-throughput-output system (De Bosscher *et al.*, 2006). However, as international comparisons of high performance sport systems show, these systems are not only sport specific but, most importantly, country specific and are shaped by cultural, economic and political processes (De Bosscher *et al.*, 2009). To that end, Part C of this book covers a variety of contemporary issues within high performance environments (e.g. globalization, media, use of performance enhancing substances), their management and the ways these areas influence athlete performance.

Lyle (1997) suggested that the terms 'performance' and 'excellence' 'are used to categorize a broad sweep of performers but further refinement is necessary to identify those who are truly engaged in extending performance levels' (p. 315). In addition, there is an emerging body of literature that identifies the management of organizational-related issues as a significant distinguishing factor in achieving Olympic success (e.g. Fletcher and Wagstaff, 2009; Gould *et al.*, 2002). As the management of organizational-related issues rests with high performance directors, it now becomes clear that a need exists to better understand their pivotal role and their contribution to athlete success. Next, the chapter exemplifies the high performance directors' roles and responsibilities within the high performance environment they operate.

HIGH PERFORMANCE DIRECTORS' ROLES AND RESPONSIBILITIES

The results from analysing the high performance directors' position description documents offer a profound insight into the various job titles (e.g. high performance director or national programme director) that are being used to refer to the role and the reporting lines between various staff involved in high performance management. The results also enable us to draw position summaries, to identify differences in the responsibilities of different roles within high performance sport and to distil detail on high performance directors' key roles and responsibilities. Most importantly, the findings highlight some qualification requirements for high performance directors, and the skills they need to possess in order to be successful and lead successful teams. While more research is needed to identify more profound information on the roles and competencies of the high performance director, the framework below provides a first compilation.

Position summaries and reporting lines

The high performance director (HPD from here on) is accountable for the ongoing development and implementation of the national high performance programme or policy and the training programmes it encompasses. He or she provides the overall leadership to produce international success as demonstrated by podium performances at Olympic Games, World Championships, World Cups and other major international events. In addition, the HPD is responsible for the development of a strong, sustainable feeder system through which the next generation of champions is produced. In the sample countries and sports, the HPD reports directly to the General Manager and/or the Executive Director of the organization and submits reports to the Board via the Administration Director. HPDs supervise staff, including programme coaches and other coaching staff, the national elite development programme coordinators, the national programme directors, the team and the support staff, and the national technical director if available. However, not all HPDs supervise that many staff. For instance, in smaller countries, like Belgium, national sports associations (or else NSOs) have one HPD and some coaches only. Hence, the structure of the NSO and its governance determine the management functions and roles of HPDs.

In sports with various disciplines (e.g. equestrian or athletics) or in nations where there are various States or Territories (e.g. Australia), sport structures sometimes allow for the incorporation of another important person in the high performance system: the national programme director. To further illustrate, the high performance structure of equestrian may include a Dressage Programme (or performance) Director and a Jumping Performance (or programme) Director under the leadership of the HPD. Equally, a sport in Australia may have a program director for each state and territory under the supervision of the HPD. Therefore, the main difference between the role of the HPD and the national programme director is the scope of activity. National programme directors have responsibility for the development and implementation of their respective programme. They maintain training, competition and performance records of athletes or teams as part of a performance analysis system. The role of the national programme director is primarily a leadership and management role and not a direct coaching role. National programme directors work with the HPD and collectively they are responsible for the planning and delivery of all major campaigns such as Olympic Games, youth championships and other competitions.

HPDs' roles and responsibilities

The results further reveal six clusters of HPD key roles and responsibilities within their portfolio. These roles revolve around the key areas of: (a) national plan and programme(s), (b) personnel management, (c) budgeting and reporting, (d) high performance system development, (e) partnerships and relations and (f) event and competitions management. Each role cluster is inclusive of various responsibilities. Figure 1.1 shows there are two key dimensions of desired HPD roles and responsibilities. These are:

■ the capacity to work and interact with staff and clients using an *internal* and/or *external* focus; and
■ the application of *performance management processes* ranging from planning, to executing and monitoring (and implementing measurements within the process).

These two dimensions help shape a four-quadrant model. Figure 1.1 illustrates the roles of HPDs and the operating context under which these roles are performed. *Budgeting and reporting*, for instance, are located within the top-right quadrant as these processes are internal and relate predominantly to implementation and monitoring processes. More specifically, Figure 1.1 is an adaptation of the competing values framework (CVF) (Quinn and McGrath, 1982), which was used in this study in order to allow the interpretation of the findings. The CVF is a behavioural model that helps explain 'what I see as my role(s) and my effectiveness in delivering my roles' and 'what others see' in that regard. The CVF is used in this study because it has scales that have been validated previously for managers (Vilkinas and Cartan,

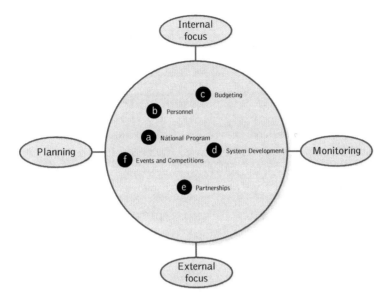

Figure 1.1 *The matrix of high performance director roles and responsibilities*

2006). Hence, the application of CVF in the context of the present study is fairly limited. To ensure the framework is appropriate to use in the content of high performance management and in order to improve the face and content validity, the required changes in language were made. The findings displayed as variables in Figure 1.1 are discussed now.

National plan and programme(s)

The HPD is 'responsible for the development, management and results of all national team programmes and initiatives and for the planning and execution of development programmes capable of producing future world-class national team athletes' (Biathlon Canada). That complicated task consists of various responsibilities. First, HPDs are responsible for designing and implementing a national elite plan as high performance development and programs are an essential part of the sports' wider policy or strategy. Second, HPDs need to continually review, refine and oversee the plan and programmes. Occasionally, and where training centres exist, HPDs are responsible for running them. HPDs need to maintain and build a strategy to ensure teams and individuals maximize their talent and achieve excellence on the international stage. Last, but not least, it is a requirement for HPDs to plan all national team or athlete activities and to document them in the high performance sections of the sports strategic, quadrennial and annual plans. As Biathlon Canada, for instance, stated it is essential that HPDs engage in 'conducting ongoing reviews and monitoring of high performance objectives contained in the approved strategic, quadrennial and annual plans, to confirm measurable outcomes'. Ensuring that the high performance programme provides a safe, respectful and appropriate sporting environment and that it is an enjoyable and rewarding experience for athletes and coaches helps focusing on a successful outcome at international level.

Personnel management

The HPD is responsible for developing and leading a team of high performance coaches and support staff, who themselves are responsible for developing junior and elite athletes from across a country (Australian Canoeing, Biathlon Canada). Developing such teams requires knowledge and understanding of staff recruitment issues including selecting carefully a team of staff members that will help achieve organizational and athlete success. Ultimately, HPDs should aim to maintain a focus of continuous improvement and build on the high standards already achieved. This focus is commonly provided through a clear and well communicated vision. Yet, the findings suggest that selection of 'the best' staff and the existence of a clear 'vision' are not adequate to lead to sustainable results and success. HPDs act as role models and use their people management skills to demonstrate a real belief in the potential of others and take active steps to encouraging others to achieve their potential. Therefore, HPDs need to inspire and lead their staff or teams to adopt leading edge approaches to their sport. Reinforcing a high performance culture is essential in that it encourages players and coaches to train and prepare like winners. It is that culture that facilitates taking risks in order to achieve personal excellence.

In order to achieve athlete and team success HPDs have to clearly articulate the rules and policies to athletes. These rules relate to athlete participation in the high performance programme(s), and establish functional communication channels and protocols with elite athletes. As HPDs work with an array of staff, it is critical to effectively communicate the goals and objectives of the organization, ensure that staff work closely with club and national coaches to help ensure athletes have proper training programmes, competitive structure planning and athletes are meeting performance targets. Overall, HPDs bring together staff and other stakeholders to work towards achieving common objectives.

Given the plethora of stakeholders that may be involved in high performance environments and the number of staff within sports organizations, HPDs need to establish effective group dynamics and be able to resolve situations of competitiveness and conflict to optimize group cohesion. Besides conflict resolution skills, HPDs are responsible for managing any issues relevant to athlete performance, behaviour or any other significant issues arising.

Budgeting and reporting

According to the position descriptions, all HPDs are required to implement the national high performance plan within the budgetary confines set by programme funding allocated and approved by the national sporting body or a national statutory authority for sports (e.g. the Australian Sports Commission). In this context, exercising appropriate financial delegation and monitoring financial operations of the high performance programmes become very important aspects of the role of the HPDs. In order to prepare annual operating reports, annual applications for financial assistance and other reports as required by all funding agencies, HPDs need sound financial and administration skills including report writing and financial analysis, accounting or financial experience. In addition, they need strong organizational skills to ensure, for instance, the maintenance of accurate and up-to-date records, database maintenance, reporting and athlete movement, and to coordinate the provision of financial reports to NSOs.

High performance system development

In most sports the well-being of the game at a junior level is a precondition for elite player professional growth and development. In order for sports to reinforce and secure a dominant position within the industry, HPDs need to build a strong youth development programme. An overarching role for HPDs is to 'serve as the lead for HP [high performance] sport development' (Biathlon Canada). In this role the HPD is responsible for systems that (a) coordinate, integrate and lead talent identification programmes, (b) develop, promote and implement structured athlete pathways to feed into the high performance system, (c) retain and nurture athletes and (d) optimize development for athletes and coaches at all levels of sport development pathways.

Talent identification, retention and transition is the process whereby a range of opportunities and other resources are offered to talented junior athletes with the ultimate aim of taking the most talented ones through to the highest levels of the professional game (Sotiriadou, 2010). The intent of the transition process is to 'fill the gaps in the elite athlete ranks, and through its pathways to the elite to produce and retain high numbers of elite athletes' (Sotiriadou, 2010, p. 207). In that process, HPDs work closely with the national coach and the high performance committee to select players for national teams and squads. During and following athlete selection, HPDs need to ensure they have developed policies, strategies and practices that improve the organization's competitive structure including, but not limited to, rankings, competitions and event management.

The transition of athletes into higher levels of performance and success and the embedded pathways required for this process to be successful are an essential job component for HPDs. The journey to the top does not occur in a vacuum. It is 'the pathways to the elite level that accommodate the retention and transition of talented athletes, their development and their smooth passage to the elite level which may foster long-term success' (Sotiriadou, 2010, p. 217).

An essential aspect of the role of HPDs is to develop resources and communication networks for athletes and officials to support their development. In their efforts to feed talent into high performance systems, HPDs are in contact and liaise with institutes and academies of sport, state associations where available, clubs, schools, talent identification programme providers and centres. In Australian Canoeing, for instance, HPDs establish relationships with surf clubs, schools and national talent identification programme providers. They engage in a network of representatives from various organizations and collaborate with Surf Life Savings Australia, state institutes and academies of sport, the Australian Institute of Sport and state sporting organizations.

Partnerships and relationships

Clearly, the range and depth of the HPDs' roles demands that they are capable of negotiating outcomes with partner organizations and optimize the contribution of a diverse range of stakeholders. Internally, for instance, they need to initiate, develop and maintain positive relationships with high performance coaches and seek their input and feedback where appropriate. Externally, they need to facilitate a collaborative and effective relationship with

9

programme partners to ensure the optimum daily training environment is available for athletes both locally and internationally. Overall, HPDs work closely with performance directors and with national head coaches, state institutes and state association and other coaches towards the coordination of athlete training and competition loads.

In that role HPDs need to establish success through agreed roles and standards around quality, quantity and type of training to be delivered by each level of coach at various times of the year. HPDs are responsible for the development of an effective communication system, information sharing and athlete tracking systems across national squads, national training centre and clubs. In this context, well-developed interpersonal, oral and written communication and people management skills are essential. Using their communication skills effectively, HPDs liaise with internal (e.g. Member Associations) and external clients (e.g. State Institutes of Sport and the Australian Institute of Sport), and a cross-section of partners including coaches, athletes, parents, peers, staff, support services personnel and other stakeholders.

Event and competition management

Competitions, events and tournaments are vital stepping stones and act as pathways to elite levels of playing a sport. The results from the position descriptions outline that HPDs are required to possess event management and coordination skills in order to plan for appropriate competitions, around the best time of the year and for the right athletes. Those skills are necessary because HPDs are asked to organize training camps, workshops, events, and establish an annual calendar of competition and training programme for athletes. In addition, HPDs may be required to help in the preparation of the various teams and players for events. Quite often they accompany teams to international competitions including World Cups, Championships and other major games. Administering aspects of competitions and travelling with teams requires HPDs not only to work under pressure to meet varying deadlines but also to be flexible, willing to work at non-business and irregular hours, and travel extensively both domestically and internationally.

DISCUSSION AND CONCLUDING THOUGHTS

The outcomes from analysing HPDs' roles and responsibilities point towards the need for HPDs to operate as a developer of human resources, and to recruit and develop staff and athletes. The findings also show that HPDs need to (a) collect data in programmes, (b) monitor how well athletes and others perform and (c) assess results and perform quality assurance. Nevertheless, what the overall findings suggest is that it all comes down to HPDs' capacity to deliver and 'get the job done'! HPDs need to ensure competitions are organized, events are set, plans and programmes are delivered. It is the HPDs' job to link the competitions calendar to the athletes' developmental programme, to send young athletes in the right competitions and to select the right athletes for providing support. Additionally, HPDs act as a broker with the external environment as they exert outside influence into professional groups, maintain external networks with organizations and institutes, and attend clinics for instance to attract athletes. All that, and much more, is usually performed under situations of high workload pressures that require HPDs to be resilient, flexible and able to travel and be called for duty at any point in time. Collectively, these traits exemplify the need for HPDs to illustrate through their roles personal drive and integrity. HPDs should display resilience, and take personal responsibility for meeting the organizations' objectives, lead by example and lead athletes to success.

In an effort to compare the findings of this inquiry with previous research, the lack of investigations on the field of high performance management from a managerial perspective leads to a broader search of literature. In that quest it was refreshing to discover the work of Fletcher and Arnold (2011) who, coming from a psychological angle, examined performance leadership and management in elite sport. In fact, scientists in organizational psychology (e.g. Fletcher and Wagstaff, 2009) seem to be leading the research in the area of managing high performance sport. Therefore, the findings of such studies propose significant messages to sport psychologists that may contribute to a more complete understanding of the psychosocial preparation of elite athletes. An added benefit of these works is advancing and broadening sport psychologists' competencies to provide more effectual support to the management staff of international sports teams. A limitation is the narrow applicability of findings to sport managers. The present study extends the implications of research findings to the discipline of sport management.

Similar to Fletcher and Arnold (2011), HPDs 'not only establish and express a team's ultimate aspiration, but also disseminate the vision, role model its message, and inspire individuals to invest in it' (p. 234). They found that one of the main roles of an HPD was the management of operations within the team, involving financial management, strategic competition and training planning, athlete selection for competition, and upholding rules and regulations. They further stress the instrumental role that HPDs have in managing these aspects of elite sport development and optimizing resources and processes. The present study adds to this knowledge as it offers key insights into these roles and details the responsibilities embedded within these roles.

A universal theme apparent throughout the work of Fletcher and Arnold (2011) was that effective performance leadership and management involves 'developing, inspiring, and challenging others to look beyond their own personal goals to the delivery of the team's vision' (p. 235). The present study complements these findings and similarly explains that influencing attitudes in terms of commitment to the team, and to a high performance culture, are important. Both studies view the creation of the team's culture as central to effective performance leadership and management. In addition, both studies reveal that creating a culture involves 'generating shared beliefs and expectations within the team via the development of role awareness and a team atmosphere' (p. 235). The findings of the present study on personnel management reveal further similarities to the findings of Fletcher and Arnold (2011). Personnel management involves recruiting the best team members, supporting and developing them continuously and enabling them to contribute in a meaningful way to the team's success.

Performance leadership at the managerial level of organizations has been considerably overlooked by sport management researchers who have tended to focus on coaching-related leadership (e.g. Chelladurai, 2007; Riemer, 2007). It is now starting to be recognized that athlete performance may not be solely the coaches' responsibility! HPDs have an increasingly significant role to play in facilitating and enhancing athlete performance. However, this premise has not been supported by adequate empirically based research. The study presented in this chapter analysed the meaning, significance and the evidence base for the ideas and terms associated with high performance management and managing high performance sport. Besides working towards shaping a definition for an emerging and distinct subfield of sport management, this chapter provides evidence on the roles and responsibilities of HPDs. These roles enhance the performance of staff, and improve high performance related operations and processes, hence the likelihood of athlete success. One of the most volatile jobs in the sport sector is the coach. Turnover is high as job retention largely depends on the performance of the team or players. As HPDs recruit the members of these teams, and that includes both staff and athletes, should then HPDs be on the lookout for new team members when their existing ones fail to live up to the expectations? More importantly, should the merit of both glory and failure of elite athlete success be shared between coaches and HPDs?

Even though this study is offering an insight into the area of high performance management, the findings and applications of the study are limited. This is due not only to the thin literature that is available in this area but also to the limited representation of the issues associated with performance in the data that were collected. As this is a preliminary study that explores the largely untapped sport management subfield of high performance management, there is a need for further research that would allow HPDs to reflect on these findings and discuss whether the identified responsibilities are a good representation of their roles per se or if there are additional required characteristics for their success. Moreover, a study that would use Personal Construct theory (Bannister and Fransella, 1986) and apply a Performance Profiling (Butley, 1989) approach to understand the way HPDs perceive their ability to perform is highly recommended as the way forward. Such study would result in more concrete interventions that focus on how leaders and managers create, optimize and maintain a high performance environment. In addition, for a fuller picture on the behaviours of HPDs and the way their performance is perceived by significant others, the CVF should be re-examined using a 360-degree feedback approach. A 360-degree feedback would include direct feedback from HPDs' subordinates, peers and supervisor(s), as well as a self-evaluation. This tool may lead to positive behaviour change and increase HPDs' performance.

At some point in its life cycle the discipline of sport management became so specialized that high performance management emerged as a new branch of learning. Such disciplinary moves may on occasions lead inquisitive researchers and practitioners who are scanning the intellectual horizons of sport management into an 'academic cul de sac'. This chapter is undoubtedly an intellectual opening to this roadblock. At the same time, the chapter represents the mere beginnings of an inquiry into this disciplinary opening on defining high performance management and the role of HPDs on athlete success. The infusion of further research and the generation of new knowledge will indeed offer confidence to translate findings into new ideas, tangible plans and actions. It is all in the years to come!

BIBLIOGRAPHY

Aguinis, H. (2009). *Performance management* (2nd edn.). Upper Saddle River, NJ: Prentice Hall/Pearson Education.

Aronson, J. (1994). A pragmatic view of thematic analysis. *The Qualitative Report*, 2(1), 1–4.

Bannister, D. and Fransella, F. (1986). Inquiring man: The psychology of personal constructs (3rd edn.). London: Routledge.

Bayle, E. and Robinson, L. (2007). A framework for understanding the performance of national governing bodies of sport. *European Sport Management Quarterly*, 7(3), 249–268.

Chelladurai, P. (2007). Leadership in sports. In G. Tenenbaum and R. C. Eklund (Eds.), *Handbook of sport psychology* (pp. 113–135). Hoboken, NJ: Wiley.

De Bosscher, V., Bingham, J., Shibli, S., van Bottenburg, M. and De Knop, P. (2008). *The global sporting arms race: An international comparative study on sports policy factors leading to international sporting success*. Aachen, Germany: Meyer & Meyer.

De Bosscher, V., De Knop, P., van Bottenburg, M. and Shibli, S. (2006). A conceptual framework for analysing sports policy factors leading to international sporting success. *European Sport Management Quarterly*, 6(2), 185–215.

De Bosscher, V., De Knop, P., van Bottenburg, M., Shibli, S. and Bingham, J. (2009). Explaining international sporting success: An international comparison of elite sport systems and policies in six countries. *Sport Management Review*, 12(3), 113–136.

Ferkins, L., Shilbury, D. and McDonald, G. (2005). The role of the board in building strategic capability: Towards an integrated model of sport governance research, *Sport Management Review*, 8, 195–225.

Fletcher, D. and Arnold R. (2011). A qualitative study of performance leadership and management in elite sport. *Journal of Applied Sport Psychology*, 23(2), 223–242.

Fletcher, D. and Wagstaff, C. R. (2009). Organizational psychology in elite sport: Its emergence, application and future. *Psychology of Sport and Exercise*, 10(4), 427–434.

Gould, D., Greenleaf, C. C., Chung, Y. C. and Guinan, D. (2002). A survey of US Atlanta and Nagano Olympians: Variables perceived to influence performance. *Research Quarterly For Exercise and Sport*, 73, 375–385.

Gibbs, G. (2007). *Analyzing qualitative data*. London: Sage.

Grude, J., Bell, D., Dodd, G. and Parker, O. (2002). Leadership: The critical key to financial success, *Drake Business Review*, 1, 1.

Hoye, R. (2007). Commitment, involvement and performance of voluntary sport organization board members. *European Sport Management Quarterly*, 7(1), 109–121.

Hoye, R. and Cuskelly, G. (2007). *Sport governance*. Burlington, MA: Elsevier.

Lyle, J. (1997). Managing excellence in sport performance. *Career Development International*, 2(7), 314–323.

Marshall, M., Wray, L., Epstein, P. and Grifel, S. (1999), 21st century community focus: Better results by linking citizens, government and performance measurement, *Public Management*, 81(10), 12–19.

Neely, A., Gregory, M. and Platts, K. (2005). Performance measurement system design: A literature review and research agenda. *International Journal of Operations and Production Management*, 25(12), 1228–1263.

Neuendorf, K. A. (2002). *The content analysis guidebook*. London: Sage.

Quinn, R. and McGrath, M. (1982). Moving beyond the single-solution perspective: The competing values approach as a diagnostic tool. *The Journal of Applied Behavioural Science*, 18(4), 463–472.

Riemer, H. A. (2007). Multidimensional model of coach leadership. In S. Jowett and D. Lavallee (Eds.), *Social psychology in sport* (pp. 57–73). Champaign, IL: Human Kinetics.

13

Shilbury, D. and Kellett, P. (2011). Sport management in Australia: An organizational overview (4th edn.). Victoria, Australia: Strategic Sport Management.

Silverman, D. (2006). *Interpreting qualitative data: Methods for analyzing talk, text, and interaction* (3rd edn.). London: Sage.

Sotiriadou, P. (2010). *The sport development processes and practices in Australia: The attraction, retention, transition and nurturing of participants and athletes*. Cologne, Germany: LAP LAMBERT Academic Publishing.

Sotiriadou, P. (2011). Improving the practicum experience in sport management: A case study. *European Sport Management Quarterly*, 11(5), 525–546.

Sotiriadou, K. and Shilbury, D. (2009). Australian elite athlete development: An organizational perspective. *Sport Management Review*, 12(3), 137–148.

Thorpe, R. and Holloway, J. (Eds). (2008). *Performance management: Multidisciplinary perspectives*. Hampshire, UK: Palgrave Macmillan.

Vilkinas, T. and Cartan, G. (2006). The integrated competing values framework: Its spatial configuration. *Journal of Management Development*, 25(6), 505–521.

Part A

High performance management of elite sport

Commercial, political, social and cultural factors impacting on the management of high performance sport

Barrie Houlihan

Loughborough University and Norwegian School of Sports Sciences

LEARNING OUTCOMES

Upon completion of this chapter the reader should be able to:

1   identify the major commercial, political and socio-cultural factors that affect high performance sport;
2   understand the relative significance for high performance sport of commercial, political and socio-cultural factors; and
3   understand the interconnection between the three sets of factors.

OVERVIEW

In the widely varying definitions of management two aspects are commonly emphasized: the first is the setting of strategic goals and the coordination of resources to ensure the achievement of those goals while the second stresses the management of the organization's relationship with its environment. Commercial, political, social and cultural factors are closely intertwined with both these aspects of the management of high performance (HP) sport and affect the operation of all sport organizations whether they are in the public, not-for-profit or commercial sectors and whether they operate at the national or international levels. Figure 2.1 provides an indication of the broad range of organizations that populate the HP policy subsector. Not only are commercial, not-for-profit and public organizations strongly represented in the HP subsector, but the interests of those organizations span a broad range from those with a direct or primary interest in HP sport (sports clubs, specialist government agencies and international federations) to those whose concern is more instrumental and arguably simply exploitative. It should be stressed that each organization in Figure 2.1 is not only affected by the environment

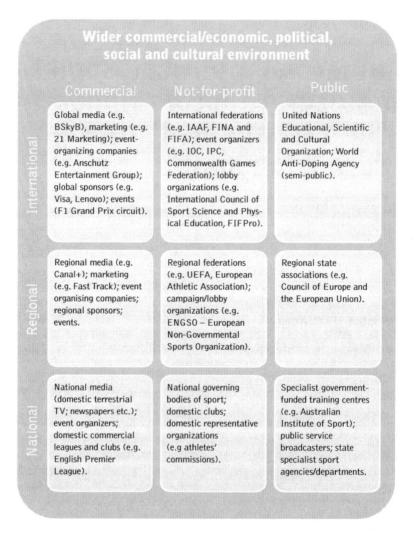

Figure 2.1 *The organizational complexity of high performance sport*

within which it functions, but also constitutes part of the environment of the other organizations. The management context of HP sport is consequently complex, densely populated and often far from benign.

Commercial factors

While it is debatable whether commercial influences or political influences are the more significant in shaping HP sport policies and determining success at the HP level, it is undeniable that these twin factors have had a profound impact on the development of sport and continue to shape contemporary global sport. It is often argued that politicians tend to view elite sport in instrumental terms – that is, as a means of achieving non-sport objectives. However, the same argument can also be made in relation to most commercial interests insofar as sport performance at the elite level is often a means to non-sport commercial objectives. Table 2.1 identifies five different types of commercial interests that impact on the management of HP sport. The list is not meant to be exhaustive, but is intended to illustrate the range of commercial interests that are associated with HP sport, their primary concerns and, more importantly, their likely impact on sport at that level.

The impact of commercialization on HP sport is neither inherently malign nor inherently benign. However, it is undeniable that the rapid growth in the 'business of sport' has had a significant impact on a series of power relationships, six of which are worthy of note.

The first relationship is that between players and their national governing bodies (NGBs) and international federations (IFs). The cumulative effect of increasingly valuable sponsorship deals and prize money, and the celebrity status of athletes in some sports, has been to strengthen the power of players in some sports, generally individual sports such as golf and tennis, at the expense of their NGBs and IFs. Professionals in both golf and tennis have formed competition circuits that have enabled them to retain a greater share of the income they generate. The development of the PGA Tour by the Professional Golfers Association in the late 1960s and the ATP Tour in 1990 by the Association of Tennis Professionals gave elite players in both sports considerable control, not only over their income, but also over where, when and how often they played. Similar, but less profound, shifts in power have occurred in a number of team sports through the formation of players' association such as the Professional Footballers Association in England and the Major League Baseball Players Association in the United States. While much of the activity of players' associations is concerned with maximizing their income, they have also addressed issues such as discrimination and poor medical treatment.

The second relationship is that between clubs and leagues on the one hand and NGBs and IFs on the other. In the United States power rests firmly with the various commercial organizations that own clubs and leagues in the major sports such as American football and baseball. The NGBs and IFs are weak and of peripheral importance to the development of the sport as illustrated by the slow pace of acceptance of the need to tackle doping. Outside the United States a similar, but less extreme, shift in the balance of power has taken place in football where the G-14 group of leading European football clubs forced concessions from FIFA regarding compensation for players injured while playing for their country.

The third relationship is that between sponsors and event organizers, leagues and clubs. While the income from sponsorship has had a number of beneficial consequences for players and spectators, those benefits, like the income from sponsorship, are unevenly spread. Estimating the total annual spend on sponsorship is difficult, but some idea of the skewed distribution of sponsorship income can be gained from Table 2.2. In 2009 football attracted almost ten times the value in sponsorship received by its nearest sport rival, rugby union, and in 2008 the sponsorship received by football almost equalled the combined sponsorship income for the next nine sports and events.

The fourth relationship is that between clubs and their fans. As the nature of sport businesses has changed, many sports have become less dependent on income from ticket sales and more reliant on income from sponsors and the sale of broadcasting rights. It is impossible

Table 2.1 Selected types of commercial interests and their relationship to high performance sport

Commercial interest	Examples	Suggested commercial priorities	Impact on high performance sport management
Non-sport businesses	Olympic sponsors: VISA, Lenovo Skiing sponsor: Audi Quattro cars Football sponsor: Barclays Bank	General: 'clean image', exciting (i.e. attractive to the media), attractive personalities Specific: image of a particular sport which complements their product For gambling: non-corrupt sports; maintenance of uncertainty of outcome	In some sports (e.g. cycling) pressure to tackle doping Demand for exclusiveness in sponsorship increases dependence by sport Gambling: increases the risk of corruption
Sports media	Television (e.g. Sky, Canal+ and ESPN), but also print and internet	Satellite broadcasters require a steady supply of attractive products which have a global market appeal. Products can be events (e.g. American Superbowl, the Olympic Games and grand slam tennis tournaments) and sports (football, rugby union, golf and motor racing)	Tendency to prioritize men's over women's events in multi-sport competitions and to give preference to the dramatic over the complex or technical
Sports leagues, clubs and individual athletes	Leagues: American NFL; Japanese J League; Spanish La Lega and English Premier League. Clubs: Dallas Cowboys, Washington Redskins, Real Madrid, Bayern Munich. Athletes: Kobe Bryant, Roger Federer and Maria Sharapova.	Protect and expand asset value e.g. by engineering competitiveness of NFL league, attempting to turn a local football club into a global brand or an athlete launching clothing ranges	Concern by leagues and clubs to protect assets can reduce willingness to release players for national teams. Improved quality of medical care of elite athletes Greater investment in talent identification and development. Transfer trade in talented athletes, e.g. in football
Sports facility providers and event organizers	Tennis academies: Evert Tennis Academy and IMG Nick Bollettieri Tennis Academy Training centres: La Manga, Spain Event organizers: Ironman triathlon series of the World Triathlon Corporation; World Series Cricket, Indian Cricket League, Professional Golf Association (PGA) Tour	Profit/income maximization; increased market share	Complement (or undermine) international federation and NGB activities in talent identification and development programmes and events, e.g. in triathlon and cricket
Equipment and sportswear manufacturers	Golf: Ping, Callaway Tennis: Dunlop, Wilson, Slazenger Swimming: Speedo General: Adidas, Nike	Profit maximization; product innovation, increased market size and share	Provide sponsorship of clubs and individual athletes. Drive equipment innovation and obsolescence

Table 2.2 *Top sponsored sports, 2009 (2008 figures in brackets), value in US$m*

Sport	Value	
Soccer (football)	2607	(2674)
Olympics	1797	(994)
Rugby Union	272	(335)
Tennis	258	(467)
Formula 1	256	(200)
Baseball	237	(214)
Cricket	227	(170)
Golf	205	(308)
American football	184	(297)
Basketball	173	(n/a)

Source: IFM Sport Marketing Surveys (2010)

to generalize the relationships between clubs (or individual athletes) and their fans. However, in a number of sports, such as football, rugby union, rugby league and cricket, fans see themselves, not simply as spectators or customers, but as having closer, and often highly emotional, relationships with their teams (Hamil *et al.*, 2010; Hassan and Hamil, 2010). In football, for example, some fan groups have become extremely assertive, often encouraged by governments or in Europe, by the European Union, and see themselves as primary stakeholders in the 'club business' rather than simply as purchasers of a sports product. However, fans generally remain confined to the margins of decision making in most commercial sports and, as some clubs attempt to develop a global fan base, traditional, locally based fans become even less significant to the club's business strategy.

The fifth relationship is that between event organizers and government. It is arguable that up until the 1990s the main aim of government involvement in elite sport was to ensure that the national squad for major events such as the Olympic or Paralympic Games performed up to or above national expectations. Since the early 1990s, governments have developed a parallel desire to host events, especially the Olympic/Paralympic Games and the football World Cup. Particularly with regard to the hosting of the Olympics and the football World Cup, there seems to be no limit to the extent to which governments will prostrate themselves before the hierarchy of the IOC and FIFA. Normal land-use planning processes are waived, streets are cleared of the homeless and laws are passed to protect the value of sponsors' investments from ambush marketing (Giulianotti and Klauser, 2009; Sugden, 2012). However, this general imbalance hides a governmental and, to a lesser extent, public resentment towards these organizations that rapidly emerges at any sign of weakness. This is exemplified by the reaction to the Salt Lake City voting scandal that engulfed the IOC in 2002 and to the allegations of corruption in voting for the 2018 and 2022 football World Cups.

The final power relationship is that within some of the major IFs and event-organizing bodies. As independent organizations, each federation can determine its own pattern of governance that reflects the balance between interests within the organization. For example, the two main multi-sport IFs for track and field (the International Association of Athletic Federations) and for swimming (Federation Internationale de Natation) both have to balance the competing interests of the various disciplines for which they are responsible, and this balancing act has often been problematic. As regards event-organizing bodies, within the IOC there has been constant concern, which was especially strong in the 1970s and 1980s, to avoid the formation of voting blocs of National Olympic Committees (NOCs) or of IFs. A number of strategies have been adopted to undermine such a development. One has been the counter-balancing of the growing influence of NOCs with an enhanced representation from the IFs. While NOC members are formally independent of the countries they represent, the IOC acknowledges that many, perhaps the majority, are either explicit state nominees or are so dependent on state support that their independence is nominal (Hill, 1992; Houlihan, 1994). A second strategy has been to increase the dependence of poorer IOC member countries on the IOC through the activities of Olympic Solidarity (formerly the Committee for International Olympic Aid established in 1961), which is the sport development agency of the IOC. The activities of Olympic Solidarity were intended to reduce the likelihood of the richer 'sports powers' creating voting blocs through the funding of sport development programmes in the poorer IOC member countries. According to Henry and Al Tauqi (2008, p. 367) 'It is clear to see that the introduction of Olympic Solidarity was intended to unify the Olympic movement by neutralizing the pressure exerted by the IFs and NOCs for a greater say in the running of the Olympic system' (see also Chatziefstathiou et al., 2008).

Political factors

While much of HP sport is intensely commercialized, it is important to bear in mind that there are still many sports and events that rely heavily on government support. Moreover, even those sports that are commercially successful are rarely immune from politics. In analysing the significance of political factors it is important to consider both the ends and means adopted by governments in relation to HP sport. While many countries have a long history of controlling or attempting to control popular sports, intervention in relation to HP sport is much more recent and is often prompted by concerns related to gambling (Forrest and Simmons, 2003) and crowd disorder (Houlihan, 1991). However, the more recent expansion of government intervention in sport can be traced to three developments in the second half of the twentieth century, namely: the Cold War; the opposition to apartheid in South Africa; and the expansion of international sports competitions, particularly when they began to be broadcast live in the early 1960s.

The onset of the Cold War in the 1950s prompted the systematic intervention in HP sport by governments in order to achieve diplomatic objectives. From the 1950s to the late 1980s the communist bloc countries of Europe, following the lead given by the Soviet Union and the German Democratic Republic (GDR), invested heavily in HP sport, at least in part to demonstrate the superiority of socialism over American capitalism (Riordan, 1978). The GDR, which refined the Soviet sports system, was also concerned to utilize sport to further its claims to be recognized as a separate country rather than simply the Russian zone of occupied Germany (Strenk, 1980). To this end the GDR established an elaborate and extremely well-funded HP sport system that involved the systematic search for talented young athletes, a network of specialist training facilities, heavy investment in sports coaching and systematic doping. As argued elsewhere, the Soviet system, as refined by the GDR, became the model for many other countries outside the communist bloc including Australia, Canada and the United Kingdom (Green and Houlihan, 2005). Even those countries, such as the United States, which did not seek to introduce their own diluted version of the communist state-centred sports systems, were not immune from the impact of Soviet and GDR success. For example, the United States intervened forcefully in the late 1970s to force American sport to restructure in order to be better able to compete effectively with the Soviet bloc countries. This was the motive behind the passing of the Amateur Sports Act 1978.

The campaign against apartheid in South Africa had an indirect impact on the role of governments in the management of HP sport. In part the impact of the campaigns to boycott various Olympic and Commonwealth Games was to make it clear to those governments who wished to take part in a boycott that in order for the threat of a boycott to have any leverage, the boycotting country had to have an elite athletic squad whose absence would clearly diminish the attractiveness of the event being boycotted. The boycott campaign also made many governments more acutely aware of the more general diplomatic benefits to be gained from attending (and being successful at) major international sports events.

A key factor that made major sports events attractive as an arena for diplomacy was their growing public profile due to the increase in live television broadcasting. The popularity of sporting boycotts, roughly from the mid 1970s to the mid 1980s, declined sharply in part because of the elimination in the late 1980s of the two main causes of boycotts – European communism and apartheid – and in part because of the rapid realization of the diplomatic benefits to be gained from being seen, and being successful, on the global stage offered by the Olympic Games and other major sports events. The need to qualify for, and succeed at, major sports events gave further encouragement to governments to intervene in the development of HP squads and teams. However, not all the motives for government intervention in HP sport were related to diplomatic objectives. Many countries including the Soviet Union, post-apartheid South Africa and Canada were keen to use sport to create a sense of national identity within culturally and/or ethnically diverse states or to construct a post-colonial identity as exemplified by Australia and many Caribbean countries (Keim, 2003; Macintosh and Whitson, 1990; Peppard and Riordan, 1993; Stoddert, 1988; Ward, 2010).

As regards the form that government intervention takes, Hood and Margetts (2007) identify four basic resources available to government: nodality (the fact that government tends to hold a central strategic position in terms of the flow of information); authority (to make and enforce regulations and laws); treasure (money that can be distributed or exchanged for other resources); and organization (administrative capacity and expertise). These resources tend to be translated into instruments that are regulatory, distributive, redistributive or organizational in character (see Lowi, 1964, 1972). Table 2.3 provides examples of the different forms that government intervention can take in relation to HP sport.

It is unlikely that there is any government in the economically developed world that does not regulate HP sport in some way. In China there is tight regulation of the movement of players to foreign teams and also of the ability of commercial sports teams, such as football and basketball teams, to remove their players from national training squads (Houlihan *et al.*,

Table 2.3 Policy instruments and high performance sport

	United Kingdom	China	Germany	United States
Regulate	1 Control over the sale of broadcasting rights for sports events of national importance, e.g. FA Cup Final, Wimbledon Championships 2 The application of the World Anti-Doping Code	1 Player transfer to foreign teams (e.g. in football and basketball) 2 Talent selection and development through a network of specialist sports schools	1 Law passed which exempted its football league from anti-cartel legislation (thus enabling the league to sell broadcasting rights collectively). There is also European Union legislation regulating the sale of broadcasting rights 2 Regulation of entry to the German lottery market	1 1961 Sports Broadcasting Act and the 1992 Cable Act regulate the sale of broadcasting rights 2 1978 Amateur Sports Act strengthened the role of the US Olympic Committee (USOC) and weakened the role of the American Athletic Union in relation to HP sport
Distribute	1 Determination of the proportion of National Lottery income to be allocated to sport 2 Select sports to be supported by lottery and exchequer funding	State funding, through the General Administration of Sport (GAS) is the key source of income for Olympic and Paralympic sports and athletes	Provision of federal funding to NGBs and the German Olympic Committee	Some indirect subsidy of the USOC through provision of training base at low rent
Redistribute	5% of Premier League broadcasting income to be allocated to grassroots football	A proportion of the earnings of elite players playing for teams outside China is redistributed to other areas of elite sport	Targeting of finance to the sports with the best medal chances	An inadvertent redistribution of funding for HP sport came as a result of the passage of Title IX of the Education Amendments 1972. One impact of Title IX was to boost funding of women's college sport (with some redistribution from men's sport) and consequently an improvement in the standard of women's HP sport.
Establish administrative structures	1 UK Sport as government agency for HP sport 2 UK Anti-Doping 3 English Institute of Sport (HP training centres)	1 GAS is the government department responsible for HP sport 2 GAS operates through a network of management centres/NGBs, which are also government administrative units	There is no federal specialist ministry although sport is the responsibility of the Ministry of the Interior, which has issued a number of policy statements related to HP sport	US Anti-Doping Agency

Sources: Cave and Crandell 2001; Bergsgard *et al.* 2007; Houlihan *et al.* 2010

2009). The instrument of distribution is also widely used with many countries, including the United Kingdom, Portugal, Norway and Japan, that have state-run lotteries which are used, at least in part, to fund HP sport. There are fewer examples of the redistribution of resources in relation to HP sport. However, in the United Kingdom there is an agreement between the government and the Premier League football clubs that the latter will pass 5 per cent of their income from broadcasting to support grassroots football, an element, albeit an increasingly minor element, in the development of future elite players (Conn, 2011). Finally, almost without exception economically developed countries have established specialist organizations either within a government department or, more commonly, as a semi-autonomous unit, to oversee HP sport. Examples include the Australian Institute of Sport, *Olympiatoppen* in Norway and the General Administration of Sport in China. In general, the growth in the cultural, diplomatic and economic significance of sport has, over the last fifty years or so, prompted a substantial increase in governmental intervention in HP sport with considerable increases in financial investment, administrative support and regulation. The only significant exception to this pattern is the United States where intervention is far less systematic, but nonetheless does occur even if only occasionally.

Socio-cultural factors

Earlier in this chapter there was a brief discussion of the interconnections between economic and political factors in shaping the development and management of HP sport. Both those factors are also closely intertwined with, and arguably the product of, deeper socio-cultural factors. To argue that the priority given to HP sport in a particular country, and the way in which that country responds to that prioritization, is simply the product of its socio-cultural history is obviously too glib, but to ignore the significance of the past would be a serious oversight. Socio-cultural factors may be divided into three very broad overlapping categories: current characteristics, long-standing values, and beliefs and recent transformative events. Current characteristics would include factors such as population size and structure, the degree of urbanization and the extent of female employment. Each of these characteristics is clearly significantly affected by the other two categories, but may also be affected by extraneous factors such as improvements in public health, labour shortages and topography. As De Bosscher (2007) noted, population size is one of the two most significant variables in influencing HP success. Together, population size and per capita Gross Domestic Product explain over 50 per cent of variation in elite sporting success. The degree of urbanization is also significant in so far as the more highly urbanized environments make access to high-quality coaches and training partners more probable.

The second category of factors refers to the long-standing values and beliefs found within communities. Acknowledging that 'socio-cultural history matters' is fairly uncontroversial. What is much more problematic is determining the extent to which history matters, and what history matters. Examples of deeply rooted values systems that have withstood wars, authoritarianism, economic collapse and invasion would include Confucianism in China, Taiwan and Japan, Protestantism in Denmark and Sweden, and Islam in the Arab world, all of which are profoundly entwined in the fabric of daily life and have been for many hundreds of years. All policy development, not just in relation to HP sport, is mediated by the historical context in which it takes place. At one level this self-evident proposition is a simple reminder that much of the explanation for such phenomena as the level of governmental enthusiasm for HP sport, the willingness of governments to intervene and the modes of intervention adopted lies in the socio-cultural history of a country and the long-established traditions and predispositions that this creates. While not denying the importance of the contemporary context (wealth, population and political party control of government, for example), it is important to investigate whether there are more deeply rooted norms, values and attitudes that are significant in shaping policy. For most countries the experience of the dominance of a particular religion, established patterns of family relations, the education system, invasion, empire and colonialism have all left their mark on broad societal values that not only influence the nature of HP policy goals, but also affect policy delivery mechanisms and management style and practices. For example, the marginal presence of women in most international and domestic sport federations is a reflection of deeply ingrained patterns of patriarchy rather than the outcome of analysis of abilities. Deep structural policy predispositions and styles of management often manifest themselves as 'storylines' (Fischer, 2003) where historical 'facts' become embroidered and take on an ideological (or mythological) status that engenders a strong commitment to particular policies and management practices irrespective of the strength of the evidence available.

The strength of these deeply rooted socio-cultural values not only helps explain current HP policy and management practice but more importantly imposes significant restrictions on future policy and management practice. Howlett and Ramesh, commenting on the significance of the institutionalization of values, emphasize 'the unique patterns of historical development and the constraints they impose on future choices' (Howlett and Ramesh, 1995, p. 27). Perhaps the most important elaboration of this view is provided by Esping-Andersen (1990, 1999) who, in his analysis of welfare regimes in Europe, provided strong support for the lasting impact of culture on policy. He argued that in many countries distinctive types of welfare regimes (liberal, conservative and social democratic) have emerged over time and generated sets of values and practices that not only influence the identification of issues as public problems, but also set the parameters of the policy response. Although he was not referring specifically to sport, his identification of distinct welfare regimes prompts consideration of whether a similar phenomenon may be evident in relation to HP sport. Thus it may be hypothesized that the extent to which HP sport and sporting success are prioritized, the treatment of HP athletes, the extent and nature of state involvement and the amount of public funding can be explained in large part by deeply rooted orientations such as those to community and the place of the individual, significant other countries and the role of the state. Cultural history, reflected in the attitudes of institutions such as religions, the military, high status groups and the education system towards sport, creates policy predispositions that are likely to be reinforced and compounded by the slow accumulation of policy decisions.

The final category of factors refers to relatively recent 'transformative' events whose origin is often external to the social system but which nonetheless leaves a profound and lasting socio-cultural legacy. The traumatic experience of Nazi occupation in Denmark and the Nazi domination of sport in Germany have led both countries to safeguard the autonomy of the sports system and made governments reluctant to become directly involved in sport, although this reluctance has clearly weakened in relation to HP sport.

SUMMARY

Although some of the bolder assertions about the homogenizing impact of globalization (see for example Korten, 1995; Ohmae, 1995) have been discredited, it is perhaps still surprising that the high level of variation found in the management of HP sport persists. The existence of monopolistic IFs, the ubiquity of a relatively small set of sports and events in the global sports media and the concentration of commercial sponsorship in a handful of mega-sports events are all powerful homogenizing forces, yet as illustrated in the foregoing discussion, politics and culture are still important mediating variables. However, it is also clear that sustaining national distinctiveness in relation to HP sport is becoming more difficult and, as De Bosscher *et al.* (2007) have shown, there has been a steady convergence in approaches to HP sport management in recent years.

The factors that are most likely to maintain a degree of heterogeneity in approaches to HP sport are culture and the attitude of government. While the former has mediated homogenizing pressures, it has not been able to withstand them to any appreciable degree. As regards the latter, with the cost of winning a gold medal at the summer Olympics approaching 40 million euros (Forrest *et al.*, 2010; Wilson, 2011) it is relevant to ask which government will be the first to declare that the return on the investment is simply not sufficient and withdraw from the sporting 'arms race'. However, it would be a brave government that would admit to its electorate that it was prepared deliberately to let the country's position in the medals table decline significantly.

DISCUSSION QUESTIONS

1 To what extent do you think socio-cultural factors can be altered to facilitate a higher policy priority for HP sport?

2 To what extent does HP sport benefit from increased commercialization?

3 Do you agree that HP sport attracts the interest and support of government primarily because it is a useful diplomatic resource?

KEY TERMS

- Commercialization
- Power
- Culture
- Policy

27

GUIDED READINGS

De Bosscher, V. (2007) provides a wide-ranging analysis of the macro-, meso- and micro-level factors that affect high performance success (see Chapters 1, 2 and 3 in particular). Green and Houlihan (2005) and Bergsgard *et al.* (2007) review high performance sport policy in a range of countries.

BIBLIOGRAPHY

Bergsgard, N. A., Houlihan, B., Mangset, P., Nødland, S. I. and Rommetvedt, H. (2007). *Sport policy: A comparative analysis of stability and change.* Oxford: Butterworth-Heinemann.

Chatziefstathiou, D., Henry, I., Al Tauqi, M. and Theodoraki, E. (2008). Cultural imperialism and the diffusion of Olympic sport in Africa: A comparison of pre and post second world war contexts. In H. Ren, L. P. DaCosta, A. Miragaya and N. Jings (Eds), *Olympic studies reader: A multi-disciplinary and multicultural research guide* (Volume 1). Beijing: Beijing Sport University Press.

Conn, D. (2011). Away from the Premier League our parks and pitches are starved of cash. *The Guardian*, Wednesday 30 April, available at www.guardian.co.uk/football/david-conn-inside-sport-blog/2011/apr/20/premier-league-cuts-funding-grass-roots, accessed 8 August 2011.

De Bosscher, V. (2007). *Sports policy factors leading to international sporting success.* Brussels, Belgium: VUBPRESS.

Esping-Andersen, G. (1990). *The three worlds of welfare capitalism.* Cambridge: Polity Press.

Esping-Andersen, G. (1999). *Social foundations of postindustrial economies.* Oxford: Oxford University Press.

Fischer, F. (2003). *Reframing public policy: Discursive politics and deliberative practices.* New York: Oxford University Press.

Forrest, D. and Simmons, R. (2003). Sport and gambling. *Oxford Review of Economic Policy,* 19(4), 598–611.

Forrest, D., Sanz, I. and Tena, J. D. (2010). Forecasting national team medal totals at the summer Olympic Games. *International Journal of Forecasting,* 26, 576–588.

Giulianotti, R. and Klauser, F. (2009) Security, governance and mega-sports events: Towards an interdisciplinary research agenda. *Journal of Sport and Social Issues,* 34(1), 49–61.

Green, M. and Houlihan, B. (2005) *Elite sport development: Policy learning and political priorities.* London: Routledge.

Guiso, L., Sapienza, P., and Zingales, L. (2006). Does culture affect economic outcomes? *The Journal of Economic Perspectives,* 20(2), 23–48.

Hamil, S., Walters, G. and Watson, L. (2010). The model of governance at FC Barcelona: Balancing member democracy, corporate social responsibility and sporting performance. *Soccer and Society,* 11(4), 475–504.

Hassan, D. and Hamil, S. (2010). Models of football governance and management in international sport. *Soccer and Society,* 11(4), 343–353.

Hill, C. R. (1992). *Olympic politics.* Manchester, UK: Manchester University Press.

Hood, C. C. and Margetts, H. Z. (2007). *The tools of government in the digital age.* Basingstoke, UK: Palgrave Macmillan.

Houlihan, B. (1991). *The government and politics of sport.* London: Routledge.

Houlihan, B. (1994). *Sport and international politics.* London: Harvester-Wheatsheaf.

Howlett, R. and Ramesh, M. (1995). *Studying public policy: Policy cycles and policy sub-systems.* New York: Oxford University Press.

Keim, M. (2003). *Nation building at play: Sport as a tool of social integration in post-apartheid South Africa*. London: Meyer & Meyer.

Korten, D. C. (1995). *When corporations rule the world*. San Francisco, CA: Bewett-Koehler.

Lowi, T. J. (1964). American business, public policy, case studies and political theory. *World Politics*, 16, 677–693.

Macintosh, D. and Whitson, D. (1990). *The game planners: Transforming Canada's sport system*. Montreal: McGill-Queen's University Press.

Ohmae, K. (1995). *The end of the nation state: The rise of regional economies*. New York: Simon & Schuster.

Peppard, V. and Riordan, J. (1993). *Playing politics: Soviet sport diplomacy to 1992*. Greenwih, CT: JAI Press.

Riordan, J. (1978). *Sport under communism*, London: Hurst.

Stoddart, B. (1988). Caribbean cricket: The role of sport in emerging small nation politics. *International Journal*, 43(4), 618–642.

Strenk, A. (1980). Diplomats in tracksuits: The role of sports in the German Democratic Republic. *Journal of Sport and Social Issues*, 4(1), 34–45.

Sugden, J. (2012). Watched by the games: Surveillance and security at the Olympics. In J. Sugden and A. Tomlinson (Eds), *Watching the Olympics: Politics, power and representation*. London: Routledge.

Ward, T. (2010). *Sport in Australian national identity: Kicking goals*. London: Routledge.

Wilson, N. (2011). The rising price of Olympic gold. http://wilson2012blog.dailymail.co.uk/2011/08/the-rising-price-of-olympic-gold.html, accessed 14 August 2011.

Chapter 3

Measuring performance and success in elite sports

Simon Shibli
Sheffield Hallam University

Veerle De Bosscher
Vrije Universiteit Brussel

Maarten van Bottenburg
Utrecht University

Hans Westerbeek
Institute of Sport, Exercise and Active Living (ISEAL), Victoria University

LEARNING OUTCOMES

Upon completion of this chapter the reader should be able to:

1   recognize different approaches to the meaning of success in elite sport;
2   identify the relative strengths and weaknesses of performance measures in elite sport;
3   propose appropriate methods of measuring elite sport success in different contexts;
4   interpret and communicate data on performance in elite sport;
5   understand the political context in which elite sport success is judged; and
6   apply the principles outlined to other relevant sporting contexts.

OVERVIEW

The purpose of this chapter is to provide a structured overview of the ways in which performance can be measured in elite sport. To illustrate the points being made, the summer Olympic Games is used as a case study throughout this chapter. The results of the 2008 Beijing summer Olympics, which provided the most up-to-date data available at the time of writing (2011), are the ones cited most frequently. The basic principles illustrated by these examples are transferable to different sporting contexts and it would be straightforward to apply the analysis used on the Olympic Games to the World Athletics Championships, the World Track Cycling Championships and many other elite sport events.

In the opening sentence we state that the chapter provides a 'structured overview' of performance and we use this term quite deliberately. It would be rather short-sighted to restrict

Figure 3.1 *The dimensions of performance*

the measurement of performance solely to an analysis of the number of medals won or a nation's ranking in the medals' table. These are valid measures of performance and are by far the most commonly used ones, but they are not the only ones. Figure 3.1 is an adaptation of a process diagram that illustrates the dimensions of performance that can be realized by elite sport development systems.

Within each section of the process diagram there is a variety of components. The components of each section are discussed in turn below.

Inputs

Inputs are the resources that are invested in an elite sport development system and are typically money (usually from governments) and the time commitments of athletes, their coaches and support staff.

Throughputs

It is evident that money and other inputs do not in isolation lead to international sporting success. Once the requisite inputs have been secured, it is the effectiveness of how these inputs are used that ultimately determines the performances of nations in elite sports. De Bosscher *et al.* (2006) propose a conceptual framework of nine pillars, which shows the interactions between inputs (Pillar 1, funding) and throughputs (or processes) (Pillars 2–9). These are illustrated and discussed in greater depth in Chapter 4.

Qualification outputs

We deliberately make a distinction in Figure 3.1 between qualification outputs and performance outputs to illustrate the various layers of performance that exist. A qualification output is the production of elite athletes who qualify to take part in international sporting competition. Counting the number of athletes from a particular nation who qualify to take part in an international sporting event, especially the Olympic Games, should be viewed as a first step in assessing that nation's performance. This is discussed in more detail later in the chapter.

Performance outputs

The classic measures of performance outputs in international sport include medals table ranking and total number of medals won. These are the most common measures but are not the only ones. Only a minority of nations win medals in the Olympic Games, so for other nations alternative measures of success are required to contextualize performance. As well as qualification outputs, other valid measures include: a season's best performance; a personal best performance; a national record; and progression to the second or subsequent rounds of competition.

Outcomes

The long-term results of qualification and performance outputs are called outcomes. Outcomes are the longer terms impacts that a country's performance in international competition has on the national funding and structure of the sport.

Having set a context for the structured measurement of performance in elite sport, we now look at qualification outputs, performance outputs and outcomes in greater depth.

QUALIFICATION OUTPUTS

In 2011 the world's population was estimated at around 6.9 billion people. In the Olympic Games the number of athletes taking part has been capped in recent times at around 11,000. Thus in simple terms, the likelihood of an individual becoming an Olympian is around one in 627,000. Clearly, this sort of statistic suggests that all things being equal, larger nations are likely to produce more Olympians than smaller nations. If we assume that athletic talent is distributed evenly across the world, then it becomes possible to compute some basic measures of performance, for example the qualification output of Olympians 'produced' by each nation. What is meant by the term 'produced' in this context is the number of athletes that qualify to take part in elite international competition. In the summer Olympic Games the majority of nations do not win a medal of any type and the vast majority (about 75 per cent) do not win a gold medal, as shown in Figure 3.2.

Since most nations don't win medals, we need other criteria for success, and the next-best thing to winning a medal is taking part in the event. In order to take part, it is necessary for athletes to meet qualification standards and this is prima facie evidence that the system a

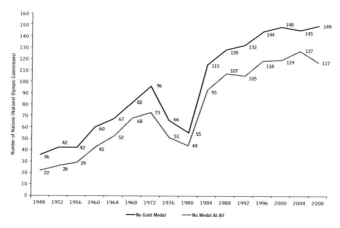

Figure 3.2 *The number of nations not winning medals in the Olympic Games, 1948–2008*

nation has used to develop such athletes has achieved a basic level of effectiveness. In practice, most international competitions in sport have qualification standards and this has the effect of limiting the number of nations and athletes that can participate. For example, in the men's 100 m sprint in athletics at the Olympic Games there is a maximum entry of eighty athletes. However, there are some 205 NOCs, most of which would like to send an athlete to take part in the 100 m. To resolve the issue of surplus demand for a limited supply of places in the competition, the market adjusts itself by raising the 'price' of entry. In the case of the men's 100 m, the price of entry is the qualifying time required to achieve a place in the starting line-up of 80. If a nation wants to send two or three athletes (the maximum from any one country), they must all achieve the A standard qualifying time of 10.21 seconds. For nations wishing to send one athlete only, the qualification criterion is the B standard of 10.27 seconds. These qualification rules ensured that athletes from sixty-four different countries were able to take part in the first round of the men's 100 m in Beijing 2008.

While we might assume that athletic talent is evenly distributed across the world, the reality is that the fifteen nations with the largest teams of athletes sent just over 50 per cent of the competitors (or qualifiers) to Beijing in 2008, as shown in Table 3.1.

By way of contrast to Table 3.1, the 124 nations, or 60 per cent of the 205 nations taking part, with the smallest delegations accounted for just 10 per cent of all competitors. Furthermore, most of these 124 nations did not qualify to take part in the Olympic Games on merit and were allowed to take part by the IOC on a concessionary (or 'wild card') basis. Consequently the Olympic Games is not based solely on merit and this is deliberately so for

Table 3.1 The fifteen largest delegations in Beijing, 2008

Nation	Athletes	Percentage of total (11,187)	Cumulative percentage
China	639	5.71	5.71
United States	596	5.33	11.04
Russia	467	4.17	15.21
Germany	463	4.14	19.35
Australia	433	3.87	23.22
Japan	351	3.14	26.36
Italy	344	3.07	29.44
Canada	332	2.97	32.40
France	323	2.89	35.29
United Kingdom	312	2.79	38.08
Spain	286	2.56	40.64
Brazil	277	2.48	43.11
Poland	268	2.40	45.51
South Korea	267	2.39	47.89
Ukraine	254	2.27	50.17

Source: http://en.wikipedia.org/wiki/2008_Summer_Olympics#Participation

two reasons. First, through the Olympic Games the International Olympic Committee (IOC) is trying to achieve what its president Jacques Rogge (2002) described as 'a real universality', by which he meant the Olympic Games being relevant to the more than 200 recognized NOCs. One method to achieve this 'real universality' is by rationing places at the Olympic Games via the use of a continental quota system whereby qualifying places are allocated, in part, on the basis of geography rather than exclusively on performance. This type of policy legislates against large nations with a strong tradition in sport such as the United States dominating the Games at the expense of smaller nations. Second, the rules for many events in the Olympic Games deliberately limit the number of athletes from any one nation taking part. The eighty athletes who contested the men's 100 m were not the fastest eighty sprinters in the world. The United States could comfortably qualify ten 100-m sprinters on merit, and some nations that actually took part in the event would not be able to qualify any at all. For this reason we find that an athlete from the Cook Islands recorded a personal best time of 11.41 seconds in the first round of the 100 m. This is considerably below the A and B qualifying times of 10.21 and 10.27 seconds respectively and would be 0.11 of a second outside the top 500 100-m sprinters in the United Kingdom. This approach has the effect of being inclusive towards smaller nations and diluting the influence of larger nations. The IOC deliberately pursues its 'real universality' approach to ensure that the Olympic Games, and its associated commercial property rights, are as relevant to as many of the world's 6.9 billion population as possible.

Nevertheless, given the difficulty of qualifying for the Olympic Games and other major sporting events, it is reasonable to conclude that of qualifying for the Olympic Games and other major sports events on merit, it is reasonable to conclude that a starting point in measuring a nation's sporting success is the number of athletes or teams it is able to qualify to take part. When qualification is genuinely on merit, this is good evidence that an elite athlete development (or production) system is functioning with a basic level of effectiveness. We now proceed to examine more demanding definitions of effectiveness in elite sport, linked to performance in competition.

PERFORMANCE OUTPUTS

For the purposes of this chapter, performance outputs are divided into two areas of interest: first, medals' table outputs; and second, contextual measures of output. What is meant by contextual outputs is evidence of performance regardless of whether it leads to the winning of a medal, such as a season's best performance.

Medals' table outputs

The measurement of performance in the Olympic Games has been a subject of considerable interest to researchers and policymakers for some time. See, for example, UK Sport (2003). It is therefore something of an irony that the IOC does not recognize the Olympic medals table as an indication of merit and that the medals' table is presented in descending order of gold, silver and bronze medals won 'for information purposes only' (De Bosscher et al., 2008). Nonetheless, outside of the IOC many nations view the final medals' table for each Olympics as an indication of merit. UK Sport (the lead agency for elite sport in the United Kingdom) described its 'ultimate goal' for London 2012 as finishing fourth in the medals' table. Similarly, China committed its national resources to finish on top of the 2008 medals table. Despite the simplicity of the medals' tables, it is not an effective measure of performance for a number of reasons. The most obvious is that a nation's ranking is to a certain extent dependent upon the performance of other nations. As an extreme example, imagine that at Beijing in 2008 China won 300 of the 302 available gold medals and the United Kingdom won the remaining two. China would still be ranked first in the table, but the United Kingdom, which won 9 gold medals in Athens in 2004, would be propelled into second place despite a decline in its gold medal tally. This shows that the simplistic nature of the medals' table means that it would be possible for a nation to win fewer medals but improve its place on the table. It would be very difficult to explain to a minister of state that despite winning seven gold medals fewer than the previous Games, the United Kingdom had in fact improved by climbing seven places up the medals table. That the Olympic medals' table itself is a less than complete measure of performance is well demonstrated by reviewing the top five nations in the Beijing 2008 table, as shown in Table 3.2.

It has been a question of some debate as to which nation was the most successful in Beijing. Using the IOC ranking system China is the top placed nation with 51 gold medals compared with the USA's 36, whereas using total medals the USA has claimed that its total of 110 is a superior performance to China's 100. When asked about this issue, IOC president Jacques Rogge is quoted in Jeffery (2008) as having said:

> I am sure each country will highlight what suits it best – one will say the gold medal tally counts, and the other will say the total medals count, we take no position on that.

A problem with both the IOC ranking system and total medals as measures of performance is that they ignore the totality of achievement by not distinguishing between the relative values of medals. One method to combat this weakness is to award points (or weights) such as three points for gold, two for silver and one for bronze, as shown in Table 3.3.

In Table 3.3 the points system shows that China (223) achieved a marginally better performance than the United States (220) and thus the average quality of medals won by China was superior to that of the United States. The strength of the points system is that it

Table 3.2 Beijing 2008 top five nations

Rank	Nation	Gold	Silver	Bronze	Total
1	China	51	21	28	100
2	United States of America	36	38	36	110
3	Russia	23	21	28	72
4	United Kingdom	19	13	15	47
5	Germany	16	10	15	41

Source: http://news.bbc.co.uk/sport1/hi/olympics/medals_table/default.stm

Table 3.3 *Beijing 2008 top five measured by points*

Nation	Gold	Silver	Bronze	Total	Points	Market share %
China	51	21	28	100	223[1]	12.0
United States of America	36	38	36	110	220	11.8
Russia	23	21	28	72	139	7.5
United Kingdom	19	13	15	47	98	5.3
Germany	16	10	15	41	83	4.5

[1]China 223 points = $((51 \times 3)+(21 \times 2)+(28 \times 1)) = (153 + 42 + 28) = 223$

takes into account the totality of achievement rather than simply gold medals won and it makes a distinction between the values of different medal types. The disadvantage of the points system is that the weights applied to medals can be arbitrary (for example, it has been argued that gold medals should be worth four points rather than three), and that the whole notion of points is harder to understand than rankings by gold medals won or total medals won.

The use of points can be developed to enable time series analysis of a nation's performance. This type of analysis is particularly useful for governments and policymakers who wish to take a consistent high-level view of the performance of a nation. In its review of how the UK elite sport development system was progressing in 2008, the National Audit Office recommended:

> they [UK Sport] should consider introducing a measure of 'market share' to reflect the Great Britain team's percentage share of all medals available at the Games, possibly based on a weighted value for each position on the podium. This would provide a more rounded measure of performance, which could be compared between Games. (National Audit Office, 2008)

By dividing the points won by a given nation by the total number of points awarded at a particular event, it is possible to compute a measure of 'market share'. As the number of events contested at the Olympic Games has grown steadily from 237 in 1988 to 302 in 2008, market share is an effective way of standardizing performance so that it can be analysed consistently over time. Figure 3.3 shows the market share of China and the United Kingdom over the period 1984 (when China first took part in the Olympic Games) and 2008 (the last data point available at the time of writing).

Since its low point in 1988 China's performance in the Olympic Games has followed an upward trajectory, culminating in a spectacular market share score of 12 per cent when it hosted the Games in 2008. In standardized terms, 2008 is confirmed as being China's best-ever performance and there is also evidence of continuous improvement from 1996. In the case of the United Kingdom, it can be seen that market share was in decline from 1984 until the low point of 1996. In 1997 the British government authorized a strategic approach to elite sport development via National Lottery funding and the establishment of UK Sport as a lead agency for elite sport. There were immediate results in Sydney 2000 (eleven gold medals

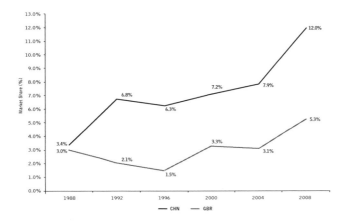

Figure 3.3 *Market share for China and the United Kingdom*
Source: IOC 1984-2004, BBC 2008

and tenth place in the medals' table). The gains of Sydney were consolidated in Athens 2004 while Beijing 2008 proved to be the United Kingdom's most successful Games for 100 years with nineteen gold medals won and fourth place in the medals' table. The evidence from previous host nations suggested that the United Kingdom should perform even better in 2012 than it did in 2008. While market share is a useful way of standardizing performance over time, it suffers from the disadvantage of being relatively difficult to understand.

It is important to be aware of what each of the four measures outlined above (gold medals, medals' table ranking, points and market share) actually reveals about sporting performance as it is possible for the various measures of performance to give conflicting results. We used total medals, points and market share to compare the performances of five countries in Athens in 2004 with their performances in Sydney 2000. As Table 3.4 shows, we found some interesting anomalies.

With the exception of Italy, whose performance declined according to every measure, the performances of the remaining nations could be said to have improved or declined, depending on the measure used. In the case of the United Kingdom, an argument can be made that overall its athletes performed better, worse or the same as they did in 2004 compared with 2000. This is a rather unclear message to give to funding bodies and policymakers. In our view the measure that gives the truest indication of performance is market share because it takes into

Table 3.4 *Change in performance 2000–2004 by measure type*

Nation	Rank	Total medals	Points (3, 2, 1)	Market share %
United Kingdom	Same	Better	Worse	Worse
Canada	Better	Worse	Better	Better
Italy	Worse	Worse	Worse	Worse
Norway	Better	Worse	Worse	Worse
Belgium	Better	Worse	Worse	Worse

37

account the totality of achievement (all medals); it distinguishes between gold, silver and bronze medals by using points; it is measurable over time on a standardized basis to test for improvement; and it is a measure of performance that is under the direct control of a nation.

It is possible to combine measures of performance to take a more rounded view of how nations have performed. In Figure 3.4 we demonstrate how plotting the change in gold medals won and the change in total medals won helps to provide a further context for analysing performance. The data illustrate the change in gold medals won and total medals won between Athens 2004 and Beijing 2008.

In Figure 3.4 China is identified as the most improved nation with an increase in gold medals won of nineteen and an increase in total medals won of thirty-seven. Other nations identified as improving on both measures are the United Kingdom, Kenya, Jamaica and South Korea. By contrast, nations losing medals on both counts include: Japan, Cuba, Greece (the previous hosts) and Russia. Some nations improve on one measure and decline on the other. In the bottom right quadrant, the Netherlands and Germany won more gold medals but fewer medals in total. This can be said to be an improvement in medal quality. France, which is in the top left quadrant, is an example of a nation that won fewer gold medals but increased its total medals won. This can be said to be an improvement in medal quantity. Similar diagrams can be drawn to show any combination of changes in rank, total medals, points or market share depending upon which aspects of performance are to be analysed.

Because the majority of nations that take part in the Olympic Games do not win medals (see Figure 3.2), it is useful to implement non-medal based measures so that these seemingly 'unsuccessful' nations are able to make an assessment of their performance, policies and investments. These contextual measures are outlined in the next section.

CONTEXTUAL MEASURES OF OUTPUT

While medals-based measures of performance are easily understood, they ignore the performance of nations that do not win medals. It is quite possible for NOCs to make considerable progress in developing a sport without increasing the number of medals

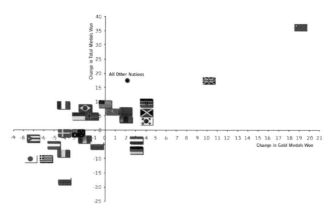

Figure 3.4 *Change in gold medals won versus change in total medals won, 2004–2008*

Source: IOC 2004, BBC 2008

38

won in elite competition. This point is made very clearly by examining the men's 100 m in the Beijing 2008 athletics programme. Of the eighty athletes who took part in the event, only three won medals. This does not automatically brand the remaining seventy-seven as failures. Examples of positive achievements in the men's 100 m by non-medallists can be seen in Table 3.5.

None of the athletes listed in Table 3.5 won a medal and only two made the final, yet all of them could find reasons to be satisfied with their efforts. They achieved milestones such as a season's best, a personal best, a national record and in most cases they progressed beyond the first round. It is difficult not to feel a degree of sympathy for Churandy Martina of the Dutch Antilles who broke his national record three times in the competition and ultimately came fourth in the final. Nonetheless for all of the athletes featured in Table 3.5 (and others as well), it is reasonable to argue that they demonstrated positive achievement despite not winning a medal. The most relevant of these measures are reviewed below.

Athletes posting seasonal best performances

In an environment of increasing global competition, the best that might be expected of an athlete would be for them to achieve a season's best performance in their event. Athletes are conditioned to peak at certain points in their training cycles and can reasonably be expected to deliver their best performance in the event that is considered to be the pinnacle of achievement in that cycle. Thus, Nawai from Kiribati in Table 3.5 who recorded a time of 11.29 seconds, which was a season's best, can feel gratified that although he was eliminated in the first round, he peaked at the right time. Similarly, Naoki Tsukahara from Japan recorded a season's best in Round 2 and then bettered this time in the semi-final.

Athletes posting lifetime best performances

A lifetime best (or personal best) performance could be considered a more significant achievement than a season's best time. This measure shows that an athlete performed better

Table 3.5 Beijing 2008 men's 100 m, non-medal based measures of success

Round	Athlete	Nation	Time	Achievement
1	Nawai	Kiribati	11.29	Season best
1	Jurgen Themen	Surinam	10.61	Lifetime best
1	Okilanu Tinilau	Tuvalu	11.48	National record
2	Naoki Tsukahara	Japan	10.23	Season best
2	Churandy Martina	Dutch Antilles	9.99	National record
Semi-final	Naoki Tsukahara	Japan	10.16	Season best
Semi-final	Churandy Martina	Dutch Antilles	9.94	National record
Final	Michael Frater	Jamaica	9.97	Lifetime best
Final	Churandy Martina	Dutch Antilles	9.93	National record

than ever before and was therefore in the best condition of his or her life. Jurgen Themen from Surinam in Table 3.5 was sixth in his first round heat and was eliminated from the competition. He and his NOC can take some pride in the fact that it was the fastest he had ever run. In the 100 m final, Michael Frater from Jamaica came sixth but also ran the fastest race of his life and would be able to reflect on that achievement as a positive measure of success.

Athletes breaking national records

An athlete's season best time or lifetime best time is a personal milestone. The extent of progress made by an elite sport development system can also be measured by examining the performance of an athlete relative to the best performance ever produced by his or her nation. Okilanu Tinilau from Tuvalu in Table 3.5 recorded a time of 11.48 seconds in the first round of the 100 m and was eliminated. This is the fastest that any athlete from Tuvalu has ever run in international competition and would provide a great sense of achievement for the athlete concerned and for those who had been involved in his training. The performance of Churandy Martina of the Dutch Antilles went almost unnoticed compared to the attention given to Usain Bolt who broke the world record in the final. However, Martina managed to break his national record three times (also lifetime and personal bests), qualify for the final and finish in fourth place. It is a remarkable achievement for a nation of 180,000 to have a competitor in the Olympics, let alone have one who finished fourth in the 100 m final.

It would be unreasonable to view Martina's performance as a failure because he did not win a medal. This type of performance indicates positive 'distance' travelled in terms of the achievement of a given nation while at the same time acknowledging that standards have improved globally. Thus, the narrowing of the gap between a national record and the level of performance required to win a medal in a major championship is also a valid measure of success.

Athletes progressing

In high profile sports such as swimming or athletics, simply qualifying for the next round or the final may well be evidence of considerable success. This point is particularly true for smaller nations that have fewer athletes and resources to draw upon than larger more affluent nations. A sprinter from the Cayman Islands (population 51,000) qualifying for the second round of the 100 m could be viewed as an achievement comparable to a large nation such as the United States having two or three athletes in the final. The concept of market share is not solely confined to the first three places. In order to measure strength in depth, it is possible to extend market share calculations to the finalists (usually the top eight) in any given event where first place is awarded eight points and eighth place is awarded one point. This type of measure provides a good insight into the overall competitiveness of nations.

OUTCOMES

Outcomes are impacts that a country's performance in international competition has on the national funding and structure of the sport. To appreciate the nature of outcomes, consider the case of the United Kingdom that has been investing in elite sport since 1997 after it finished in thirty-sixth place on the medals' table for the 1996 Atlanta Olympic Games in what was perceived as a national humiliation. As a result of a huge improvement in Sydney 2000 (eleven gold medals and tenth place in the medals' table), there have been two key outcomes. First, the elite sport development system in the United Kingdom has been shown to be effective and therefore increased funds have been secured from government to maintain the performance of the system. Second, sustained success has enabled the development of what is known as the World-Class Performance system that has continued to produce world-class athletes with the potential to reach the podium. British Rowing is a good example of a national governing body of sport being able to develop a strategy that consistently produces elite talent. The United Kingdom's rowing prowess is such that it has won at least one gold medal in every Olympic regatta since 1984, mainly in the coxless pairs and fours events. The continued funding of British Rowing and the development structure that gives British rowers a competitive advantage in international competition are both classified as outcomes. Qualifying for international competitions, and consistently winning medals in those competitions, ensures continued funding, which in turn means the maintenance of the development structure. For smaller nations, such as the Cayman Islands, creditable performances can also lead to outcomes. These include continued government support for elite sport as well as social impacts such as more people taking part in sport, which in turn may help in the production process of generating more future Olympians.

SUMMARY

At the start of the chapter we set out to provide a structured overview of performance in elite sport. The basic point is that performance should not be measured solely by the number of medals won. In the case of the Olympic Games there are around 205 NOCs and for most of them just producing athletes who qualify for Olympic events is a significant achievement. Even for the nations whose athletes do not qualify on merit alone, it is still likely that their representatives at the Olympics are the best their country has to offer and that they may achieve significant outcomes such as progression to the second round of competition, a season's best, a lifetime's best or a national record.

For the minority of nations that win medals in the Olympic Games, simplistic measures such as medals' table ranking or total medals won are at best only partial measures of performances. Concepts such as awarding points to account for the relative values of medals and the calculation of market share to measure performance over time help to address the weaknesses of the simplistic measures. Different measures can give conflicting assessments of performance and thus it is important to be clear about the purpose of performance measurement and how the results of any analysis are to be interpreted. Combining measures of performance, as shown in Figure 3.4, can help to provide a structure for interpreting results.

Most nations do not win medals at the Olympic Games and thus there needs to be an alternative set of measures that enable such nations to gauge their performance in a way that does not brand them as failures and enables relative performance measures to be used.

Achievements such as posting creditable performances are the building blocks for continued funding. This funding in turn acts as the basis for developing a long-term system that continues the production of internationally competitive athletes. These athletes build a sustained record of success, which in turn drives a virtuous cycle of competitive advantage, success (in its various forms) and funding.

The most important points are that successful performance means different things to different nations and that to measure performance effectively requires an appreciation of the context in which nations operate. The techniques used to measure international sporting success are relatively straightforward. The real skills lie in being able to apply the appropriate techniques for a given set of circumstances and to interpret the results accordingly.

DISCUSSION QUESTIONS

Building on what has been discussed and illustrated in this chapter, test your understanding of the principles involved by tackling the following questions and tasks.

1 For a successful sporting nation of your choice (ranked in the top ten in the Olympic Games medals' table), write a brief assessment of its performance in the most recent Olympic Games.

2 Now conduct a similar analysis for a nation that sent ten or fewer athletes to the same Games.

3 Why is Question 2 more difficult than Question 1?

4 Apply the analysis of medals' table ranking, total medals, points and market share to a single sport of your choice (e.g. the World Track Cycling Championships)? Do the basic principles described in this chapter transfer well to your chosen context?

5 Apply the concept of market share to a nation of your choice in the last five editions of an event of your choice. For example, you might look at China's performance in the World Athletics Championships 2003–2011. What is your interpretation of this nation's performance in this event?

6 For two consecutive editions of an event of your choice, can you replicate the analysis shown in Figure 3.4? Choose an event that has a manageable number of events, for example the World Badminton Championships.

7 To what extent do you agree with the IOC's policy to allow smaller nations to take part in the Olympic Games even though many of these nations are unable to qualify athletes on merit?

8 To what extent are the principles outlined in this chapter applicable to large events in which there is only one winner, for example the FIFA World Cup?

KEY TERMS

- Performance
- Olympic Games
- Success

- ■ Measures
- ■ Medal
- ■ Qualification
- ■ Outputs

GUIDED READINGS

1   The initial research on which this chapter is based was published by UK Sport in 2003. In Sydney 2000 Team GB improved from thirty-sixth place in the medals' table to tenth and won eleven gold medals compared with just one in Atlanta 1996. Despite this improvement, five European nations (Russia, Germany, France, Italy and the Netherlands) were all ranked higher than Great Britain. UK Sport wanted to know why these countries performed better than Team GB and if there was anything that could be learnt from the literature on elite sport policy at the time. In this report our thinking on performance measurement and concepts such as points and market share were first developed.
UK Sport (2003) *European sporting success: A study of the development of medal winning elites in five European countries*, London: UK Sport.

2   Chapter 4 of *The Global Sporting Arms Race* extended our thinking on performance measurement and applied it to different areas such as the Olympic Winter Games and the World Sporting Index (a portfolio of sixty sports that reveals a nation's overall strength in sport). It was in this chapter that we demonstrated the different measures of performance that can give different diagnoses of how well a nation has performed. For example, the number of gold medals won can decline and yet medals' table ranking can stay the same, as was the case for Great Britain between 2000 and 2004.
De Bosscher, V., De Knop, P., van Bottenburg, M., Bingham, J. and Shibli, S. (2008) *The global sporting arms race: Sports policy factors leading to international success.* Brussels, Belgium: Meyer & Meyer.

3   A further application of performance data is using it to make forecasts of how nations might be expected to perform in forthcoming events. In the paper referenced below we forecast that China would win forty-six gold medals in Beijing in 2008. This figure was derived by simple linear regression of performance over time and the addition of a host nation factor. Globally this proved to be the best forecast of China's performance, which was actually fifty-one gold medals.
Shibli, S. and Bingham, J. (2008) A forecast of the performance of China in the Beijing Olympic Games 2008 and the underlying performance management issues. *Managing Leisure: An International Journal*, 13(3–4), 272–292

Recommended websites

www.olympic.org
For the definitive list of all Olympic medals that have been won since 1896 in both Summer and Winter Olympic Games, see the IOC's official website. It has a searchable database of medals that can be searched and filtered in many ways.

http://news.bbc.co.uk/sport1/hi/olympic_games/default.stm

    The BBC has an excellent range of Olympic related pages on its website, including medals' tables and results with innovative ways of analysing the data at the click of a mouse. For example, if you wanted to see a table for performance by men and women at Vancouver 2010 Olympic Winter Games, the data are there to be experimented with.

http://sports123.com/

    For almost unlimited sports results and tables, visit www.sports123.com. This would be a useful starting place for readers wanting to tackle Outcome Questions 4, 5 and 6 at the end of the chapter.

BIBLIOGRAPHY

De Bosscher, V., De Knop, P., van Bottenburg, M. and Shibli, S. (2006). A conceptual framework for analysing sports policy factors leading to international sporting success. *European Sport Management Quarterly*, 6, 185–215.

De Bosscher, V., De Knop, P., van Bottenburg, M., Bingham, J. and Shibli, S. (2008). *The global sporting arms race: Sports policy factors leading to international success*, Brussels, Belgium: Meyer & Meyer.

Jeffery, N. (2008). We're beating drug cheats: Rogge, The Australian, 25 August 2008. Available at www.theaustralian.com.au/news/were-beating-drug-cheats-rogge/story-e6frg7mo-111111728 9173, accessed 29 March 2011.

National Audit Office (2008). Preparing for sporting success at the London 2012 Olympic and Paralympic Games and beyond, report by the Comptroller and Auditor General, The Stationery Office, London.

Rogge, J. (2002). The challenges for the Third Millennium. Opening speech made at the International Conference on Sports Events and Economic Impact, Copenhagen, 18 April 2002.

UK Sport (2003). *European sporting success: A study of the development of medal winning elites in five European countries*, London: UK Sport.

Chapter 4

Managing high performance sport at the national policy level

Veerle De Bosscher
Vrije Universiteit Brussel

Maarten van Bottenburg
Utrecht University

Simon Shibli
Sheffield Hallam University

Paul De Knop
Vrije Universiteit Brussel, Belgium

LEARNING OUTCOMES

Upon completion of this chapter the reader should be able to:

1 recognize and understand the policy factors influencing international sporting success and how the success can be managed;
2 define what an elite sport policy is; interpret and explain the critical success factors (CSFs) used to assess such policies; and
3 apply the policy dimensions (called pillars) and its CSFs outlined to other relevant sporting contexts.

OVERVIEW

In strategic management literature, several authors take the view that performance is constructed by the management system and by managers. According to this view, performance management precedes performance measurement and gives it meaning (Lebas, 1995). Similarly, in high performance sport – also called elite sport in this chapter – systems are created and programmes are developed for young talented athletes, elite athletes, their coaches and organizations because there is a growing belief among policymakers that the international success of athletes is 'developable' and that it can thus be influenced by human intervention. Studies show that nations who plan for success increase their chances of success (De Bosscher *et al.*, 2008). This has led to increasing competition in international sports with extensive investment via Exchequer and lottery funding. The purpose of this chapter is to identify how high performance sport can be managed at the national policy (meso) level and to define what an elite sport policy is.

We present a conceptual framework, the Sports Policy factors Leading to International Sporting Success, also known as the SPLISS model (De Bosscher et al., 2006). This model is the result of joint efforts of a consortium group of international researchers who wanted to develop a model that could be used by policymakers and high performance managers to compare and benchmark nations in elite sport, to measure the performances of their organizations and to evaluate the effectiveness of national elite sport policies (e.g. De Bosscher et al., 2011). While the model addresses the evaluation at the national level of elite sport policy, it is also designed to be implemented at other levels, for example by national sport organizations (sports federations) (Brouwers et al., n.d. (Tennis); Sotiriadou et al., n.d. (Canoe); Truyens et al., n.d. (Athletics)), commercial teams (Boogerd, 2010) and at the city level (De Meyer, n.d.; Van Rossum, n.d.).

THE CONTEXT OF ELITE SPORT

Competition in international sport has increased considerably during the last decade. While Hogan and Norton (2000) found that during the nineties there was a significant linear relationship between money spent and total medals won in Australia, there is evidence that in the period 1980–1996, this has become less valid. De Bosscher et al. (2008) found that none of the nations in a sample of six (Belgium, Canada, Italy, the Netherlands, Norway and United Kingdom) improved its market share of medal points[1] between 2000 and 2004 even though their expenditures on elite sport (from government funding and lotteries) had increased during the same period. There are diminishing returns on investment and it is necessary to continue investing in elite sport simply to maintain existing performance levels (De Bosscher et al., 2008). The fundamental principle of what has been described as 'a global sporting arms race' is that international sporting success can be produced by investing strategically in elite sport (De Bosscher et al., 2008; Oakley and Green, 2001b). A key feature of this 'arms race' is that the rules are determined by what rival nations are doing now, rather than by what an individual nation did in the past (De Bosscher et al., 2008). Just as it is in strategic management literature, the focus is on future performance rather than past achievements (Lebas, 1995). Therefore, because standards are continually improving, standing still means going backwards in elite sport. As a result nations are searching for the most effective keys to strive to differentiate themselves from their competitors and gain a competitive advantage. The focus has moved more and more from a simple input–output relationship towards investing in a blend of 'pillars' or policy dimensions, which are the processes or throughputs, that aim to turn inputs into the desired outputs (Chelladurai, 2001). This was the starting point of the SPLISS model, which will be explored further in this chapter.

THE SPLISS MODEL AS A FRAMEWORK TO MANAGE HIGH PERFORMANCE SPORT AT NATIONAL LEVEL: WHAT IS AN ELITE SPORT POLICY?

The elite sports policies of nations have one common aim: to perform successfully against the best athletes, mostly during international competitions. In spite of increasing competition and high investments in elite sports systems by many countries, the optimum strategy for delivering international success is still unclear. This makes it difficult for sports managers and policymakers to prioritize and to make the right choices in elite sports policy. The lack of an empirically grounded, coherent theory on the factors determining international sporting success lies at the root of the SPLISS model. The aim was to develop a model that clusters all these factors. The basic ideas of this model are related to the generic competitiveness literature, in which researchers seek to determine what makes one firm or nation more successful than its competitors. The measurement of world competitiveness is routinely used in economic studies to provide a framework 'to assess how nations manage their economic future' (Garelli, 2008, p. 1). In the SPLISS study we attempted to replicate this approach in an elite sport setting. Accordingly we developed a framework and explored a method 'to assess how nations can manage their future success in international sporting competitions'. The term 'manage' indicates that the focus is at the meso-level factors, or those determinants that can be influenced by human intervention, in this case by national elite sport policies. Macro-level factors of which population and wealth are identified as the most important and explain more than 50 per cent of international sporting success (e.g. Bernard and Busse, 2004; van Bottenburg, 2000; De Bosscher et al., 2003) were therefore excluded from this model, as well as the micro-level factors, such as genetics, which can explain differences in success between individuals, but not between nations.

From (a) a comprehensive body of literature on different elite sport systems over the past twenty years (e.g. Clumpner, 1994; Digel et al., 2006; Green and Houlihan, 2005; Oakley and Green, 2001a; Riordan, 1989) and (b) supplemented by studies at the micro-level that attempt to understand success determinants for individual rather than nations (e.g. Conzelmann and Nagel, 2003; Duffy et al., 2006; Greenleaf et al., 2001), all 'manageable' key determinants of success were clustered using inductive procedures. Additionally two experimental studies were conducted, one with international tennis coaches from twenty-two nations, and one with 114 Flemish elite athletes and coaches to identify key success drivers from a consumer perspective (Chelladurai, 2001). We refer to earlier publications for more information about the methods used to develop the SPLISS model (De Bosscher et al., 2006). From these different sources, it was concluded that all sports policy factors commonly considered to be important for international sporting success can be classified into nine dimensions, or 'pillars', situated at two levels according to the effectiveness literature: inputs (Pillar 1, financial support) and throughputs (Pillars 2–9), indicating the processes that may lead to certain outputs (successes). These pillars are presented in Figure 4.1 and will be explained in the next section. The input–throughput–output model can be accepted as a way to evaluate effectiveness of elite sport policies of countries from a multidimensional approach (Chelladurai, 2001; De Bosscher and Croock, 2010).

When these nine pillars are compared to recent international comparative studies on elite sport systems (e.g. Bergsgard et al., 2007; Digel et al., 2006; Houlihan and Green, 2008), they show a high degree of overlap with what other authors consider to be the elements of an elite sport system. The main difference is that the nine pillars in the SPLISS study are underpinned by more than 100 critical success factors (CSFs, see below) (De Bosscher et al., 2009) and that the focus is at meso-level factors in relation to success of countries, unlike the more generic literature that attempts to explain elite sport policies in their broader political or historical context.

47

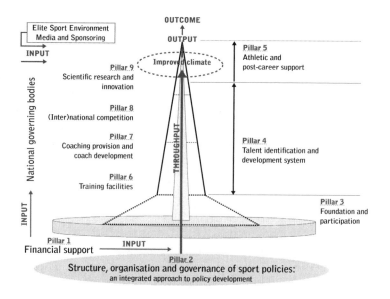

Figure 4.1 *The SPLISS model: theoretical model of nine pillars of sports policy factors influencing international success*

Reprinted with permission from Taylor & Francis Ltd, http://www.informaworld.com, and slightly adapted from De Bosscher *et al.,* 2006

THE CRITICAL SUCCESS FACTORS THAT ARE NEEDED TO MANAGE PERFORMANCE

If you can't measure it, you can't manage it. (Holbeche, 2007, p. 247)

Input–throughput–output models, such as the SPLISS model, are also well known in strategic management literature. With the advent of total quality management (TQM), statistical process control (Deming, 1986) and the balanced scorecard (Kaplan and Norton, 1996), the emphasis in strategic management has shifted away from output measures (such as success) and input measures (such as financial resources) to measures of processes and strategy (Neely *et al.,* 2005). Processes (or throughputs) are much more difficult to measure. For example, companies have often failed at this point because of a lack of aligned performance measures and a linkage with the strategic plans (Kloot and Martin, 2000). The linkage between strategy and performance is also the cornerstone of the Kaplan and Norton (1992) balanced scorecard and the business excellence model (EFQM, 2001) (Wongrassamee *et al.,* 2003). Accordingly, in the SPLISS model each pillar is operationalized into measurable concepts by identifying detailed CSFs.[2] 'Critical success factor' is the term for a critical factor or activity required for ensuring the success of a company or an organization. CSFs are elements that are vital for a strategy to be successful, to an organization's current operating activities and to its future success. A CSF drives the strategy forward; it makes or breaks the success of the strategy (hence 'critical') (Friesen and Johnson, 1995).[3] CSFs should not be confused with key performance indicators (KPIs) that are measures that quantify management objectives and enable the measurement of strategic performance. Accordingly, the CSFs identified in the SPLISS model are vital for the evaluation of each pillar, but are not essentially performance indicators (such as the number of medals). The term 'Leading' in the SPLISS acronym can be misleading in this respect and does not point out cause–effect relationships. Instead, it concerns the factors that are needed to measure each pillar rather than KPIs.

In the second stage of the SPLISS study, the conceptual framework was tested empirically in an international comparative pilot study with six nations (De Bosscher *et al.*, 2008): Belgium (treated separately as two regions, Flanders and Wallony), Canada, Italy, the Netherlands, Norway and the United Kingdom. Using mixed research methods, each CSF was measured by means of four research instruments: an overall sport policy inventory and surveys with athletes, coaches and performance directors. In this respect, the study included 'feedback of the users' as an important element of a multidimensional approach to effectiveness (Chelladurai, 2001). One of the key elements in this study was that, after collecting qualitative and quantitative data in the sample nations, the CSFs were subsequently transformed into a scoring system for each pillar by country. By doing this, the study attempted to move beyond the descriptive level of international comparisons and assess the extent to which nations with good elite sport policies perform better in the international arena than nations with less-developed elite sport policies. We refer you to De Bosscher *et al.* (2007, 2009) for a fuller explanation of this international comparative study in nine pillars and the scoring system.

Including the findings of this study (referred to as De Bosscher *et al.*, 2008), the nine pillars and its content will be discussed according to the CSFs used in the next part. A list of all CSFs is included in Appendix A, as a guide for the reader who wants to apply this in an elite sport setting.[4] As elite sport is dynamic, and as research is still in a developmental stage, these CSFs have changed slightly over the past four years. In 2011–2012 this study with six nations is being repeated at a larger scale, called SPLISS-II. At the time of writing (2011), SPLISS-II involved fifteen nations. There are 133 CSFs measured in the nine pillars and clarified below.

Inputs

Pillar 1: Financial SUPPORT for sport and elite sport

It is an undisputed fact that countries that invest more in elite sport can create better opportunities for athletes to train under ideal circumstances and thus improve their chances of success. There are many examples of countries that have performed better after increasing their investments in elite sport. For example, the United Kingdom set up their World-Class Performance Programme in the build-up to the Sydney 2000 Olympics after disappointing performances in Atlanta in 1996. De Bosscher *et al.* (2008) found that nations who had invested most in elite sport (Italy, the United Kingdom and the Netherlands in their study) also performed best.

Making cross-national comparisons of expenditure on sport is a notoriously difficult exercise, in terms of consistency of what nations include in their definition of expenditures (De Bosscher *et al.*, 2008). In most successful nations except for the United States, high performance sport is financially supported directly through government tax revenues or lotteries and there is considerable political control over elite sport policies. In Appendix A, twelve CSFs, in four categories, have been identified for Pillar 1. The categories include national level expenditures and support for NGBs, both for sport in general and for elite sport. To keep our analysis as simple and consistent as possible, we focus mainly on nations' public expenditure on sport at the national level – that is, expenditure derived from the central government and/or national lotteries. While we acknowledge that, in most nations, expenditure by local government (mainly in grassroots sport development – see CSF 1.8 in Appendix A) and/or the private sector (see CSF 1.9–1.10) is greater than that provided by national government, data are usually unavailable or insufficiently comparable on a like-for-like basis.

Throughputs

In order to achieve the desired results, the outputs, it is important not only to consider the 'what' of investment but also the 'how', or the throughputs. The next eight pillars contain criteria that are indicators of the throughput stage.

Pillar 2: The governance, organization and structure of elite sport: an integrated approach to policy development

As a consequence of internationalization, successful nations' elite sport systems have been copied all over the world. Consequently, in their search for the best pathway to success, elite sport systems and policies are converging into uniform models, with room for variation. Nations differ in the ways the ingredients of success are applied (De Bosscher *et al.*, 2009a). Defining success criteria for Pillar 2 is a complex task due to variations in the sport system of countries, due to how these systems are embedded in a larger system of values and beliefs and due to the difficulty of measuring intangible services. We refer to Appendix A for the twenty-two CSFs have been included in Pillar 2. One important issue is that there needs to be a strong coordination of all agencies involved in elite sport; they need to have clear task descriptions and no overlap of tasks (Clumpner, 1994; Oakley and Green, 2001a). Therefore, sports systems need long-term strategic planning, a good communication system, with simplicity of administration through common sporting and political boundaries (Oakley and Green, 2001a) and elite sport must be recognized as a valuable component of a politician's portfolio of responsibilities (De Bosscher *et al.*, 2008; Houlihan and Green, 2008). According to Houlihan (1997), there is no consensus that there is a need to centralize elite sports policies or have high levels of government intervention. Although federal/central governments in Australia, Canada and the United Kingdom are characterized as 'least centralized states', they have exerted considerable influence in developing elite sport policies (Green and Houlihan, 2005). However, as can also be found in political science studies, centralization facilitates the decision-making process in areas where a higher level of specialization is required (Mintzberg, 1994; Slack, 1997). De Bosscher *et al.* (2008) support this perception and argue that it is a strength to have elite sport coordinated primarily by one organization at the national level, such as UK Sport (UK), *Olympiatoppen* (Norway), NOC*NSF (the Netherlands) and CONI (Italy). Another interesting point of variation (heterogeneity) was noted in the United Kingdom and Norway where UK Sport and *Olympiatoppen* are only responsible for elite sport at the national level, whereas NOC*NSF (the Netherlands), Bloso (Flanders), Adeps (Wallonia), CONI (Italy) and Sport Canada also have responsibilities for general sport development (De Bosscher *et al.*, 2008). This dual responsibility may lead to tension between the development of the two areas, resulting in a slowing down of the decision-making processes.

Another important element of Pillar 2 is the involvement of stakeholders as mechanisms to evaluate the governance assumptions, processes, structures and outcomes, so that members have some say in the strategy of an organization (Hoye and Cuskelly, 2007). Therefore the SPLISS model takes the view that elite athletes, coaches, performance directors and others should be formally invited to be involved in governance, and these groups should also have representatives in the NGBs and have voting rights (Thibault *et al.*, 2010). They should be involved in this way prior to, during and after policy planning and implementation (Dooms, 2010).

Finally, the prioritization of elite sport disciplines is a characteristic of elite sport development in many nations. In an increasingly competitive environment with diminishing returns on investments one may support the policy of investing in 'focus' sports in which there is a track record of prior success and a reasonable probability of future success, rather than spreading resources thinly across all twenty-eight Olympic sports (e.g. Clumpner, 1994). This view has been an element of elite sport policy development in many nations, leading to worldwide debates on prioritization versus diversification.

Pillar 3: Sport participation

Literature is still ambivalent about the relationship between sport for all and elite sport (Green, 2005; Sotiriadou *et al.*, 2008). Van Bottenburg (2003) finds a significant correlation between mass participation and medals won during the Olympic Games (Barcelona and Sydney) especially when sport practising is 'intensive and competitive'. Although this relationship is often contradictory (Green, 2005), the viewpoint of the SPLISS study is that most top athletes have their roots in sport for all. In this respect – compared with other comparative elite sport policy literature – the SPLISS model appears to be standing alone in its view that sport participation should be included as a key to success, and it is even identified as a pillar with which nations, particularly small ones, can gain a competitive advantage over others (De Bosscher *et al.*, 2008). This pillar was measured by twenty-one CSFs (see Appendix A) at three different levels: opportunities for children to engage in sport during school time, opportunities for sport participation outside school time (organized and non-organized) and sport delivered by sport clubs. De Bosscher *et al.* (2008) found that time devoted to physical education (PE) was roughly similar in most of the nations in their sample (on average two times a week for about one hour each time). Slight differences were found in the compulsory nationally determined amount, and in the organizational structures of school sport. The authors found that there were variations in the number of sport club members as a percentage of the population. The percentage was highest in Norway (48 per cent) and lowest in Italy (14 per cent). This finding is consistent with the findings of international comparative studies on sports participation in Europe (van Bottenburg *et al.*, 2005; COMPASS, 1999).

51

Pillar 4: Talent identification and development systems

Once young people have chosen to participate in a sport on a regular basis, it is an important part of NGBs' planning processes to ensure talented young athletes can be identified and developed further. During this stage, performance becomes more important, and requires involvement in formal, competitive sport, primarily with a view to moving towards excellence. De Bosscher *et al.*'s (2008) study found that this pillar was relatively underdeveloped in most nations. The authors conclude that:

> if larger nations, like Italy and the United Kingdom, take a more systematic approach towards talent development, the future prospects for smaller nations are poor as they will find it even more difficult to compete in the escalating global sporting arms race (p. 133).

This pillar consists of two different stages:

(1) Talent identification

Notably there is no consensus in the literature about the exact meaning of different terms (Vaeyens *et al.*, 2008). This stage includes four elements in the SPLISS model, identified through nine CSFs: talent recognition (i.e. monitoring systems and the criteria that are needed to recognize young sports people as being talented), talent detection (the identification of talents from outside a sport participants basis), talent scouting (the processes undertaken to identify young talents) and selection processes (the process of selecting young talents for specific purposes such as competitions and training activities). Most talent identification issues need to be analysed on a sport-specific basis, as in most nations, talented athletes are usually recruited from the existing participation base of a sport. However, some nations have nationally coordinated projects to recruit athletes with a system-related scientific selection process (from a non-participant base, e.g. through schools), or through sport transfer (athletes moving from one sport to another) (UK Sport, 2008).

(2) Talent development

The fourteen remaining CSFs in this pillar are used to measure the second part of Pillar 4. During the talent development phase, athletes become highly committed to their sport, train more and become more specialized. Athletes face a number of transitions during this stage, at the academic level, the athletic level and the psychosocial and psychological levels (Wylleman and Lavallee, 2003). Each transition requires special attention. At the national level, it is important that coaches and NGBs can get information, guidance and possibly financial support to build an optimal approach for planning talent identification and talent development. For athletes it is important to receive multidimensional services appropriate to their age and level. Furthermore, the dual responsibilities of being a student and a young athlete should be recognized by a nationally coordinated system and by a legal framework, both at secondary and higher education levels (Aquilina and Henri, 2010; De Bosscher and De Croock, 2009).

Pillar 5: Athletic and post-athletic career support

Pillar 5 is the stage of excellence: it is the stage at which athletes attain publicly recognized excellence and represent their club or country at national or international level. While different models on athletic development have been formulated, all identify a specific period and/or point of transition whereby youth/junior athletes (are expected to) transfer into the senior elite/professional level. Many athletes drop out of their elite athletes career during this stage (Wylleman and Lavallee, 2003). Various support systems have been set up by nations to increase their numbers of elite athletes, and to provide an optimal elite sport climate.

Many nations have adopted a holistic approach to athletic development and athletes are supported by a multidisciplinary staff for the creation of an optimal environment, including career coaching, legal advice, media training, coaching support (specialist coaches), training and competition support (training facilities, training camps), sports science support (strength and conditioning, nutrition, mental coaching) and sports medicine support (medical specialists, physiotherapists, etc). There are only a few sports where athletes can earn enough money to live and pay for all the costs they incur. Therefore athletes pursuing their sport are treated as employees who receive funding for living and sporting costs, which is sometimes linked to a minimum wage (De Bosscher et al., 2008). This subsidy is often not sufficient to enable elite competitors to be financially independent, and so many continue to work in other employment, or rely on parental support or commercial sponsorship (Green and Houlihan, 2005). The SPLISS model takes the view that the individual living circumstances of athletes need to be provided in a way that enables them to concentrate on their sport full time.

Finally, many athletes are insufficiently prepared for life after sports (Conzelmann and Nagel, 2003). Most athletes face the end of their careers around their mid to late twenties, much earlier than is the case in a regular career (Sinclair and Hackfort, 2000). While they are still engaged in their athletic careers athletes need to be offered appropriate training and given opportunities to prepare for their life after they retire.

Pillar 6: Training facilities

The sixth pillar is concerned with elite sport facilities and infrastructure. These factors were identified as being important by, among others, Oakley and Green (2001a) who identify 'well developed and specific facilities with priority access for elite athletes' as one of the ten characteristics commonly found in elite sports development systems. In addition to sport-specific training facilities, elite sport institutes also have administrative headquarters and close links with education and sports medicine/science facilities. The components of this network can be centralized or decentralized. These elite sport institutes are costly and in many smaller nations less expensive facilities may still be beneficial. The large institute networks such as those in France and Australia have evolved from large centralized systems funded by public means towards commercial partnerships, and from centralized systems to both central and regionally spread networks (Oakley and Green, 2001a). Key reasons for this include reducing distances and travelling times for athletes between their homes and their training venues, and reducing 'homesickness' and under-performance, particularly in young athletes. These elements are measured by ten CSFs in Pillar 6. The 2008 SPLISS study (De Bosscher et al.,

53

2008) suggested that nations that are smaller in area may have a competitive advantage in this pillar, as athletes and coaches don't have to travel so far for training. This pillar also looks at coordination and planning for building and renovating facilities and for creating conducive 'work' environments for elite athletes.

Pillar 7: Coach provision and coach development

The quality and quantity of coaches is important at each level of sport development. In some countries, like France and Australia, certification of coaches is required in sports clubs (López de D'Amico, 2000). Eighteen CSFs are used to measure this pillar, divided in two parts. The first considers the quality and organization of training certification systems, the opportunities delivered to coaches to become world-class experts in their fields and how nations try to develop or attract the best coaches. The second is concerned with the individual living circumstances of elite coaches, including the amount of status attached to being a coach, the pay they receive, social security services and other initiatives that determine how attractive coaching is as a profession. In many countries it is often hard to become a professional coach, due to a lack of recognition for the job by the state, and insufficient social security support systems or opportunities for career development (De Bosscher et al., 2008). Many hours must be invested in training and considerable individual talent is required to become a top-level coach. The system for training and supporting elite coaches seems to be relatively immature in most nations (De Bosscher et al., 2008). It is difficult for coaches to carry out the role on a full-time basis, even though there seems to be a general agreement that athletes as well as coaches need to apply themselves full time to achieve their potential. Furthermore, access to world-class coaching is widely accepted by athletes as the most important support service that they receive (De Bosscher, 2007). This finding is confirmed by Green and Houlihan's study (2005) in which it is stated that:

> There is an acceptance of coaching as an important, if not essential, ingredient in elite success and, more importantly, an ingredient that required status and investment was slow in developing . . . the supporting services of coaching, sports science and medicine were generally and afterthought (2005, p. 175).

Pillar 8: National and international competition

Competition, both at national and international levels, is an important factor in the development of athletes (e.g. Crespo et al., 2001; Green and Houlihan, 2005). It allows athletes to measure themselves against rivals, individually or as a team. Opportunities for international competition for athletes can be enhanced when major sports events are organized in their own nation, as has been shown in many studies on the Olympic Games (e.g. Bernard and Busse, 2004). The eight CSFs in Pillar 8 are classified into three key areas: first, the extent to which there is a national policy and support system for the organization of major international sports events; second, the opportunities for athletes to participate in international competitions; and third, the standard of the national competitions in which athletes participate.

Pillar 9: Scientific research and innovation

Pillar 9, which has ten CSFs, is concerned with the scientific input into elite sport. In this pillar we examine the extent to which nations take a coordinated approach to the organization and dissemination of research and scientific information. Digel *et al.* (2006) found that the systems of high performance sport were all supported by scientific expertise in the eight nations they compared. In Australia, for example, there are more than 100 experts who work in the field of sport science (at the Australian Institute of Sport and in regional institutes) and sport organizations collaborate with the science departments of Australian universities (Russell, 2004). This pillar is one that nations can use to gain a competitive advantage over others, according to the results of the SPLISS 2008 study. The search for innovation and the use of applied scientific research in the development of high performance sport is one of the key indicators that show that nations are strategically developing elite sport (De Bosscher *et al.*, 2008). This pillar is concerned with the development of research, and the collection, coordination and dissemination of scientific research and innovation.

CASE STUDY 4.1

TALENT IDENTIFICATION AND DEVELOPMENT IN ATHLETICS: A COMPARISON OF FLEMISH AND DUTCH POLICY INITIATIVES

Jasper Truyens, Veerle De Bosscher and Bruno Heyndels
Vrije Universiteit Brussel

The 'global sporting arms race' has thwarted the sporting ambitions of many countries (De Bosscher *et al.*, 2008; Oakley and Green, 2001a). Success in international competition can no longer be achieved simply by spending more government money (van Bottenburg, 2009). A crucial question for national sporting organizations is how to develop a performance-driven management system that will bring success on the world stage. Although most elite sport systems have common policy characteristics, there is a lack of scientific research on the performance of national governing bodies (NGBs), which are the main organizations responsible for delivering success at the elite level (Sotiriadou and Shilbury, 2009). NGBs have specific tasks and aims in developing elite sport in their disciplines. The main question addressed in this case study is: What are the organizational tasks and processes in the quest for international sporting success at sport-specific level? To be successful, elite athletes need access to high-quality facilities, qualified coaches, a national competition structure and opportunities to compete internationally, but the sport-specific organizational requirements to achieve these aims remain largely unknown. The role and function of NGBs regarding sport-specific policies tend to be heterogeneous among different countries. Nevertheless, these organizations have an opportunity to play an important role in the development of resources and a competitive advantage. NGBs are characterized by increasing professionalism, a costumer orientation, modernization of management and greater accountability and transparency in their use of public funds (Bayle and Robinson, 2007). As a result these

NGBs have the following tensions due to conflicting aims: (1) a tension between elite development and club development; (2) a tension between the individualized programmes of elite athletes on the one hand, and the collective needs of club members and the social values of sport participation and development on the other; and (3) a tension between the move towards a professional/bureaucratic model of management and the voluntary model of decision making found in many sports (Green, 2008). National sport-governing bodies are moving towards a more business-like approach (Arnott, 2008).

How do these sport organizations construct strategic activities, practices and priorities to achieve elite success? What is their role apart from providing administrative units and national sport agencies directing national elite sport policies? What are the key determinants or priorities in the development of elite success at sport-specific level? This is a case study on athletics in Flanders and the Netherlands. Rather than evaluate the trends of professionalization and bureaucratization, the aim of this case study is to evaluate the organizational performance of the Flemish (*Vlaamse Atletiekliga*) and Dutch (*Atletiekunie*) athletics associations with regard to their elite athletics development processes.

Because of the lack of an appropriate theoretical model of sport policy resources at the sport-specific level, the SPLISS model (Sport Policy factors Leading to International Sporting Success) and the resource-based perspective was used as a starting point to evaluate the nations' competitive advantage in athletics (De Bosscher *et al.*, 2006; De Bosscher, 2007). The added value of this perspective consists of a functional framework of key policy factors describing the overall organizational structure of national elite development (Sotariadou and Shilbury, 2009). Additionally, a resource-based perspective will be applied to identify organizational resources and capabilities that contribute to the development of a competitive advantage in elite athletics. The resource-based perspective aims to explain the relationship between organizations' internal characteristics, the interaction of its resources and its performance (Helfat and Peteraf, 2003). Thereby, capabilities represent a relationship between resources embedded in the policy process (Wang and Ahmed, 2007). Elite sports development is a complex and multidimensional process and the pillars or common features of development systems are highly interdependent (Digel, 2002). Rather than the existence of different pillars and the elite system as such, the strategic management of these resources become more important (Böhlke and Robinson, 2009; De Bosscher *et al.*, 2009). This perspective affirms the crucial importance of organizational capabilities in the development of a competitive advantage.

Based on the nine pillars of the SPLISS model, CSFs were developed representing the policy resources and dynamic capabilities for elite athletics development. In addition to an extensive literature review on elite athletics development, we conducted an exploratory study involving twenty-one interviews and fourteen digital surveys with international high performance directors in athletics in order to develop a model of the sports policy factors that determine international success in athletics. Using inductive analysis, specific policy dimensions and practices in athletics were categorized into eleven different groups or pillars of policy practices that contribute to the organizational strength of the elite athletics policy system.

The following paragraphs describe the policy structures and processes used in athletics in Flanders and the Netherlands. We focus on just two important dimensions, the identification and development of elite athletes. To do so we refer to the organizational structures of the athletics federations (*Vlaamse Atletiekliga* in Flanders and the *Atletiekunie* in the Netherlands). The identification and development of elite athletes is represented by Pillar 4 of the overall SPLISS model, but was separated in the analysis of policy resource in athletics. Talent detection refers to the discovery of potential performers currently not involved in any sport programme (De Vos, 2009; Lidor *et al.*, 2009; Mohamed *et al.*, 2009) and is more focused on athletics participation and talent identification. Talent selection is 'the ongoing process of identifying players at various stages who demonstrate prerequisite standards of performance for inclusion in a particular team' (Mohamed *et al.*, 2009) and represents a structural element in the development of young talented athletes. An overview of the CSFs for talent identification and development can be found in Appendix B.

Talent detection and identification

With regard to talent identification, thirteen CSFs have been identified. Overall, the Flemish *Atletiekliga* has more organizational resources than the Dutch federation for making multidimensional evaluations of athletes' potential. The specific starting age for the talent identification phase in Flanders is determined by the age at which club-level talent tests are first used to provide a first indication of an athlete's potential. Based on these club-level tests, athletes between 12 and 15 years of age are selected to participate in annual regional talent days followed by regional-level training days. An additional test battery at the regional level is the main way of selecting athletes for national talent development programmes. Scouting and competition results are additional ways of selecting future talent.

In 2010, the *Atletiekunie* in the Netherlands introduced different talent tests for clubs, which became operational in 2011. Besides these tests, the *Atletiekunie* itself has no specific resources to identify or detect athletics talent. At a regional level, clubs are stimulated to cluster training activities for young athletes and organize identification tools themselves.

While there is a much broader approach to detecting future talent in Flanders based on club- and regional-level talent tests, detection and selection criteria in the Netherlands refer to specific competition results.

Talent development in athletics

Both athletics federations have multiple development paths to include young talented athletes in their development structures. The development process of the *Atletiekunie* (Netherlands) starts with talented athletes being invited to participate in (a) regional training sessions or (b) central training sessions. Regional coaches provide regional training sessions in four different regions, with up to twenty different training sessions for specific discipline groups (middle- and long-distance running, hurdles, sprinting, throwing events and combined events). These sessions are provided to 14- to 19-year-old junior athletes. Athletes are selected for these training courses according to their development stage (a subjective evaluation by coaches) or, in most cases, by competition results. Additionally, the *Atletiekunie* provides development training plans for different disciplines on their website.

In the talent development process in Flanders, three parallel lines of support can be distinguished: (a) an initial trajectory of regional training and national talent days, followed by a federal talent group structure; (b) two elite athletics schools in Ghent and Hasselt for 12- to 18-year-old athletes; and (c) additional training and completion training camps for the national top fifty athletes (juniors over 14 years of age).

An additional part of the picture in the Netherlands is the secondary LOOT-talent schools (a local cooperation between sports and education), where young students may receive additional training, combined with flexible educational arrangements. As students need a national status to participate in these LOOT-talent schools, these facilities do not add competitive value to the development process. As was stated by a federation talent coach: 'the talents do not need a topsport talent school, as their status allows them to train nationally, where more facilities are provided' (Interview 2).

Figure 4.2 provides an overview of federation resources used to identify and develop athletics talents in Flanders and the Netherlands. Both countries' athletics development processes are characterized by multiple, interchangeable development pathways, which are crucial to the efficiency of the talent development process. As the talent detection process is better developed in Flanders, its process runs more easily as different development pathways are provided. The *Atletiekunie* has a more decentralized and club-based approach to talent identification and develops athletes in regional or national training sessions according to their performance levels.

The Flemish *Atletiekliga* has more organizational resources within the federation to make a multidimensional evaluation of an athlete's talent potential. The Flemish athletics association has more specific human resources (relative to the number of youth athletes) and policy tools (talent identification battery tests and training days) at its disposal to identify and recruit young athletes to its development process. As a consequence, the *Atletiekliga* more easily connects talent identification programmes to its talent development process and

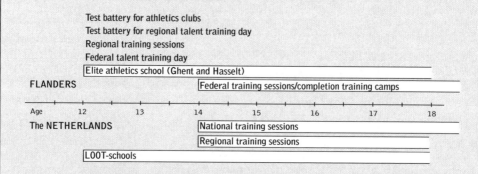

Figure 4.2 *The different development pathways in athletics in Flanders* (Vlaamse Atletiekliga) *and the Netherlands* (Atletiekunie)

is therefore able to use a multidimensional selection strategy, which is a crucial aspect of elite sport development (Vaeyens *et al.*, 2008). Both federations are able to provide training and development support systems for talented athletes, organized in high-level training facilities and by discipline-specific coaches.

Concluding comments

Although both organizations successfully organize an adequate number of talent programmes and develop national athletes, we can't evaluate the development process without bearing in mind the other policy dimensions on the path to success. For example, what is the role of coaching in this process? How are athletics clubs involved in the development of talented athletes? Checking the box on the presence of different policy determinants is an important step to improving the policy development process, but a strategic recipe is probably the most crucial ingredient to international sporting success.

SUMMARY

The nine pillars outlined in this chapter capture all the factors that can be affected by sports policies or sport organizations and that may influence the potential of athletes to perform at international level. The SPLISS model was identified as a functionalist model (Boogerd, 2010). It is applied at the national level, and accepting a high level of institutionalization and government involvement. In an escalating global sporting arms race (De Bosscher *et al.*, 2008) governments in many nations are more willing to intervene directly in elite sport development by investing large amounts of money and expecting a higher return on their investments. However, the SPLISS model may not yet be applicable to other sporting contexts, for example the United States, where governments are generally less involved and where elite sport development is delegated to sport organizations (Sparvero *et al.*, 2008). In the United States sport is highly embedded in the school system that is designed to feed athletes into the university system. There is no sport club tradition in the United States that is comparable to the kind found elsewhere in the world (Sparvero *et al.*, 2008). While the United States is one of the most successful countries, this success is hardly the result of any national policy. On the other hand, elite sport in China (number one in market share in Beijing) has a highly centralized and governmentalized elite sport system. Ergo, it is obvious that 'there are several ways to skin a cat'. It may well be that an optimal environment or elite sports climate for a talented athlete does not deliver the desired success and vice versa, and that athletes without support from government or sport structures emerge naturally. Therefore the SPLISS model may be identified as a useful model for policymakers who want to have an impact on elite sport policies. The model should be further validated in other sporting contexts, such as at the sport-specific level, in commercialized sports, in Paralympic Sports and at the regional level. Exploratory studies have therefore been set up in athletics (2009–2011), tennis (2010–2012), commercial skating teams (2010) and at the city level (2012) to test whether the nine pillars and its CSFs can be a useful tool for the evaluation of performance systems in any elite sport context.

Furthermore, it was concluded from the SPLISS study that the development of athletes with medal-winning capabilities is increasingly the product of a long-term strategic planning process. But in a rapidly changing sport environment this model may be subject to revision over time, when nations find other strategies to gain success. Competition is profoundly dynamic in character, and organizations in every sector, including sports, therefore have to adapt just to maintain their competitive position (Holbeche, 2007). Sustaining advantage requires continual change and innovation that logically implies continuous revision of the critical success indicators used to measure each pillar. Another key element influencing the strategic planning processes of nations is that the rules of the game are dictated by what rival nations are doing, not by what an individual nation is doing at present compared with what it did in the past. Performance is therefore not so much about past achievements, but about the future.

DISCUSSION QUESTIONS

1   What is an elite sport policy?
2   Take one or more pillar and its CSFs and apply them to a specific elite sport setting of your choice, e.g. a sports federation (national sport organization, national governing body), a sports club, city, sports academy or a commercial sport team. Collect data through several sources, such as the Internet, secondary sources and interviews. How and to what extent does this organization apply the pillar(s)?
3   Make a critical evaluation on the usefulness of the pillars and CSF to your context. Which CSFs can be applied, and which cannot?
4   Is the SPLISS model and its CSF applicable to contexts other than national level elite sport policies?

PS: You can always email your findings to the authors.

KEY TERMS

- Inputs
- Throughputs
- Elite sport policies
- Competitiveness
- Managing high performance sport

GUIDED READINGS

De Bosscher, V., Bingham, J., Shibli, S., van Bottenburg, M. and De Knop, P. (2008). *The global sporting arms race. An international comparative study on sports policy factors leading to international sporting success.* Aachen: Meyer & Meyer.

Houlihan, B. and Green, M. (2008). *Comparative elite sport development. Systems, structures and public policy.* London: Elsevier.

Oakley B. and Green, M. (2001a). The production of Olympic champions: International perspectives on elite sport development system. *European Journal for Sport Management*, 8, 83–105.

NOTES

1 Market share as the term is used here is a standardized measure of total achievement in an event whereby total medals won are converted into 'points' (gold = 3, silver = 2, bronze = 1), and the points won by a given nation is subsequently expressed as a percentage of the total points awarded (SIRC, 2002).

2 In the SPLISS pilot study (De Bosscher, 2008) 144 CSFs were identified as important. After reorganization, validation in specific contexts and taking into account the dynamic character of elite sport policies, 133 CSFs now remain and are measured in the SPLISS-II study.

3 The concept of 'success factors' was developed by D. Ronald Daniel of McKinsey & Company in 1961. This process was refined by John F. Rockart in 1981. In 1995, James A. Johnson and Michael Friesen applied it to many sector settings, including health care (Wikipedia, 2011).

4 It should be noted that this model was developed in order to compare nations, and therefore it focuses on the national level of elite sport policies. Further validation is needed to use the model in other sporting contexts or at other levels.

BIBLIOGRAPHY

Aquilina, D. and Henry, I. (2010). Elite athletes and university education in Europe: a review of policy and practice in higher education in the European Union Member States. *International Journal of Sport Policy*, 2(1), 25–47.

Arnott, I. (2008). An understanding towards organisational change in swimming in the United Kingdom. *International Business Research*, 1(2), 110–123.

Bayle, E. and Robinson, L. (2007). A framework for understanding the performance of national governing bodies in sport. *European Sport Management Quarterly*, 7(3), 249–268.

Bergsgard, N. A., Houlihan, B., Mangset, P., Nodland, S. I. and Rommetveldt, H. (2007). Sport policy. A comparative analysis of stability and change. London: Elsevier.

Bernard, A. and Busse, M. (2004). Who wins the Olympic Games? Economic resources and medal totals. *Review of Economics and Statistics*, 86, 413–417.

Boogerd, R. (2010). Twee kanten van de medaille. Sleutelfiguren uit de schaatssport over de gevolgen van de ontwikkeling van merkenteams voor het topsportklimaat van het langebaanschaatsen en talentontwikkeling in het bijzonder [Two sides of the medal. Key figures in skating about the consequences of the development of branding teams for the elite sport climate and talent development in particular]. Unpublished master's thesis.

Böhlke, N. and Robinson, L. (2009). Benchmarking of élite sport systems. *Management Decision*, 47(1), 67–84.

van Bottenburg (2003). Top- en breedtesport: een Siamese tweeling? [Elite sport and sport for all: a siamese twin?] In K. Breedveld (Ed.), *Rapportage Sport 2003* (pp. 285–312). Den Haag, the Netherlands: Sociaal en cultureel planbureau.

van Bottenburg, M. (2009). *Op jacht naar goud. Het topsportklimaat in Nederland 1998–2008.* Nieuwegein: Arko Sports Media.

van Bottenburg, M. (2000). *Het topsportklimaat in Nederland* [The elite sports climate in the Netherlands]. 's-Hertogenbosch, the Netherlands: Diopter-Janssens and van Bottenburg bv.

van Bottenburg, M., Rijnen, B. and Van Sterkenburg, J. (2005). *Sports participation in the European Union. Trends and differences.* 's Hertogenbosch: W.J.H. Mulier Institute and Nieuwegein: Arko Sports Media.

Chelladurai, P. (2001). *Managing organisations, for sport and physical activity. A system perspective.* Scotsdale: Holcomb Hathaway Publishers.

Clumpner, R. A. (1994). 21st century success in international competition. In R. Wilcox (Ed.), *Sport in the global village* (pp. 298–303). Morgantown, WV: FIT.

COMPASS (1999). *Sports participation in Europe.* London: UK Sport.

Conzelmann, A. and Nagel, S. (2003). Professional careers of the German Olympic athletes. *International Review for the Sociology of Sport*, 38, 259–280.

Crespo, M., Miley, D. and Couraud, F. (2001). An overall vision of player development. In M. Crespo, M. Reid and D. Miley (Eds.), *Tennis player development* (pp. 13–18). London: ITF.

De Bosscher, V. (2007). *Sports policy factors leading to international sporting success.* Brussels, Belgium: VUBPRESS.

De Bosscher, V., Bingham, J., Shibli, S., van Bottenburg, M. and De Knop, P. (2008). *The global sporting arms race. An international comparative study on sports policy factors leading to international sporting success.* Aachen: Meyer & Meyer.

De Bosscher, V. and De Croock, S. (2010). *Effectiviteit van de Topsportscholen in Vlaanderen* [Effectiveness of the elite sport schools in Flanders]. *Research report for the department CJSM, Flemish government.* Brussels, Belgium: Vrije Universiteit Brussel.

De Bosscher, V., De Knop, P. and Heyndels, B. (2003). Comparing relative sporting success among countries: Create equal opportunities in sport. *Journal of Comparative Physical Education and Sport*, 3(3), 109–120.

De Bosscher, V., De Knop, P. and van Bottenburg, M. (2009). An analysis of homogeneity and heterogeneity of elite sport systems in six nations. *International Journal of Sports Marketing and Sponsorship*, 10(2), 111–131.

De Bosscher, V., De Knop, P., van Bottenburg, M. and Shibli, S. (2006). A conceptual framework for analysing sports policy factors leading to international sporting success. *European Sport Management Quarterly*, 6(2), 185–215.

De Bosscher, V., De Knop, P., van Bottenburg, M., Shibli, S. and Bingham, J. (2009). Explaining international sporting success. An international comparison of elite sport systems and policies in six nations. *Sport Management Review*, 12, 113–136.

De Bosscher, V., Shilbury, D., Van Hoecke, J., Theeboom, M. and De Knop, P. (2011). Effectiveness of national elite sport policies: A multidimensional approach applied to the case of Flanders. *European Sport Management Quarterly*, 11(2), 115–141.

Deming, W. E. (1986). *Out of the crisis.* Cambridge, MA: MIT Press.

Digel, H. (2002). A comparison of successful sport systems. *New Studies in Athletics*, 17(1), 37–50.

Digel, H., Burk, V. and Fahrner, M. (2006). High-performance sport. An international comparison. *Edition Sports International*, 9. Weilheim/Teck: Bräuer.

Dooms, M. (2010). Crafting the integrative value proposition for large scale transport infrastructure hubs: A stakeholder management approach. Brussels, Belgium: VUBPRESS.

Duffy, P., Lyons, D., Moran, A., Warrington, G. and McManus, C. (2006). How we got here: Perceived influences on the development and success of international athletes. *Irish Journal of Psychology*, 27(3–4), 150–167

Friesen, M. E. and Johnson, J. A. (1995). *The success paradigm: Creating organizational effectiveness through quality*. Westport, CT: Greenwood Publishing Group.

Green, B. C. (2005). Building sport programs to optimize athlete recruitment, retention and transition: toward a normative theory of sport development. *Journal of Sport Management*, 19, 233–253.

Green, M. (2008). Non-governmental organizations in sports development. In V. Girvinov (Ed.), *Management of sport development* (pp. 89–108). Oxford: Elsevier.

Green, M. and Houlihan, B. (2005). *Elite sport development. Policy learning and political priorities*. London: Routledge.

Greenleaf, C., Gould, D. and Diefen, K. (2001). Factors influencing Olympic performance with Atlanta and Nagano US Olympians. *Journal of Applied Sport Psychology*, 13, 154–184.

Helfat, C. E. and Peteraf, M. A. (2003). The dynamic resource-based view: Capability lifecycles. *Strategic Management Journal*, 24, 997–1010.

Hogan, K. and Norton, K. (2000). The 'price' of Olympic gold. *Journal of Science and Medicine in Sport*, 3, 203–218.

Holbeche, L. (2007). The high performance organisation. Creating dynamic stability and sustainable success. London: Butterworth-Heinemann.

Houlihan, B. (1997). *Sport, policy and politics. A comparative analysis*. London: Routledge.

Houlihan, B. and Green, M. (2008). Comparative elite sport development. Systems, structures and public policy. London: Elsevier.

Hoye, R. and Cuskelly, G. (2007). *Sport governance*. Oxford: Elsevier.

Kaplan, R. and Norton, D. P. (1996). Using the balanced scorecard as a strategic management system. *Harvard Business Review*, 74(1), 75–85.

Kloot, L. and Martin, J. (2000). Strategic performance management: A balanced approach to performance management issues in local government. *Management Accounting Research*, 11, 231–251.

Lebas, M. (1995). Performance measurement and performance management. *International Journal of Production Economics*, 41, 23–35.

López de D'Amico, R. (2000). *Organisation and regulations in National Sport Bodies: A comparative study in artistic gymnastics*. Published doctoral thesis, Sydney University, USA (UMI No. 3001249).

Mintzberg, H. (1994). *Organisatiestructuren* [Organisational structures]. Schoonhoven: Academic Service.

Neely, A., Gregory, M. and Platts, K. (2005). Performance measurement system design. A literature review and research agenda. *International Journal of Operations and Production Management*, 25(12), 1228–1263.

Oakley, B. and Green, M. (2001a). The production of Olympic champions: International perspectives on elite sport development system. *European Journal for Sport Management*, 8, 83–105.

Oakley, B. and Green, M. (2001b). Still playing the game at arm's length? The selective reinvestment in British sport, 1995–2000. *Managing Leisure*, 6, 74–94.

Riordan, J. (1989). Soviet sport and perestroika. *Journal of Comparative Physical Education and Sport*, 6, 7–18.

Russell, A. (2004). Sports institutes, science and government funding: A key to Australia's sporting success? In R. Philippaerts (Ed.), *Proceedings of the 9th annual symposium of the Association for Kinesiology in cooperation with the Belgian Association of Sports Medicine and Sport Science, from science to medals* (pp. 23–25). Ghent: VKS.

Sinclair, D. A. and Hackfort, D. (2000). The role of the sport organisation in the career transition process. In D. Lavallee and P. Wylleman (Eds.), *Career transitions in sport: International perspectives* (pp. 131–142). Morgantown, WV: Fitness Information Technology.

Slack, T. (1997). Understanding sport organizations: The application of organization theory. Champaign, IL: Human Kinetics.

Sotiriadou, P. Shilbury, S. and Quick, S. (2008). The attraction, retention/transition and nurturing process of sport development: Some Australian evidence. *Journal of Sport Management*, 22, 247–272.

Sotiriadou, K. and Shilbury, D. (2009). Australian elite athlete development: An organisational perspective. *Sport Management Review*, 12(3), 137–148.

Sparvero, E., Chalip, L. and Green, C. (2008). United States. In B. Houlihan and M. Green. Comparative elite sport development (pp. 243–293). London: Elsevier.

Thibault, L., Kihlb, L. K. and Babiak, K. (2010). Democratisation and governance in international sport: Addressing issues with athlete involvement in organisational policy. *International Journal of Sport Policy*, 2(3), 275–302.

UK Sport (2008). The elite coach. Available at www.uksport.gov.uk/pages/elite_coach/, accessed 10 December.

Vaeyens, R., Lenoir, M., Williams, A. M. and Philippaerts, R. (2008). Talent identification and development programmes in sport: Current models and future directions. *Sports Medicine*, 38(9), 703–714.

Wang, C. L. and Ahmed, P. K. (2007). Dynamic capabilities: A review and research agenda. *International Journal of Management Reviews*, 9(1), 31–51.

Wikipedia (2011) Critical Success Factor. Available at http://en.wikipedia.org/wiki/Critical_success_factor#cite_note-1, accessed October, 2011.

Wongrassamee, S., Simmons, J. E. L. and Gardiner, P. D. (2003). Performance measurement tools: The balanced scorecard and the EFQM excellence model. *Measuring Business Excellence*, 7(1), 14–29.

Wylleman, P. and Lavallee, D. (2003). A developmental perspective on transitions faced by athletes. In M. Weiss (Ed.), *Developmental sport and exercise psychology: A lifespan perspective*. Morgantown, WV: Fitness Information Technology.

Chapter 5

Comparative high performance sports models

Winston Wing Hong To
University of Western Ontario

Peter Smolianov
Salem State University

Darwin Michael Semotiuk
University of Western Ontario

LEARNING OUTCOMES

Upon completion of this chapter the reader should be able to:

1   identify various approaches to comparing high performance sport systems (HPS);
2   define strengths and limitations of various approaches to comparing HPS;
3   profile HPS systems in the former USSR and current Russia, United States and Canada; and
4   discuss the challenges the above countries face and their international sporting performance in the future.

OVERVIEW

This chapter discusses different models that have been used to compare high performance sport (HPS) systems. It includes case studies covering the USSR and Post-Soviet Russian HPS systems, the Canadian HPS system and the US HPS system. The chapter includes a comparison of these case studies.

ANALYSING SELECTED HPS COMPARATIVE MODELS

There is no perfect model for international comparative sport analysis, let alone one that focuses solely on HPS (De Bosscher *et al.*, 2010). The most recent attempts include studies by academic researchers such as Green and Oakley (2001), Baumann (2002), Digel (2002),

Houlihan and Green (2008), Smolianov and Zakus (2008), Platonov (2010) and De Bosscher *et al.* (2010).

Mainly, comparative HPS models focus on descriptive explanations of the selected ingredients (usually sport policies) that are deemed to contribute to successful performance in international sport. These models are validated by using case studies of countries that have demonstrated international sporting success. HPS systems are dynamic, complex and varied in design. This is due to the ever-changing sport environment, and the cultural and political dimensions that need to be considered when conducting a comparative research study (De Bosscher *et al.*, 2010; Digel, 2002).

The criteria for cross-country analysis in this chapter are based on an investigation of the comparative studies mentioned above and shown in Table 5.1.

Past models seem to reflect the views of the authors' countries to a certain degree, in the history of their sport systems and what they are trying to achieve. This could be the reason why some models give more emphasis to macro-level aspects such as partnerships or financing, while other models focus more on meso-level factors such as coaching expertise or micro-level practices such as post-career athlete support.

Comparative models are challenged by the constant innovations introduced in the attempt to provide maximum support of HPS. Therefore a progressive comparative framework should be flexible enough to encompass the similarities and differences of sport systems and to deal adequately with unique and innovative strategies. The following broad HPS areas are used in the case studies of this chapter: organization and financing, facilities and competitions, talent identification and development, sport science, medicine, education and other support of athletes. Three successful but very different HPS systems are featured: the centralized governmental system of the former USSR and present-day Russia, the decentralized governmental system of Canada and the decentralized non-governmental system used in the United States.

THE USSR AND POST-SOVIET RUSSIAN HPS SYSTEM

The USSR and Unified Team[1] competed in the Summer Olympics ten times from 1952 to 1992, winning the highest number of medals eight times and being second in the total medal tally twice. In the Winter Olympics, the USSR and Unified Team competed ten times from 1956 to 1992, topping the total medal tally seven times and coming second three times. The USSR placed second in 1964 and 1968 as a result of the short-lived governmental policy of relying more on volunteer instructors and less on paid coaches. Soviet sport dominated global competition when its system was in the hands of professional coaches and sport scientists, and when everyone was encouraged to participate in sport at no or minimal cost. The commitment to these conditions lessened in post-Soviet Russia, which placed third in the total medal count at the 1996 Summer Olympic Games, second in 2000 and 2004 and third in 2008. In the Winter Olympics Russia was third in 1994, third in 1998, sixth in 2002, fifth in 2006 and sixth in 2010.

Organization and financing

The present-day Russia inherited a holistic Soviet HPS system, where athlete preparation had been managed by the national government from the top down, driven primarily by political imperatives, where common goals were put above the interests of national sport organizations (NSOs) and clubs, and where coaches, in consultation with physicians and scientists, played a critical role in identifying athletes who were likely to win. These athletes were given more opportunities for progression (Platonov, 2010).

The following organizational structures important for HPS in the USSR were developed after 1917 and reached their peak in the 1980s:

- multi-sport clubs supported by workplaces;
- uniform athlete and coach classification and rewards; and
- athlete paths from sport clubs through sport schools to sport colleges and sport universities.

HPS had been supported by mass participation and was financed by the government to provide free or heavily subsidized coaching, facilities and competitions for all. Construction of facilities was driven by the central government, and planning of sport programmes and competitions was coordinated by national and local sport commissions across municipalities. Each organization received awards and increased budgets to reward them for the sporting achievements of their employees. The Soviet government introduced a national lottery called Sportloto in 1970, which is still one of the most important support mechanisms for sport in Russia.

After the dissolution of the Soviet Union in 1991, Russian sport lost much of its public funding. Sport started to regain its importance in the year 2000. HPS development has been emphasized more strongly since 2007 when Sochi won the bid to host the 2014 Winter Olympics, with increased sport funding of US$3 billion announced in 2011 (Mackay, 2011).

Events

Spartakiads – multi-stage national festivals that included more sports than Olympic Games – were important in the Soviet system of competition. The four-yearly finals of the Spartakiads were a rehearsal, one year before the Olympics. In 1956, 20 million people participated in Spartakiads and by 1975 the number had grown to 80 million – one-third of the population (Isaev, 2002; Riordan, 1980). Post-Soviet Russia revived the Spartakiads in 2002, and made them annual events and integrated them with student competitions. The 2011 Youth Spartakiad had four tiers of competition: first at individual educational institutions, then in municipalities, in regions and culminating in the national finals (Ministry for Sport, 2011).

The Soviet Olympic preparation began five years ahead of each Games, and included the previous Games. The plans integrated medal objectives, training programmes and competition calendars. In the 1970s, the Soviet annual sports calendar included 300 different competitions. The Ministry for Sport coordinated 10,000 competitions and training camps in 132 sports in 2011.

Table 5.1 Summaries and observations of comparative HPS models

Models	Observations (strengths and limitations)
Bauman (2002) • Coaching expertise • Decentralization and regionalization • Leading-edge support services • Partnerships • Talent search • Interventionism	*Strengths* • Simple, clearly explained actions that lead to successful high performance *Limitations* • Based primarily on Australia
Digel (2002) • Resource model for successful top-level sport (3 levels): • Level of society (vary from country to country): politics, population, economics, employment, education, mass media, standard of living, life satisfaction of the population • Level of sport organization (important for success in international competitions): ideological preconditions, definition of priorities, Olympic tradition, athlete services, coaches, sports facilities, funding, talent identification, the competition system, reward systems, anti-doping fight • Level of the relationship between the top-level sport system and its environment: relationship of the level of society's elements (i.e. politics, population, economics) to its environment (the population)	*Strengths* • Identifies commonalities and differences across countries • Focuses on macro-level factors that affect high performance sport *Limitations* • Hard to use as a guide for meso- and micro-level practices
Houlihan and Green (2008) • Support for 'full-time athletes' • A hierarchy of competition opportunities centred on preparation for international events • Elite facility development • The provision of coaching, sports science, and sport medicine support services	*Strengths* • Focus on the athletes, particularly on meso-level support • Easy to understand practices of different countries *Limitations* • No conclusions on how to achieve success
Smolianov and Zakus (2008) • Funding and organization of mass and elite sport • Partnerships with supporting agencies • Educational, scientific, medical, philosophical and promotional support • Competition systems • Training centres • Talent identification and development • Advanced athlete preparation and support	*Strengths* • Integration of Western and Eastern European approaches • Identification of desired practices *Limitations* • Some practices are difficult to implement

Platonov (2010)
- Theoretical, methodological and organizational foundations
- Material and technical provisions, concentration of financial resources
- Human resources and athlete development
- Training process, competition activities
- Science and methodology support, medical service

Strengths
- Specific ways to win Olympic medals
- Histories of HPS development capturing the uniqueness of nations

Limitations
- No uniform comparison structure

De Bosscher et al. (2010), referring to De Bosscher et al.'s (2006) SPLISS model
- Financial support
- Organization and structure of sport policies
- Foundation and participation
- Talent identification and development system
- Athletic and post-career support
- Training facilities
- Coaching provision and coach development
- National and international competition
- Scientific research

Strengths
- Detailed explanation of the success factors with sub-criteria allowing for quantitative analysis and specific actions for developing an HPS system
- Focus on meso- and micro-level of HPS
- Allows operationalisation and measurement of HPS

Limitations
- The highly detailed criteria may not capture unique or new practices

Facilities

The development of the USSR training centres peaked during the preparation for the 1980 Olympic Games in Moscow. A water sports facility developed in the 1970s included twelve swimming pools of four sizes for different levels of swimming, as well as a multi-speed transparent treadmill pool. Seven of these pools operate in 2011. Current Russia also retained the Soviet system of schools integrated with sport facilities to offer special academic schedules, nutritional and other services to accommodate athletes training twice a day, as well as boarding schools and colleges that provide nurturing conditions for up to three daily sport practices.

In the 1970s, a network of training centres for all Olympic sports had been developed for different geographic, climatic and altitude conditions. Ten centres for the centralized training of national teams had been developed. Sports that could benefit each other had been placed together. The Ministry for Sport (2011) coordinates facilities and programmes at 781 Olympic Reserve Schools, 40 Olympic Reserve Colleges and 25 regional Olympic training centres.

Talent identification and development

One of the responsibilities of coaches in the USSR and in present-day Russia has been to scout for potential athletes at schools. Guidelines for 18-year athlete progression include minimum safe starting ages for each sport as well as training, competition and recovery methodologies. The system of uniform nationwide athlete ranks developed by the USSR scientists included three junior, three senior and four master ranks with minimum performance requirements and competition achievements. Twenty-first century Russia extended the USSR system of ranks from 60 sports in 1980 to 143 in 2011. Pools of participants are gradually reduced through the ten ranks by coaches who use anthropometric, medico-biological, pedagogical, psychological and sociological tests.

To help coaches, the Russian sport authorities provide a genetic test based on the analysis of blood and hair, accompanied by recommendations from sport scientists regarding the right sport for particular individuals, specialization within the sport, and optimal training and lifestyle programmes. The test is also available to parents to have their children tested for US$2,000.

Comprehensive support of athletes

The USSR sport system was operated by qualified paid professionals at all participation levels. Coaches had to pass fitness tests in addition to academic exams to enter sport universities for five-year long programmes; coaches competed in and studied a particular sport and then progressed through a five-stage qualification system. Post-Soviet Russia continues to provide coaches with this guided progression in 117 sports. The same curriculum and sport-specific education is retained by thirteen sport universities across Russia. The leading sports university in Moscow, the Russian State University of Physical Education, Sport and Tourism, was established in 1918. It has 43 departments offering 100 specializations including coaching degrees in 55 different sports. HP athletes are able to attend one of the country's forty Olympic Reserve Colleges, which integrate high school and college education, awarding degrees in physical education, coaching and sport management.

In the USSR, research on all aspects of sport was coordinated by the Central Scientific Research Institute of Physical Culture established in 1933 and undertaken at 28 sport research institutes and sport universities. In the 1970s and 1980s, scientific groups were formed to advise sports teams. The USSR wrestling and boxing teams were serviced by a group of forty specialists in pedagogical science, medicine, psychology, physiology, biomechanics, biochemistry and engineering. Four- to eight-year plans were prepared for individual athletes. In the 1970s, 1980s and 1990s, the USSR/Unified wrestling team won more gold in each Olympics they attended than the wrestlers of any other country. The Russian scientists of the twenty-first century have applied the wrestling research to thirteen other disciplines (Ippolitov *et al.*, 2009). The scientific support is still centrally coordinated and financed by the Ministry for Sport. In 2011, Summer Olympic sports were supported by forty-one science groups, winter sports by fifteen and Paralympic and other special needs sports by twenty-six.

In the 1920s and 1930s, free medical service for all USSR sport participants was established, including physicians at sport facilities. From 1946, sport clinics were created where a full spectrum of specialist doctors detected early symptoms of overtraining and corrected training regimes. A 'doctor-coach' degree was developed to combine medical training with sport-specific coach education. Retaining the USSR focus on preventative medicine, in 2011 the hydrothermal complex at the Sochi national training centre was equipped with seven different kinds of hot rooms and saunas as well as pools for hydromassage and rooms for other types of massage. As part of the increased governmental support of sport, sports medicine received US$83.4 million in 2011 (Mackay, 2011).

The USSR sport system seemed to be more successful in preventing doping scandals than post-Soviet Russia. One week before the Beijing 2008 Olympics, seven Russian contenders for Olympic medals were suspended for tampering with their urine samples. The Russian performance at the 2010 Vancouver Winter Games also suffered after seven skiers were disqualified, mostly for taking the banned drug EPO. Subsequent measures by the Ministry for Sport (2011) included stricter penalties for doping violations and closer cooperation with event organizers and regional sport authorities. Also, Russian authorities decided to start teaching courses in the prevention of doping at schools and universities, and to feature anti-doping material on television.

Modern Russia increasingly offers monetary incentives to athletes, promising Olympic gold medallists US$150,000–250,000 each from such sources as national and regional governments. The governmental monthly allowance for athletes was increased in 2011 from US$400–670 to US$1,170–4,000 (Mackay, 2011).

The future of Russian HPS

The government neglected sport for a decade following the 1991 dissolution of the USSR and this caused a deterioration in the foundations of HPS. Mass participation decreased as did the expertise of coaches, managers and scientists. However, if the country continues to increase its investments into reconstruction and modernization of the former Soviet sport system,

Russia's second placing in the medal tallies at the 2010 Youth Olympic Games and at the 2011 World Summer Universiade could be indicative of the country's potential to perform among the world's top three sporting nations.

THE UNITED STATES' HPS SYSTEM

The United States (US) has won more medals than any other country in the Summer Olympic Games and it has the second highest overall medals tally for the Winter Olympic Games. However, as the US is the only successful sport nation where the federal government does not develop sport, the country's sport performance is not stable. The US grew to own the Olympic podium for most of the first half of the twentieth century, but after 1952 the USSR led the Games, except in 1964 and 1968 when the Soviet government reduced its support for sport. After the disintegration of the USSR, the USA led the Olympic medals tallies from 1996 until 2008 when China started to overpower in international sport.

Organization and financing

HPS in the US is under the sway of market forces more than in other countries, and is managed from the bottom up by the organizations governing individual sports, most importantly NSOs under the coordination of the United States Olympic Committee (USOC). The National Collegiate Athletic Association (NCAA) and the National Federation of State High School Associations (NFHS) play important roles. Professional leagues, such as the National Basketball Association (NBA), Major League Baseball (MLB) and the National Hockey League (NHL), allow their athletes represent the country and develop players through minor leagues. Governmental control is minimal, and so the functions of sporting organizations are not constrained but often chaotic, and international sport success depends largely on the nation's level of interest in sport, organizational, economic and technical abilities, the role of sport in education, and the budgets and competence of NSOs, as noted by Platonov (2010).

The US sport system is driven by competition rather than by cooperation among sport organizations, programmes and coaches. This provides opportunities and stimulation for unique approaches, but means there is a lack of coordination and uniform standards, which has resulted in diminishing performance since the Second World War (Coyle, 2007; Sparvero et al., 2008), despite the following measures.

A US law passed in 1950 enabled the US Olympic Committee (USOC) to solicit tax-deductible contributions as a private, non-profit corporation. However, with the lack of governmental funding and the absence of a sport lottery, USOC raises most of its money from broadcast fees and sponsorships, which makes athlete preparation dependent on the economic climate, and forces some athletes to spend time on fundraising instead of training (Michaelis, 2009).

The US government has been supporting HPS through the military since 1947. President Kennedy requested that the military concentrate on minor sports in the Olympics. Conditions for full-time paid Olympic preparation in the military were created during the 1960s and from the 1990s onwards these conditions have been strengthened. Since 1948, 615 military personnel have represented the US at the Olympics as athletes and coaches, winning 142 medals.

Events

The US has hosted the Olympic Games on eight occasions, four times each for the Summer and Winter games. National multi-sport festivals were organized by the USOC from 1978 to 1995 and were held annually in the three years between Summer Olympics. National State Games have been held biennially since 1999, serving as finals for state-level games. Annually, more than 400,000 athletes compete in state games nationwide. Medal winners from forty-five state games earned the right to compete in 24-sport 2011 State Games of America.

US national competitions are run in a limited range of sports compared to the thirty-five disciplines of the 2012 Olympics. National competitions are held in about fifteen professional sports, twenty-four sports in the national state games and twenty sports in the NCAA. In the 2008 Olympics, China won medals in twenty-five different sports, while the USA won medals in twenty-one.

In the market-driven professional US sport system, it is a particular challenge to integrate competitions across all levels of each sport. The NBA integrated their competitions for the 2008 Olympics, but the MLB did not; the US Basketball team won two gold medals (men and women), the US Baseball team were placed third and the US Softball team were placed second.

Facilities

The network of Olympic training centres provides top-level centralized athlete preparation in different geoclimates and altitudes in Colorado, New York and California. The centre at Northern Michigan University services sports not well developed at other US universities. There are also twelve Olympic training sites.

The USOC has been assisting intermediate-level athletes through its Community Olympic Development Program (CODP). The CODP started in 1998 and partnered with fourteen NSOs and seven community sports groups. There were 217 CODP training centres with 250,000 participants in 2011 (CODP, 2011). Facilities in schools, colleges and universities also play a critical role in the USA's sporting success.

Talent identification and development

Talent searches by coaches and scouts, try-outs as well as minor leagues, developmental competitions and camps are all used to identify potential high performers. However, the primary means of athlete selection in the US is competition within the following talent pools:

- elite athletes: national team, Olympic, professional
- advanced athletes: college, semi-professional leagues
- adolescent athletes: high school
- young athletes: recreational programs, grassroots leagues

(Grasso, 2008)

Atlas Sports Genetics offers a US$149 test to children from infancy to about 8 years old using a swab inside the child's cheek and along the gums to collect DNA. Atlas provides advice on whether the child will be suited to sprints, power and strength sports, endurance sports or activity sports. Atlas recommends which sports will be the most appropriate and what paths to follow so the child reaches his or her potential (Markur, 2008).

US NSOs are starting to establish systematic athlete development methodologies. USA Hockey adopted a long-term athlete development (LTAD) model to create the American Development Model (ADM). Launched in 2009, ADM provides a nationwide blueprint for age-appropriate training.

Academies play an increasingly important role in the development of talented US athletes, but mostly in a private capacity. The International Management Group Academies in Florida provide pre-school, elementary, middle, high school and college preparation education integrated with sport training in seven sports. Only top athletes receive scholarships here to cover costs, which can be over US$50,000 a year.

Comprehensive support of athletes

USOC relies on NSOs to decide the amount and type of support each athlete should receive, including health insurance, direct athlete support, grants for education and Operation Gold rewards from US$2,000 for eighth place to US$25,000 for the first place in global competitions. USOC also provides NSOs with experts in nutrition, biomechanics, physiology, psychology, strength and conditioning, performance technology, sports medicine, recovery services, library services, a quarterly Olympic coach e-magazine and conferences (USOC, 2011).

US universities have conducted some of the world's leading sport-related scientific studies with practical applications, particularly in the Fatigue Laboratory at Harvard University from 1927 to 1946 and the Massachusetts Institute of Technology's Institute for Soldier Nanotechnologies founded in 2002. There is great potential for better partnerships between sporting organizations and scientific groups in the US.

Corporations increasingly support elite US athletes. The Nike Oregon Project started in 2001 by building a house where oxygen was removed from the air, simulating high altitude, as well as using other advanced methods of performance and health enhancement (Track Town USA, 2011).

Before Home Depot ended its sponsorship in 2009, the company provided Olympic athletes with part-time jobs, flexible hours and full-time pay. The US Army World-Class Athlete Program (WCAP) was established in 1997 to employ Olympic and Paralympic hopefuls and release them from service for training and competition. The largest fitness chain in the United States, 24 Hour Fitness, also employs Olympic athletes.

US sports authorities have worked successfully with the IOC to include in the Olympics programme sports that are popular in the US, such as beach volleyball, triathlon and golf. US athletes also have noticeable protection from doping control. American cyclist Tyler Hamilton was accused of blood doping during the 2004 Athens Games, but kept his medal because of a 'faulty back-up sample'. He later served a two-year ban from the sport for a similar offence and surrendered the medal in 2011, admitting the use of the banned drug EPO (Herrmann, 2011). Another US cyclist with an estimated income of US$20 million in 2010, Lance Armstrong, was reported to use drugs and have a 'financial arrangement' with an official from the International Cycling Union to cover up a positive test for EPO during the 2002

Tour of Switzerland (Hart, 2010). One of the US challenges is to make all sport organizations' policies consistent with international anti-doping standards, particularly for professional athletes who compete in Olympic Games, such as NHL players.

The future of US HPS

The USOC and NSOs are improving conditions for the comprehensive long-term nurturing of athletes. The interdependent systems of health care, education and sport in the US are more private, market driven, expensive and less coordinated than in other successful sport nations. However, governmental and corporate initiatives contributing to national fitness and sport performance are on the rise. If the US government continues to stimulate these emerging trends and USOC continues to increase its efforts to bring about greater cooperation for a more cohesive pyramid of athlete development, Team USA might be able to achieve the country's ambition of being the best in the world. If history repeats itself, US elite sport development may be accelerated by China's challenge, just as it was in the past by the challenge from the USSR.

CANADA'S HPS SYSTEM

Since the inception of the Olympic Games, Canada has won an average of eleven medals at each Summer Olympic Games and seven medals at each Winter Olympic Games. The focus on HPS by the Canadian government was started in 2005 when Canada won the bid to host the twenty-first Winter Olympic Games. The Canadian government and the Canadian public wanted the country to do well on home soil as Canada did not win a gold medal at the 1976 and 1988 Olympics in Montreal and Calgary. Prior to 2005, the Canadian government did not attach a great deal of importance to its public sport policies on HPS, due to the doping scandal of Canadian track and field sprinter Ben Johnson at the 1988 Seoul Olympic Summer Games.

Organization and financing

The Canadian sport system has a complex decentralized structure with many key players. It is a decentralized sport system as it is a shared system with state and public support for HPS. The Government of Canada gives limited funding to NSO and certain programmes such as Sport Canada and Own the Podium (OTP). Public support is usually sought by HPS athletes, NSOs and the Canadian Olympic Committee (COC) and Canadian Paralympic Committee (CPC) for additional financial support. An example of this is the Royal Bank of Canada (RBC) sponsorship of Olympic athletes called RBC Olympians.

The organization that mainly focuses on Olympic sports is called Own the Podium (OTP). OTP programme was a national initiative started in 2005 by the COC based on the recommendations of an independent consultant (Cathy Priestener Allinger) to increase the performance results of Canadian athletes for the 2010 Vancouver Winter Olympic Games. In 2006, the programme was extended to summer Olympic sports. Today, both the winter and summer programmes are under the operational name of OTP.

In 2011 to 2012, the funding provided by OTP to winter Olympic sports from Sport Canada (which is an entity of the Government of Canada) was C$20,549,050. The 2010 Vancouver Olympics received approximately C$54 million more than the 2006 Torino Games, and Paralympic Sports funding increased by approximately C$8.5 million in the same period. The amount allocated by OTP to summer sports in 2011 to 2012 was C$34,749,500, split among twenty-four summer Olympic sports. Although there was a significant increase in funding in winter sports, this was not the case in the allocation of funding by OTP to summer sports. The allocation of funding for the 2008 Beijing Olympics compared to the 2012 London Olympics only increased by about C$4 million, and in Paralympic Sports, there was an increase of approximately C$3 million (VANOC, 2010 and OTP, 2010, 2011).

Events

Each NSO and PSO is responsible for creating provincial and national championships for their sport (Canadian Heritage, 2011). Canada does have multi-sport national games (Canada Summer and Winter Games) that are held every two years, alternating between summer and winter sports and are open only to amateur athletes (Canadian Games Council, 2011). Since their inception in 1967, over 75,000 athletes have participated in the Canada Games.

The Department of Canadian Heritage of the Canadian federal government recognized the importance of hosting sporting events, as it stimulates sport development within the country and has a positive economic impact and builds community cohesion. The government has developed a federal policy for hosting international sport events that has been in effect since 1 January 2008.

Facilities

Seven high performance centres have been established across Canada (Calgary, Montreal, Ontario, Manitoba, Saskatchewan, Atlantic Canada, Pacific Canada) and are supported by Sport Canada, OTP, COC, CAC and provincial governments to:

- support the achievement of HPS excellence by Canadian athletes;
- contribute to the holistic development of HPS athletes;
- provide an enriched training environment in key locations across the country;
- promote the profession of coaching;
- stimulate sport development across the country.

(Canadian Heritage, 2011)

The facilities provide targeted athletes with services such as sport science, medicine and research services. The facilities also give opportunities for athletes (of any sports) to base their training at these centres. It is not a requirement for carded athletes (elite and development targeted athletes) to train at these facilities, and many Canadian elite athletes are involved in post-secondary education and are recruited to universities in Canada and the United States to compete for university teams. These athletes will normally access what is provided by their universities (e.g. strength and conditioning facilities, coaches and training programmes sport psychology services).

Talent identification and development

Canada has adopted the LTAD model to create a systematic streamlined approach to developing sport and physical activity skills in incremental stages. There are seven stages in the Canadian LTAD model:

1. Active Start (0–6 years)
2. FUNdamentals (girls 6–8, boys 6–9)
3. Learning to Train (girls 8–11, boys 9–12)
4. Training to Train (girls 11–15, boys 12–16)
5. Training to Compete (girls 15–21, boys 16–23)
6. Training to Win (girls 18+, boys 19+)
7. Active for Life (any age participant)

(Canadian Sport Centres, 2011)

It is left to the NSO to implement and develop an LTAD model. All Olympic sports have created and implemented an LTAD model, as it is a requirement for funding and for being recognized as a sport by the Department of Canadian Heritage and Sport Canada (Canadian Heritage, 2011).

Each NSO determines talent identification strategies and techniques with regard to HPS (VANOC, 2010 and OTP, 2010, 2011). It is up to each sport to determine how they identify potential elite athletes and who represents teams at provincial and territorial, national and international competitions. There are differences in how sports identify athletes, as some sports within the country identify athletes earlier (e.g. swimming and gymnastics) than other sports (e.g. bobsleigh).

Comprehensive support of athletes

OTP recognizes that without world-class coaches, Canada's athletes will not achieve top podium results at competitions. To ensure the continual development of coaches, OTP has created a programme in association with Coaching Association of Canada (CAC) called the OTP Coach Professional Development Program. The aim of this programme is to provide opportunities for:

- customized training and education;
- exchange of ideas with international colleagues;
- courses that include completion of the National Coaching Certification Program (NCCP);
- team professional development opportunities to enhance the preparation of the national team coaching staff (training courses, interaction with elite coaches from other backgrounds, fostering innovative and new ideas to improve coach effectiveness);
- customized seminars at national conferences

(VANOC 2010 and OTP 2010, 2011)

The CAC is responsible for training coaches and providing coaching certification in Canada. The coaching certification is called the National Coaching Certification Program (NCCP). The NCCP is divided into three streams (community, competition and instruction) and five levels (pre-trained, trained, certified, advanced and master) (Coaching Association of Canada, 2011).

Talented athletes can be funded through the Athlete Assistance Program (AAP). A funded and financially supported athlete through the AAP is referred to as a carded athlete (Canadian Heritage, 2011). Each NSO creates and implements the criteria on how carded athletes are selected and it is the responsibility of the NSO to select them.

In terms of services for carded athletes, Integrated Support Teams (ISTs) have been developed by OTP, COC, NSOs and provincial governments at Canadian Sport Centres to make sure Canadian athletes are healthy, fit and psychologically ready for optimal performance and to provide elite Canadian athletes with services such as:

- physiologists
- sport psychologists
- biomechanists
- nutritionists
- physical therapists/therapists
- physicians

(VANOC, 2010 and OTP, 2010, 2011)

In 2004, OTP created a five-year, C$8 million project called Top Secret Project to use science and technology to help Canadian winter athletes perform to their optimal level at the 2010 Winter Olympic Games in Vancouver. The project combined ideas from Canada's thirteen national winter sport organizations, businesses and universities, and recruited the top researchers in Canada to work on fifty-five prioritized projects in four areas (competition clothing, ice sports, snow sports and performance) (Khoshnevis, 2010).

The future of Canadian HPS

By investing in the Canadian HPS system, the Government of Canada is promoting the Canadian values of personal excellence, creativity, diversity, achievement and leadership. At the 2010 Winter Olympics, Canada won fourteen gold medals, the most gold medals ever by a nation at a Winter Olympics. This is an amazing turnaround, as past Olympics hosted in Canada did not result in any gold for the country. Canada could remain among top three nations in overall medal count at major winter and in top fifteen at major summer sporting competitions if the nation continues to improve communication among its HPS stakeholders and to increase financial assistance to sport, particularly to preparations for such events as Olympics, Paralympics, Commonwealth Games, Pan and Parapan American Games.

Table 5.2 *Summary of HPS in Canada, USA and USSR/Russia*

	Canada	USA	USSR/Russia
Organization and financing	Managed bottom-up by government, decentralized, partly integrated	Managed bottom-up with little leadership from government, decentralized, disintegrated	Managed top-down by government, centralized, highly integrated
Events	Sport-specific events by NSOs, professional teams, universities and schools, and national multi-sport events	Multi-sport two-level State Games; sport-specific events led by NSOs, among professional teams, universities and schools	Multi-sport multi-level Spartakiads among all organizations and regions; sport-specific events led by NSOs, among professional teams and universities; government coordinates and supports most events
Facilities	Provincial training centres coordinated by multiple Canadian HPS stakeholders for high performers and developing talent, often with athlete and support services	National and regional training centres coordinated by NOC, NSOs and some universities for high performers and sometimes for developing talent, sometimes integrated with education and athlete services	National government coordinates network of national, regional and local training centres for high performers and developing talent integrated with education and athlete services
Talent identification and development	Primarily selection through competitions; NSOs implement long-term athlete development methodologies for age-appropriate training	Primarily selection through competitions; emerging academies where expert coaches train top talent; NSOs start to use long-term athlete development methodologies	Expert coaches use scientific tests as part of 18-year path to high performance supported by age-specific training, recovery and education methodologies and by 10 athlete ranks with rewards for specific results in each sport
Comprehensive support of athletes	Governmental and non-profit organizations provide educational and scientific support to coaches and athletes; corporations and governmental and non-profit organizations assist elite athletes by partially covering expenses such as education, coaching, facilities, sport sciences and medicine, psychology, and nutrition	NSOs start to educate coaches in specific sports; NOC provides on-the-job educational and scientific support to top coaches through NSOs; NOC assists top athletes in covering educational expenses and finding jobs, and provides medical services to top athletes; NOC provides NSOs with scientific support	Government educates coaches in specific sports and related sciences, employs coaches and provides on-the-job educational and scientific support; nurtures athletes through education and career paths, particularly for sport-related professions; integrates sport-specific medical service and preventative medicine with training; employs scientists for sport-specific research and individualized assistance to each national team member

CASE STUDY 5.1

STRATEGIES FOR PREPARING INTERNATIONAL WINNING TEAMS AND ATHLETES

Bill Sweetenham

Gold Coast, Queensland

This case study explains some of the strategies I put in place when I was the National Performance Director (NPD) for British swimming. My role as the NPD was to ensure podium-winning performances on a consistent basis at the Olympic level.

In any sport, prior to any implementation of strategy the sport environment must be understood in detail. That environment as it relates to swimming has the following characteristics:

- Swimming is an early specialization sport.
- Elite swimmers around the world commonly swim 70,000–100,000 m per week.
- Elite swimmers may train up to 30 hours per week.
- Medal winners in swimming are usually aged 22 or younger.
- Females typically begin to win medals at younger ages than males.
- Swimming is a highly specialized sport in which the fundamentals are acquired at a very early age (children can learn to swim between the ages of 4 and 7).

One of my biggest challenges was to lead Britain swimming third in the medal tally at the Beijing Games in 2008. Additionally the British team became one of the best prepared and respected teams in the world and I describe here the strategies that were used for the preparation and management of our team.

Strategies for preparation

Six areas of Britain's swimming structure were identified that needed radical change. The changes in each of these areas were carried out in coordination with each other, and they ensured a clear strategy for achieving our goal of preparing British swimming to achieve podium performances.

1 Winning staff

The key priority is simple: people are what make things happen. I ensured that Britain had the world's best staff in place to drive every aspect of the British performance programmes. I developed each staff member as a leader with performance expertise and my motto was: 'employ the right person and then develop their skills'. The team consisted of management, swimmers, coaches, specialists in sports science in a range of disciplines, team managers (logistics and camp operations) and support staff. However, the two critical positions for appointment were:

- The lead coach – this effectively was the number one coaching position and was critical in producing results.
- The lead manager – this person would work with the coaches and swimmers to ensure that all other needs were catered for.

2 Squad selections

Decision making and policies for squad selection included:

- using 200-m events to develop skilled and versatile swimmers and British relay teams;
- selecting athletes to form squads solely for their potential to perform in Olympic events;
- selecting a squad based on times from events at world standards; and
- ensuring that swimmers' times improved between heats, semi-finals and finals, and that selections were only made from finals.

To bring squads of swimmers together (squads consisting of distance swimmers, sprinters or swimmers of individual strokes) we created specialist camps and training events. These occasions created natural competition allowing swimmers to specialize and train against each other, and at the same time helped coaches to specialize in managing swimmers of a particular gender or skill level.

3 Talent

Previous experience in coaching national teams indicated that young development swimmers are able to attain world standards. This is due to refined skill development, a professional approach to training and coaches that lead the swimmers. The British swimming strategy relied upon a strong talent programme with a six-year timescale and selected boys aged 16 and girls aged 14 to ensure that their potential could be fulfilled prior to the age of 22. The talent strategy in Britain considered the following:

- using a battery of tests to ensure effective selection;
- selecting the best environment for each individual and gender to excel;
- deliberately creating adversity in training and competition in order to create challenge and a sense of achievement;
- competing against the opposition;
- competing against world-class competitors; and
- providing exposure to a variety of positive and negative experiences in a wide range of countries including poor swimming environments.

The rate of improvement of these two groups was continuously measured through world results and world rankings to ensure British swimming stayed on target to achieve its goals at the Beijing Olympic Games.

4 Responsibility for winning performances

Competition for elite performers is greater now than ever, and each programme must have the best people managing, organizing and providing leadership. Throughout this structure and at all levels (from national structures through to clubs) individuals responsible for high performance results should be held unconditionally accountable.

5 Building a winning team

The make-up of the British team was as follows:

■ Twenty per cent of the team consisted of talented swimmers, coaches and scientists, and team support members. This group created winning opportunities for themselves and the team. These people are naturally talented and possess inherent winning strategies. When it counts they consistently perform above and beyond their talent levels.

■ Forty per cent of team membership was made up of those people who could achieve a goal. This 40 per cent supported the top 20 per cent of the team. This 40 per cent being able to perform when it counted was made possible by strong leadership. This leadership came in the form of strong coaches and management who were able to make the right decisions under pressure. I found that if mental, emotional and physical stress was minimized it was likely that a 1 per cent performance improvement would occur. This could in turn deliver a 70 per cent winning performance outcome as opposed to a 60 per cent outcome. The coach must form winning and unbreakable partnerships with each athlete and with the team, and must understand the hearts and minds of the athletes and the competition.

■ The talent programme played a role in delivering a constant stream of individuals to inject over the remaining 30 per cent of the team.

■ The team operated with the understanding that winning teams are superior at all levels and in every way possible.

■ The team operated with clearly defined roles and responsibilities to work towards a common purpose.

6 Plan for performance

■ Plans were made a minimum of 6 years in advance of the final outcome.

■ Talent must be identified and recruited 4–6 years prior to the event.

■ 18–24 months in advance of the event a campaign group is formulated.

■ The campaign group is made up of sport scientists, logistics personnel, coaches, swimmers and support staff. These individuals possess the experience to set in place methods that will produce a winning outcome.

■ This campaign group reduces in size as you move towards the main event.

■ At 8–12 months prior to the event the camp team reduces in size by 40–50 per cent.

■ As the size of the group reduces, selected expertise is refined, and potential winners and their individual support staff are identified.

■ The final stage begins 6 months from the event. A smaller and more outcome-focused and driven group of experts was put in place to deliver the winning strategies for the swimmers.

■ The selection of these people was based around a swimmer's trust, faith and belief in them.

■ Each group member had to clearly show by performance and commitment that he/she was able to deliver winning strategies. For a member to keep his/her place in the group, this winning philosophy had to be consistently demonstrated over a period of time.

The world's best team needs to be superior to its opposition in talent, ability, preparation and expertise. Coincidentally, you often find that failing teams operate in reverse. They get bigger, expertise is diluted and at the most important competitions there is a sense of the uncontrollable that causes panic. To conclude, creating a winning team started with understanding the working environment and having a clear goal. This was supported by the following:

1   the selection of world leading staff;
2   squads of swimmers selected using world-class principles;
3   a strong talent identification programme to continue to feed the high performance system;
4   accountability throughout the team to ensure consistent efforts towards achieving the team goal;
5   the ability to create winning teams through strong leadership and an understanding of how to structure a team;
6   a well-planned and carefully scheduled approach to achieving the ultimate goal;
7   flexibility, which is crucial given that high performance at any level of endeavour is vulnerable to change due to international circumstances – an example of this may be the provision of sponsorship and funding or the lack of it;
8   accuracy and precision in all decision making.

These principles are applicable to all sports and have been proven to be effective.

SUMMARY

This chapter reviewed three HPS models and suggested a broad flexible analysis structure covering key HPS elements. As Table 5.2 shows, the three sport nations examined here are all trying to advance their HPS systems in the key areas shown.

The fundamental question for HPS professionals is usually: Which practices could I adopt? The three cases above identified a number of useful practices for HPS managers across the world:

■ governmental funding and support;
■ specialized HPS facilities and comprehensive training centres;

- multi-sport multi-level events;
- integrated management of competitions and camps in all sports at professional and amateur levels;
- talent identification and LTAD methodology;
- multidisciplinary science groups;
- uniform education and certification of coaches;
- medical support for illness prevention and training correction of athletes at all stages of development;
- educational and career path for athletes through specialized sport classes in regular schools, special sport schools, sport colleges and sport universities.

DISCUSSION QUESTIONS

1 Define advantages and disadvantages of various approaches (comparative HPS models) to comparing HPS systems in different countries.
2 Identify similarities and differences in the HPS management of the former USSR and current Russia, USA and Canada.
3 Discuss the challenges the former USSR and current Russia, USA and Canada face and their international sporting performance in the future.

KEY TERMS

- Comparative HPS model
- HPS system
- Elite athlete

GUIDED READINGS

Douyin, X. (1988). A comparative study on the competitive sports training systems in different countries. *Journal of Comparative Physical Education and Sport*, 2, 3–12.

Houlihan, B., and Bloyce, D. (2009). Developing the research agenda in sport policy. *International Journal of Sport Policy*, 1(1), 1–12.

Kihl, L., Kikulis, L., and Thibault, L. (2007). A deliberative democratic approach to athlete-centred sport: The dynamics of administrative and communicative power. *European Sport Management Quarterly*, 7(1), 10–30.

Zeigler, E. (2009). *International and comparative physical education and sport*. Victoria: Trafford Publishing.

Recommended websites

www.roc.ru
http://government.ru/eng/power/60
www.teamusa.org
www.pch.gc.ca/sportcanada/index-eng.cfm
http://ownthepodium.org
www.olympic.ca/en

NOTE

1 At the 1992 Summer Games the Unified Team included twelve of the fifteen former USSR republics and at the 1992 Winter Olympics it included six.

BIBLIOGRAPHY

Baumann, A. (2002). Developing sustained high performance services and systems that have quality outcomes. *12th Commonwealth International Sport Conference Abstract Book*, 62–71.

Canadian Games Council (2011). Canada games: Introduction. Available at www.canadagames.ca/content/Games/Home.asp.

Canadian Heritage (2011). Canadian heritage website. Available at www.pch.gc.ca.

Canadian Sport Centres (2011). LTAD stages. Available at www.canadiansportforlife.ca/learn-about-canadian-sport-ife/ltadstages.

Coaching Association of Canada (2011). NCCP training: What is NCCP. Available at www.coach.ca/what-is-the-nccp—s12507.

CODP (2011). Community Olympic development program 2011 fact sheet. Available at http://s3.assets.usoc.org/assets/documents/attached_file/filename/41103/2011_CODP_Fact_Sheet.pdf?1302640380%20.

Coyle, D. (2007). How to grow a super-athlete. *The New York Times*. Available at www.nytimes.com/2007/03/04/sports/playmagazine/04play-talent.html?emc=eta1.

De Bosscher, V., Shibli, S., van Bottenburg, M., De Knop, P. and Truyens, J. (2010). Developing a method for comparing the elite sport systems and policies of nations: A mixed research methods approach. *Journal of Sport Management*, 24, 567–600.

Digel, H. (2002). *Resources for world class performances in sport: A comparison of different systems of top level sport policy*. Institut National du Sport Expertise in Elite Sport 2nd International Days of Sport Sciences, 46–49.

Grasso, B. (2008). Talent identification & development on an international basis, athletes' acceleration. Available at http://www.athletesacceleration.com/youthtalentidentification.html, accessed July 1, 2008.

Green, M. and Oakley, B. (2001). Elite sport development systems and playing to win: Uniformity and diversity in international approaches. *Leisure Studies*, 20, 247–267.

Hart, S. (2010). Floyd Landis puts Lance Armstrong at the centre of new drug allegations. Available at www.telegraph.co.uk/sport/othersports/cycling/lancearmstrong/7746819/Floyd-Landis-puts-Lance-Armstrong-at-the-centre-of-new-drug-allegations.html.

Herrmann, L. (2011). In latest cycling doping scandal, Hamilton gives up gold. Available at http://digitaljournal.com/article/307004.

Houlihan, B. and Green, M. (2008). *Comparative elite sport development systems, structures and public policy*. London: Elsevier.

Ippolitov, J. A., Mishin, A. A., Novikov, A. A., Tarasova, L. V. and Shamilov, G. S. (2009). Innovative technologies of athletic preparation. *Sports Science Bulletin*, 5, 3–5.

Isaev, A. A. (2002). *Sports policy of Russia*. Moscow: Soviet Sport.

Khoshnevis, K. (2010). Top secret contributions. Available at www.capitalnews.ca/index.php/news/top-secret-contributions.

Mackay, D. (2011). Putin backs Russian athletes preparations for Sochi 2014 with massive cash injection. Available at www.insidethegames.biz/olympics/winter-olympics/2014/11683-putin-backs-russian-athletes-preparations-for-sochi-2014-with-massive-cash-injection.

Markur, J. (2008). Born to run? Little ones get test for sports gene. *The New York Times*. Available at http://www.nytimes.com/2008/11/30/sports/30genetics.html?th&emc=th, accessed November 29, 2008.

Michaelis, V. (2009). U.S. Olympic athletes help pitch fundraising campaign. *USA Today*. Available at http://usatoday30.usatoday.com/sports/olympics/2009-06-02-usolympiccampaign_N.htm, accessed June 3, 2009.

Ministry for Sport, Tourism and Youth Policy of the Russian Federation (2011). Available at http://sport.minstm.gov.ru.

Platonov, V. N. (2010). *High performance sport and preparation of national teams for Olympic Games*. Moscow: Soviet Sport.

Riordan, J. (1980). *Sport in Soviet society: Development of sport and physical education in Russia and the USSR*. Cambridge: Cambridge University Press.

Smolianov, P. and Zakus, D. H. (2008). Exploring high performance management in Olympic sport with reference to practices in the former USSR and Russia. *The International Journal of Sport Management*, 9, 206–232.

Sparvero, E., Chalip, L. and Green, B. C. (2008). United States. In B. Houlihan and M. Green (Eds.), *Comparative elite sport development: Systems, structures and public policy*. Burlington, VT: Butterworth-Heinemann.

Track Town USA (2011). Nike Oregon project: Salazar applies the latest technology to distance training. Available at www.tracktownusa.com/track.item.5/the-oregon-project.html.

USOC (2011). United States Olympic Committee. Available at www.teamusa.org.

VANOC 2010 and OTP 2010 (2011). Own the Podium. Available at http://ownthepodium.org.

Chapter 6

Quality and performance management of national sport organizations

Measuring and steering the performance of the distribution network

Jo Van Hoecke, Hugo Schoukens and Paul De Knop

Vrije Universiteit Brussel, Belgium, and Double PASS

LEARNING OUTCOMES

Upon completion of this chapter the reader should be able to:

1   define a strategy to control and steer the organizational performance of a federation's system;
2   discuss the importance of a well-functioning youth development system for a national sport federation/professional league;
3   examine the critical success factors of the academy system related to the clubs of the professional league in your country; and
4   develop quality standards and performance indicators for the youth department of a specific segment of sport clubs.

OVERVIEW

A number of national sport federations and professional leagues have introduced the 'Professional Academy Support System' (PASS) as their system of quality assurance regarding youth development. They are working with Double PASS – a spin-off of the University of Brussels – for the objective auditing of the academies in their clubs. The role of this independent standards organization (ISO) is to measure the actual and potential performance of these youth academies with a set of relevant and mutually agreed standards and indicators. By monitoring the critical success factors (CSFs) and key performance indicators (KPIs) of the academy system, these national sport organizations try to control and improve their distribution network. Strategies to award the best performing clubs with quality labels and grants can help them with the further professionalization of their sport and talent development system in particular.

The implementation of a system of effective measurement and quality assurance with regard to talent identification and development is essential to guarantee the future success of a sport, including its structures and competitions. Many researchers and practitioners believe that well-defined performance dimensions and CSFs can help develop specific measures to monitor progress and performance towards excellence. For most national team sport federations it is one of their responsibilities to ensure a successful national team, beside club teams that are at least competitive in the highest international competitions. Another essential element is an attractive national competition with financial stable clubs and players with which fans can identify themselves. For this, it is important that there is a consistent production of excellent home-grown players gaining contracts in the clubs. Critical to success is the quality of the distribution network and the academy system in particular.

The popularity of a team sport in a country often depends on the results of the national team and the results of professional club teams. International sporting success has a major impact on the media attention given to a sport, and generally results in higher participation figures and greater interest on the part of stakeholders (administrators, private sponsors, fans, the general public, etc.). As a result, performance indicators like sport results at the elite level, the number of licensed teams and the numbers of members that clubs have are frequently used as measures of the performance of the coordinating bodies responsible for the organization and promotion of a sport in a country or region. However, this limited managerial approach is only one method of measuring the success of a national sport federation.

In order to obtain a broader picture of the performance and the potential of such sport organizations, it is a good idea to consider the internal and external factors influencing these results as well. Chappelet and Bayle (2005) propose a multidimensional performance measurement tool that includes organizational, financial, promotional and internal social and societal indicators in addition to measures of performance in competition. Moreover, achieving competitive success is a more complex task for a federation of associations than it is for a single association. For the national federation of a team sport, competitive success requires all the members (i.e. clubs) of the federation and its decentralized bodies (i.e. leagues) to play a crucial role. For this reason Chappelet and Bayle also speak about the organizational performance of the federation's system, referring to the federations' dependence on these partner organizations.

According to Chappelet and Bayle (2005) the quality of services and partnership relations, as well as the satisfaction of stakeholders, is an essential measure of the performance of a national sport federation. Providing services to members can reinforce the quality of the distribution network and increase the legitimacy of the federation. Such practices as offering seals of approval and supporting services to clubs are justified in order to maintain control of an environment that could otherwise escape the control of some national sport federations. Given the sometimes erratic behaviour of those involved in sport, it is important that the beneficiaries of a federation's certification can create fidelity among its stakeholders. Other elements that are pushed forward by Chappelet and Bayle for justifying a seal of approval concerns a better awareness of the structure, of its means and of its results for local partners, permitting these latter to evaluate the reliability of possible collaboration with the federation's system, which is the guarantee of professionalism, effectiveness and control of the product.

QUEST FOR QUALITY AND PROFESSIONALIZATION

The high visibility and value of sport has encouraged governing bodies at different levels to pressure sport organizations into assuming a more professional approach to the delivery and design of the sport product (Kikulis *et al.*, 1995). Moreover, since the sector has evolved into a differentiated buyers' market with service and quality as the most CSFs, the need for professionalization has increased considerably. Governing bodies expect that the products delivered by the sport organizations will meet the expectations of the intended customers, and that the product will be generated in an effective and efficient way, using the capacities of the employees in the most optimal manner, conforming to predetermined specifications and developed with respect for the legitimate expectations of the stakeholders (Lucassen *et al.*, 2007). This demand for quality is also shared by public authorities and other institutions in exchange for grants and other forms of support. In this context the principles of quality and performance management have been introduced systematically into the various sport structures in order to improve and control the quality and performance of the sport system.

The principles of quality and performance management

Performance Management (PM) is defined by Neely *et al.* (1995) as the process of quantifying action, where measurement is the process of quantification and action leads to performance. At the heart of the PM process is the performance measurement system, which is of critical importance to the effective and efficient functioning of PM. As Deming points out, without measuring something, it is impossible to improve it. Kueng (2000, p. 70) explains it in sporting terms:

> Imagine an athlete or an athletic team which does not measure its performance. What would happen? They could not motivate themselves, they could not judge their training methods, and they certainly would not be able to achieve world-class standards.

Traditionally, performance measurement is understood to be an a posteriori evaluation of the results obtained by an organization, but much research work has also presented it as the measurement of the factors upon which successful performance depends (Chappelet and Bayle, 2005). By identifying what is really required to achieve excellence, an organization can find out what areas it needs to improve in and how its limited resources can be more effectively directed to achieve this improvement (Kanji, 2002). It follows that, if it is to be effective, the system must be based on the 'true' performance drivers – and those, according to most literature, reflect a set of practices and core concepts like customer satisfaction, process

89

management, teamwork, empowerment and continuous improvement (Kanji and Sa, 2007). When it is based on these true drivers, performance measurement can be carried out by means of a systematic approach to assessing the actual and potential performance of the organization. When this is done with a managerial approach, performance measurement is consistent with the ideas of total quality management (TQM).

A primary strategy of TQM is to encompass a set of critical factors to achieve and maintain excellent organizational performance (Zakaria and Zulnaidi, 2006). In this approach the focus is on the use of systems and procedures for controlling quality. As Dale (1994) points out, a quality control system is widely understood to be a fundamental pillar in an organization's holistic approach to quality management and can help in ensuring that any improvements made are held in place. Systems of quality assurance entail having the organizational structure, responsibilities, procedures, processes and resources for implementing quality management, such that there is a guiding framework to ensure that every time a process is performed the same information, methods, skills and controls are used and practised in a consistent manner.

Integrating PM with TQM concepts becomes an imperative in the pursuit of excellence. 'Business excellence', regarded as the simultaneous satisfaction of key organizational stakeholders, requires the measurement of performance based on CSFs – that is, 'the limited areas in which results, if they are satisfactory, will ensure successful competitive performance for the organization' (Kanji and Sa, 2007). Therefore, to improve organizational performance it is essential to determine the TQM criteria and measure their effect on organizational performance (Gadenne and Sharma, 2002). Such an integrated approach to TQM and PM clearly shows why continuous improvement is central to TQM philosophy. It highlights the value an organization gives to its various stakeholders by focusing on quality (Sitkin *et al.*, 1994; Soltani *et al.*, 2004). According to Pun (2002), the ultimate objective of TQM/PM integration is to assist organizations in their quest for continuous improvement and better organizational performance and results.

The integration requires a thorough definition of the measures and indicators used to monitor the TQM implementation process and corporate performance from a stakeholder perspective. Kanji and Sa (2001) argue that the criteria for PM are rooted in the CSFs of the organization and ultimately correspond to the determinants of business excellence. The integration should align with corporate missions and strategies, and intertwine with the operation goals, management systems, measurements and practices. TQM/PM integration also demands continuous self-assessment to identify relevant factors that help with organizational changes. Since the award criteria of the Malcolm Baldrige National Quality Award (MBNQA) and the European Quality Award (EQA) are generic and well documented, they have been the most commonly used models for self-assessment (Kueng, 2000). These performance measurement frameworks of TQM have been followed by other PM systems like the Balanced Scorecard (Kaplan and Norton, 1996) and the HR Scorecard (Becker *et al.*, 2001). These advances in measuring performance and TQM outcomes and their effects on work organization have been enthusiastically reported by many authors and researchers (e.g. Bititci *et al.*, 1997; Capon *et al.*, 1995; Dale, 1999; Neely, 1998; Neely *et al.*, 2000; Wilkinson, 1993) who comment on the future of PM and measurement issues in business organizations.

The specific context of a federation's system

Most European team sports are organized in the same basic pyramid structure. The supporting framework of this structure is formed by clubs, regional associations, leagues and national federations. The clubs form the foundation of the pyramid and have a central position in the distribution network. These private organizations are responsible for the deliverance of most of the sport services to the different consumers – that is, active sportsmen and women, and sports spectators. Accordingly, most sport consumers have access to their sport product via a network of professional and amateur clubs that form the basis of the traditional sport system. Furthermore, these sport clubs also contribute significantly to the initiation and training of young athletes or players so they also determine the future of the sport. This fundamental role is also underlined in the Nice Declaration (2000):

> Training policies for young sportsmen and women are the life blood of sport, national teams and top level involvement in sport and must be encouraged. Sports federations, where appropriate in tandem with the public authorities, are justified in taking the action needed to preserve the training capacity of clubs affiliated to them and to ensure the quality of such training, with due regard for national and community legislation and practices.

This explains the significant dependence of the team sport federations on their associated clubs for the fulfilment of their core activities and the realization of their mission.

Football as an example

As indicated by Arnaut (2006), football is a good working example of this interlinked pyramid structure. Elite, professional, semi-professional and amateur football are inextricably linked through the pyramid and each level supports the other levels. For instance, the ability of football authorities to invest in the grassroots of the game is directly related to their ability to generate revenue from the competitions they organize. It follows, therefore, that any diminution in the revenue from these competitions will translate into less spending on the sport. This connection between the professional and grassroots sectors is fundamental to European sport and, referring to the Nice Declaration, the federations are seen as the key organizations to ensure the maintenance of this sporting cohesion and participatory democracy.

This is also confirmed in the vision statement of the Union of European Football Associations (UEFA) (2005):

> UEFA – and the overall football system – will only be as strong as the national associations who make it up. Therefore, the functioning of the system at all levels of the pyramid should be improved on a continuous basis. There is pressure from both inside and outside the football family for some member associations to modernise and be more efficient – and for many it is also considered a necessity.

In this sense, football and its structures have changed considerably during the last few decades. Through the years, football clubs have frequently been subject to external influences from national and international organizations and ruling bodies (Relvas *et al.*, 2010). From a broad European perspective, these influences essentially have come from UEFA. As a consequence of the incremental player and market movements following the European Union legislation and the Bosman ruling, which guaranteed the free movement of players to clubs in all EU countries, UEFA introduced a club licensing system. It was introduced at the start of the 2004/2005 season with the goal of encouraging European club football to look beyond the short term and consider underlying long-term objectives essential for the game's continued good health (UEFA, 2011).

In 2010, a new set of Club Licensing and Financial Fair Play regulations were approved. They continue the existing annual licensing by national licensing bodies, and also ensure continued monitoring by an independent club financial control panel for clubs qualified for UEFA competitions. The annual licensing is based on a series of defined quality standards, which each club must fulfil to gain admittance to UEFA's club competitions, and on the key principles of transparency, integrity, credibility and capability. The criteria of the licensing system can be broken down into five principal categories: sporting, infrastructure, personnel, legal and financial. As reported by the UEFA (2011), these requirements have helped to improve the business credibility of club operations and have led to better transparency and governance by clubs and national associations.

A licence granted to a club by the national association proves that the club is achieving a minimum quality level. Further checks coordinated by UEFA in cooperation with independent partners on the proper application of the system at each association reinforce the Europe-wide nature of the system. To help the system take root across Europe, UEFA provides the national associations with the technical and financial support required to establish an adequate infrastructure. By the end of the 2010/2011 season, associations had received €90 million from UEFA's solidarity fund.

The benefits of this system have gained further recognition on a broader international level. As a consequence, in 2007 FIFA presented their Club Licensing Regulations as a framework for better corporate governance on a worldwide scale. The regulations safeguard the credibility and integrity of club competitions, and promote sporting values as well as transparency in the finances, ownership and control of clubs, and they improve the level of professionalism within the football family (FIFA, 2007).

MANAGING THE QUALITY OF THE DISTRIBUTION NETWORK OF A NATIONAL FEDERATION

At a local level, clubs have also been subjected to the influence of national governing bodies and local authorities. In some countries several ministries and sport governing bodies have defined a general legal environment, which includes regulations for operation, recognition and/or subsidization. For example, in France, training centres for high-level athletes must fulfil specific requirements, which are regularly checked by the Ministry.

More often, a basic framework is given to the national federations who are responsible for the administration of the sport. The national federations aim to assert their control over the sport's administration and over the links between the various levels of competition. This encourages a professional approach throughout the sport. The centralized control involved in this arrangement requires the cooperation of the main actors and induces generalized professionalism within the system. The structure assumes a clearly defined and global strategic project on the part of the federations and one that is formalized and shared by its various components.

Often, special attention is given to youth sport and the optimization of the youth development system. After all, investing in youth academies is seen as an essential strategy to ensure the future success of a sport (federation) in a country or region. According to a study on training of young football players in Europe conducted by Ineum Consulting and Taj (2008), various actors operating on different levels are defining requirements or standards for training structures, which make up the so-called books of specifications. These books differ from one country to another and are sometimes used as a classification system for certification. According to this exploratory study, one-third of the European countries do not have other training specifications besides the UEFA licensing system. On the other hand, the study found that two-thirds of European national football federations had introduced other specifications in the form of licensing systems. In half of these countries a classification system has been set up in parallel to the licensing system, defining a large number of quality criteria and different categories of clubs (Ineum Consulting and Taj, 2008).

For instance, in 1997 the English Football Association introduced 'A Charter for Quality', including specific proposals for the FA's Programme for Excellence, the Young Player Development programme in the Professional Game. The Charter for Quality listed specific environmental and operational criteria relating to such things as facilities, staff, medical provision, practice and legislation. These criteria are considered essential to provide for appropriate player development (Relvas *et al.*, 2010). As formulated in the Lewis Report (2007), since the publication of the Charter of Quality a great deal has been achieved in young player development in professional football. There has been considerable investment in, and by, football in the building of facilities and fostering expertise in Football Academies and Centres of Excellence. Currently, forty clubs are licensed to operate a Football Academy and fifty-one clubs are licensed to operate a Centre of Excellence.

In England each league (i.e. the Premier League and the Football League) operates its own internal monitoring system in respect of compliance by their member clubs with the league's rules and regulations. However, as part of a new strategic plan to modernize youth development in English professional football, it is the intention to coordinate these rules and regulations to ensure that the modernized academy system functions in a coherent and unified manner.

One of the CSFs of the Elite Player Performance Plan is the implementation of a new system of effective measurement and quality assurance. With Foot PASS England, independent quality control will be implemented to ensure impartiality and absolute objectivity. By choosing Foot PASS, English Professional Football has appointed Double PASS as an ISO to undertake the auditing of Academies under the new youth development system. This was one of the key recommendations of Lewis who argued that:

> A culture of excellence demands that high standards are set, that measurement is against these standards and progress and achievement is recorded. Where progress is stagnant or in reverse, action must be taken. At the heart of this drive for improvement and progression is the use of quality assurance. (Lewis, 2007, p. 22)

93

In this way the Premier League, the Football League and the FA are following the lead of the Belgian, Finnish and German federations and leagues who have installed the Foot PASS system in their clubs for more than five years. In the German *Bundesliga* the independent auditing and certification of academies at professional clubs is considered to be a key element in their further development and German football as a whole. As a director of the *Deutsche Fußball-liga* said (DFL, 2011):

> With the certification of our Academies, again, we have made a step forward in ensuring sustainability in youth development. The systematic implementation of the quality and performance system 'Foot PASS' has significantly increased the potential of these training structures what already results in more home-grown players.

With this certification project, and others, it was the aim of the *Deutsche Fußball-liga* and the *Deutscher Fußball-Bund* to guide the clubs through the process of professionalization and to emphasize the importance of a high-quality academy system with regard to a more efficient development of 'home-grown' talent. As a consequence, since the installation of the elite academies in the professional clubs ten years ago, German professional football has invested more than half a billion euros in their professional academy system (DFL, 2010). In 2010, a second round of independent audits began and grants of the UEFA Solidarity Fund (7.5 million euros in 2009/10) were distributed based on the results of the audits carried out by Double PASS (more information is given in the case studies).

The Professional Academy Support System (PASS)

Several sport federations and leagues are using the 'Professional Academy Support System' (PASS) as their system for quality assurance and performance measurement with regard to youth sport and talent development in particular. PASS is based on a framework that can be translated into different sport concepts (i.e. sport services for youth players in professional and amateur clubs within the different team sports) in order to assess and improve the management of the training system and processes in these sport structures. It is important that audits are conducted by an independent body, not only to guarantee the objectivity of the results, but also to keep the functions of assessor and supporter clearly separated. Support staff of the federation can help the clubs to work on the suggestions for improvement formulated by the external audit body. In this manner they can improve the quality of their distribution system in the most effective way.

At first the focus of this PASS quality and performance system is on professional team sports, such as football (Foot PASS), basketball (Basket PASS) and ice hockey (Hockey PASS). In these traditional competition-oriented sports, academies aspire to develop players for the first team or (at least) generate income through the sale of marketable assets (Stratton *et al.*, 2004). This direct 'return on investment' explains why a youth academy is generally seen as the R&D department of these organizations, engaged in the business of performance, entertainment and financial profit. Therefore, all primary, supporting and managerial processes of this particular department have to be designed in a professional way to provide more and better home-grown players and increase the efficiency of youth development investment.

For this kind of sport federation the installation of a specific quality assurance system like PASS can help them to:

- introduce and implement the principles of TQM and PM systematically in the federation's sport system;
- inform all the stakeholders of the federation's network about the CSFs of the different sport concepts and the corresponding training systems and processes;
- measure the quality and performance of their clubs objectively with respect to the particular requirements of the sport;
- classify and benchmark with regard to the certification of the clubs and the distribution of grants and awards;
- provide the clubs with professional advice and support to optimize their organizational structures and processes, especially with regard to youth development;
- improve the management of these sport systems in terms of a higher degree of professionalization to enhance the permanent output and outcome.

The PASS framework

At the core of these quality projects is a functional and relevant measurement tool (Van Hoecke *et al.*, 2009). The PASS measurement tool consists of checklists monitoring CSFs to evaluate the potential performance of the youth academy and a performance measurement with KPIs to evaluate the actual performance of the club with regard to youth development (Van Hoecke *et al.*, 2006, 2007, 2008). In this context, CSFs can be considered as elements that are vital to success whereas KPIs are used to evaluate the success of the club's youth development. Most of the measures of productivity are related to the central goal of these youth academies – that is, the result of the talent identification and development system, indicated by the transition of talented players to the senior teams of the club and/or other comparable teams.

As presented in Figure 6.1, the CSFs and KPIs are clustered in eight interconnected dimensions, which form the basic structure of the current PASS framework (Van Hoecke *et al.*, 2010).

As far as the operationalization is concerned, these dimensions are further divided into significant subdimensions, which form the base of a scoring system:

1　strategic and financial planning (STRA): mission and vision of the club with regard to the central role of the academy, and strategic and financial plan of the academy;
2　organization and decision making (ORG): organizational structure, position of the academy within the club structure, leadership and formal decision-making;
3　talent identification and development system (DEV): coaching philosophy and programme, planning and evaluation, access to coaching and games, internal and external scouting;
4　athletic and social support (SUP): medical, psychological, academic and social supervision;
5　academy staff: availability and specialization of the academy management team and the coaching staff;

95

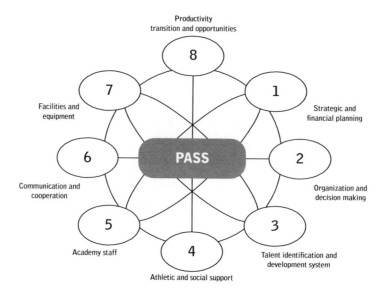

Figure 6.1 The eight dimensions of the PASS framework
Source: Van Hoecke et al., 2010

6   communication and cooperation (COM): internal and external communication, player
    progression meetings, staff appraisal, cooperation with local authorities, schools and
    other relevant organizations;
7   facilities and equipment (FAC): academy facilities, playing surfaces and training
    premises, supporting facilities and equipment;
8   productivity (PRO): in this last dimension the actual results of the youth development
    processes are evaluated on the basis of KPIs related to the central goal of the
    organization with regard to youth development; for instance, in a professional club
    these indicators focus on the transition of talented players (e.g. movement upwards to
    the senior teams of the club or other comparable teams, appearances and playing time
    of home-grown talent in senior teams, selections for national teams, etc.).

A digital logbook, attuned to the dimensions of the PASS framework, lists the club's material
and resources in order to establish a structured evaluation of the actual and potential
performance of the academy in question. Academy managers can also use this digital tool to
perform a self-assessment and learn about their strengths and weaknesses.

In order to calculate scores for each dimension and subdimension, a number of weighted
standards and indicators are selected. These standards are further unravelled into concrete
and measurable criteria, which are assessed by independent auditors during documentary and
practical audits. These are organized to check the implementation of the theoretical procedures
in real-life conditions. In order to help the external auditors do their job effectively, as well
as to increase the reliability of the evaluation, specific software has been developed that guides
them through the complete procedure. The activation of digital checklists with criteria for
the objective assessment of documents, observations and interviews automatically results in
quantitative and qualitative reports for the clubs.

Stages of implementation

In order to guarantee a sustainable installation of this PASS quality assurance system with regard to a long-lasting upward spiral towards excellence in youth development, a procedure for implementation has been developed consisting of three major stages:

1　'Defining the quality standards and performance indicators': the first thing that is needed in order to improve and ultimately achieve excellence is to develop an appropriate system for performance measurement. In this preparatory stage it is imperative to involve various stakeholders (quality evaluators) in the determination of the sport-specific standards relevant for the sport organizations in question. Taking into account this principle of 'fitness for use', it is essential to discuss the standards and indicators with experts and partners of the federation involved in this particular matter. Moreover, in order to create a solid basis for the next phases, it is also important to involve the clubs in these discussions in order to come to a set of mutually agreed standards that are relevant for these organizations. This way, there is a higher chance that it is considered a relevant tool and a common project to guarantee and improve the quality of the distribution network.

2　'Improving through evaluation': in the first implementation the focus is on measuring with the intention of improvement (bridging the gap). In order to improve, an organization needs to know its main strengths and weaknesses, not only from an internal perspective, but also, and essentially, from its 'key stakeholders' points of view. That is the major role of quality and PM. Consequently, in this stage the adapted PASS, customized to the situational context of the sport and type of organizations, is primarily used as a tool for self-assessment and external audits with regard to change management and benchmarking. Individual reports from external auditors about relative strengths and weaknesses usually form the base for the creation of specific action plans to improve the quality in the club. Counselling by professional consultants is recommended to guide the clubs in this process of change towards a higher degree of professionalism. These supporting activities can be organized individually, but also collectively as management courses or by means of quality manuals that outline best-practice standards (Schoukens and Van Hoecke, 2005).

3　'Positioning by quality': in the next stage(s), the PASS system for quality assurance and performance measurement can also be used as a marketing tool for the certification and promotion clubs with excellent youth academies. Quality awards and labels (seals of approval) – whether or not listed in a catalogue – can be important cues for external stakeholders because they are testaments to the reliability of the clubs concerned. As indicated by Chappelet and Bayle (2005), the use of these labels and awards can be considered to be an accelerator of promotional activity, a vector of external communication, and a federative and stabilizing element in managerial behaviour. Adding together all the structures that have received a seal of approval or quality label constitutes a relatively uniform, standardized network from a quality point of view. Other incentives, like grants, can be linked to certification systems in order to keep them motivated all the time.

In Belgium and Finland Foot PASS is also used to evaluate the quality and performance of football academies in amateur clubs. The youth development system of these clubs is measured with a modified set of standards and indicators, relevant to this type of sport organization. The procedure is almost the same as with the one for professional clubs. External auditors go on-site for the verification of the information provided by the club, including the interviews with different stakeholders (the Board, management, coaching staff and players) and a practical audit of facilities and delivery. At the end an audit report is produced with notes and qualitative feedback on the different dimensions of the PASS system. Finally, a 'double pass' is made between the external audit body and the federation in question. By organizing supporting activities (post-audits, management courses, quality manuals with best practices, etc.) and distributing incentives (quality labels and awards) based on the results of these external audits, these federations can stimulate their clubs to implement the recommendations of the auditor. In this way these federations try to reinforce the quality of their distribution network by inspiring, stimulating, advising and rewarding the academy staff in these clubs.

The football cases described above demonstrate that in order to promote the quality and performance of the federation's network, national sport organizations need to understand and control their local sport structures. As indicated by Chappelet and Bayle (2005), this control must involve monitoring the application of the federation's policy and, above all, it must involve verifying the quality of the services supplied and thus the capacity to achieve fidelity and growth. For this, it is important that sport organizations understand the services and benefits their stakeholders really expect and it is important that they understand the key factors that influence the performance of their sport system. These criteria for measuring the potential and actual performance must be sensitive to the specificity of the sport organization in question and should reflect the whole input–process–output cycle and not just the end result. In this way, it is possible to develop the right conditions for well-functioning organizational and operational processes, and to achieve the desired outcomes associated with quality and added value for all stakeholders.

Strategies to create a seal of approval or quality labels aim to improve and promote the quality of services offered by the clubs. By offering such a quality assurance system to clubs or other training structures, a federation's ability to control the sport system can be greatly strengthened. For this reason, most strategic plans to promote the development of a sustainable academy in the clubs are inextricably linked with the implementation of a system of performance measurement and quality assurance.

The PASS system has been adopted by several federations and league associations in different countries (Belgium, Finland, Germany and England). This system of quality assurance has been adapted to several sports based on, among other factors, the type of sport, segmentation (elite, national, provincial, etc.), the club orientation (competition, recreation or a combination) and organizational culture of the clubs involved.

An evaluation of the football-related projects in Germany and Belgium has shown that Foot PASS is generally accepted in the field as a relevant and effective system for quality and PM of football academies in professional and amateur clubs. In general, most of the clubs have rated the certification process as good to very good. It is important to note that in both countries the added value as perceived by the clubs primarily lies in the qualitative part of the reporting and the suggestions for further improvements. Most of the youth academy

Table 6.1 *Evolution of the Performance Indicators of Productivity between 2007 and 2010*

KPIs – Productivity	Mean 2007	Mean 2010	Max. 2010
'Local players' in 1st team	5.6	6.8	13
Home-grown (>:= 4 years in YA) players in 1st team	4.7	6.5	12
Home-grown players in 1st and 2nd team	10.7	13.3	22
Min. 3 appearances for home-grown players	2.3	3.0	8
Min. 3 matches for home-grown players	–	2.5	7
Home-grown players in *Bundesliga*	10.8	13.7	30
Min. 3 appearances for home-grown players (*Bundesliga*)	6.7	9.6	23
Players of U19 – min. 5 yrs in Academy	4.6	5.1	11

managers confirmed that the project has changed the management of their departments dramatically, especially with respect to the standardization of procedures and the specialization of the staff. In the German *Bundesliga* the certification of the academies is considered as an important key to success. Referring to Table 6.1, which represents the evolution of some KPIs between the first and the second measurement (2007 and 2010), it can be concluded that all the investments and efforts they have done were certainly not without consequences.

According to Chappelet and Bayle (2005), the German football federation and professional league consider Foot PASS as a system akin to franchising that unifies and favours the development of the sports in question based on a more qualitative and professional approach, but with respect for the individual cultures, values and means of the clubs. This way they recognize the diversity and individuality of each club while providing a national benchmarking system fit for purpose. The ability to develop mutually agreed upon performance standards, to measure them independently and to record progress and achievement is seen as the success factor of their quality assurance system.

CASE STUDY 6.1

FOOT PASS: MANAGING PERFORMANCE IN THE *BUNDESLIGA* THROUGH THE CERTIFICATION OF THE YOUTH ACADEMIES

Hugo Schoukens and Jo Van Hoecke
Double PASS and Vrije Universiteit Brussel

German Football was in crisis around the turn of the century. The German national team was eliminated in the first round of EURO 2000, the European championships for national teams organized in the Netherlands and Belgium. The cry to develop better and more youth academy players was heard at all levels of German football.

The leaders of German football (i.e. the *Deutsche Fußball-liga* and the *Deutscher Fußball-Bund*) took the initiative and defined the performance objectives of German football for the next ten years, thereby highlighting the transition of more and better youth academy players into the elite teams (professional senior team) of the *Bundesliga* and *2. Bundesliga* clubs as a way of guaranteeing the creation of a successful national squad (with the aim of attaining the number one position in world football).

Youth development became a top priority and in 2001 a youth development task force (*die Kommission Nachwuchsförderung*), composed of football experts of the league and the football association, created a master plan, *Der weite Weg zum Erfolg* ('The long road to success') and the vision that each professional football club had to establish a youth academy, considered to be the R&D department of the club with specified minimum requirements for infrastructure and staff. In addition the football association installed 366 regional centres of development all over the country with at the leading 29 regional youth directors and 992 coaches deployed in these centres.

The leitmotivs of the master plan were:

1 youth development is based on an individual approach for each youngster, i.e. an emphasis on individual development and progression;
2 personality development and promotion on and off the field;
3 the coach has a key position; the better the coach, the better the development of the youngsters.

Today, more than 8,800 players benefit from a first-class professional and full-time development programme in the forty-seven youth academies (Leistungszentren) of the professional clubs and about 14,000 players participate in the part-time development programmes of the regional centres. Both these youth development channels are fundamental components of the development pyramid and they supply talented players for the national youth teams and the national senior squad.

In 2006, after running this project for five years, the youth development task force decided to measure and optimize the quality of youth development in the *Bundesliga* and *2. Bundesliga* academies. In collaboration with Double PASS Ltd (www.doublepass.com) the quality and PM system 'Foot PASS' was installed in the clubs.

What are the objectives of Foot PASS Germany?

One of the primary goals of Foot PASS is to give the youth academy managers and their teams a guiding tool (i.e. a management system) to optimize the development process in their academies. The aim is to help them to identify and address their shortcomings in achieving an effective throughput of talent (i.e. the transition of more and better academy players to their first teams).

The certification of the youth academies based on their quality is a second objective. The role of the certification is to stimulate the intrinsic motivation and work done by the academy staff through extrinsic motivation means, i.e. the attribution of quality labels (quality stars) and the distribution of important grants emanating from the UEFA Solidarity Fund.

What are the implementation stages of Foot PASS Germany?

The implementation began in 2006 and has been conducted in order to create a long-lasting upward movement towards excellence in youth development. The three major stages in this process:

1   **Defining the standards:** in this first stage (2006–2007) it was imperative to involve various stakeholders in the definition of the sports-specific standards in order to obtain a Gestalt view of these organizations.
2   **Improving through evaluation:** the main objective of this second stage (2007–2010) was to objectively assess the youth development processes and productivity of the clubs. Data were collected during standardized documentary audits (analysis of the formal and informal process by interviews) and practical audits (by visiting games and training sessions) with an eye to improvement. The Foot PASS evaluation instrument was primarily used as a tool for self-assessment, change management and certification.
3   **Positioning by quality:** in the third stage, after a refinement of the audit tool (standards and process), Foot PASS is still used for continuous improvement, benchmarking and stimulating extrinsic motivation through certification and the distribution of grants. Last but not least the quality stars were used by the clubs as a marketing tool for positioning themselves in the business of youth development.

What has the impact been?

First of all, a comparison of the results over the years clearly shows an improvement of the operational system. This is confirmed by the academy managers who indicate that Foot PASS has stimulated them to take action and has guided them through the process.

In the 2002/2003 season the number of German academy players in the *Bundesliga* was 50 per cent of the total and in the *2. Bundesliga* it was 63 per cent. In the 2010/2011 season the figures had improved significantly and 57 per cent of *Bundesliga* players were German academy players and 71 per cent in the *2. Bundesliga* were German academy players.

In 2008 the U19 national team became European champions and in 2009 the U17 team and the U21 teams did the same. This had never happened before in the European championships for youth teams.

Last but not least, the German national team won the bronze medal at the World Cup in 2010 in South Africa and was recognized as the most creative, attacking and attractive team of the tournament.

CASE STUDY 6.2

ARE NATIONAL COORDINATED SYSTEMS FOR THE COMBINATION OF CAREER AND EDUCATION EFFECTIVE? A CASE STUDY ON THE ELITE SPORT SCHOOLS IN SECONDARY EDUCATION IN FLANDERS

Veerle De Bosscher and Stephanie De Croock

Vrije Universiteit Brussel

The purpose of this text is to examine the systems that have been developed by countries to enable the combination of elite sport and study in order to increase the potential for athletes to perform in the international arena. Findings from a recent study in Flanders[1] are used to discuss whether these elite sport systems – called elite sport schools in the text – have been effective, in terms of sport results, study results and processes.

The general context

It has become commonly accepted that roughly 8–10 years and 10,000 hours of deliberate practice are required to reach the elite level in a sport (Bloom, 1985; Ericsson, 2003; Ericsson and Charness, 1994). Much of this development occurs during secondary school and higher education. Research conducted on talented, elite and former elite athletes shows that a sports career occurs in phases, and that these phases are parallel to, and influenced by the athlete's development in other domains, such as the academic development (Bloom, 1985; Wylleman and Lavallee, 2003). The transition out of secondary education may entail a diversification in career paths for talented athletes. Some may choose to end their academic pursuits and to move into a professional sport career. However, most athletes have little prospect of a full-time professional athletic career and will probably discontinue participation in high-level competitive sport altogether to look for or engage in a part- or full-time professional occupation (Wylleman and Lavallee, 2003).

To cater for these athletes, in the past decade various countries had systems to enable the combination of elite sport and academic activities. These systems have been the subject of a number of studies (e.g. Aquilina, 2009; European Commission, 2004; Radtke, 2010; Radtke and Coalter, 2007; Wylleman and De Knop, 1995). Talented athletes in Flanders are given the opportunity to complete their secondary education in a 'topsport' school that provides 'pupil-athletes' with a weekly 20-hour academic programme similar, albeit in a compressed form, to that of their non-athletic peers. Similar schools exist in France, Australia and the Netherlands (De Bosscher *et al.*, 2008). Initiatives to optimize the conditions for student-athletes can be displayed on two axes. The first axis relates to the promoter of the initiative (i.e. academic or athletic governing bodies), and the second axis relates to the degree of localization of the initiative (i.e. on a continuum from centralized to decentralized). The Flemish policymakers and the elite sport schools run a centralized system in which athletes (ages 12–18) are encouraged to follow the trajectory of talent development primarily via these elite sport schools. In 2009–2010, the elite sport schools in Flanders started their twelfth operational year. The number of participating national sport organizations (federations) grew from 12 to 17, spread over six recognized 'elite sport schools'. Also the number of registered elite athletes has increased significantly (from 201 to 683) throughout the years and subsidies have increased exponentially (from 0.18 million euros to 2.25 million euros in 2009).

Table 6.2 summarizes the characteristics of the Flemish elite sport schools.

Table 6.2 *Characteristics of elite sport and study systems in Flanders*

Positive aspects	Negative aspects
• Centralized: the best elite athletes train together • Financial resources from both sport and educational sector • Athletic guidance/training by the national sport organization; educational guidance by the school • All ages (< 12–18), depending on sport-specific requirements • Living, studying and training at one location (no displacement time) • Legal structure	• Boarding school. Children away from home • Limited choice of studies: not all young talents are reached • Relatively recent initiative (1998)

Source: De Bosscher *et al.*, 2008

This table shows that it is difficult to have an optimal system for elite sport and study. The LOOT schools in the Netherlands, for example, are very decentralized (regionally spread), so that young people can train in their home environment. However, this means that the best athletes don't train together in one centre and sport-specific coaching is provided by local sports clubs, who don't always have the best coaches and other support services. To address this issue, the Netherlands recently established a centralized system, called CTO (Centres for Topsport and Education).

Evaluation of elite sport schools in Flanders

After twelve years' investment, Flemish policymakers felt the need to evaluate the effectiveness of the elite sport schools. They surveyed 408 elite athletes (a 64 per cent response rate) who attended elite sport schools since their inception in 1998, as well as 341 who were eligible for elite sport schools but preferred not to enter (a 69 per cent response rate). The participants completed a written online survey. The results show that at the time of the survey, 61 per cent of former sport school students and 85 per cent of those who chose not to attend a sport school were still active as elite athletes. They are involved in a total of sixteen different sports.

The effectiveness is approached using the SPLISS model (Sport Policy factors Leading to International Sporting Success) in which all CSFs of the policy are listed in nine pillars. It shows the performance determining factors of elite sports and the policy effectiveness at three levels inputs (resources),throughputs (processes) and outputs (results) (De Bosscher *et al.*, 2006). This study focuses on: (1) the outputs (athletes' results) and four pillars: P4: talent development, P5: athletic career, P6: training facilities and P7: trainers' expertise.

Output

What counts in elite sport is national achievements, expressed as numbers of medals, top eight listings or other criteria in international competitions. Since 2005, thirty-five Flemish elite athletes have reached a top eight position in Europe. Nineteen of them (54 per cent) went to an elite sport school. This is 4.6 per cent of the 408 surveyed athletes. These figures are higher than a few years ago, where 33 per cent of the elite athletes went to an elite sport school (De Bosscher *et al.*, 2008). This shows that elite sport schools are growing, which is also reflected in the growing amount of elite athletes who perform during important youth championships. Our analysis reveals that there were only slight differences between the success rates of those who attend elite sport schools and those who did not. These are salutary lessons for Flemish policymakers who invest yearly 2.25 million euros a year in these schools. However, the results also showed that significantly more athletes from elite sport schools won a medal on a European, or World championship. There were ten medal winners from elite sport schools and only two medal winners from among those who did not attend elite sport schools. Furthermore, the conclusions are very sport-specific; for some sports the elite sports schools appeared to be a necessary tool for performances, while for other sports they were not (see Table 6.3).

Table 6.3 *Overview of sports that performed better or not through the trajectory of an elite sport school*

Sports in Flanders . . .	
that *only* performed through an elite sport school	triathlon (since 2005); gymnastics
with *better* performances in an elite sport school	badminton; table tennis
performing in *both* paths: with and without elite sport school	athletics; swimming; judo; tennis
with better performances *next to/without* following a path through an elite sport school	cycling
with *no* performances at all	handball

The original purpose of elite sport schools was to ensure that athletes were well prepared for professional life and for life after their athletic career. As a second measurement of output, the study revealed that there was no significant difference in the number of elite athletes who continued with higher education after the age of 18. Seventy-nine per cent of the elite athletes who went to an elite sport school went to a university or other tertiary institution, compared to 74 per cent of those who did not attend an elite sport school.

What does an elite sport school mean in a total athletic career?

One contentious issue among researchers examining expertise from a developmental perspective (e.g. Baker, 2003) is whether aspiring elite athletes need to limit their childhood sport participation to a single sport or not – that is, whether it is better to specialize early or whether it is better to play a number of different sports before specializing in the later stages of development (Gould, 1987; Wiersma, 2000). A closer look at the career trajectories of elite athletes in Flanders shows that, as young athletes, 41 per cent had practised another sport alongside their current elite sport, and this on average for a period of six years. However, the results are very sport-specific. Figure 6.2 provides an overview for Flanders.

The so-called initiation stage starts earliest in tennis, gymnastics and swimming (ages 5–7) and latest in cycling (11 years). The average entry age to the elite sport school was 14–16 years. In sports requiring early specialization like tennis and gymnastics, over 50 per cent of the athletes had already entered the sport school at the age of 12 while in cycling, 50 per cent of the athletes entered at 16 years of age. Sixty per cent ($n = 201$) of all respondents believed that their entry age was just right while 24 per cent considered it to be too late and 16 per cent too early.

Another point emerging from the study was that, on average, a student spent only 2.8 years at the elite sport school, varying from 2 years in cycling to 4.3 years in table tennis. This shows that the impact of elite sport schools should not be underestimated or overestimated as athletes had already gone through 6 years of specialization in their sport before they entered an elite sport school.

Processes

Last but not least, the next section summarizes the results on the processes, or how elite athletes, whether or not in the context of an elite sport school, received support services and faced problems during their talent development stage.

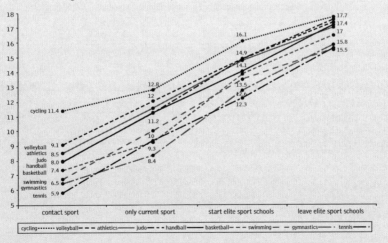

Figure 6.2 Career trajectory of Flemish elite athletes in nine sports

Generally, elite athletes were very satisfied with the elite sport schools. Sixty-six per cent were highly satisfied, 20 per cent were reasonably satisfied and only 14 per cent were unsatisfied. Moreover, 66 per cent believed that the elite sport school made a positive contribution to their achievements in sport and the sport-specific guidance was highly rated. Only 11 per cent were dissatisfied about this. However, apart from sport-related issues, only 13 per cent of the questioned athletes believed that the elite sport school contributed to their study achievements.

Compared to athletes who did not go to an elite sport school, results were also striking: only 35 per cent of talents that had chosen a different educational trajectory received extra support services, such as training more often and more intensively, better training facilities, extra condition- and strength training. After leaving the elite sport school, they also indicate that the support and extra sportive guidance is insufficient.

Conclusion: are the elite sport schools effective then?

While high-quality support services are delivered to elite athletes in elite sport schools, after twelve years of existence it appears that there are only slight differences between the two groups in terms of both sport and study performances. The most significant conclusion from this study is that not all sports require the specialized facilities that are offered in an elite sport school. For policies and national governing bodies this may imply that in some cases they should focus on more decentralized and market-led systems, where local sports clubs have a fundamental role and receive support services accordingly. Government support is needed to improve the quality of the sport clubs, support services during talent development at young ages, as many characteristics (e.g. coordination) are best trained before the age of twelve and as elite athletes spend most of their careers in their local clubs.

CASE STUDY 6.3

ORGANIZATIONAL STRUCTURE AND DRIVERS FOR SUCCESS IN HIGH PERFORMANCE SPORT: THE CASE OF THE QUEENSLAND ACADEMY OF SPORT

Jeff Greenhill and Sue Hooper

Centre of Excellence for Applied Sport Science Research, Queensland Academy of Sport

The organization

The Queensland Academy of Sport (QAS) is an initiative of the Queensland government aimed at supporting the State's high performance athletes. Officially launched in May 1991, the

QAS has strived to ensure that Queensland remains at the forefront of domestic and international sport through an athlete-focused, coach-centred approach to high performance sport management. As a result, Queensland athletes, teams and coaches have enjoyed tremendous success at world championships, Commonwealth Games and Olympic Games. Talented Queensland athletes and their coaches have benefited from the support of the QAS and its provision of sport science, medicine, nutrition, psychology, physiotherapy, strength and conditioning, athlete career and education guidance, applied research, information services and access to state-of-the-art training and recovery facilities.

QAS has grown significantly since 1991 and now supports more than 600 athletes through programmes in eleven primary sports and eleven partnership sports. QAS also provides individual scholarships in other sports. Primary sport programmes include athletics, canoeing, cycling, gymnastics, hockey, rowing, sailing, swimming, triathlon, volleyball and water polo. QAS partnership sport programmes include baseball, basketball, cricket, diving, football, golf, netball, softball, tennis, rugby union and rugby league. Athletes competing in sports not covered by a QAS programme are eligible for assistance under the QAS Individual Scholarship Programme.

QAS primary sport programmes are programmes with athletes in the top four high performance sport categories as defined by Australia's National Elite Sports Council (i.e. world class, international class, developing international and potential international). These programmes receive the services described above as well as specialist equipment, coaching and travel assistance. Partnership sport programme athletes are athletes identified for elite youth development that are below senior state representation. Partnership sport programmes receive significantly less QAS support than the primary sport programmes.

In assisting Queensland high performance sport, the QAS three primary objectives are:

1 having Queensland athletes in Australian teams;
2 achieving world-class performances in international competition; and
3 being regarded as the knowledge and resource hub for the development of elite athletes in Queensland.

A secondary objective is to augment the performance and development of Queensland's high performance sports system. In achieving these objectives, the success of the QAS has not been achieved in isolation. It relies on Queensland government support and on close collaboration with stakeholders such as state and national sporting organizations, other state and national institutes and academies of sport, and other organizations such as schools and universities.

QAS structure

Leadership of the QAS is provided by the QAS Executive Director who receives strategic advice from the QAS Board (usually eight people) and reports to the Queensland government's Deputy Director-General for Sport and Recreation Services under the State Minister for Sport. A challenge for the QAS Executive Director and QAS senior managers is to provide a structure for the QAS to meet the needs of Queensland's high performance sport economy while providing a tailored, individualized approach to supporting athletes and coaches.

QAS has four operational units: the QAS Business Services Unit; the Centre of Excellence for Applied Sport Science Research (CoE); and two High Performance Teams. Each unit has a director or manager who reports directly to the QAS Executive Director as shown in the organizational structure (see Figure 6.3).

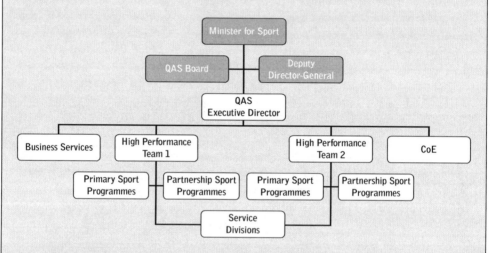

Figure 6.3 *QAS organizational structure*

Source: QAS High Performance Framework 2012 (available online at http://www.qasport.qld.gov.au/resources/qasport/publications/qas-hpf-jan2012.pdf)

The QAS Business Services Unit provides support in areas of finance, human resources, public relations and facilities. The CoE operates as a strategic alliance between QAS and universities to facilitate high-quality research outcomes aimed at improving athlete, team and coach performances. The two High Performance Teams oversee twenty-two primary and partnership sport programmes and four service divisions (i.e. sport science, sports medicine, strength and conditioning, and athlete career and education). At a deeper operational level, the QAS structure has a matrix configuration with service personnel in service divisions working across and up and down the matrix. For example, in the sport science service division, sport scientists report to the High Performance Team Director responsible for the sport they work with and the Sport Science Senior Adviser. Figure 6.4 illustrates the matrix configuration for primary sport programme service divisions.

Reporting and communication processes can be complex, and good information sharing is essential in this structure. The matrix structure has helped QAS staff to work together in collaborative ways, increasing benefits to athletes, teams and coaches.

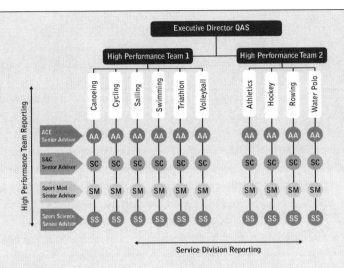

Figure 6.4 *Matrix configuration*

Drivers for success

One goal of the QAS is to have over 25 per cent of athletes selected for Australian senior teams coming from Queensland. The QAS strategic plan provides specific drivers to achieve this goal:

- sustainable QAS growth (enhancing services so that they best support athletes);
- effective and efficient management (providing a strong organizational support base and financial and human resource management);
- wise innovation (striving for new knowledge and skills that provide a competitive advantage); and
- optimizing QAS programmes and services to support athlete preparation and performance (controlling to maintain the highest standards of specialist services).

High performance sport management

The QAS organizational structure was put in place to help improve vertical and horizontal lines of communication and collaboration among service providers and high performance sport programmes. It requires the two High Performance Directors to manage the organization's drivers for success, and to be vigilant in encouraging staff, service providers and coaches to work together in highly collaborative ways.

The established communication style of collaboration and integration flows outward from the organization to build strong relationships with government, state and national sport organizations, industry and other partners. These relationships are essential to QAS success because they set the stage for the innovation and best practices needed for the QAS to stay at the forefront of international sport performance.

SUMMARY

Referring to Chappelet and Bayle (2005), the primary task of a national sport federation is to federate. Given their complex structure as a network organization, this means that they also have to manage the quality and performance of their distribution network. This assumes a clearly defined and global strategic project that is formalized and shared by its various components, like regional associations, leagues and clubs. In this chapter it is explained how a sport federation or professional league can install its system of measurement and quality assurance in order to control and improve the performance of its sport system. It is illustrated by the case of the PASS that has been implemented by several national sport organizations in order to improve their talent development system. First, it is essential to have an appropriate system for performance measurement that is fit for purpose and mutually agreed. For this it is crucial to understand the key factors behind the performance of the sport system in question. When it is based on true drivers, performance measurement can be carried out by means of a systematic approach to assessing the actual and potential performance of the organizations. In this stage, it is important that external audits are conducted by an independent body, not only to guarantee the absolute objectivity of the results, but also to keep the functions of assessor and supporter clearly separated. In this way, the federation can assist their clubs and guide them through the process of change. This can and must be stimulated by a proper certification strategy to promote these actions. The implementation of such a system of quality assurance will strengthen the ability of a national sport organization to control and steer the performance of their distribution network.

DISCUSSION QUESTIONS

1   Why should a national sport federation install a system of quality assurance and measure the performance of its distribution network?
2   What is the role of the federation in this process of quality management?
3   Think about some possible success factors and pitfalls when installing such a quality and performance measurement system in your sport organization.
4   What is the difference between quality standards and performance indicators? Define some of both for your sport organization.

KEY TERMS

■   Quality and performance measurement
■   Quality assurance system
■   Sport organization
■   Football
■   Youth development

■ Academy system
■ PASS

GUIDED READING

Strategic and Performance Management of Olympic Sport Organisations (2005) by Jean-Loup Chappelet and Emmanuel Bayle offers valuable guidance on strategically evaluating, managing and driving the performance of sport organizations. It defines critical strategic management principles and methods and teaches managers how to implement them to improve performance.

Recommended websites

www.doublepass.com
http://ec.europa.eu/sport/pdf/doc512_en.pdf

NOTE

1 Flanders is the northern, Dutch-speaking part of Belgium.

BIBLIOGRAPHY

Aquilina, D. (2009). Degrees of success: Negotiating dual career paths in elite sport and university education in Finland, France and the UK.

Arnaut, J. (2006). Independent European Sport Review. Final version October 2006. 175 pp. Available at http://www.independentfootballreview.com.

Bititci, U., Carrie, A. and McDevitt, L. (1997) Integrated performance measurement systems: A development guide. *International Journal of Operations & Production Management*, 17(5), 522–534.

Baker, J. (2003). Early specialization in youth sport: A requirement for adult expertise?

Becker, B., Huselid, M. and Ulrich, D. (2001). *The HR scorecard: Linking people, strategy and performance.* Boston, MA: Harvard Business School Publishing.

Bloom, B. S. (1985). Developing talent in young people. New York: Ballantine.

Capon, N., Kaye, M. and Wood, M. (1995). Measuring the success of a TQM program. *International Journal of Quality and Reliability Management*, 12(8), 8–22.

Chappelet, J.-L. and Bayle, E. (2005). *Strategic and performance management of Olympic sport organisations.* Champaign, IL: Human Kinetics.

Chelladurai, P. (1992). A classification of sport and physical activity services: Implications for sport management. *Journal of Sport Management*, 6, 38–51.

Chelladurai, P. (1994). Sport management: Defining the field. *European Journal for Sport Management*, 1, 7–21.

Dale, B. (1994) Quality management systems. In B. Dale (Ed.), *Managing quality.* Hemel Hempstead, Prentice Hall.

Dale, B. (1999). *Managing quality.* Oxford, Blackwell Publishers.

111

De Bosscher, V., De Knop, P. and Heyndels, B. (2006). En de winnaar is . . . Rusland. Een methode om het relatief succes van landen te bepalen [And the winner is. . . Russia. A methodology to determine relative success of nations]. In P. De Knop, J. Scheerder and B. Vanreusel (Eds.), *Sportsociologie. Het spel en de spelers [Sport sociology. The game and the players]* (pp. 213–229). Maarssen: Elsevier.

De Bosscher, V., De Knop, P. and van Bottenburg, M. (2008a). *Vlaanderen sport. Ook aan de top. Een internationale vergelijking van het topsportbeleid en topsportklimaat in zes landen.* Nieuwegein: Arko Sports Media.

De Bosscher, V., De Knop, P. and van Bottenburg, M. (2008b). *Vlaanderen sport, ook aan de top.* Nieuwegein: Arko Sports Media.

DFL (2010). *Bericht des Ligaverbandes zum DFB-Bundestag 2010 in Essen.* Frankfurt/Main: DFL Deutsche Fussball Liga.

DFL (2011). *10 Jahrre Leistungszentren. Die Talentschmieden des deutschen Spitzenfussballs [10 Years of Academies. The Development of German Elite Football Players].* Frankfurt/Main: DFL Deutsche Fussball Liga.

Ericsson, K. A. (2003). Development of elite performance and deliberate practice: An update from the perspective of the expert performance approach. In K. Starkes and K. A. Ericsson (Eds.), *Expert performance in sports. Advances in research on sport expertise* (pp. 49–85). Champaign, IL: Human Kinetics.

Ericsson, K. A. and Charness, N. (1994). Expert performance. Its structure and acquisition. *American Psychologist*, 725–747.

European Commission (2004). Education of young sports persons. Final report (lot1), in the European Year for Education and Sport, Report by PMP in partnership with the Institute of Sport and Leisure Policy, Loughborough University, Loughborough, UK.

FIFA (2007). Club Licensing Regulations. Zurich: FIFA. Available at http://www.fifa.com/mm/document/affederation/administration/club_licensing_v4_en_33721.pdf.

Gadenne, D. and Sharma, B. (2002). An inter-industry comparison of quality management practices and performance. *Managing Service Quality*, 12(6), 394–404.

Gould, D. (1987). Understanding attrition in children's sport. In D. Gould and M. R. Weiss (Eds), Advances in pediatric sports sciences (pp. 61–85). Champaign, IL: Human Kinetics.

Heinemann, K. (1998). Sport clubs management. In D. Soucie (Ed.), *Research in sport management: Implications for sport administrators*, Schorndorf, Hofmann.

Horch, H.-D. (1996). The German sport club and the Japanese firm. *European Journal for Sport Management*, 3(1), 21–34.

Horch, H.-D. (1998). Self-destroying processes of sport clubs in Germany. *European Journal for Sport Management*, 5(1), 46–58.

Ineum Consulting and Taj (2008). *Study on training of young sportsmen/women in Europe. Extension - Part I: Home grown player rule.* Paris: Ineum Consulting.

Kanji, G. (2002). Performance measurement system. *Total Quality Management*, 13(5), 715–728.

Kanji, G. and Sa, P. (2001). Measuring leadership excellence. *Total Quality Management*, 12(6), 701–718.

Kanji, G. and Sa, P. (2007). Performance measurement and business excellence: The reinforcing link for the public sector. *Total Quality Management and Business Excellence*, 18(1/2), 49–56.

Kaplan, R. and Norton, D. (1996). *The balanced scorecard: Translating strategy into action.* Boston, MA: Harvard Business School Press.

Kikulis, L., Slack, T. and Hinings, C. (1995). Sector-specific patterns of organizational design change. *Journal of Management Studies*, 32(1), 67–100.

Kueng, P. (2000). Process performance measurement system: A tool to support process-based organizations. *Total Quality Management*, 11(1), 67–85.

Lewis, R. (2007). A review of young player development in professional football. Report for the FA, the Premier League and the Football League.

Lucassen, J., van Bottenburg, M. and Van Hoecke, J. (2007). *Sneller Hoger Ster Beter. Kwaliteitsmanagement in de sport [Faster higher stronger better: Quality management in sport].* Nieuwegein: Arko Sports Media.

Neely, A. (1998). *Measuring business performance: Why, what and how.* London: The Economist Books.

Neely, A., Bourne, M. and Kennerley, M. (2000). Performance measurement system design: Developing and testing a process-based approach. *International Journal of Operations and Production Management,* 20(10), 1119–1145.

Neely, A., Gregory, M. and Platts, K. (1995). Measuring performance system design: A literature review and research agenda. *International Journal of Operations and Production Management,* 15, 80–116.

Pun, K. F. (2002). Development of an integrated total quality management and performance measurement system for self-assessment: A method. *Total Quality Management,* 13(6), 759–777.

Radtke, S. and Coalter, F. (2007). Sports schools: An international review. Report to the Scottish Institute of Sport Foundation.

Relvas, H., Littlewood, M., Nesti, M., Gilbourne, D. and Richardson, D. (2010). Organizational structures and working practices in elite European professional football clubs: Understanding the relationship between youth and professional domains. *European Sport Management Quarterly,* 10(2), 165–187.

Schoukens, H. and Van Hoecke, J. (2005). *Droit au but. Gérer avec succès une formation des jeunes [With youth to the top. Effective management of a youth academy],* Antwerpen: F&G Partners.

Sitkin, S., Sutcliffe, K. and Schroedern, R. (1994). Distinguishing control from learning in total quality management: A contingency perspective. *Academy of Management Review,* 19(3), 537–564.

Slack, T. and Hinings, B. (1994). Institutional pressures and isomorphic change: an empirical test. *Organization Studies,* 15(6), 803–827.

Stratton, G., Reilly, T., Williams, A. and Richardson, D. (2004). *Youth soccer – from science to performance.* London: Routledge.

Soltani, E., van der Meer, R. and Williams, T. (2004). Challenges posed to performance management by TQM Gurus: Contributions of individual employees versus systems-level features. *Total Quality Management,* 15(8), 1069–1091.

UEFA (2005). Vision Europe. The direction and development of European football over the next decade. Nyon: UEFA. Available at http://www.uefa.com/newsfiles/374875.pdf.

UEFA (2011). Available at www.uefa.com/uefa/footballfirst/protectingthegame/clublicensing/index.html, accessed 1 September 2011.

Van Hoecke, J., De Knop, P. and Schoukens, H. (2009). A decade of quality and performance management in Flemish organized sport. *International Journal of Sport Management and Marketing,* 6(3), 308–329.

Van Hoecke, J., Schoukens, H. and De Knop, P. (2006). Foot PASS: A constructive and distinctive quality system for youth academies of professional football clubs. In D. Papadimitriou (ed.), *Proceedings of the 14th Congress of the European Association for Sport Management,* Nicosia, EASM, 278–279.

Van Hoecke, J., Schoukens, H. and De Knop, P. (2007). The impact of the quality management system Foot PASS on the structural dimensions of a professional football academy. In *Proceedings of the 15th Congress of the European Association for Sport Management,* Torino, EASM and SUISM, 382–384.

Van Hoecke, J., Schoukens, H., Lochmann, M. and Laudenklos, P. (2008). Foot PASS Deutschland: Managing performance in the Bundesliga through the certification of youth academies. In H. Preuss and K. Gemeinder (Eds). *Book of Abstracts of the 16th Congress of the European Association for Sport Management,* 447–449. Heidelberg: GSM mbH.

113

Van Hoecke, J., Schoukens, H., Simm, S., Isakowitz, M. and De Sutter, R. (2010). Refinement of the Foot PASS model for a high quality certification of professional football clubs. In *Proceedings of the 18th Conference of the European Association for Sport Management*. Prague: EASM, 167.

Wiersma, L. D. (2000). Risks and benefits of youth sport specialization: Perspectives and recommendations. *Pediatric Exercise Science*, 12, 13–22.

Wilkinson, A. (1993). Managing human resource for quality. In B. Dale (Ed.), *Managing quality*. Hemel Hempstead, Prentice Hall.

Wylleman, P. and De Knop, P. (1995a). *Athlètes de haut niveau et enseignement: Perspective Européenne sur la combinaison d'etude et sport de haut niveau* (High-level athletes and education: European perspective on the combination of study and high-level sport). Paper presented at the conger d'Etude et Sport (Congress Study and Sport), Montréal, Canada: Université de Montréal-Ecole de Mortagne, 27–29 January 1995.

Wylleman, P. and De Knop, P. (1995b). The influence of the social network on young student-athletes. Paper presented at the International Congress on Physical Education and Sport of Children, Bratislava, Slovakia: FIEP, 13–16 August 1995.

Wylleman, P. and De Knop, P. (1996). Combining academic and athletic excellence: The case of elite student-athletes. Paper presented at the International Conference of the European Council for High Ability 'Creativity and Culture', Vienna, Austria: ECHA, 19–22 October 1996.

Wylleman, P. and Lavallee, D. (2003). A developmental perspective on transitions faced by athletes. In M. Weiss (Ed.), *Developmental sport and exercise psychology: A lifespan perspective*. Morgantown, WV: Fitness Information Technology.

Zakaria, A. and Zulnaidi, Y. (2006). Exploring the relationships between Total Quality Management (TQM), Strategic Control Systems (SCS) and Organizational Performance (OP) using a SEM Framework. *The Journal of American Academy of Business*, 9(2), 161–166.

Chapter 7

The governance of high performance sport

Lesley Ferkins
Deakin University

Maarten van Bottenburg
Utrecht University

LEARNING OUTCOMES

Upon completion of this chapter the reader should be able to:

1   discuss meanings and definitions associated with the governance of sport in the high performance setting;
2   distinguish between organizational governance and systemic governance in relation to the evolving nature of high performance governance practice; and
3   discuss issues and trends associated with the governance of high performance sport on the international stage.

OVERVIEW

We begin by providing some context to the notion of governance, and how we have come to use the concept in connection with the management of high performance sport. We then set out more specific meanings and definitions associated with the concept of governance, followed by a discussion of some of the theories that can help make sense of governance issues in high performance sport. We then examine two modes of governance: governance *of* organizations (referring to corporate or organizational governance) and governance *between* organizations (referring to systemic, network or configurational governance). We conclude the chapter with an analysis of the issues and trends associated with the governance of high performance sport on the international stage. The case study and examples embedded within the chapter serve to exemplify the concepts, issues and practices introduced and discussed.

Almost thirty years ago, when the Cold War between the East and the West was still being waged, the Finnish sociologist Kalevi Heinilä noticed that high performance sport had evolved from being a contest between individuals and teams into a battle between systems. Talented athletes still competed against each other, he argued, but their success increasingly depended on the performance capacity of the system they represented, including all the organizing resources, the means of regulation, and the interest groups that maintained and promoted high performance sport at that time (Heinilä, 1982).

The Cold War is over, but the 'Gold War' continues. The struggle to win major sport competitions has intensified. Elite athletes still need talent, spirit and dedication, but they increasingly rely on a network of sport organizations, governments, sponsors and other stakeholders to reach the top (De Bosscher and van Bottenburg, 2011). This has been accompanied by rapidly escalating investments and the involvement of a growing number of people and organizations. As a result, there is now a greater need for coordination and control in high performance sport (De Bosscher *et al.*, 2008; Oakley and Green, 2001). This intensification of competition has also raised the expectations placed on board members of sport organizations to deliver improved elite sport performances and to meet demands for efficiency, effectiveness, stakeholder representation, transparency and accountability (Hoye and Cuskelly, 2007). These issues are directly linked to the central theme to be discussed in this chapter: the governance of high performance sport. We now turn our attention to the meanings and definitions associated with this concept of governance.

DEFINING GOVERNANCE AND SPORT GOVERNANCE

Etymologically, the term 'governance' derives from the Greek *kubernân* and *kybernetes*, which mean to 'steer' and 'pilot' or 'helmsman' respectively (Rosenau, 1995). The derivatives of this term were used mainly in the sense of 'the act or manner in governing', and as a synonym for government (Kjaer, 2004). However, since the 1980s scientists from diverse disciplines (political sciences, public administration, organizational studies, business studies and international relations) have come to refer to governance as something broader than government (Rhodes, 1996; Stoker, 1998). They have increasingly come to use the term to mean a process in which an organization, network of organizations or a society steers itself, allocates resources and exercises control and coordination (Rhodes, 1996; Rosenau, 1995).

Today, the concept of governance is widely used in public, non-profit and the private sectors. It 'generally refers to the means for achieving direction, control, and coordination of wholly or partially autonomous individuals or organizations on behalf of interests to which they jointly contribute' (Lynn *et al.*, 2000, p. 235). All sport organizations, from local clubs to national bodies, government agencies, sport service organizations and professional teams around the world, need to be directed, controlled and regulated (Ferkins and Shilbury, 2010). However, none of these sport organizations can act independently of other sporting agencies. The International Olympic Committee (IOC) determines, for example, whether cricket will be included in the Olympic programme, with far-reaching consequences for national and local cricket organizations, individual cricket players and other stakeholders. Yet, the international governing body in cricket (i.e. the International Cricket Council, ICC) is the leading organization in the regulation of its competition rules, whether this concerns the Olympic Games or any other international tournament.

When a major crisis erupts in international cricket, such as allegations of match fixing, it is the ICC that takes action in sanctioning such behaviour. But if such a crisis were confined to Australia, the national sport federation (e.g. Cricket Australia) would be expected to intervene. Cricket Australia also has leadership responsibilities for the sport in Australia and, as such, plays a governing role across organizational boundaries exercising coordination with and control over state- and club-level cricket. However, when it comes to raising the overall level of Australia's high performance sport, including cricket, this responsibility is scattered among numerous agencies, from government agencies (e.g. the Australian Sports Commission and the Australian Institute of Sport) to voluntary sport associations (at national, state and local levels), the corporate sector (e.g. sponsors) and many other stakeholders (e.g. sport science institutes, physical educationalists and coaches associations). In such a configuration, it could be argued that there is no one agency that is hierarchically subordinated to another. Thus, central steering is replaced by another mode of governance, based on joint action, mutual adjustment and networking (Kooiman, 1993).

To get to grips with issues of steering, accountability and responsibility in high performance sport, we will concentrate in this chapter on the distinction between governance *of* organizations and governance *between* organizations. Governance *of* organizations refers to corporate and/or organizational governance. These terms encompass the governance issues, practices and processes of a specific organization, such as a local sport club or national sport organization. Corporate governance points to large commercial organizations. Organizational governance is broader and can also concern non-profit organizations, which are very prominent within the sport sector. Governance *between* organizations is related to the governance of high performance sport in a system, network or configuration of institutions. It encompasses, for example, governance issues within a nation and across sports (e.g. the governance of high performance sport in the United Kingdom), or within a sport or group of sports across nations (e.g. the governance of football by FIFA or of the Olympic movement by the IOC). Depending on their inter-organizational relationships and the theoretical framework used to analyse them, these latter modes of governance can be characterized as systemic, network or configurational governance,[1] or, at the highest level, global governance.

Before exploring organizational and systemic governance in more depth, we will first introduce you to some theories that can help you understand the implications and complications of these modes of governance in high performance sport.

HELPFUL THEORIES IN THE GOVERNANCE OF HIGH PERFORMANCE SPORT

The application of theory can help make sense of these tensions and dilemmas, and at least in part, explain why things occur in the way they do. If we are lucky, a good theory can also help guide good practice. While there is no agreed universal theory of governance (Huse, 2009), researchers are starting to gather together a suite of theories, borrowed from other elements of organizational studies, public management and international relations. Some of these major theories include agency theory, stewardship theory, resource dependence theory, institutional theory, stakeholder theory, network theory and international relations theory.

117

Table 7.1 *Helpful theories in the governance of sport*

Theory used in governance	Premise for governance	Implications for board role and function
Agency theory	Owners have different interests from those who manage (Fama and Jensen, 1983)	To control and monitor the actions of the CEO
Stewardship theory	Owners have similar interests to those who manage (Davis and Schoorman, 1997)	To partner with CEO in the interests of the organization
Institutional theory	Design of the governance model is the result of external pressures to conform (Hoye and Cuskelly, 2007)	To conform to external expectations
Resource dependence theory	Organizations are dependent on others for survival (Pfeffer and Salancik, 1978)	To build relationships with other organizations
Stakeholder theory	A diverse range of interests exists among stakeholders (Hung, 1998; Oliver, 1990)	To incorporate stakeholder perspectives into the governing role and to balance stakeholder needs
Network theory	There is interdependence between organizations (Henry and Lee, 2004; Kooiman, 1993)	To facilitate networks between organizations and individuals
International relations theory	The governance structure is fragmented and has multiple centres (Kjaer, 2004; Rosenau, 1995)	To link and change between several networks with different governance structures

Source: Adapted from Cornforth, 2003; Hoye and Cuskelly, 2007

While this may mean there are a large number of theories to come to grips with, leading authors in governance such as Pye and Pettigrew (2005), Cornforth (2003), and Hoye and Cuskelly (2007) encourage us to use a multi-theoretical approach. This is because agency theory has, until now, dominated our thinking about the governing role and arguably this has created some limitations in our understanding of governance, particularly in the non-profit setting (Cornforth, 2003). The use of multiple theories can help us understand individual theories by highlighting contrasting approaches, while each theory also offers something different in our endeavours to make sense of the various modes, tensions and dilemmas of governance in high performance sport. Table 7.1 summarizes these theories and also relates them to the role and function of the board (in a generic sense) in organizations.

TWO MODES OF GOVERNANCE: ORGANIZATIONAL AND SYSTEMIC GOVERNANCE

With reference to these theories we now explore in more depth the two modes of governance outlined earlier (organizational and systemic). We start with organizational governance that focuses on the role of the board as it relates to high performance sport (governance of organizations), and then discuss systemic, network and/or configurational governance practices across high performance sport systems (governance between organizations).

Organizational governance in high performance sport

The governing responsibilities of a sport organization vary considerably between the different contexts of commercial elite sport and non-profit elite sport. In the commercial setting, a dominating reason for existence is, by definition, commercial gain for those who have invested financially in the sport. Examples of commercial entities in sport are all around us and include teams in the English Premier League (e.g. Manchester United Football Club), teams in the Australian National Rugby League (e.g. the Melbourne Storm) and teams in the US National Basketball Association (e.g. the Boston Celtics). In these instances the sport team or club is owned (in a governance sense) by shareholders who, while often indulging in a passion, also seek a financial return on their investment. Therefore, the board's role is to *set the direction*, *account for* and *control* activities, and *regulate* behaviour on behalf of the owners (i.e. shareholders).

Much of our understanding of organizational governance in high performance sport is grounded in what we know about governance in the corporate setting outside of the sport context. The notion of organizational governance has come about because of the separation of ownership between those who traditionally owned the corporation and those who manage it (Fama and Jensen, 1983). As a result of growth, a company becomes too large for the commercial owners to also manage, so oversight of the entity is delegated to a group known as the board of directors. This group is usually made up of shareholders, the CEO and independent or non-executive directors.

In the high performance sport domain, who *owns* the sport organization (in a governance sense) is not clear cut. While we certainly have commercial or 'corporate sport', the industry globally is also heavily dominated by sporting entities that have a 'not-for-profit' legal constitution. Commonly referred to as NPOs (non-profit organizations), the profits generated by these organizations are returned, not to the shareholders, but back to the organization for its ongoing viability and development. Our global sport system is replete with NPO sport entities with responsibility for governing high performance sport. Examples of such organizations include the IOC and international governing bodies of sporting codes such as football, tennis, netball, triathlon, rugby union (i.e. FIFA, ITF, IFNA, ITU, IRB, etc.). Accordingly, the national governing bodies of the sport codes, and the corresponding provincial, regional or state bodies and finally, local clubs, are almost always NPOs.

WHO HAS THE RIGHT TO GOVERN?: BOARD COMPOSITION AND MEMBER 'OWNERSHIP' OF SPORT ORGANIZATIONS

So, who has the right to govern a non-profit sport organization? You might assume that the key stakeholders have places on the board just as the majority shareholders do for a commercial sport entity. In fact, there are multiple stakeholders, including sponsors, funders, fans, athletes and the media. Determining who has a place on the governing board can sometimes be a vexed question (Ferkins and Shilbury, 2010). Traditionally, those who are the legal 'members' have been considered equal to shareholders in a commercial sense with the right to govern or have governing representatives. Usually, the members of an international body, such as the International Rugby Board, are organizations representing the member nations (e.g. the New Zealand Rugby Union, the Irish Rugby Union). Similarly, with a national sport organization, the state/provincial/regional entities are usually the legal members. In turn, the local clubs are usually the members of the regional entity, and individuals are members of the local clubs.

It is becoming increasingly obvious within high performance sport, however, that the system of governance whereby the member associations, who have traditionally had their representative on the board, is creating tensions in the prioritizing of resources (Ferkins and Shilbury, 2010). Consider, for example, the priorities of a local tennis club and regional tennis association, and how their priorities may differ from those of the national body such as the French Tennis Federation, or Tennis Australia. The local clubs and associations primarily exist for the purposes of participation in tennis. On the other hand, Tennis Australia is one of Australia's largest national sport organizations and has responsibility for elite player development and, of course, the Australian Open Grand Slam event. Traditionally, the Tennis Australia board has been made up of elected members drawn from its state bodies who, historically, have held the view that the state bodies 'own' Tennis Australia. However, Tennis Australia has recently sought to move to an independent board to allow it to focus in a more professional and corporate way (Shilbury and Kellett, 2011).

Indeed, an increasing trend in non-profit sport organization governance is the restructuring of representative boards (Ferkins and Shilbury, 2010). Many NSOs in New Zealand and Australia, for example, now have what has come to be known as a 'hybrid board' composition (Ferkins and Shilbury, 2010). Set out below are three options for board composition of non-profit sport organizations:

1 a *representative board* – where board members are elected from specific member organizations/entities to represent those members;
2 a *hybrid board* – where there is a mix of elected board members and appointed board members; and
3 an *independent board* – where board members are appointed, usually by an appointments panel to govern on behalf of the membership at large.

One of the dilemmas of sport governance is that we tend to deal in uncertainties when it comes to the notion of ownership. In addition, the tensions between priorities of high performance sport and sport participation are reflected in the governing role. This brings us back to the question, who has the right to govern high performance sport? As you can see, the notion of ownership is closely associated with the complexities of understanding who governs sport. Carver (2002, p. 66), a well-known governance specialist, urged, 'Determining ownership isn't always easy, but it's an absolute necessity for boards who wish to get in touch with the true source of their authority and their own true governing power.' Indeed, there are no easy answers to the question of who has the right to govern high performance sport. Shilbury (2001) noted that, in sport governance, there is usually no one individual or group of individuals who legally own the organization and, as a consequence, the concept of control is often blurred.

120

THE ROLE AND FUNCTION OF THE BOARD IN HIGH PERFORMANCE SPORT

Having established some of the challenges in determining who has the right to govern, the nature of member 'ownership' and how boards are constituted, we now turn our attention to board function. What might the board of a sport organization with responsibility for elite athlete development or high performance competitions, actually do? Not surprisingly, there is a range of perspectives in the literature, and thus far, empirical research efforts to describe and analyse the role and function of the board in sport organizations have been limited (Hoye and Doherty, 2011). However, in considering the literature on board roles per se (i.e. including and looking beyond sport), Kilmister (2006) established a comprehensive list of key elements applicable to sport organizations with responsibility for high performance. These roles/functions included:

- overseeing the organization's systems, processes and actions to ensure that there is compliance with externally imposed requirements and that the organization's internal policies and rules are honoured (e.g. compliance with government legislation such as a ban on tobacco sponsorship, or internal athlete selection policies);
- managing the relationship with the chief executive – this includes hiring, firing and setting performance criteria for the Chief Executive Officer (e.g. the paid CEO of a national sport organization, such as England Squash and Racquetball, is accountable to the volunteer board);
- setting the organization's mission, vision and strategic direction, that is, the upper level components of the organization's strategy (e.g. the Tennis Australia board provides direction with regard to the prioritization of resources for high performance sport vs. sport participation);
- setting and monitoring policies, including risk management policies (e.g. the board of the Australian Olympic Committee approves selection standards and policies for the Australian Olympic and Commonwealth Games teams);
- monitoring progress towards long-term strategic objectives and monitoring short-term results (e.g. the board of the International Federation of Netball Associations monitors progress against established strategic priorities such as the globalization of netball);
- expressing accountability to members and other key stakeholders (e.g. the board of the New Zealand Rugby Union reports at its Annual General Meeting to its member regions and other stakeholders, such as media, government, sponsors, etc.);
- accepting ultimate responsibility for all organizational actions (e.g. members of the board of the Melbourne Storm Rugby League Club accepted ultimate responsibility after major breaches in the salary cap were revealed despite the board being found to have had no prior knowledge of the breaches).

For those countries where the government plays a major role in fostering and funding the sport system (e.g. the United Kingdom, France, Canada, New Zealand and Australia), the central governance agencies responsible for sport have established guidelines to assist national sport organizations develop their governance capability. These guidelines give us some insight into the desired role of the board from the perspective of these funding agencies. UK Sport, for example, details the board's role as, '(1) to set the organization's strategic aims; (2) to provide the leadership to put those aims into effect; (3) to supervise the management of the entity; and (4) to report to members on their stewardship' (UK Sport, 2004, p. 6). The Australian Sports Commission (2007, p. 6) describes the board's role as 'determining the organization's strategic direction, core values and ethical framework, as well as key objectives and performance measures'. It also notes that the board has 'ultimate authority and responsibility for financial operations and budgeting to ensure the achievement of strategic objectives' (p. 6). Finally, Sport and Recreation New Zealand offers a similar definition, in describing the role of a governing board as the process by which the board sets strategic direction and priorities, establishes policies and performance expectations, characterizes and manages risk, and evaluates and monitors organization achievements 'in order to exercise its accountability to the organization and its owners' (Sport and Recreation New Zealand, 2006, p. 16).

While the governance of high performance sport requires that the board cast a long-term view of the organization's future (i.e. often in four-year Olympic or world championship cycles), some governance scholars have argued that we need a greater focus on the strategic role of the board (Ferkins et al., 2009) and that we need to better understand what this aspect of the board's role actually entails (Hoye and Cuskelly, 2007). Carver (2002), a well-known governance specialist, also emphasizes the strategic role of the board. Carver argues that the board's job is to create the future, and not to mind the shop. This statement accentuates the forward-looking role and the need for the board to contribute at the strategic level, and cautions against being captured by the day-to-day demands of the organization.

Garratt (2005) also emphasizes the board's strategic role and claims that many boards find it difficult to balance their monitoring and accountability role with the need to consider the organization's future. In an earlier insightful text, he describes the role of the board in the following way (1996, pp. 3–4):

> As I see it, the key to organizational health is a committed and thoughtful board of directors, not managers, at the heart of the enterprise. It is the board's job to keep striking balances between the external and internal pressures on the organization to ensure survival. The board must give a clear direction to the business and create an emotional climate in which people can align and attune to that direction . . . Directing is essentially an intellectual activity. It is about showing the way ahead, giving leadership.

> This is a big challenge for boards that have responsibility for high performance sport and overseeing all of the demands that this entails, not the least of which is often balancing the priorities for sport participation and elite development and competition. The case study on British Cycling exemplifies the board's strategic role in balancing these two priorities. Table 1, which sets out governance theories, also highlights the potential challenges in balancing different board roles. We now turn our attention to the relationships between organizations that are involved in the governance of high performance sport.

Systemic governance: governing across organizational boundaries

A peculiar feature of the sport sector in most countries is that it has evolved from the 'bottom-up'. Predominantly, in the late nineteenth century, private citizens founded local voluntary clubs to practise their sport. These local clubs established national governing bodies to codify the rules, organize competitions, sanction their sporting practice and preserve its social exclusiveness (Houlihan, 1997). This development was rapid. Within less than a generation after the first clubs had sprung up in most sports, major regional and national competitions were held. Soon afterwards, the governance of many of these sports was internationally standardized by the foundation of international sport federations. The Federation of International Football Associations (FIFA), for example, was founded in 1904 by six national football associations, while football had been unknown to those countries a mere thirty years before (van Bottenburg, 2001).

In countries all over the world, sporting practices were initiated, regulated, organized and standardized by individual citizens with shared interests. Collectively, they created a global sporting system characterized by a hierarchy of vertically integrated associations and federations, in which separate national governing bodies (e.g. the Brazilian Volleyball Federation) and international governing bodies (e.g. the International Volleyball Federation, FIVB) obtained jurisdiction over each sport. These organizations were mainly based on a system of indirect democratic decision-making by their members (as noted earlier). Club members elected the members of their local boards and representatives of these boards had the right to appoint the board members of their national sport federations. The national representatives of these federations were, in turn, eligible to vote for board candidates of the international federation to which they were affiliated.

In this predominantly 'bottom-up' global sport system, the organization of the 'top-down' Olympic movement is an exception. The IOC was founded before National Olympic Committees (NOCs) were established all over the world, at the instigation of the IOC. Moreover, board members of the IOC and the NOCs are not democratically elected representatives of lower bodies; instead, they are appointed by what is referred to as a system of cooptation. This system of appointment (rather than election) has been criticized because of a lack of democracy and transparency, but has also been defended on the grounds that it guarantees the independence of the IOC. It is argued that under this system, groups of nations cannot collude to elect the IOC members they want for political reasons.

Nation states hardly played a role in the formation of this global sporting system. Until deep in the twentieth century, sport in general and elite sport in particular were considered to be the responsibility of sport organizations, whereby governments rarely interfered. In most countries, the development of both club sport and elite sport was left in the hands of voluntary bodies. Wherever there was some government support for elite sport, it was ad hoc and limited, such as assistance with travel costs to support the participation of national teams in the Olympic Games or other international sport events (Houlihan, 1997; Stewart, 2011).

This situation changed in the second half of the twentieth century and central government intervention in elite sport became commonplace. Among the reasons for this transformation, the Cold War was the most prominent. During the 1950s and 1960s, the Soviet Union and other communist European countries embraced elite sport as a medium through which they could prove their excellence and raise their international status. They created a high performance model that was directed towards the systematic identification and nurturing of talented athletes. This model contrasted sharply with the rest of the world. Against the state-led 'system-related' model of the East, the West still relied on a 'person-related' model, where talented athletes had to emerge spontaneously from sport competitions ordered on the basis of age, gender, region and standard of play (Fisher and Borms, 1990; Green and Houlihan, 2005). The success of the Eastern European model, and particularly the success of Soviet and East German athletes at Olympic Games, prompted increased concern in other countries about the need for a more strategic, planned and coordinated approach to high performance sport (Bergsgard *et al.*, 2007).

In this competition for international prestige, government interference was no longer taboo. In many countries, high performance sport became institutionalized. Governments and the governing bodies of sport developed policies and established new organizations. As a result of these changes,

> Specialist elite sport policy units have been established; elite centres have been created; scientific methods have increasingly been adopted; programmes for the professional education of coaches have been developed; and policies for identification, selection and training of talented athletes have been designed. (Bergsgard *et al.*, 2007, p. 154)

CONTRASTING SYSTEMS OF HIGH PERFORMANCE GOVERNANCE

The introduction of a systematic approach and abandonment of the principle of non-interference by the state altered the relationships between sport organizations within nations (e.g. NOCs, National Sport Governing Bodies, local sporting clubs) and between sport organizations and national, provincial and local governments (Houlihan, 1997). These changes raised several new questions about governance in high performance sport. First, who was legitimized to set national goals, objectives and priorities for the high perform-ance system? Second, who was responsible and accountable for achieving these goals, and how was that related to other sport policy goals such as club development and sport participation? Third, how and to what extent should the high performance system be altered from an amateur, voluntary and decentralized activity to a professional and centralized undertaking? Finally, how and to what extent should the sport system prioritize and thus focus funding on sports that have delivered success or shown medal potential, and what might such a policy mean for less-developed sports and other sport policy goals, such as raising sport participation?

Such questions have important implications for the notion of governance. Consider the earlier definitions of governance as expressed by Lynn *et al.* (2000), Rosenau (1995) and Rhodes (1996). In other words, how did countries set about steering, allocating resources and exercising control and coordination (as per Rosenau's 1995 definition of governance)? In response to these questions, every country developed its own system characterized by a

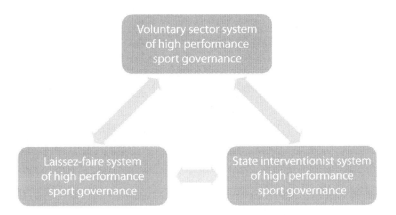

Figure 7.1 *Contrasting systems of high performance governance within countries*

specific configuration of governmental institutions, voluntary sport organizations and business partners. Schematically, these configurations can be represented within a triangle, in which a laissez-faire model, a state interventionist model and a voluntary sector model form the hypothetical extremes (refer to Figure 7.1).

In this triangle, the United States differs most from other countries. Consistent with the ideological foundations of American government, the federal government is hardly involved in elite sport. In contrast to the increasing governmental interference in elite sport throughout the world, there is hardly any policy coordination and thus no 'system' for high performance development in the United States. Athletes have multiple pathways to and through elite sport, but there is no well-mapped road to elite status. Each sport must develop its own system. National performances continue to rely overwhelmingly on school, university and professional systems. For specific sports, these systems indeed offer a structured pathway from talent to elite athlete. However, sports that lack professional or university opportunities are at a distinct disadvantage and produce few medals (Sparvero *et al.*, 2008).

At another corner of the triangle (see Figure 7.1), we find countries with interventionist high performance systems. Poland, China and other former or current communist countries are good examples of this. Jolanta Żyśko (2008, pp. 190–191) characterized Poland, for example, as 'interventionist, centralized, bureaucratic, intensely formalized but unstable' and 'moving towards greater centralization and a strengthening of the state administration's grip of the management of sport'. Today, state sport policy in Poland is formalized and regulated by an Act of parliament. This Act stresses the role of the state and state administration in sport in general, and high performance sport in particular. At the national level, Poland has a governmental body dedicated exclusively to sport, which is meant to be the only decision centre for the entire field of high performance sport (Żyśko, 2008). For China, elite sport has been an effective way to boost its image on the international stage. Since the country started its 'open-door' policy in the late 1970s, success in the Olympic Games became the highest aim of Chinese sport. To achieve this goal the government directed increasing amounts of money (from general revenue and from lotteries) to elite sport, and expanded its centralized administrative and management system. Priorities for financial support within this system included talent selection and development, full-time professional athletes, a strenuous training system, coaching and sport science research, and national and regional training facilities (Hong, 2008, 2011).

Less obvious is the crucial role of the state in high performance sport in liberal welfare states, such as New Zealand, Australia, Canada and the United Kingdom. Green and Houlihan (2005, p. 63) describe Australia and Canada 'as the "early Western adopters", and the UK as a "late adopter" of many of the principles of organization and administration developed by former Eastern bloc countries'. Evidently, the high performance system of the Eastern Bloc proved to be successful, leading to a period of dominance at the Olympic Games, which began in the 1950s and lasted into the 1980s. This was accompanied by a strong decline in the 'market share' of Western countries in Olympic medals. The Eastern Bloc system, however, was not easy to emulate, as its interventionist, centralized and bureaucratic governance structure was diametrically opposed to the fragmented, decentralized and voluntary organization based governance structure that prevailed in Western countries. The solution to this problem was found in the growth of commercial patronage on the one hand and the creation of a variety of new administrative infrastructures for high performance sport on the other (Houlihan, 1997).

These changes altered the relationships between federal governments and national sport organizations. The creation of Sport Canada in the 1970s, the Australian Institute of Sport in 1981, the Australian Sports Commission in 1984, the Hillary Commission in 1987 in New Zealand and UK Sport in 1997 were turning points in these countries. They reflected not only a much more interventionist stance by their governments but also a decline in the autonomy of the national sport organizations regarding high performance sport. The provision of funds by the government means that national sport organizations have become increasingly dependent on the government contributions to a centralized, professionalized and successful high performance system (Houlihan, 1997; Green and Houlihan, 2005).

In most social-democratic countries in Western Europe, central governments intervene less in the voluntary sector. High performance sport remains, in principle, the responsibility of relatively autonomous sport organizations in Germany, the Netherlands, Denmark and Norway. In these countries, central governments have also expressed increased ambitions to promote professional and structured elite sport policies and achieve success in the international arena. However, compared to the liberal welfare states mentioned earlier (e.g. Australia, New Zealand, Canada, the United Kingdom), they have tried to realize these ambitions in a more indirect way, that is, through financial support of the organized sport system, and in particular through direct subsidies of the umbrella sport organizations that bear responsibility for high performance sport. In Germany, Norway and the Netherlands, these umbrella organizations have a far-reaching influence on the distribution of the gaming profits (mainly from lotteries) allocated to sport in their countries (Augestad and Bergsgard, 2008; Augestad et al., 2006; Bergsgard et al., 2007; Petry et al., 2008).

This section has discussed the three contrasting systems of high performance sport governance that are seen in different countries around the world (as encapsulated in Figure 7.1). In this, the notion of systemic governance is considered in terms of a network of organizations, each contributing to the steering, allocation of resources and exercise of control and coordination of high performance sport. In staying with a macro view of governance, in other words systemic governance, our attention now turns to future issues in the governance of high performance sport.

FUTURE ISSUES AND TRENDS IN THE GOVERNANCE OF HIGH PERFORMANCE SPORT

Houlihan and Green (2008, p. 291) conclude in their comparative study of elite sport development that, 'increasing global competition is encouraging a growing number of nations to adopt a more strategic approach to the development of elite athletes in order to differentiate themselves from "rival" countries'. Other studies endorse this view and show that national approaches are based increasingly on a homogeneous model of elite sport development, although each country still shows domestic variations (De Bosscher et al., 2008; Houlihan and Green, 2008; Oakley and Green, 2001). What almost all countries have in common is a trend towards growing interference of governments and a perceived need for more effective coordination, central control and governance of high performance sport.

This trend has put pressure in many countries on the relationship between the governance of high performance sport and the governance of sport-for-all. With respect to high performance sport, questions such as, 'how to steer', 'how to increase efficiency', 'how to improve accountability' and 'how to gain and maintain legitimacy' increasingly result in different answers from when considering sport-for-all. Increasing expenditure on elite sport has forced many countries not only to prioritize elite sport over sport-for-all but also to target a minority of (elite) sports for funding (e.g. see Ibsen et al., 2011, for Denmark, and Stewart, 2011, for Australia). This tendency of exclusion and priority setting increasingly conflicts with the principles of sport-for-all policies that are directed towards inclusion and diversity. If the demand for success is increased, or if governments allocate less to elite sport, this tension will further intensify and provoke a fierce discussion in many countries about the fundamentals of both high performance and sport-for-all policies.

Undoubtedly, such a discussion will touch upon other core concepts in governance theory: legitimacy and accountability. As Collins (2007) concludes with respect to New Zealand, elite sport funding is increasingly driven by the expectation of a 'return of investment' and the achievement of clearly identified goals (i.e. an output-orientated focus). Legitimacy and accountability in sport-for-all funding, on the other hand, are based on arguments concerning democratic procedures, social justice, fairness and equality (i.e. an input-orientated focus). Here again, it can be expected that this difference will reinforce the tension between high performance sport and sport-for-all policies. In high performance sport governance structures it is tempting to respond to the pressure to succeed by centralizing the decision-making processes and shortening the lines of responsibility. The input-oriented focus of sport-for-all policies, however, can easily provoke the opposite response – calls for decentralization and extensive stakeholder participation. In high performance sport governance, one of the biggest challenges, for governments and sport governing bodies alike, is how to cope with this fundamental tension. After all, in the end, they have a dual responsibility.

127

CASE STUDY 7.1

THE GOVERNANCE OF BRITISH CYCLING

Adam Karg

Deakin University

British Cycling, based in Manchester, is the governing body for cycle sport in the United Kingdom. At the elite level in cycling, the United Kingdom is a world leader. The British team won thirty-four medals in the 2008 Olympic and Paralympic Games and half of the available gold medals at the World Championships in the same year. In the run-up to the London 2012 games, British Cycling boasted strong participation growth and considerable strength in its elite programmes, underpinned by innovative partnerships and a clear and transparent strategic plan within a complex multi-national and regional governance framework.

History and role

The aim of British Cycling is to inspire participation in cycling as a sport, for recreation and for sustainable transport through achieving worldwide success. The organization, formerly known as the British Cycling Federation (BCF) was formed in 1959 following a merger of the National Cyclists Union, the Road Time Trials Council and the British League of Racing Cyclists. Prior to this, the presence of these multiple organizations had fragmented the sport, resulting in conflicts about regulation, selection of national teams and who should control national governance responsibilities for the sport. The move to a more unified approach was complete when the British Mountain Bike Federation, Cyclo-Cross Association, BMX Association and Cycle Speedway Councils became commissions within the BCF.

Governance structure

A multi-tiered governance structure incorporating international, national and regional bodies is evident in the sport. British Cycling is a member of the international federation, the Union Cycliste Internationale (UCI) as well as the European Cycling Union. It has associations with the British Olympic Association. The organization itself is governed by a board of eight directors, led by an executive president. In 2010 the CEO and senior management team led a total of 226 employees, which represented a staffing growth of 13.5 per cent for the year (British Cycling, 2010).

Reflecting its wide coverage, and exemplifying the notion of 'systemic governance' (refer to the main body of the chapter), there is a network of multiple regions that are interlinked in the British Cycling governance structure. Representative regions include Central, Eastern, East Midlands, North East, North, South, South West, South East, West Midlands and Yorkshire regions, as well as the Scottish and Welsh Cycling Unions (British Cycling, 2011a). The British Schools Cycling Association and British Universities and Colleges Sport are also affiliates of British Cycling. As such, British Cycling is the governing body for the sport in the home nations and also acts as the UCI member for overseas British territories. The Isle of Man and the Channel Islands are recognized as regions under the national governing body of British Cycling (British Cycling, 2011b). While this fosters a centralized and standardized approach to Olympic team representation, the situation becomes more complex when countries compete as individual nations, as is the case at Commonwealth Games events. Below the regional level, around 1,500 cycling clubs or teams are affiliated to British Cycling to enable their athletes to hold licences, race in events and become members of the national organization. In total, British Cycling has over 33,000 members, of which around two-thirds are affiliated with clubs (British Cycling, 2010).

The board's strategic role

A critical role of the board of an organization is to set the organization's mission, vision and strategic direction, and, in the case of British Cycling, the overall strategy for the sport in the United Kingdom. The environment for cycling in the United Kingdom, prior to the 2012 London Olympic Games, presented a clear opportunity for the governing body to capitalize on the design of its strategy. In a press release, the CEO of British Cycling highlighted the opportunities for the sport and summarized the strategic, whole-of-sport approach the organization has taken to deliver across multiple disciplines and multiple regions: 'We have a once in a lifetime opportunity in the run up to London 2012 to really engage Britain with cycling and turn our "medal success" into a "people success" by inspiring mass participation in our sport' (British Cycling, 2009b). The development of a clear strategic plan has been identified as a vital component of the sport's short- and long-term success. The sport's coordinated governance approach is highlighted by the Whole-of-Sport Plan spanning a five-year period from 2009. The plan sought to 'grow cycling as a sport, recreational activity and as sustainable transport by leveraging the worldwide success of its athletes' (British Cycling, 2009a).

Another important function of the board of British Cycling is the monitoring of progress towards long-term strategic objectives as well as monitoring short-term results. In the opening years of the plan, British Cycling demonstrated considerable achievement in key areas including institutional goals related to high performance and mass participation as well as an increased profile through the promotion and the development of partnerships. At the elite level, British Cycling has greatly improved its standing in world events with its success at the Olympics and at UCI World Championships, most notably in track and mountain biking. The provision of the best possible equipment (NASA and the McLaren Group are key technology partners) and progressive and structured sport development and high performance programmes, including Olympic talent, development, academy and podium programmes for elite performers, has aided this success.

Additionally, a partnership with British Sky Broadcasting (BSkyB) has seen the creation of a professional cycling team formed as part of British Cycling that competes globally as a registered Pro Tour team in events such as the Tour de France (British Cycling, 2010,

2011c). This partnership, which involves collaboration at the participation and development levels as well as sponsorship of the elite national team, provides a great profile for the sport, and an avenue to promote and develop its athletes at the highest level. This principal partnership has been further supported by UK Sport, the high performance sports agency responsible for investing in lottery and public funds, and by Sport England that invests funds in organizations and projects that will grow and sustain participation in grass-roots sport and create opportunities for people to excel at their chosen sport (British Cycling, 2011c).

Key 'takeaways'

British Cycling:

- unified what were once separate bodies and cycle disciplines to provide coordinated leadership and governance for the sport;
- unified a number of regions, thereby achieving efficiencies as part of a multiple-level governance network including international, national and regional bodies;
- has a clear and transparent whole-of-sport strategic plan structured around key sport and business outcomes that the board uses to 'steer' the organization; and
- has achieved high performance, sport organization performance and promotional outcomes for cycling.

Case study discussion questions

1. Select cycling or another sport in your country and investigate the way the sport is governed. In what ways is the structure similar to that of British Cycling? In what ways is it different?
2. Identify the role(s) governance plays in British Cycling's Whole-of-Sport Plan.
3. Despite the coordination of various regions and disciplines within cycling, complexities remain in the structure of British Cycling. What potential problems exist given this structure?

SUMMARY

This chapter began with providing some context to the notion of governance and how we have come to use the concept of governance in studying the management of high performance sport. We then discussed more specific meanings and definitions of governance, and sport governance in particular. Table 7.1 summarized the examination of theories considered to be relevant for our understanding of governance. The distinction between organizational governance (governance *of* organizations) and systemic governance (governance *between* organizations) was also highlighted. In our discussion of organizational governance, we detailed the role and function of the board for sport organizations, noting the challenge for voluntary board members in balancing a strategic focus with the monitoring and accountability role. In the discussion of systemic governance, a much broader interpretation of governance was offered. In contrasting the systems of governance within countries, elements of sport policy and sport development were integrated in order to understand the network of organizations responsible for the governance of high performance sport.

The issues and trends highlighted near the end of the chapter concentrate primarily on systemic governance, but also come back to the notion of organizational governance in noting that those who govern high performance sport have to grapple with the fundamental tension between elite sport and sport-for-all in the allocation of limited resources. Finally, the case study, which primarily exemplified organizational governance in focusing on British Cycling, also demonstrated the networked approach to the governance of cycling within the United Kingdom. In many respects, we only really notice the work of the board and the governing system when things go wrong in sport. A deeper understanding of both organization governance and systemic governance of high performance sport brings to light the tensions and complexities of this critical aspect of the management of high performance sport.

DISCUSSION QUESTIONS

1   Distinguish between what the authors describe as 'organizational governance' and 'systemic governance'. Explain how both views of governance relate to high performance sport.
2   Who has the right to govern a sport organization? Explain the composition of a governing board that has responsibility for high performance sport. In your answer, refer to the board composition models of representative, hybrid and independent.
3   Why might sport governing bodies struggle in the future with maintaining control and legitimacy over their respective sporting code? Consider both organizational governance and systemic governance in your answer.

KEY TERMS

- ■ Governance
- ■ Organizational governance
- ■ Member 'ownership'
- ■ Board composition
- ■ Representative board model
- ■ Hybrid board model
- ■ Independent board model
- ■ Role and function of the sport board
- ■ Systemic governance

- Contrasting systems of governance
- Laissez-faire sport governance system
- State interventionist sport governance system
- Voluntary sector sport governance system

GUIDED READING

Sport Governance (2007) by Russell Hoye and Graham Cuskelly provides a very good overview of organizational governance in sport. It summarizes relevant theories and salient topics related to the governance of sport organizations such as the roles and responsibilities of boards, board behaviour and culture, strategic sport governance, the sharing of leadership between the board and the CEO, and conformance and evaluation.

The Governance of Public and Non-profit Organisations: What Do Boards Do? (2003) edited by Chris Cornforth covers issues of organizational governance. While it is not sport specific, it is highly relevant for the governance of non-profit and voluntary sport organizations.

Corporate Governance: Principles, Policies and Practices (2009) by Bob Tricker is another helpful text on organizational governance. While it is primarily focused on the governance of commercial organizations, the issues, practices and processes discussed relating to the role of the board are a useful foundation for understanding the governance of high performance sport.

John Carver on Board Leadership: Selected Writings from the Creator of the World's Most Provocative and Systematic Governance Model (2002) by John Carver is a comprehensive text capturing Carver's publications over two decades. While Carver primarily concentrates on elements of organizational governance, such as board–CEO relationships, board involvement in strategy and board composition, there are sections also relevant for the issues embedded within systemic governance.

'Studying Governance and Public Management: Challenges and Prospects' by Laurence Lynn, Carolyn Heinrich and Carolyn Hill (2000) is an article published in the *Journal of Public Administration Research and Theory* that explains the notion of systemic governance, as derived from the public sector. The article pursues the question of how the myriad of agencies within the public sector can be coordinated to achieve public purpose.

'Governance and Ethics in Sport' by Ian Henry and Ping Chao Lee (2004) is a very useful chapter in the text, *The Business of Sport Management* by John Beech and Simon Chadwick. The chapter explains the notion of network governance as it applies to professional sport.

NOTE

1 Here, we use these terms interchangeably.

BIBLIOGRAPHY

Augestad, P., Bergsgard, N. A. and Hansen, A. Ø. (2006). The institutionalization of an elite sport organization in Norway: the case of 'Olympiatoppen'. *Sociology of Sport Journal*, (23)3, 293–313.

Augestad, P. and Bergsgard, N. A. (2008). Norway. In B. Houlihan and M. Green (Eds), *Comparative elite sport development. Systems, structures and public policy* (pp. 194–217). London: Elsevier.

Australian Sports Commission (2007). *Governance principles: A good practice guide for sporting organisations.* Canberra, Australia: Author.

Bergsgard, N. A., Houlihan, B., Mangset, P., Nodland, S. I. and Rommetveldt, H. (2007). *Sport policy. A comparative analysis of stability and change.* London: Elsevier.

British Cycling (2009a). *The whole sport plan 2009–2013.* Manchester, UK: British Cycling.

British Cycling (2009b). *Whole sport plan for cycling published.* Press release, 23 September 2009. Available at www.britishcycling.org.uk/about/article/bc20090917-British-Cycling-s-Whole-Sport-Plan-0, accessed 21 July 2011.

British Cycling (2010). 2010 *Annual report.* Manchester, UK: British Cycling.

British Cycling. (2011a). *British cycling – about us.* Available at www.britishcycling.org.uk/about, accessed 21 July 2011.

British Cycling (2011b). *British cycling – memorandum of association.* Available at www.british cycling.org.uk/zuvvi/media/bc_files/corporate/02Memorandum_of_Association_2010.pdf, accessed 21 July 2011.

British Cycling (2011c). *British cycling – partners.* Available at www.britishcycling.org.uk/staticcontent/bcst-British-Cycling-s-Partners, accessed 21 July 2011.

Carver, J. (Ed.). (2002). *John Carver on board leadership: Selected writings from the creator of the world's most provocative and systematic governance model.* San Francisco, CA: Jossey-Bass.

Collins, C. (2007). Politics, government and sport in Aotearoa/New Zealand. In C. Collins and S. Jackson (Eds), *Sport in Aotearoa/New Zealand society* (2nd edn, pp. 208–226). Auckland: Thomson.

Cornforth, C. (Ed.). (2003). *The governance of public and non-profit organisations: What do boards do?* London: Routledge.

Davis, J. H. and Schoorman, D. F. (1997). Toward a stewardship theory of management. *Academy of Management Review,* 22(1), 20–48.

De Bosscher, V., Bingham, J., Shibli, S., van Bottenburg, M. and De Knop, P (2008). *The global sporting arms race: An international comparative study on sports policy factors leading to international sporting success.* Oxford: Meyer & Meyer.

De Bosscher, V. and van Bottenburg, M. (2011). Elite for all, all for elite? An assessment of the impact of sport development on elite sport success. In B. Houlihan and M. Green (Eds), *Routledge handbook of sport development* (pp. 575–595). London: Routledge.

Fama, E. F. and Jensen, M. C. (1983). Separation of ownership and control. *Journal of Law and Economics,* 26, 307–325.

Ferkins, L. and Shilbury, D. (2010). Developing board strategic capability in sport organisations: The national-regional governing relationship. *Sport Management Review,* 13, 235–254.

Ferkins, L., Shilbury, D. and McDonald, G. (2009). Board involvement in strategy: Advancing the governance of sport organizations. *Journal of Sport Management,* 23, 245–277.

Fisher, T. J. and Borms, J. (1990). *The search for sporting excellence.* Schorndorf: Verlag Karl Hofmann.

Garratt, B. (1996). *The fish rots from the head.* London: HarperCollins Business.

Garratt, B. (2005). The real role of corporate directors: Balancing prudence with progress. *Journal of Business Strategy,* 26(6), 30–36.

Green, M. and Houlihan, B. (2005). *Elite sport development. Policy learning and political priorities.* London: Routledge.

Heinilä, K. (1982). The totalization process in international sport. *Sportwissenschaft,* 12(3), 235–254.

Henry, I. and Lee, P. C. (2004). Governance and ethics in sport. In J. Beech and S. Chadwick (Eds), *The business of sport management* (pp. 25–41). Harlow, UK: Pearson Education.

133

Hong, F. (2008). China. In B. Houlihan, and M. Green (Eds), *Comparative elite sport development. Systems, structures and public policy* (pp. 27–52). London: Elsevier.

Hong, F. (2011). Sports development and elite athletes in China (pp. 399–417). In B. Houlihan and M. Green (Eds), *Routledge handbook of sports development* (pp. 386–399). London: Routledge.

Houlihan, B. (1997). *Sport, policy and politics: A comparative analysis.* London: Routledge.

Houlihan, B. and Green, M. (2008). *Comparative elite sport development. Systems, structures and public policy.* London: Elsevier.

Hoye, R. and Cuskelly, G. (2007). *Sport governance.* Sydney: Elsevier.

Hoye, R. and Doherty, A. (2011). Nonprofit sport board performance: A review and directions for future research. *Journal of Sport Management, 25,* 272–285.

Hung, H. (1998). A typology of theories of the roles of governing boards. *Corporate Governance,* 6(2), 101–111.

Huse, M. (2009). The value-creating board and behavioural perspectives. In M. Huse (Ed.), *The value creating board: Corporate governance and organizational behavior* (pp. 3–9). New York: Routledge.

Ibsen, B., Hansen, J. and Storm, R. K. (2011). Elite sport development in Denmark. In B. Houlihan and M. Green (Eds), *Routledge handbook of sports development* (pp. 386–399). London: Routledge.

Kilmister, T. (2006). Governance. In L. Trenberth and C. Collins (Eds.), *Sport business management in Aotearoa New Zealand* (pp. 184–201). Palmerston North: Dunmore Press.

Kjaer, A. M. (2004). *Governance.* Cambridge: Polity Press.

Kooiman, J. (1993). Social-political governance: Introduction. In J. Kooiman (Ed.), *Modern Governance* (pp. 1–6). London: Sage.

Lynn, L. E., Heinrich, C. J. and Hill, C. J. (2000). Studying governance and public management: challenges and prospects. *Journal of Public Administration Research and Theory,* (10)2, 233–261.

Oakley B. and Green, M. (2001). The production of Olympic champions: International perspectives on elite sport development system. *European Journal for Sport Management, 8,* 83–105.

Oliver, C. (1990). Determinants of interorganizational relationships: Integration and future directions. *Academy of Management Review, 15,* 241–265.

Petry, K., Steinbach, D. and Burk, V. (2008). Germany. In B. Houlihan and M. Green (Eds), *Comparative elite sport development. Systems, structures and public policy* (pp. 115–146). Amsterdam: Elsevier.

Pfeffer, J. and Salancik, G. (1978). *The external control of organizations: A resource dependence perspective.* New York: Harper & Row.

Pye, A. and Pettigrew, A. (2005). Studying board context, process and dynamics: Some challenges for the future. *British Journal of Management, 16,* S27–S38.

Rhodes, R. A. W. (1996). The new governance: governing without government. *Political Studies,* (44)4, 652–667.

Rosenau, J. N. (1995). Governance in the twenty-first century. *Global Governance,* (1)1, 13–43.

Shilbury, D. (2001). Examining board member roles, functions and influence: A study of Victorian sporting organisations. *International Journal of Sport Management, 2,* 253–281.

Shilbury, D. and Kellett, P. (2011). *Sport management in Australia: An organisation overview* (4th edn). Crows Nest: Allen & Unwin.

Sparvero, E., Chalip, L. and Green, C. (2008). United States. In B. Houlihan and M. Green (Eds), *Comparative elite sport development* (pp. 243–293). London: Elsevier.

Sport and Recreation New Zealand (2006). *Nine steps to effective governance: Building high performance organisations.* Wellington, New Zealand: Author.

Stewart, B. (2011). Sports development and elite athletes: The Australian experience. In B. Houlihan and M. Green (Eds), *Routledge handbook of sports development* (pp. 418–432). London: Routledge.

134

Stoker, G. (1998). Governance as theory: Five propositions. *International Social Science Journal*, 155(50), 17–28.

Tricker, B. (2009). *Corporate governance: Principles, policies and practices*. Oxford: Oxford University Press.

UK Sport (2004). *Good governance guide for national governing bodies*. London: UK Sport.

Van Bottenburg, M. (2001). *Global games*. Urbana and Chicago: University of Illinois Press.

Żyśko, J. (2008). Poland. In B. Houlihan and M. Green (Eds), *Comparative elite sport development. Systems, structures and public policy* (pp. 166–193). London: Elsevier.

Part B
Managing high performance athletes

Chapter 8

Sport development in high performance sport
The process of attracting, retaining and nurturing athletes

Popi Sotiriadou
Griffith University

David Shilbury
Deakin University

LEARNING OUTCOMES

Upon completion of this chapter the reader should be able to:

1   understand the critical role of sport development as the backbone of athlete development in HPS;
2   define sport development and athlete development, and understand the various types and goals of sport development;
3   recognise the benefits of the attraction, retention/transition and nurturing of athletes framework (aka ARTN processes);
4   understand sport management and science-based sport development frameworks, their strengths and weaknesses; and
5   identify sport development stakeholders, the ways they are involved and the impact of their involvement with athlete development.

'The man who will use his skill and constructive imagination to see how much he can give for a dollar, instead of how little he can give for a dollar, is bound to succeed.'

Henry Ford

OVERVIEW

Chapter 8 focuses on the importance of sport development in high performance sport. The chapter will present sport development processes and practices as the basis and backbone of athlete development in high performance sport (HPS). HPS is the top end of sport development and encapsulates any athlete who competes at an international and national level. The chapter will examine who (what sporting organisations and other stakeholders) is involved in the various stages of athlete development, including the attraction, retention and nurturing process, in what ways (roles) and with what outcomes/pathways.

Elite athletes are those who compete at the Olympic Games and various World Championships or play professional sports such as cricket, football and rugby. According to Dr Phil Jauncey, a sports psychologist with the Australian baseball team and the Queensland Bulls Cricket team, the current number of elite athletes in the United States is somewhere between 12,000 and 15,000 and these athletes participate at the elite level for an average of between three and five years depending on the sport. Given that the population of the United States is about 300 million, this means that the percentage of the US population that comprises elite athletes is less than 0.005 per cent. If that is the case, how do these athletes defy the odds and make it to the top? Is success dependent on a mix of nature and nurture, and being at the right place at the right time? Or is success in elite sport a systematic process involving more than genetics, upbringing and luck? This chapter discusses the significance of sport development in the development of athletes. Sport development is an indispensable contributor to athletes' initial attraction to their sport and it is essential to the retention of these athletes in the sport system, to their transition to higher levels of competition and to the nurturing of their long-term performances and international success. Sport development is explained as being a management process and not solely a product of biological, psychological and physical attributes.

EARLY DAYS OF DEFINING SPORT DEVELOPMENT

Sport development is about helping people from all backgrounds to start, persevere with and succeed in sport. The area of sport development has received increasing scholarly attention since the 1970s. The term has been defined by Collins as 'a process of effective opportunities, processes, systems and structures that are set up to enable people in all or particular groups and areas to take part in sport and recreation or to improve their performance to whatever level they desire' (1995, p. 3). It is generally accepted that sport development has three goals: a public health goal that involves participation for personal well-being; an educational goal where grassroots participants may achieve personally referenced excellence by improving personal best performances in sports; and an elite performance goal involving competing on the international stage or at other high levels (Siedentop, 2002).

These three goals can be grouped into two types of sport development: development *through* sport, which places an emphasis on the social objectives achieved through physical activity (the first and second goals in the above list); and development *of* sport (the third goal), which applies to talented and elite athlete development. Development *through* sport focuses on the role that sport can play in contributing to community wellness, but the development *of* sport focuses on the 'need for sporting organisations to ensure a sustainable future by attracting and nurturing participants likely to progress through the system and represent a sport at the elite level' (Shilbury *et al.*, 2008, p. 218). The latter type of sport development, development *of* sport, is the focus of this chapter.

Elite athlete development

Researchers have made many attempts to provide a definition of talent or elite athlete development and to identify what is necessary for the development of elite athletes. Vaeyens *et al.* (2008) argued that talent is an extremely complex concept to define and that it lacks an agreed theoretical framework. A key contributing factor in this lack of consensus is the perennial debate regarding the relative contribution of nature and nurture in the development of elite athletes. In his interpretation of the roles of nature and nurture in the development of elite athletes, Bloom (1985) maintained that ultimately, performance is the outcome of a combination of (a) initial aptitude based on natural motor and cognitive skills, as well as psychological and physiological make-up and (b) a process that recognises the role of practice, coaching, training, familial influences and other options that can nurture nature. This is the athlete development process that encompasses 'the use of sports science, sports medicine, talent identification, and coaching' (Martin *et al.*, 2005, p. 2) targeted to those athletes competing (or with the potential to compete) at the international level for their countries. Cashman and Hughes (1998), however, argued for a broader definition of athlete development, one that encompasses wider and more lasting indicators and factors such as facilities construction and their legacy to sport. This call for a broader definition shows the impact on athlete development of factors other than sport science and medicine.

Most studies on talent and athlete development draw a distinction between the role of sports sciences/sport medicine and the role of sport management. This is because sports sciences/sport medicine and sport management are viewed as separate bodies of knowledge. Much greater emphasis is placed on sport sciences/sport medicine than on sport management. Williams and Reilly (2000) maintain that sports scientists have a role to play in working with coaches and sport managers to ensure adequate attention is given to key elements of the talent and athlete development process. Hence, a definition of athlete development should reflect this combination of science and management for maximising athlete development.

Sotiriadou *et al.* (2009) argued that in addition to sports sciences and medicine, elite development requires the contribution of two things. First, the direct or indirect involvement of other interested groups and stakeholders (e.g. spectators and management), and second, specifically designed strategies and programmes (e.g. competitions) that facilitate athlete development and success. This success, in turn, has the potential to increase the sport's profile and further stimulate the involvement of sponsors, participants, spectators and supporters. Sotiriadou (2010) considered these two factors together with the factors presented by Martin *et al.* (2005). Combined, these factors suggest that *athlete development* is a process that encompasses the use of sport sciences, sport medicine, talent identification and coaching; requires the contribution of various interested groups in an array of specifically designed strategies and programmes targeted to those athletes who compete nationally and internationally, with the potential to create and regenerate involvement from governments, sponsors, participants, spectators, sports supporters and athletes themselves.

This understanding of what is necessary for the development of elite athletes recognises the multifaceted and not always acknowledged factors involved. This more detailed understanding may enable high performance managers, sport development officers and policymakers to capitalise on elite athletes' success in new ways. For instance, sport managers may capitalise on (a) *direct outcomes* (e.g. athletes' involvement with coaching/clinics); (b) *indirect outcomes* (e.g. public interest/awareness); and (c) *financial benefits* (e.g. sponsorship) of elite development and success (Sotiriadou and Shilbury, 2009). Taking into account these outcomes of elite success may result in elite development funding being based on factors other than just medals won at Olympic Games.

Sport and athlete development frameworks

Providing a holistic and all-inclusive model for athlete development has challenged exercise physiologists, coaches, social psychologists, educators, sport managers, governments and policy planners for over 35 years. Currently, there is a plethora of athlete development frameworks highlighting various key features or development stages as being important for athlete progress depending on the disciplinary background. These include the works of Balyi (2002), Bloom (1985), Bramham *et al.* (2001), Côté (1999) and Wylleman and Lavallee (2004), and most of them are discussed in this section. Collectively, these models start from an athletic (i.e. micro-level) perspective, and look at how young people go through the different development stages. This literature has added much to the practice of elite athlete development. However, as this section will demonstrate, what is lacking in these studies is the organisational/ management perspective (i.e. meso-level). At a meso-level sport managers are interested in knowing the ways sport organisations structure the different development stages, and the kinds of processes and strategies that are necessary to attract, retain and nurture athletes. Therefore, the attraction, retention/transition and nurturing (ARTN) framework (Sotiriadou, 2010; Sotiriadou and Shilbury, 2009) is a necessary addition to the literature and complements the micro-level models.

Even though identifying and developing talented athletes is a well-researched field from a sport sciences viewpoint, the talent development process has rarely been explored from an organisational perspective. Various sport and support organisations help young talented participants to become elite athletes by implementing specially designed programmes and other development opportunities. Hence, sport and support organisations play a central role in developing talented athletes. The contribution of the ARTN framework is that it extends the existing knowledge of sport development by considering the effects and outcomes these organisations have on talent development. As the case study in golf at the end of the chapter demonstrates, the ARTN framework can be used as a planning tool to assess the ability of stakeholders and development programmes to achieve predetermined key performance indicators (KPIs). As such, the ARTN framework may be useful to staff ranging from development officers at the grassroots level to high performance managers at the elite level who have adopted a linear approach to sport development planning. Linear approaches to sport development might be inadequate because they prevent us from thinking outside the sport development pyramid and from examining sport development as a reciprocal process in which supporting one process at the expense of others might result in fragmented outcomes.

Initial efforts to depict sport development opportunities resulted in a view of sport development that is represented by the participation pyramid and the sports development continuum (Bramham *et al.*, 2001). The base of the pyramid represents mass participation and the top represents elite participation. In the sports development continuum there are four phases: *Foundation*, which involves the development of basic movement; *Participation*, which entails playing sport for social and health benefits; *Performance*, which is a more structured environment that delivers high standards of performance through commitment to training and competition, and *Excellence*, which is the pinnacle of sporting performance at the national and international levels. The sport development pyramid and the continuum are not empirically derived models, yet they have shaped the thinking, conceptualising and planning for sport development in various countries.

Basing his research on the perspectives and insights of elite athletes, Bloom (1985) developed a model of talent development through interviews with twenty-one Olympic swimmers and eighteen world-class tennis players. This model outlines three critical stages of talent development. The early years (or initiation stage) are characterised by fun, playful activities with guidance, stimulation of interest and support from parents and participants. The middle years (or development stage) occur when children become more achievement-orientated and serious about their activity. They practise more and have more dedication to succeed. The late years (or perfection stage) occur when individuals become more autonomous and knowledgeable about their training and competition, and the chosen activity dominates all aspects of their lives. The model is based on athletes' experiences of their development and highlights the importance of transition between stages.

Côté (1999) builds on Bloom's model and identifies three stages of participation. The first stage is the sampling years (ages 6–12) and consists mostly of play, with enjoyment, as well as experimentation in different sports. The second stage is the specialising years (ages 13–15) when athletes choose one or two sports and focus their skills with more structured practice. The third stage is the investment years (after the age of 16) and is characterised by the quest for an elite level of performance with more time, effort and intense deliberate practice needed. In his development model of sport participation (DMSP), Côté (1999) describes how deliberate play (i.e. activities that are intrinsically motivating and are specifically designed to maximise enjoyment) and deliberate practice (i.e. activities that require effort specifically designed to improve performance) vary during the transitions between the sampling, specialising and investment years (Ericsson *et al.*, 1993).

Balyi (2002) also observed participant practice and, using an exercise physiology approach, conceptualised the long-term athlete development (LTAD) model that includes four stages for early-specialisation sports and six stages for late-specialisation sports. These stages include: fundamental and learning to train (only for late specialisation sports); training to train; training to compete; training to win; and retirement/retainment. The LTAD is a sports development framework that is based on human growth and development. It is about adopting an athlete-centred approach to guide coaches in the training and development of the sport and its athletes. An LTAD plan creates a gradual progression in which coaches teach athletes the game in stages, rather than all at once, coordinating the instruction and programmes with the athlete's motivations and developmental phases.

REDEFINING SPORT DEVELOPMENT

The aforementioned studies that have focused on the development *of* sport and its applications to athlete development 'have provided significant insight but have been ad hoc insomuch as sport development has so far lacked a theoretical framework' (Green, 2005, p. 234). Perhaps the most notable omissions in all these models are the lack of theoretical input from management and organisational studies, and the failure to identify who is involved with sport development, in what ways they are involved and with what outcomes. Even though Collins' (1995) definition of sports development portrays it as a process that creates opportunities for participation, it is only recently that sport development has come to be more inclusive in its roles, practices and outcomes. It is now understood that it involves various stakeholders, and numerous strategies, systems and pathways that facilitate athlete development. Houlihan and Green (2011) argued that sport development is highly contested in terms of what its objectives and practices are and who its practitioners are. The objectives that have been identified by writers in the field include talent identification, talent development and enhanced health. Practices they have identified range from the development of sport-specific technical skills to recreational fun days, and the practitioners that have been identified range from development officers and coaches to religious missionaries.

In recognition of the evolving nature of sport development, and of its various objectives, practices and stakeholders, Sotiriadou (2010) provides an interpretation of sport development from a different perspective that complements the existing one. After examining the sport development processes of thirty-five sporting organisations over a period of four years, she defined *sport development* as a dynamic process, in which stakeholder involvement (inputs) provides the necessary sport development strategies (throughputs) and pathways (outcomes) that facilitate the ARTN (i.e. sport development processes) of participants. More specifically, Sotiriadou *et al.* (2008) explain that the term 'sport development stakeholders' is inclusive of all the 'parties' involved in the delivery of sport development processes. The case study in golf at the end of the chapter exemplifies the intricacies involved with offering successful pathways to amateur players. The case study gives examples of the processes and strategies undertaken by golf organisations to keep young talented golfers in the sport system.

There are generally two types of sport development stakeholders. The first is the group of individuals or organisations that support sport financially or operationally, and initiate and shape policies, programmes and other sport development strategies. Examples of these organisations include government departments responsible for sport policy such as Sport England, the Australian Sports Commission, Sport Canada, state departments for sport and recreation, Olympic committees and international federations. The second is the group of organisations or individuals that help implement these policies, programmes and other sport development strategies. For instance, coaches, umpires, athletes, sponsors, volunteers, high performance managers, team leaders and other staff are involved with various activities including the maintenance of facilities, the organisation of competitions or events, umpiring games and the running of training sessions.

While the two groups of sport development stakeholders provide the input, sport development strategies offer the throughput for athlete development. Lyle (1997), in his description of the United Kingdom's system of managing excellence in sports performance, acknowledges the importance of sport development programmes, facilities, competitions and other factors for the structural progression of athletes. He calls these factors delivery mechanisms or structural strategies. Sport development strategies are the actions taken by the sport development stakeholders for successful sport development. Hence, sport development strategies (throughput) represent the ways in which the sport development stakeholders put sport policies and programmes into practice or any other ways they are involved with athlete development. These strategies consist of the programmes, initiatives, objectives and tools of sport development. They are used to cater for player development, and to provide facilities, coaches, umpires, administration, management, promotions, competitions and events. Strategies in the above areas determine who gets what (in terms of resources), when and how. The formulation and maintenance of strategies for sport support the establishment and sustainability of sport development. Sport development pathways represent the output of sport development stakeholder input and throughput, and are defined as the means to move from one sport development process to another.

SPORT DEVELOPMENT PROCESSES: THE ARTN FRAMEWORK

Sport development processes are the stages that sport participants and athletes may find themselves in during their engagement with sport and careers. There are three sport development processes: attraction, retention/transition and nurturing (Figure 8.1). Since sports cannot retain or nurture participants or athletes they have not attracted, it is logical to examine the attraction process first.

Attraction is the process whereby sport development strategies draw new sport development segments or target groups and provide quality experiences to existing ones. The attraction process involves five sport development segments. These are members/participants, juniors, youth, elite athletes and supporters/spectators regardless of the demographic and socioeconomic factors that define them. The attraction process has a twofold aim: to increase awareness, participation and membership of general participants, and to nurture large numbers of young participants destined to be elite performers. The attraction process is

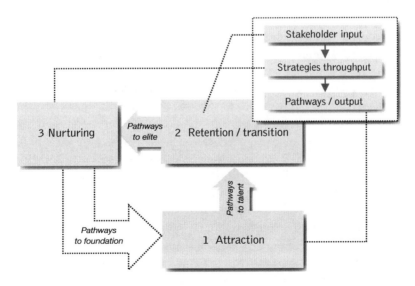

Figure 8.1 *An overview of the attraction, retention/transition and nurturing processes framework*

achieved through various strategies and programmes that sport development stakeholders create and enforce. Sport organisations, for instance, coordinate 'come and try' sessions to attract members.

The *retention/transition* process involves a number of groups of participants including volunteers and umpires. An important part of the retention/transition process is talent identification and development, and the process has a particular focus on junior participants (rather than participants in general). Hence retention/transition for the purposes of this chapter may be defined as the process whereby a range of policies, including development programmes and competitions/events, are implemented to identify talented junior athletes and to coach and train them with the ultimate aim of taking the most talented athletes through to the highest levels of the sport. The retention and transition process aims to capitalise on the identification of the most talented, to retain them and to help them to obtain the skills required to achieve high standards of performance.

As with the attraction process, to create a successful retention and transition process, sport development stakeholders adopt various strategies. For instance, sport organisations create opportunities for existing members to participate through consistent, quality competition, and producing quality services such as coaching and development programmes in order to retain their interest. It is important to note that the sport development strategies used in the retention and transition process such as player development programmes, competitions and coaching requirements are adapted to a level that reflects the needs and requirements that athletes have at various stages of their development. This is essential in order to avoid losing talented athletes due to injury, burn-out or loss of interest in the sport.

A condition for successful retention and transition is a successful attraction process. Once sport participants move beyond the attraction process, the pathways to retention/transition might act as an entry point for the talented athletes to move to a higher level of participation. The intention of a well-established retention and transition process is to cater for all participants but particularly juniors, and to provide a springboard for progression to being elite athletes and succeeding at the national and international levels. More specifically, the outcomes of a successful retention and transition process, and the strategies embedded within that process, are the pathways to the nurturing process. They involve talented participants who are ready to move to a higher level of competition and success in sport. Talented participants therefore progress via these pathways to the nurturing process.

Nurturing is defined as the process whereby development programmes and practices are tailored to the individual athlete, team or sport to achieve best performances on the national and international sporting stage. The nurturing process is the stage in athlete development when stakeholders coordinate their efforts to tailor sport development for specific sports and individuals or teams. The aim is to nurture the finest athletes, to work towards their success at prestigious international events and competitions, and to sustain a culture of continued success at the highest levels. The pathways to the nurturing process are crucial to achieving this aim and to obtaining well-prepared and skilled athletes. The success of the elite athletes who take part in the nurturing process is a testament to their talent and their commitment to training and competition. It is a tribute to the coordinated efforts of the various stakeholders. Support staff such as nutritionists, physiotherapists and psychologists all influence elite athlete performances. Skilled, professional, committed and knowledgeable coaches also play a significant role. Spectator support can also make the difference between winning and losing, and sponsors are more likely to finance successful athletes and teams. An example of sponsor support in the nurturing process is the financial and in-kind assistance usually provided at various events and competitions. Elite success may increase the potential for the publicity a sport receives. It creates further interest in the print and electronic media, and may boost overall revenue. Increased awareness, interest and inspiration, if exploited appropriately and in a timely manner, may boost participation and increase audiences and spectator bases. Hence, the nurturing process might facilitate the pathways to the attraction process. These pathways offer opportunities for retiring athletes to remain in the sport system and participate in various ways. For instance, retiring athletes may get the opportunity to participate at a community level, to act as coaches or umpires or to be involved in clinics for the attraction process.

THE BENEFITS OF USING THE ARTN FRAMEWORK

The ARTN framework is inclusive of the three key areas that Green (2005) believes sport development efforts should address: the attraction, retention/transition and nurturing processes. These processes highlight the importance of understanding that athlete development occurs as a process through different stages that are characterised by transitions (Bloom, 1985). Transitions are a major characteristic of talent and athlete development (Tebbenham, 1998), and when successful these transitions can ensure future athlete success (Sinclair and Orlick, 1993).

The ARTN shows that sport development can be a cyclic rather a linear process and that it incorporates the notion of transition through pathways. Of particular interest in that regard is the nurturing process that demonstrates the potential for elite success to influence community sport or else the 'demonstration effect' (Weed, 2009). The cyclic nature of sport development is proof that the two ends of sport development, grassroots and elite, do not operate in isolation from each other. In light of this coexistence and interdependence of sport development processes, governments should re-evaluate the priorities they assign to the various sport participation phases. The ARTN framework provides clarity on athlete development pathways in terms of who is involved in them, and in what ways. An essential characteristic of these pathways is that they link one development process to the following process, illustrating participant movement and the impact that each process might have on other facets of sport development. Consequently, the ARTN framework strengthens the argument that elite and mass participation are not in conflict – they complement each other. The implication of this for sport development practitioners is recognition of the extent to which elite and mass participation are mutually dependent. Contrary to research claiming to demonstrate that elite development can be definitively assessed by using measures such as the number of medals won or the number of athletes that qualify for elite competition (De Bosscher *et al.*, 2008, 2009), the outcomes of elite athlete development and success are multifaceted and cannot always be clearly measured. For example, it is common for elite athletes to be involved with community programmes, such as clinics, which facilitate the pathways to attract young or new participants. This is clearly a positive outcome that is not reflected in medal tallies.

Collectively, sport development opportunities offer what are universally known as the pathways to participation. The importance of elite athlete pathways in sport development

147

lies in the premise that the well-being of a sport at the junior level is in a lot of sports a precondition for elite professional growth and development. In order for sports to reinforce and secure a dominant position within the sport industry, they need to build a strong youth development programme to ensure a good flow of well-grounded athletes likely to perform at the highest international level. The pathway to continued success at the elite level is a practical plan to ensure that an outstanding record of sporting achievement is maintained and that a new generation of athletes is given even greater opportunities to participate and improve their performances.

Sport sciences and medicine are essential for athlete development and success. However, successful sport development requires more than science and medicine. Sport development starts at an organisational level. It involves policymakers, sport managers and other personnel, and it involves strategic, operational and financial planning. These plans set goals, objectives and policies, and they involve the use of sport science together with specific training programmes. While the role of chance and human nature in talent and athlete development is indisputable, this chapter focuses on athlete development from an organisational and managerial perspective. Studying sport development from a management point of view allows us to examine the role of sport development stakeholders, their practices, and the outcomes of their efforts to attract, retain/transit and nurture elite athletes. The ARTN approach to sport development offers sport organisations and the people that work within those organisations a framework for approaching sport development.

CASE STUDY 8.1
ATHLETE DEVELOPMENT PATHWAYS IN GOLF
Popi Sotiriadou
Griffith University

The ARTN framework was tested in different contexts, and on a sport-by-sport basis. Liebenau (2010), for instance, tested the ARTN properties of the model in golf. More specifically, the purpose of her study was to examine the development pathways available for amateur golfers in Queensland, Australia, as well as relevant inputs and strategies required by sport development stakeholders for successful progression to become an elite player. Such testing revealed gaps in the way golf organisations pursue sport development in amateur golf, and assisted these organisations to understand how to build a sustainable sport development system, improve their current pathways and practices, and optimise the use of the government funding they receive.

The results of that study revealed that the most common development pathway for amateur golf is a government-related one, mostly because this pathway is financially supported by the government. Following an introduction to golf usually at public courses, amateur golfer development then starts with club and district programmes for an early introduction to the game. The focus is to ensure that young players maintain their interest in the sport as they develop. At this stage coaching is essential in order to lay the foundations and fundamentals of the game, such as basic rules, scoring and fundamental motor skills. Modified tournaments are also critical to expose amateur golfers to competition from a young age. District golf development programmes expose players to more advanced tournament play, such as club-versus-club matches. Despite two further pathway options (i.e. independent golf coaching academies and public and private golf-specific colleges), a progression into the Golf Queensland development programme/Queensland academy of sport (QAS) programme is encouraged because it provides maximum development opportunities. The programme provides input and strategies necessary for amateur development and meets the athletes' financial needs that are essential for successful advancement within the pathway. The main input and strategies include access to high quality facilities, a coaching panel, sport psychologists, physical conditioning programmes as well as potential equipment scholarships, while funding is provided for travel to compete in tournaments.

Talent identification is important to ensure talented amateurs are provided with the best development opportunities to represent Australia internationally in future. Although the government-supported development pathway is encouraged, funding from the government for golf, in particular elite golf is lacking. This could be partly due to the government's focus on Olympic and Commonwealth Games sports and its measurement of success by medal counts. In light of golf having been admitted to the 2016 Olympic Games, and considering the Australian government's suggestion that greater pools of early identified talent lead to more elite athletes, an increase in funding allocations for golf should be expected.

The results of the study also reveal a lack of tournaments for amateur golfers to compete in, and a lack of four-round tournaments, both due to lack of funding and course availability. While amateur golfers may be given the opportunity to develop their skills with the right inputs and strategies, the inability to apply these skills on a regular basis through tournament play inhibits optimum development. The majority of professional golf tournaments are played over four rounds. As such, Australian elite golfers seem restricted in their preparation for professional competition as the majority of amateur events in Australia are played as two-round events. State and national ranking amateur events are held over four days playing four rounds; however, these are not scheduled on a frequent basis. The aforementioned lack of funding further limits amateur players' exposure to international competition. Players from wealthier backgrounds have an advantage, as do those who travel as part of the national or state team. Talented players not selected for the Golf Queensland development programme are disadvantaged if they come from less well-off families and have difficulty seeking external funding sources.

Golf in Queensland is one of the greatest sport industry contributors to the Australian economy, yet it lacks funding on both amateur and professional levels. With an increase in amateur and professional tournaments for elite golfers, an increase in participation and greater pools for talent identification could potentially follow. In order to do so a restructure of the current event/tournament provision and the introduction of more tournaments and competitions are essential. Companies and businesses should consider golf tournaments as a sponsorship client. Also, golf companies should concentrate their input on two areas other than equipment: tournaments and player support for travel. These companies could invest more into becoming (main) sponsors of tournaments, rather than continually supplying amateur golfers with seemingly excessive golf equipment, such as golf clubs and golf bags. They could also support amateur players through offering a scholarship programme regardless of the chosen pathway. The scholarship could be partly in kind to include an initial set of equipment and continual accessories (e.g. golf gloves and golf balls), but with greater focus on providing the player with the opportunity to gain exposure to more tournaments, nationally and internationally. On the other hand, if golf companies opt to remain focused on golf equipment alone, they could align themselves with pathway providers other than the Golf Queensland development programme, such as public and private golf-specific colleges and independent golf coaching academies in order to provide talented amateur players with basic golf development needs.

CASE STUDY 8.2

ARE PERFORMANCES AT YOUNG AGES A GOOD PREDICTOR OF LATER SUCCESS?

Hebe Schaillée and Veerle De Bosscher
Vrije Universiteit Brussel

An important change in the career of an athlete is the transition from junior to senior competition. Many have the potential to become elite athletes, but only a few attain this high level and fewer still can sustain it. Several factors influence the achievement of high level performance (Martindale *et al.*, 2005). Research suggests that athletic potential in the long term is neither readily nor accurately assessed (Abbott and Collins, 2002; Howe *et al.*, 1998). Although not much is known about the extent to which performances at young ages are good indicators of later success, these performances are frequently used as a criterion for talent identification (Brouwers *et al.*, 2010). This case study is concerned with a project in Flanders, which developed a youth performance sports index (YPSI). This YPSI aimed to enable us to detect a critical moment at which athletes must start to succeed at international (youth) competitions. It was anticipated that such a YPSI would enable the evaluation of the performances of top young athletes over a period of several years with regard to their potential to become world-class athletes.

The preliminary research consisted of a Europe-wide analysis[1] of four sports: judo, tennis, gymnastics and athletics. This case study uses a top-down approach to collect data, to answer the question: how did good performing senior elite athletes perform during youth tournaments? The sport-specific principles of the YPSI (tournaments, see Table 8.2) were chosen in consultation with representatives of the Flemish Sport Federations. The purpose of this contribution is twofold. We will shortly focus first on correlations[2] between performances on youth tournaments and professional level. Second, we will shed light on how elite athletes performed in the selected youth tournaments (top-down approach).

The conducted correlations (see Table 8.1) were all significant (0.01 level), but ranged from very weak to weak correlations. As a result, junior athletes with better performances at the selected youth tournaments appear to have a slightly greater chance to be successful at the elite athlete level. Notwithstanding, in sum we conclude that there is a great uncertainty about the relationship of performances on youth tournaments and success of elite athletes.[3]

Table 8.1 Correlations between performances on youth tournaments and professional level

	Correlations	Correlation coefficient	r^2	Population
Athletics[iv]	♀: Total junior score – Total Senior Score	−0.088*	0,008	♀ = 238
	♀: Av. Junior score – Total Senior Score	−0.093*	0,009	
Gymnastics[v]	♂: Total junior score – Total Senior Score	0.214*	0,046	♂ = 232
	♂: Total junior score – Total Senior Score	0.203*	0,041	♂ = 93
Judo[vi]	♀: Total Junior score – Total Senior Score	−0.021*	0,000	♀ = 250
	♂: Total Junior score – Total Senior Score	0.101*	0,010	♂ = 209
Tennis[vii]	♀: Av. Junior score – Best Rank	−0.284*	0,081	♀ = 1624
	♀: Highest junior – Best Rank	−0.296*	0,088	
	♂: Av. Junior Score – Best Rank	−0.192*	0,037	♂ = 1897
	♂: Highest junior – Best Rank	−0.208*	0,043	

* = Significant correlation (0.01 level)
▨ = 0.00 < r < 0.20 Very low correlation
▧ = 0.20 < r < 0.40 Low or weak correlation

Figure 8.2 shows how many senior elite athletes performed at least once in a selected youth tournament. Sports should not be compared in this analysis, due to the different ages and tournaments. With the exception in tennis U14 tournaments, these figures ranged between 65 and 81 per cent.

Since these results give no indication with regard to the importance of each tournament, the next table shows the performances of elite athletes for each selected youth tournament (Table 8.2).

In two cases, European Junior Cup (EJC) < 23 for athletics and EJC for Judo, results showed that the participation level of elite athletes turned out to include more than half of all elite athletes, who had performed at these tournaments at younger ages. For all other tournaments participation levels have been found to be less revealing with regard to future senior success. These are salutary lessons for policymakers and national governing bodies who often use performances as one of the selection criteria for selection. The results also

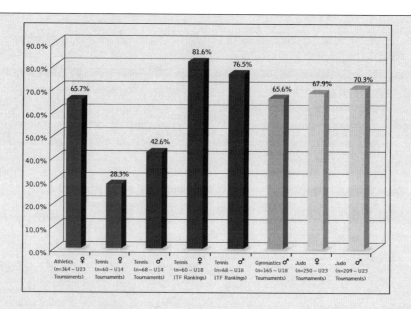

Figure 8.2 *Percentage of elite athletes who performed at least once in a selected youth tournament*

revealed that approximately a third of all world-class athletes for athletics, judo as well as gymnastics did not perform or even participate in the selected youth tournaments. Besides more than half of all male and female Senior Top 20 tennis players never participated in one of the selected U14 youth tennis tournaments. Some additional analysis led to some interesting sport-specific facts, which are summarised below.

- **Athletics:** Most of all athletes (a minimum of 70 per cent) who performed at any of the youth tournaments reached the top 8 as a senior athlete.[4]
- **Gymnastics:** Results indicated that from the senior top 8 gymnasts 66 per cent reached the top 8 when young and less than half of these athletes won a medal when young (39 per cent). Notably, from all top 3 senior athletes 67 per cent reached the top 8 as a junior athlete and 49 per cent won a medal when young.[5]
- **Judo:** Interestingly, the performance pattern during youth tournaments for the ten most successful judoka ($\female_n = 77 - \male_n = 77$) from 1997 to 2007 in all weight categories is very similar in comparison to the whole population of 77 judoka.[6]
- **Tennis:** Fifteen per cent male and 13 per cent of the female senior top twenty players (ATP/WTA) reached a final in one of the selected youth tournaments, or, in other words, were also successful at junior level (finals of U14 tournaments).[7]

These results indicate the general good to put into perspective the relative importance of performances at young ages. Moreover, a mixture of physical and mental skills into

Table 8.2 *Overview of performances of elite athletes on the selected youth tournaments*

	Population top-down analysis	Youth tournaments used in the YP SI	Senior tournaments used in the YP SI	Athletes who did perform at young age %	Athletes who haven't performed %
Athletics	♀ = 364 Top 8 1990–2009 Born after 1974	European Youth Olympic Festival (U18) World Youth Championships (U18) European Junior Championships (U20) World Junior Championships (U18) European Junior Championship (U23)	European Championships (EC) World Championships (WC) Olympic Games (OG)	♀ : 2 ♀ : 10 ♀ : 28 ♀ : 32 ♀ : 57	♀ : 34
Gymnastics	♂ = 165 Top 8 1996–2008	OBI Team Cup GWG Cup European Junior Championships (U18)	European Championships World Championships Olympic Games	♂ : 13 ♂ : 9 ♂ : 38	♂ : 34
Judo	♂ = 209 ♀ = 189 Top 7 1997–2007	European Youth Olympic Festival European Junior Championships (U23) World Junior Championships European Junior Championships < 23 years	European Championships World Championships Olympic Games	♂ : 5 ♀ : 15 ♂ : 57 ♀ : 51 ♂ : 33 ♀ : 38 ♂ : 20 ♀ : 17	♂ : 33 ♀ : 30
Tennis	♂ = 68 ♀ = 60 WTA Top 20 1999–2007 ATP Top 20 2000–2008	U-14 International Youth Tournaments (Les Petits As Tarbes, European Championship, BNP Paribas Rankings of the international tennis federation	World rankings (Top 200): Women's Tennis Association (WTA) Association of Tennis Professionals (ATP)	♂ : 43 ♀ : 28 ♂ ITF Top 200: 76 ♂ ITF Top 100: 66 ♂ ITF Top 50: 56 ♂ ITF Top 20: 44 ♀ ITF Top 200: 82 ♀ ITF Top 100: 75 ♀ ITF Top 50: 60 ♀ ITF Top 20: 40	♂ : 57 ♀ : 72

▨ = Most important tournament based on the percentage of performing elite athletes when young

appropriate action is common for all sports and each sport is marked by a singularity of required sport-specific elements for successful performance (Baker and Horton, 2004). The ages at which transitions occur as well as the duration of the stages are sport-specific (Wylleman *et al.*, 2004). Therefore, it should be indicated that the YPSI is only one out of many parameters evaluating the development of young athletes and that perhaps other factors such as physical skills, psychological preparation and social support should be taken into account while analysing youth performances (Lidor *et al.*, 2009). The YPSI should be completed annually, in order to enlarge the research populations. It should also be noted that although the selection of tournaments took place in consultation with high performance directors and other representatives of the Flemish Sport Federations, other regional, national or international tournaments might be regarded as important by other nations.

Acknowledgements

We acknowledge the Ministry of Culture, Youth, Sport and Media from the Flemish Government for their support in this study. Besides, we would like to thank Jessie Brouwers, Elke Van Camp and Erik Blondeel for their support with regard to data collection as part of their masters thesis as well as Dr Jasper Truyens for his assistance in the preliminary stage of the project.

SUMMARY

Sport development is described in this chapter as being the backbone of athlete development. It is viewed as a sport management process rather than solely as a product of biological, psychological or physical attributes. Sport development facilitates the attraction of participants to sport, their retention in the sport system and their transition to higher levels of competition, and the nurturing of their long-term performances and international success. These processes are outlined in Figure 8.1. Figure 8.1 also indicates that each sport development process has three properties: sport development stakeholders (input); the sport development strategies or practices they initiate or implement (throughput); and the outcomes of their input (pathways).

The types of stakeholders involved with sport development may vary from organisations and government agencies to individuals working for, or within, those organisations and government agencies. Stakeholders have various roles and responsibilities (e.g. initiating and/or implementing sport development practices, such as programmes and competitions). Sport development practices and strategies (e.g. facilities and venues, competitions and events, promotions and public relations, management/administration, and athlete/coach development programmes) are required for sustainable sports. The transition from one sport development process to the next is facilitated by pathways. These pathways link the nurturing to the attraction process, the attraction to the retention/transition process and the retention/transition to the nurturing process. In conclusion, sport development stakeholders and their involvement in sport lead to the availability, implementation and evaluation of sport development strategies and the provision of appropriate sport development pathways for the ARTN processes.

There are five clear reasons for using the ARTN framework in the development of sport:

■ to establish a clear development pathway;
■ to identify gaps in the current development pathway;
■ to realign and integrate the programmes for developing sport;
■ to provide a planning tool, based on scientific research, for coaches and administrators; and
■ to guide planning for optimal performance.

DISCUSSION QUESTIONS

1   Examine the attraction, retention/transition and nurturing process (ARTN) and pathways of a sport, and analyse the roles and responsibilities of sport development stakeholders (input), their strategies (throughputs) and the outcomes of their involvement (output) with the ARTN processes.

2   Discuss how the ARTN processes and the sport development pathways (i.e. the pathways from one sport development process to another) across different sports may vary. Consider drawing comparisons between (a) individual and team sports, (b) Olympic and high profile versus non-Olympic or low profile sports and (c) sports that require large numbers of grassroots participants from which to draw talented athletes versus sports that do not rely on grassroots participation for elite success.

3   Analyse the barriers to participation for individuals from different sport development segments or target groups (e.g. female or older participants) at different levels of participation (attraction, retention/transition and nurturing) and provide realistic and effective ways of overcoming these barriers.

4   Given the challenges that golf organisations are presented with in the case study, what strategies would you recommend these organisations and stakeholders should follow in order to optimise athlete development pathways?

KEY TERMS

■ Sport development stakeholders
■ Sport development strategies
■ Sport development pathways
■ Athlete development
■ Attraction, retention/retention and nurturing process
■ Transition

GUIDED READINGS

Bailey, R., Toms, M., Collins, D., Ford, P., MacNamara, A. and Pearce, G. (2011). Models of young player development in sport. In I. Stafford (Ed.), *Coaching children in sport* (pp. 38–56). London: Routledge.

Lang, M. and Light, R. (2010). Interpreting and implementing the long term athlete development model: English swimming coaches' views on the (swimming) LTAD in practice. *International Journal of Sports Science & Coaching*, 5(3), 389–402.

Shilbury, D. and Kellett, P. (2011). *Sport management in Australia: An organisational overview.* Crows Nest, NSW: Allen & Unwin.

Sotiriadou, P. (2010). *The sport development processes and practices in Australia: The attraction, retention, transition and nurturing of participants and athletes.* LAP Lambert Academic Publishing.

Wolstencroft, E. (2002). *Talent identification and development: An academic review.* Edinburgh: Sport Scotland.

Recommended websites

www.sportscoachuk.org
www.ausport.gov.au
www.sportengland.com

NOTES

1   The data analysis comprises descriptive statistics as well as several statistical tests for which the statistical package for social sciences, 'SPSS 16.0 for Windows®', was used. The multiple analysis for these four sports were various and not always similar as a result of the sport-specific data collection (e.g. judo: weight categories; athletic disciplines: sprint, 1/2 fond, fond, jump, throw; . . .). Therefore, a comparison between the four sports might not always be relevant.

2   The Spearman rank correlation coefficient was used because index points at youth tournaments as well as rankings, are data at ordinal level.

3   Perhaps the low correlations can be attributed to the fact that these are based on performances of a small number of youth tournaments, respectively five youth tournaments for athletics and three for gymnastics, judo and tennis.

4   Athletics' correlations include all athletes who performed on a senior tournament as well as on one junior tournament.

5   Gymnastics' correlations include on one hand all selected junior athletes ($n = 232$) and on the other hand all junior athletes who reached the top 8 at a senior tournament ($n = 93$).

6   Judo correlations include all selected judo athletes.

7   Tennis correlations include all youth tournament players who have reached the top 200.

BIBLIOGRAPHY

Abbott, A. and Collins, D. (2002). A theoretical and empirical analysis of a 'state of the art' talent identification model. *High Ability Studies*, 157–178.

Baker, J. and Horton, S. (2004). A review of primary and secondary influences on sport expertise. *High Ability Studies*, 211–228.

Balyi, I. (2002). Long-term athlete development: The system and solutions. *Faster, Higher, Stronger*, 14, 6–9.

Bloom, B. S. (1985). *Developing talent in young people*. New York: Ballantine Books.

Bramham, P., Hylton, K., Jackson, D. and Nesti, M. (2001). Introduction. In K. Hylton, P. Bramham, D. Jackson and M. Nesti (Eds.), *Sport development: Policy, process and practice* (pp. 1–6). London: Routledge.

Brouwers, J., De Bosscher, V., Schaillée, H., Truyens, J. and Sotiriadou, P. (2010). The relationship between performances at U-14 International Youth Tournaments and later success in tennis. *Journal of Medicine and Science*, 21–25.

Cashman, R. and Hughes, A. (1998). Sydney 2000: Cargo cult of Australian sport? In D. Rowe and G. Lawrence (Eds), *Tourism, leisure, sport: Critical perspectives* (pp. 216–225). Sydney: Hodder.

Collins, M. (1995). *Sport development locally and regionally*. Reading, MA: ILAM.

Côté, J. (1999). The influence of the family in the development of talent in sport. *Sport Psychologist*, 13(4), 395.

De Bosscher, V., Bingham, J., Shibli, S., Van Bottenburg, M. and De Knop, P. (2008). *The global sporting arms race. An international comparative study on sports policy factors leading to international sporting success*. Aachen: Meyer & Meyer.

De Bosscher, V., De Knop, P., van Bottenburg, M., Shibli, S. and Bingham, J. (2009). Explaining international sporting success: An international comparison of elite sport systems and policies in six countries. *Sport Management Review*, 12(3), 113–136.

Ericsson, K. A., Krampe, R. T. and Tesch-Römer, C. (1993). The role of deliberate practice in the acquisition of expert performance. *Psychological Review*, 100(3), 363.

Green, B. C. (2005). Building sport programs to optimize athlete recruitment, retention, and transition: Toward a normative theory of sport development. *Journal of Sport Management*, 19(3), 233–253.

Houlihan, B. and Green, M. (2011). Routledge handbook of sports development. New York: Routledge.

Howe, M., Davidson, J. and Sloboda, J. (1998). Innate talents: Reality or myth? *Behavioral and Brain Science*, 399–442.

Lidor, R., Côté, J. and Hackfort, D. (2009). ISSP position stand: To test or not to test? The use of physical skill tests in talent detection and in early phases of sport development. *International Journal of Sport and Exercise Psychology*, 1367–1380.

Liebenau, L. (2010). Sport development pathways for amateur golfers: The case study of Queensland. Unpublished Honours Thesis, Bond University, Gold Coast, Australia.

Lyle, J. W. B. (1997). Managing excellence in sports performance. *Career Development International*, 2, 314–323.

Martin, S. G., Arin, K. P., Palakshappa, N. and Chetty, S. (2005). *Do elite sports systems mean more Olympic medals?* (pp. 1–14). Auckland, NZ: Massey University, Department of Commerce. Available at http://commerce.massey.ac.nz/research-outputs/2005/2005031.pdf, accessed 2 May 2009.

Martindale, R. J., Collins, D. and Daubney, J. (2005). Talent development: A guide for practice and research within sport. *Guest*, 353–375.

Shilbury, D., Sotiriadou, P. and Green, C. (2008). Sport development. Systems, policies and pathways: An introduction to the special issue. *Sport Management Review*, 11(3), 217–223.

Siedentop, D. (2002). Junior sport and the evolution of sport cultures. *Journal of Teaching in Physical Education*, 21(4), 392–401.

Sinclair, D. A. and Orlick, T. (1993). Positive transitions from high performance sport. *The Sport Psychologist*, 7 (20), 138–150.

Sotiriadou, P. (2010). *The sport development processes and practices in Australia: The attraction, retention, transition and nurturing of participants and athletes*. Cologne, Germany: LAP LAMBERT Academic Publishing.

157

Sotiriadou, P., Quick, S. and Shilbury, D. (2009). A framework for the retention and transition of talented athletes in Australia. *Journal of Economy and Sports,* 9(3), 30–39.

Sotiriadou, P. and Shilbury D. (2009). Australian elite athlete development: An organisational perspective. *Sport Management Review,* 12(3), 137–148.

Sotiriadou, K., Shilbury, D. and Quick, S. (2008). The attraction, retention/transition and nurturing processes of sport development: Some Australian evidence. *Journal of Sport Management,* 22, 247–272.

Tebbenham, D. (1998). The nature of talent development and the importance of athletic transition in UK sport. Unpublished Master's dissertation, Manchester Metropolitan University, Alsager.

Vaeyens, R., Lenoir, M., Williams, A. M. and Philippaerts, R. (2008). Talent identification and development programmes in sport: Current models and future directions. *Sports Medicine,* 38 (9), 703–714.

Weed, M. (2009). *The potential of the demonstration effect to grow and sustain participation in sport.* Report to Sport England. Available at www.sportengland.org/about_us/sport_england_conferences/idoc.ashx?docid=b97bc095-eb32-4c20-91d4-5943b85e9462&version=2.

Williams, A. M. and Reilly, T. (2000). Talent identification and development in soccer. *Journal of Sport Sciences,* 18(9), 657–667.

Wylleman, P. and Lavallee, D. (2004) *Career transitions and sport: Research and applications.* Morgantown, WV: Fitness Information Technology.

Wylleman, P., Alfermann, D. and Lavallee, D. (2004). Career transitions in sport: European perspectives. *Psychology of Sport and Exercise,* 7–20.

Chapter 9

A developmental and holistic perspective on athletic career development

Paul Wylleman, Anke Reints and Paul De Knop
Vrije Universiteit Brussel

LEARNING OUTCOMES

Upon completion of this chapter the reader should be able to:

1   understand the difference between a developmental and a holistic perspective of the athletic career;
2   identify normative transitions in athletes' development in the athletic, psychological, psychosocial, academic and vocational domains;
3   understand how the HP manager, using the lifespan model, can formulate a developmental/holistic profile of athletes that takes account of the transitions they face; and
4   identify the benefits of using a lifespan approach in the HP system so as to maximize athletes' opportunities to prepare for and/or cope with transitions.

OVERVIEW

High performance (HP) requires both talent and a system. In sport, the HP manager must establish a system that maximizes not only talented athletes' development to the elite level, but also the maintenance of a superior internationally competitive level of performance by its elite athletes. This chapter describes how the success of strategies to achieve these aims is influenced by the transitions and stages athletes face in different domains of development (e.g. athletic, psychological, academic). Using a lifespan model that allows for a developmental (i.e. start-to-finish) as well as a holistic (i.e. multilevel) perspective on the development of the elite athletic career, several strategies are identified for how HP managers can use a developmental and holistic approach within their HP system in order to optimize the development of athletes.

159

To achieve at the highest level in any field, talent is not enough. An appropriate HP system is also required (Bolchover and Brady, 2002; Holbeche, 2005). The HP manager must thus establish a system that maximizes not only the development of talented athletes to the elite level, but also the maintenance of superior performances at the international level by its elite athletes. Both aims require the HP manager to use a 'beginning-to-end' approach to the development and use of their HP system.

As there is a need among HP managers for more knowledge on how to identify and implement such an approach (e.g. Wylleman, 2004, 2008; Wylleman *et al.*, 2001), this chapter does two things. First, it describes a *lifespan model* that will enable HP managers not only to identify the normative (i.e. predictable) stages in elite athletic careers using such a 'start-to-finish' or *developmental* approach, but also to develop a *holistic* approach with which they will be able to incorporate the influence of other domains of athletes' development (e.g. psychological, psychosocial, academic) as the elite athletic career progresses. Second, several strategies will be described which HP managers can use to apply this lifespan model within the HP system in order to optimize the continued development of the athletes' elite sport careers.

The first section of the chapter provides an overview of the research that led to the use of a lifespan approach. Extracts from former elite athletes' autobiographies are used to illustrate the relevance of these research findings. In the following two sections, the lifespan model is described, and its application to the four athletic career stages is explained. This is followed with a section describing how HP managers can use this lifespan model within their HP system in order to optimize their athletes' continued development. Some final thoughts on the support services required within an HP system are followed with a case study illustrating the use of the lifespan model with a talented adolescent swimmer.

RESEARCH ON THE DEVELOPMENT OF THE ELITE ATHLETIC CAREER

The interest of sport scientists, and especially sport psychologists, in the development of athletic careers can be traced to research in the 1960s and 1970s on the incidence of distress among retired professional athletes (e.g. Haerle, 1975; Mihovilovic, 1968). This research revealed that athletes often retired from elite sport unexpectedly and that they had not prepared themselves for the changes involved. As a result they were prone to having problems in coping and adjusting. It became clear that the end of an athletic career should be treated as a 'transition' that required coping strategies on the part of the athlete. This line of thought could also be applied to the process of dropout among young athletes.

According to Schlossberg, a transition is 'an event or non-event [which] results in a change in assumptions about oneself and the world and thus requires a corresponding change in one's behaviour and relationships' (Schlossberg, 1981, p. 5). For athletes, transitions involve a conflict between what she or he is or was, and what they want or believe they ought to be (Alfermann and Stambulova, 2007). As this developmental conflict brings up sometimes turbulent emotions, athletes need to mobilize resources to help them cope with the demands of transitions such as retirement. If coping is effective, then the athlete will progress in their development (e.g. by successfully initiating a post-athletic career). If coping is ineffective, then the athlete will be confronted with a crisis or undergo an unsuccessful transition that may lead to subclinical or clinical problems such as depression (Stambulova, 1994, 2000).

Researchers have found that athletes face other transitions *throughout* their athletic careers (Wylleman *et al.*, 1999).

> Five-time Olympic gold medal winner Steve Redgrave says his career had many significant transition events including, for example, a disappointing experience during his first junior world championships, winning his first Olympic medal, ending the collaboration with a rowing partner, establishing a new rowing partnership, his decision to continue his career after his fourth gold medal amid expectations that he would retire, the turbulent periods in his marriage and his 'date with destiny' when going for his fifth gold medal at the 2000 Olympic Games (Redgrave and Townsend, 2001).
>
> Legendary tennis player Pete Sampras (2008) linked his career to events and periods such as starting out in tennis, a period of wavering commitment, the winning moments at Wimbledon and setting down a new record of winning fourteen Grand Slam titles.

Alfermann and Stambulova (2007) found that athletes need to cope with these transitions in order to progress in their athletic careers and overcome problems such as a decline of athletic performance, overtraining and injuries or even clinical psychological issues.

Moreover, these transitions can be categorized according to their degree of predictability. Some are 'normative' transitions, which are generally predictable and anticipated (e.g. the transition from junior to senior ranks, athletic retirement), and 'non-normative' transitions, which are the result of important events that are unpredicted, unanticipated and involuntary (e.g. a season-ending injury, the loss of a personal coach, an unanticipated 'cut' from the team). Perhaps less obvious, research showed that athletes also referred to events that did not occur (e.g. not winning the Olympic gold).

> Despite winning a gold and a bronze medal, Dutch long track skater Sven Kramer looks back at the 2010 Winter Olympic Games in Vancouver with a feeling of disappointment because he unexpectedly failed to win the gold medal in the 10,000 m – an event Kramer saw as 'one of the most important moments in my life' (Grijsbach, 2010).

Research has shown that athletes face both normative and non-normative transitions throughout their athletic careers (e.g. Sinclair and Orlick, 1994; Wylleman *et al.*, 1993).

During the 1990s, this approach to transitions meshed with research in the domain of talent development (e.g. Bloom, 1985; Salmela, 1994) and the athletic career came to be described in terms of normative transitions (e.g. junior-to-senior transition, retirement) and stages (e.g. the stage from initiation to development, the stage from development to perfection).

Using this transition approach, researchers showed that athletes also face normative and/or non-normative transitions in a range of other aspects of their lives (e.g. psychological, psychosocial) that strongly influenced the continued development of their athletic careers (Wylleman *et al.*, 1999).

Pete Sampras introduced his autobiography with the statement that he also wanted to acknowledge those events which 'aren't the things that come to most people's minds at the mention of my name' (i.e. fourteen Grand Slam titles) but of which he wanted to 'reveal what they meant and how they affected me' (e.g. his first coach spending time in jail, his mentor being stricken by cancer and dying at an early age, a career-threatening injury).

Twelve-time Olympic medallist Dara Torres (2009) emphasized the role of her motherhood, as well as the social aspects of the age difference with other swimmers when competing (and winning three silver medals) at the age of 41 in the Beijing 2008 Olympic Games.

This brief overview underlines that in order to better understand the transitions faced by athletes at the elite level, a better understanding is required, not only of *athletes' development in other domains* (e.g. academic, psychological), but also of how this development affects (or is affected by) the development of their athletic careers.

For English Rubgy Union player Jonny Wilkinson, a serious neck injury meant not only going into surgery, but also not playing which 'does odd things to your head . . . It is funny how quickly you can begin to doubt yourself' (Wilkinson, 2006, p. 181).

American US Olympic swimmer Dara Torres' motherhood made her realize that 'becoming a mother changes everything . . . It forces you to weed out distractions from your life. It compels you to define your values, to figure out who you are' (Torres, 2009, p. 79). When she returned to competitive swimming she found that 'I'm a mom first and a swimmer second' (p. 87).

For Pete Sampras, the loss of his mentor-coach resulted in him developing 'from a boy into a man' (p. 167) and developing a new coach–player relationship in which the coach was now more of 'a companion and an adviser, an equal who understood me' (Sampras, 2008, p. 167).

A DEVELOPMENTAL AND HOLISTIC PERSPECTIVE ON THE ATHLETIC CAREER

Based on research with student-athletes, elite athletes and former Olympians, and complemented with experiential knowledge from applied sport psychology and career/lifestyle service provision, Wylleman and Lavallee (2004) presented a lifespan model. Their model integrated the normative transitions that occur in any athletic career (e.g. Bloom, 1985) with the normative transitions and stages that athletes face in other aspects of their lives. This model,

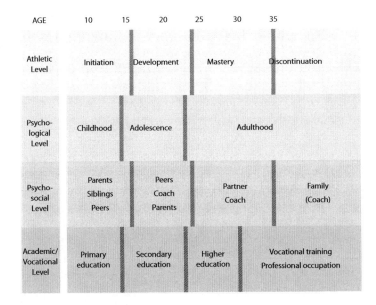

Figure 9.1
A developmental perspective on transitions faced by athletes at athletic, individual, psychosocial and academic-vocational levels

Source: P. Wylleman and D. Lavallee in Weiss, M.R. (2004) *Developmental sport and exercise psychology: A lifespan perspective.* Morgantown, WV: Fitness Information Technology, Inc. (pp. 507–527). Reproduced with permission

which describes four domains of development (athletic, psychological, psychosocial, academic/vocational) (see Figure 9.1), reflects a 'whole career/whole person' approach (Alfermann and Stambulova, 2007).[1]

The top layer in Figure 9.1 represents the development of an athlete's athletic career, including: (a) the 'initiation' stage during which the young athlete is introduced into organized competitive sports (from about 6 to 7 years of age); (b) the 'development' stage during which the athlete is recognized as being talented, and training and competition intensifies (from about 12 to 13 years of age); (c) the 'mastery' stage in which the athlete participates at the highest competitive level (from about 18 to 19 years of age); and (d) the 'discontinuation' stage which describes the elite athlete's transition out of competitive sports (from 28 to 30 years of age). The transitions between these stages are normative, but the specific ages at which they occur may vary depending upon the type of sport, and the athletes' characteristics (e.g. early vs. late maturation or gender). For example, at age 18–19 the mastery stage among female gymnasts may be coming to an end (Kerr and Dacyshyn, 2000), while for male rowers this may be the start of their mastery stage (Wylleman *et al.*, 1993).

The second layer represents the developmental stages and transitions occurring at the psychological level and is based on the different conceptual frameworks of psychological development (e.g. Erikson, 1963). The stages include childhood, adolescence and (young) adulthood.

The third layer shows the changes that can occur in an athlete's psychosocial context relative to her or his athletic involvement and identifies those individuals who are perceived by athletes as being the people most significant to them during that particular stage. These changing contexts include the athletic triangle (athlete–parent, athlete–coach and coach–parent relationships), the athlete's relationships with the family, peer relationships, marital or lifetime partner relationships and other significant interpersonal relationships (e.g. Jowett and Meek, 2000; Smith, 2003; Wylleman *et al.*, 2006).

163

Finally, the athlete's vocational stages are represented in the fourth level. As most countries have compulsory education up until the age of 16 or 17, athletes will be confronted with a major overlap between their academic and athletic development (De Knop *et al.*, 1999). For example, the normative transitions in the sport life cycle of a basketball player in the United States will run parallel to transitions at academic levels – from young children's sport to junior high school to senior high school to college and, finally to the professional level (Petitpas *et al.*, 1997). This layer therefore reflects the stages and transitions at the academic level, and includes the transitions into primary education/elementary school, the stage of secondary education/high school and the move into higher education (college/university). However, as vocational training and the development of a professional occupation may also have a strong influence on a talented athlete's sport career, the final stage in this fourth layer represents their vocational training and/or a professional occupation.

The model shown in Figure 9.1 has been used not only in research (e.g. Bruner *et al.*, 2008; Pummell *et al.*, 2008; Reints *et al.*, 2008) but also in applied settings. Using its holistic/developmental view of athletes' careers and their social environments (Alfermann and Stambulova, 2007), it has provided HP managers, career support service providers and sport psychologists with a better overview and understanding of the (multilevel) transitional demands on athletes and the resources available to them (Stambulova, 2000). At the operational level it has been used in the development and provision of career support services to elite athletes and former elite athletes in Scotland, France and Flanders (Bouchetal Pellegri *et al.*, 2006; Van Aken *et al.*, 2008; Wylleman and Debois, 2007; Wylleman and Taelman, 2007). At the strategic level it has been proposed to the Athletes' Commission of the International Olympic Committee (Wylleman and Waser, 2007) and the International Athletes' Forum (Wylleman and Parker, 2004) as a conceptual framework for support services to elite athletes, former elite athletes and Olympians, and it has been presented at the European Parliament (Wylleman, 2011) in view of the development of a European sport policy regarding 'dual careers' in elite sport (e.g. the combination of an elite sport with an academic career).

TRANSITIONS THROUGHOUT THE ATHLETIC CAREER

As the development of the athletic career cannot be seen as separate from athletes' development in other domains, it is important to recognize the interactions between these different domains as they can occur in each of the four athletic career stages.

During the initiation stage of the athletic career

During the initiation stage young talented athletes face at the psychological level the need for motivational and cognitive readiness for structured competitive sport. From a motivational point of view, young athletes' participation in competitive sport can be linked to, among other factors, internally driven motivators (e.g. interest in the sport and friendship relations). As intrinsic motivation provides for a stronger and more long-lasting impetus involvement, it is essential that young talented athletes are embedded in an environment that reinforces this type of motivation. It is important to acknowledge that the development of motivational readiness may be enhanced (or challenged) by the strong but generally well-meant involvement of the young athletes' parents (Wylleman *et al.*, 2006). From a cognitive point of view, readiness refers to young athletes' capacity for abstract reasoning, as well as for an understanding of roles, responsibilities and relational characteristics relevant to the setting of athletic competition. As a child's ability to adopt a variety of roles is not fully developed until 8–10 years of age (van der Meulen and Menkehorst, 1992), young athletes may experience considerable frustration because they do not fully understand their own roles and those of the adults involved in competitive sports. They may thus lose interest because they do not have the cognitive capacities to handle the demands placed on them. Moreover, as children do not effectively distinguish among the various contributors to achievement outcomes until around age 10–12 years (Fry and Duda, 1997), young athletes may not be able to estimate accurately their own ability or understand the causes of performance outcomes.

During the development stage of the athletic career

At the end of the development stage, 16- to 18-year-old talented athletes face the transition from junior level competitions into senior level or professional sports. They enter in this way a more high level of competition. While many have been at the top end as junior elite athletes, as first-year senior athletes they will generally be at the lower end in terms of athletic prowess and achievement. In fact, one novice senior in two has been reported to experience this transition as difficult due to such challenges as financial problems, illnesses, injuries or self-doubts. Young athletes entering the senior ranks may even experience a career-high injury-rate (Australian Sports Commission, 2003). Many first-year seniors may also need to move away from home (e.g. into a professional football academy, or to their own private accommodation). It should not be surprising therefore that, on average, only one junior elite athlete in three actually makes a successful transition into the senior elite ranks (Australian Sports Commission, 2003; Bussmann and Alfermann, 1994). Successfully completing the junior–senior transition takes novice senior athletes an average of 2.1 years (Australian Sports Commission, 2003), and involves having supportive and transition-related assistance for first- and second-year seniors, but also a supportive family and financial support (Robertson-Wilson and Côté, 2002).

During the mastery stage of the athletic career

During the mastery stage elite athletes will encounter several transitions, including those at the academic level. In view of the value attributed by parents, and by society at large, to the acquisition of academic qualifications, and taking into account the risks (e.g. career-ending injury) and the possible disadvantages (e.g. unfulfilled academic potential, lack of financial security and stability) of elite sport, many athletes will continue their academic development into higher education. Parents play an important role in this transition. They have been shown to 'gently' pressure their children into continued formal education on the way to a professional future (Koukouris, 1991). However, their guidance, support and involvement have also been related to transition distress among student-athletes (Zaichkowsky *et al.*, 1997). Moreover, because only 5 per cent of high school athletes play in one of the four major US team sports

165

(football, baseball, basketball and ice hockey) at the collegiate level (Leonard, 1996), most student-athletes will need to learn to cope with not making the team or not progressing to the next athletic career level. This can affect an identification with athletic achievement that may have been strongly reinforced at the high school level by successful performances (Danish *et al.*, 1993; Finch and Gould, 1996).

In contrast to their secondary education, student-athletes need to be more personally involved in developing their academic careers. The relatively high degree of freedom at college or university requires a stronger personal investment from student-athletes to attend classes, to plan their course of study and to commit to allocating sufficient time to academic activities (De Knop *et al.*, 1999; Donnelly, 1993). De Knop *et al.* (1999) compared student-athletes' adherence to academic activities with that of students involved in non-academic activities (e.g. sororities, fraternities) and found that although both groups of students invested a similar amount of time to academic activities, student-athletes reported more academic problems caused by a lack of time and physical fatigue related to their sports involvement. Student-athletes are required to cope with changes to their social environment, which at the tertiary level is very different from school. Although student-athletes rated the support provided by their academic institute, their coaches and their parents as influential in their academic and athletic success, the role of their peers was also perceived to be crucial in sustaining their efforts in both fields.

During the discontinuation stage of the athletic career

In many sports, about 5 to 7 per cent of elite athletes retire each year (North and Lavallee, 2004). Depending upon the type of sport, the age of retirement varies (Wylleman *et al.*, 1993). For example, North and Lavallee (2004) found that elite athletes from gymnastics, diving, swimming, ice skating and judo planned to retire in the 24–30 year age category, while those from sailing, golf, equestrian and shooting planned to retire well after 40.

Transitional challenges faced by retiring/retired elite athletes include: adjusting to a new life in which they are suddenly 'like everyone else', missing the sport atmosphere and the competition, dealing with bodily changes and changes in subjective well-being or adapting to a new social status and new vocational responsibilities (e.g. Cecić Erpič *et al.*, 2004; Stephan *et al.*, 2007). Reints *et al.* (2008) found that seven out of fifteen former elite judokas reported problems (e.g. increases in responsibilities, changed financial situations, lack of goal-oriented work, working with fixed hours) in adapting to their post-athletic life. Former elite athletes often face 'occupational delay' (Naul, 1994) as few will have had the opportunity to actively employ the knowledge and skills gained in higher education (e.g. via summer jobs or vocational or in-service training). Consequently, retired elite athletes may lack the relevant professional skills, experience and relational networks necessary for vocational success. They may therefore need to return to higher education or to basic vocational training in order to gain professional knowledge and skills. Once they enter the job market, they may find themselves 'at the bottom of the ladder', earning lower wages than younger colleagues with more work experience. Former elite athletes will need motivational readiness and interpersonal skills to integrate into such a professional setting. Former elite athletes may, in fact, turn to their families for support, or even 'return home' to live with their parents and may then also experience

166

interpersonal (or intergenerational) problems. Taking into account these challenges, it should not be surprising that vocational training is an important part of career support services for athletes (Reints and Wylleman, 2009).

If HP managers aim at providing their athletes with optimal opportunities for sustained progress, then this lifespan model will assist them in identifying the normative transitions that athletes will face during each of the athletic career stages, as well as the interactions between these domains of development and the influence they may have on the development of athletes' athletic careers. Each transition will require athletes to cope with specific situations, and the way in which athletes cope will determine the extent to which they will continue to develop. With this in mind, HP managers may use this approach to identify, develop and use specific support services within the HP system.

THE HP MANAGER AND THE DEVELOPMENT OF THE ATHLETIC CAREER

HP managers who want to optimize the support the HP system provides to their athletes have a range of options.

While many HP managers will be knowledgeable about athletic development, not many will have a similarly thorough understanding of athletes' development and the transitional challenges they face in each of the domains of their lives.

As a first step, HP managers can use the model to *increase understanding* of each of the four domains of development (athletic, psychological, psychosocial, academic/vocational) from a developmental perspective. HP managers may gather more detailed information through the use of literature and/or consultations with career support experts and sport psychologists. For example, HP managers can gain more insight into the role and influence (or lack of influence) of interpersonal relationships and social networks (e.g. parents, peers, coaches) throughout the athletic career using publications reflecting experiential knowledge (e.g. former elite athletes' biographies) or empirical knowledge (e.g. Wylleman *et al.*, 2006). Gaining a better developmental perspective may assist HP managers in establishing a continuous system of support, starting with young athletes entering the competitive system, up to elite athletes and Olympians, and athletes entering retirement.

Research into the needs of elite athletes, and the systems supporting them, have developed more and more into separate domains of expertise such as genetics, skill acquisition, sports psychology and sports medicine (Baker, 2012; De Bosscher *et al.*, 2008; Gould *et al.*, 2002; Wylleman *et al.*, 2009). As a result, it can be said that HP managers are in need of a framework to join the 'pieces of the puzzle'.

Because this model provides a developmental and holistic perspective on the athletic career, HP managers may in a second step use it to draw up a *developmental/holistic profile* of each athlete. This enables HP managers to identify more easily those factors that do have an influence on athletes' development, but that are not always obvious to HP managers. Analysing an athlete's development in this way may assist HP managers to develop a useful 'helicopter' view. In fact, experience (Wylleman, 2005, 2009; Wylleman and Debois, 2009) with HP managers and elite coaches shows that using this approach raises awareness about things that are relevant to athletes' development but which are generally 'taken for granted'.

167

For example, the junior-to-senior transition is seen to be such a natural part of the athletic career that in many cases HP managers do not fully consider the transitional challenges involved. One example at the psychological level is the challenge of moving from being the best at junior level to being one of the many talented senior athletes. An example at the psychosocial level is the search for independence from home and parents. The model also draws the HP manager's attention to factors that they may feel are not within the original remit of their job (e.g. assisting elite athletes to look for an optimal way of combining an athletic and an academic career). An additional benefit of using this model is that it gives all stakeholders (including the athlete, the coach, the HP manager, parents and representatives of national Olympic committees) a similar conceptual framework and a 'common language' to identify and attend to the challenges an elite athlete faces.

In a third step, the developmental/holistic profile can be used in combination with the generic lifespan model, which is a tool that makes it possible to envisage the forthcoming normative transitions. By using these approaches in combination, HP managers can draw up a mid- to long-term *plan of support provision* specific to the stages and transitions the athlete will face. For example, if an athlete has planned (after consulting with her parents and coach) to continue her studies and combine an athletic career with an academic career, the HP manager can look into measures that will assist her to cope with the impact of this choice on her academic development (e.g. during training camps having time for self-study and for online work using the university's digital platform), on her psychosocial development (e.g. moving away from the family home, integrating in the group of students), on her psychological development (e.g. requiring time-management skills, coping with stress related to her studies) and the possible impact on athletic progress (e.g. change to a university coach, being required to compete in other levels of competition, physical training on campus).

As a fourth step, and on the basis of the previous step, HP managers can *plan career transition programmes and career support services* which should increase athletes' ability to cope with the challenges they will face in the different domains of development. Such programmes and services are generally aimed at supporting athletes' personal growth, balancing their lifestyle and helping them to prepare for their post-athletic career life (Lavallee *et al.*, 2001). These programmes may include, for example, career planning, goal setting, mentoring and life development interventions, and are usually delivered via a combination of workshops, seminars, face-to-face counselling and multidisciplinary support services (e.g. on developmental and lifestyle issues, on academic and vocational development). In the developmental approach to athletic career development (i.e. 'beginning-to-end'), career support should be aimed not only at elite senior athletes, but also at young talented athletes, prospective junior athletes, student-athletes and retiring/retired elite athletes. Supports that cater for the particular needs of elite female athletes should be provided.

Illustrating this 'beginning-to-end' approach, Wylleman (2008) delineated three major career support stages: (a) from age 9 onwards – the stage of education (including primary, secondary, higher); (b) from age 14 to 16 onwards – the stage of athletic development; and (c) 26–28 years onwards – the post-athletic career. These career support stages have been used to develop the career support services *Carrièrebegeleiding Topsport* ('career support services in elite sport'). Adopting a holistic approach, Wylleman identified for each stage a set of skills aimed at preparing the athletes to cope with the normative transitions they will face.

These included time management skills (to be mastered from age 10 onwards), transition skills (taught at age 14), media skills (to be used from age 16 onwards), relationship skills (to be used from age 18 onwards), financial management skills (relevant from 22 years of age onwards) and networking skills (to be used from the age 26 onwards).

CASE STUDY 9.1

HOW ATHLETES CAN BE COACHED DURING/THROUGH THE TRANSITION INTO HIGHER EDUCATION: STRUCTURE AND CONTENT OF CAREER SUPPORT IN FLANDERS

Kristel Taelman

Bloso, Belgium

THE ESTABLISHMENT OF CAREER COUNSELLING IN FLANDERS

In 2004 Wylleman and Lavallee introduced a comprehensive model of career support for elite athletes. Based on the experience and expertise of these authors, the Flemish[2] policymakers for sports established in 2007 *Carrièrebegeleiding Topsport*, a career support service in addition to career support for professional athletes (since 1995) and student/athletes (since 2003–2004), set up by the Flemish sport administration Bloso. The project was assigned to the Vrije Universiteit Brussel and started with one dedicated career counsellor, focusing on supporting the transition into higher education. After three years, a second counsellor was added, focusing on the combination of employment and high level sport and on the termination of the high level sport career. Since January 2011, *Carrièrebegeleiding Topsport* has been integrated in the Flemish sport administration (BLOSO), conducted by the same two career counsellors.

There are many other countries that have had similar systems for a long time. Flanders copied and adapted some elements of their systems to the Flemish situation. This case study will focus on the specific context of Flanders.

In 2011, approximately sixty high level athletes – selected on performance and personal need for counselling – received individual career coaching. As Wylleman and Lavallee's 'Developmental model' is the basis of the daily work of the service, the individual counselling and the supply of information is focused on athletes who are facing a transition (Wylleman and Lavallee, 2004).

Purpose

This case study describes the approach of *Carrièrebegeleiding Topsport Bloso* with regard to the transition of elite athletes into higher education. First we explain the procedures, and then we describe by a concrete example of coaching over several years.

169

Sport careers contain both normative (predictable) and non-normative transitions (Schlossberg, 1984), and so career counsellors have to support athletes through both predictable and less predictable transitions. An academic year also contains fixed and less-fixed elements. Hence, only some career support interventions can be planned.

The experience of four years of counselling elite athletes resulted in a roadmap (see Table 9.1), based on the organization of the academic year. The roadmap outlines the structure and content of the initiatives taken by the career counsellors regarding the transition into higher education. It is an important tool to inform not only the athletes, but also parents, coaches, sport directors and policymakers about career support.

The identification of promising athletes that might need career support is done mainly inside the 'Topsportschool' (i.e. the original Dutch name of the adapted high schools for pupils involved into high level sports in Flanders), which are high schools for students aged 12–18 that are involved in elite sports. Selected talented young athletes receive support services and have 12 hours a week reduced education without losing credits at school. To anticipate the transition into higher education, an information session is organized in each 'Topsportschool' (January). Because of the importance of support that parents and coaches provide, they are invited to a separate information session about the common problems athletes experience in their transition after high school and what needs to be considered when combining higher education and high level sport. Additionally, a comprehensive information brochure is made available, in order to reach maximum numbers of young athletes, parents and coaches.

Case study: Tom's career transition from junior to senior

An information session on the combination of high level sport and higher education in the 'Topsportschool' was the first contact between Tom and the counsellor. Tom was a member of the national junior volleyball team. As 18-year-old volleyball players leaving elite sport schools are not always ready to be active players in a professional club, the volleyball federation, supported by the government and the Belgian Olympic and Interfederal Committee, organized a project in which the most talented players are trained by professional trainers from the Flemish volleyball federation and counselled on how to combine training, competition and higher education studies. All the players involved in the project were required to study at one university, and that university cooperated closely and consistently with the career counsellor and the federation. Academic planning, schedules and logistics were prepared and organized in detail at least six months before the start of the academic year.

The first individual session that Tom had with the career counsellor took place when he was still in his elite sport schools. The counsellor has a short session with every pupil about leaving the Topsportschool, checking the plans of the talented youngsters regarding sports, higher education, residence, transport and coaching. For an experienced counsellor, it is pretty easy to spot those athletes who will need support during the transition.

In July, the counsellor met with Tom for an intake session to get detailed information about him, to explain how the counselling would be conducted and for Tom and the counsellor to get to know each other better.

Table 9.1 Roadmap of individual career support

Transition into higher education	Oct	Nov	Dec	Jan	Feb	Mar	Apr	May	Jun	Jul	Aug	Sep	Oct	Nov	Dec	Jan	Feb	Mar	Apr	May	Jun	Jul	Aug	Sep	Oct
	Year x-1										Year x												Year x+1		
Workshop: 'What after the "Topsportschool"?' (x6)	x	x	x	x																					
Ind. sessions pupils of the last year of the 'Topsportschool'							x	x	x																
Proposal list of supported athletes to Taskforce Topsport									x																
Meeting with the institution of higher education											x	x	x												
Proposal action plan to the sport directors											x	x	x												
Time management skill training												x													
Communication skill training												x													
Goal setting and problem-solving skill training													x												
Study planning and study skill training														x											
Follow-up study planning and problem-solving support															x										
Follow-up exam period																x									
Evaluation exams and planning 2nd semester																	x								
Goals for personal improvement																		x							
Goals for personal improvement																			x						
Follow-up study planning and problem-solving support																				x					
Follow-up exam period																					x				
Evaluation exams and planning exams of August																						x			
Follow-up exam period																							x	x	
Evaluation academic year and planning next academic year																							x	x	
General feedback to the sport directors																							x	x	

Academic year x + (year x+1)

Source: BLOSO

In September, the career counsellor organized an information session for Tom and his team to explain their specific academic programme. The counsellor explained the procedures they had to respect, their schedule (training sessions, attendance of classes, study time, rest, meals and transport).

During the first four months of the academic year, Tom attended monthly individual training sessions on time management, communication, goal setting, problem solving and study methods. There was intensive feedback (rather informal) on his way of acting through which Tom learnt the skills in a more informal way. The combination of the formal sessions (monthly) and the informal follow-ups yielded excellent results.

Naturally, the exam periods in January, June and August were prepared (study method, time schedule and study planning) and evaluated with Tom. As the regular exam periods conflicted with the competition schedule of Tom's team, his exams were rescheduled. Tom managed to achieve very good marks in his studies and to fully participate in all of the team's training and competitions.

As the goal of career support is to guide athletes to the most optimal self-support, after one year of intensive counselling, the support changes to e-coaching with the possibility of a limited number of one-on-one counselling sessions. Every athlete in the programme was able to contact the counsellors for advice later on in his/her career. Tom has had regular email contact with the career counsellor, and one face-to-face meeting in his fourth year of higher education.

CASE STUDY 9.2
TALENT TRANSFER

Lisa Gowthorp
Australian Sports Commission

Elite athletes spend many years training in order to reach the standard required for success in the international sporting arena. Sports where technique and skill are crucial, such as gymnastics, often require even more years of training and commitment to reach an international standard. Elite gymnasts commence training as young as 7 years of age, with a full-time training programme of up to 7 hours a day by the age of 10 or 11. It is not until the age of 16–18 years that they are at the senior international competition level.

Gymnastics is a sport where athletes gain strength, flexibility, coordination and develop a dedication to training and hard work. All of these are qualities desired in many sports. As gymnasts are typically very young when they commence their training, many of them transfer to other sports very successfully. In Australia, gymnasts have been successful in aerial skiing, shooting and diving. In addition, many ex-gymnasts now have successful careers in Cirque du Soleil, a performance arts company with over twenty shows performing around the world.

One such athlete who has successfully transitioned to another sport is Alexandra Croak. Alex is the only Australian athlete to win gold medals at the Commonwealth Games in two different sports. Alex started her gymnastics training at a young age and was offered a scholarship at the Australian Institute of Sport (AIS) in 1994 at the age of 10. She trained at the AIS until 2002, during which time she competed at the Sydney 2000 Olympic Games and the 2002 Commonwealth Games in gymnastics. The Australian gymnastic team won a gold medal at the 2002 Commonwealth Games, with Alex winning an individual bronze medal on the vault. She retired from the sport soon afterwards.

Following an 18-month break (or semi-retirement from gymnastics), Alex decided to take up diving, due mainly to the many gymnastics skills she could transfer across. 'Things like body awareness, body control, routine, strength and motivation were all traits that were transferrable,' says Alex. However, the idea of landing upside down was a challenge, especially after training for ten years to land your feet! But as a determined, competitive and highly motivated athlete, Alex was destined to be a success. Her dedication to training, her good self-management abilities and her technical skill were key factors in her success – skills and qualities gained during her time as an elite gymnast.

The NSW Institute of Sport (NSWIS) provided Alex with a 'talent transfer' scholarship, recognizing the skill and talent she brings with her to the new sport, even though she had no experience or technical abilities in the sport of diving. Training with Chava Sobrino, one of Australia's best coaches, and with a squad of elite athletes ensured Alex developed as an elite diver very quickly. The scholarship covered all training costs, provided access to sports science and sports medicine facilities, assistance with career and education as well as nutrition and strength and conditioning training.

Talent transfer is a successful means of achieving international success in a variety of sports. Research indicates that in 2004, 72 out of 256 athletes in the AIS or State Institutes of Sport (SIS) who transferred to a new sport represented Australia within four years of the transfer (Australian Institute of Sport, 2011). However, an athlete cannot expect immediate success when commencing another sport. A dedicated coach must understand the athlete's history, identify their ability and fast track their development in the new sport.

Alex believes 'getting involved in another sport has been an absolute highlight as I have had better results as a diver than as a gymnast'. In addition, she believes, that as an older athlete, she is able to balance all areas of her life and dive to the best of her abilities. Alexandra Croak was training at the NSW Institute of Sport and was preparing for her third Olympic Games in London 2012.

Questions

1   Why is talent transfer a popular and successful way of developing athletes in different sports for international success?
2   What are the key factors that made Croak's transition to diving so successful?
3   Identify links between sports in which athletes could make an easy transition. Explain why you believe there is a link.

CASE STUDY 9.3
A DEVELOPMENTAL AND HOLISTIC PERSPECTIVE ON ATHLETIC CAREER DEVELOPMENT

Paul Wylleman, Anke Reints and Paul De Knop
Vrije Universiteit Brussel

The following case study reflects how an HP manager can use the lifespan/holistic model in order to:

(a) gain a holistic understanding of the transitional challenges that athletes face;

(b) formulate specific recommendations on how the HP system can provide optimal support to the athlete; and

(c) assist in and/or take charge of the provision of career support services which will optimize the way in which the athlete can cope with the identified transitional challenges and thus keep making progress.

Background information

Tim is 16 years old, and he has recently taken his school examinations, achieving results that exceeded his expectations. As an international swimmer, he had been training for about 18 hours per week, getting up at 5.30 am four mornings a week and training after school on each of the five weekdays with his teammates. This year had been especially demanding because additional training was required to gain selection for a major championship. Tim was selected and performed creditably. Tim is very mature for his age and has a desire to do everything perfectly as evidenced by his acute frustration when he does not meet his personal standards. On the other hand, he sometimes disagrees with what he considers to be an unrealistic training load that the coach imposes upon him that disregards other demands upon his time. It is clear that he is talented both academically and athletically, with the capacity for hard work and a strong desire to lead an organized life. He says he is especially 'stressed out' when hard physical demands are placed upon him in training, and he is currently considering whether he should continue to focus on his swimming as much as he previously has or whether he should dedicate more time to his studies. His parents are very supportive and have not pressured him either way, although Tim sometimes perceives pressure to focus more on his swimming from his coach.

Questions

The first step consists of situating Tim's athletic career stage in the developmental model based on his age and various levels of development. In the second step, Tim's current profile is described briefly by identifying:

(a) the people who are significant in Tim's life; and

(b) the principal issues that Tim faces.

The third step involves describing in more detail Tim's development by answering a number of questions that are summarized below.

With regard to Tim's athletic development:

■ Is Tim in the stage of athletic development as identified in the model based on his chronological age, his athletic experience or his level of athletic achievements?
■ To what extent are the people who are significant in Tim's life (his parents and coach) influential in his athletic development?
■ What does Tim's coach need to take into account for Tim to further his athletic development?
■ How can the coach cooperate with Tim's parents in maximizing positive outcomes in Tim's athletic development?

With regard to Tim's psychological development:

■ In what way does Tim's athletic identity influence the quality of his athletic involvement?
■ Is Tim psychologically ready to cope with the requirements of competitive sport?
■ What does Tim's coach need to take into account with regard to Tim's psychological development for him to successfully develop as an athlete?
■ How can the coach cooperate with Tim's parents in this?

With regard to Tim's social development:

■ What is the quality of Tim's relationships with significant persons in his life?
■ In what way do these relationships influence Tim's athletic development?
■ What does Tim's coach need to take into account with regard to his social development for him to successfully develop as an athlete?
■ How can the coach cooperate with Tim's parents in this?

With regard to Tim's academic development:

■ To what degree is Tim able to combine his academic and athletic careers?
■ How does the combination of academic and athletic activities influence Tim's athletic development?
■ What does Tim's coach need to take into account with regard to his academic development for him to successfully develop as an athlete?
■ How can the coach cooperate with Tim's parents in this?

Brief report

Several steps can be taken in order to report on Tim:

Step 1. Using his age to present a profile across each level of development reveals that Tim has reached the mastery level in terms of his athletic development:

(a) Tim is psychologically at the adolescent level;

(b) the key people in his life should be peers, coach and parents; and

(c) Tim is at the secondary education level.

Step 2. Tim's coach and parents play important roles in his current situation. (Could we not expect that his peers such as swimming teammates should also be an important part of Tim's life?) The principal issues reflected in the case description are Tim's desire to perform perfectly, his coach's unrealistic expectations and pressure to focus more on his swimming, and Tim being 'stressed out' as a result of self-imposed and coach-imposed expectations and standards.

Step 3. Tim has performed exceptionally well as a swimmer to date. His athletic development reflects that he has reached the mastery level at a relatively early age. (Was the development stage too brief?) Tim has shown a high level of commitment to his sport, including a capacity for hard work and for organizing his life. (Does this cause him to be 'stressed out'?) Tim sees his coach as imposing too heavy a burden upon him. (Has he always worked with his current coach? If not, why and since when did he switch coaches?) His parents have influenced his development as a swimmer to a great extent and are not perceived as putting pressure on him to perform. (In what way are his parents actually involved in his swimming: emotionally, logistically and financially?) Tim's coach could look at the way in which the mastery stage could be planned over a period of three to five years. (Given that his development stage was relatively short, can we expect that Tim's mastery stage will end earlier than is usual for a typical elite swimmer?) What are the expectations of Tim's parents with regard to their son's future swimming career?

In terms of his psychological development, the degree to which Tim identifies with his role as a swimmer has significantly influenced the quality of his involvement. Before reaching this transition in his career, he has coped reasonably well with the requirements of competitive sport. (Does he feel 'stressed out' due to a lack of readiness to cope at the mastery level?) In order for Tim to continue to develop as an elite-level swimmer, his coach will need to take into account his athletic identity and work with Tim's parents in developing a balanced plan for his future. On a social level, the quality of Tim's relationships with his coach and parents appears reasonably sound (see earlier question about the actual involvement of Tim's parents in his swimming career). These particular relationships have influenced his athletic development in significant ways, although we know little about his teammates and peers. (Does Tim have any intimate same- or opposite-sex relationships?) The coach could envisage that Tim may need and want to relate more with his peers from inside and outside the world of swimming. The coach could consult with Tim's parents about how to enable Tim to have more time for interacting with his peers.

Finally, Tim has been able to combine his academic and sporting careers quite successfully up until this point, having achieved better grades in school than expected (for someone who has already achieved the elite level in his sport). Tim's capacity to work hard and his strong desire to organize his life help him to combine athletic and academic pursuits. (To what extent do the physical training demands leave him enough time for schoolwork and recuperation?) The coach should take into account that Tim is a good student, so he will probably want to continue into higher education. The coach and Tim's parents could inform him of the possibilities available for him to select a university or college that will allow him to develop fully, both in athletics and in his studies.

SUMMARY

While HP managers can use the above four steps to maximize the support they provide to athletes for equipping them to cope with transitional challenges, three final notes are warranted. First, as the lifespan model is generic, HP managers need to adapt it to the athlete concerned and, where required, add other levels that are relevant to the athlete's development (e.g. financial level).

Second, as this model reflects normative (i.e. predictable) transitions, HP managers need to remain aware of the significance of more or less unpredicted, unanticipated, and involuntary or 'non-normative' transitions (e.g. a season-ending injury, unanticipated deselection from the team, loss of a personal coach). Conferring with athlete and coach, the HP manager can use the model to estimate the probability of these 'unforeseen' transitions occurring. For example, with regard to the possibility of athletic injury, while not fully predictable, research reveals that the likelihood of getting injured increases during the transition from final year junior to first year senior (Australian Sports Commission, 2003). In view of this, the HP manager may provide final-year juniors with a programme that increases their knowledge about and skills related to injury prevention, as well as knowledge, skills and support to cope with possible injury and rehabilitation.

Third, while HP managers should take centre stage in applying the HP system in line with such a lifespan approach, they should also confer and, if possible, rely on several experts who can assist them in establishing an interdisciplinary approach covering the needs and challenges of the athlete in all domains and stages of development. Assistance from applied sport psychologists, career counsellors and career support providers should enable HP managers to develop and provide tailor-made support to their athletes.

The international 'battle for medals' (De Bosscher et al., 2009) requires an HP system that not only allows for a sustained level of superior performances but also for the continued development of talented athletes to the elite level. Optimizing the HP system so as to maximize athletes' opportunities to prepare for and/or cope with transitions that may otherwise slow down, arrest or even cut short the development of the athletic career of athletes, should therefore be an essential approach in elite sports. The use of a lifespan approach, as described in this chapter, should provide HP managers with more knowledge on how to fulfil this vital requirement.

DISCUSSION QUESTIONS

1   The lifespan model describes in a generic way the normative transitions occurring in four domains of an athlete's development. Discuss what other domains of development could be added to this model and what normative transitions each of these domains would consist of.
2   The transitions described in the lifespan model are normative; that is, they are predictable and anticipated. Describe which 'non-normative' transitions athletes could face throughout their athletic career using the lifespan model – that is, transitions that do not occur in a set plan or schedule but are the result of important events that take place in an individual's life and are thus unpredicted, unanticipated and involuntary.
3   The lifespan model has been developed for athletes. Discuss what a lifespan model for a coach would look like.

KEY TERMS

- Lifespan model
- Career transition
- Holistic
- Development
- Normative
- Higher education
- Retirement
- Support service

GUIDED READING

A good follow-up to this chapter is not only to get closer to understanding the real-life relevance of this holistic and developmental perspective to working with talented, elite and retired athletes, but also to actually practise using it. One way is by reading (retired) athletes' (auto)biographies. Some of the ones I enjoyed reading included *Serious: The Autobiography* by John McEnroe (2003; Sphere) and *A Golden Age* by Steve Redgrave and Nick Townsend (2001; BBC Books). In fact, reading the autobiographies of two teammates of Steve Redgrave – *A Lifetime in a Race* by Matthew Pinsent (2005; Ebury Press) and *Four Men in a Boat: The Inside Story of the Sydney 2000 Coxless Four* by Tim Foster – allows to compare and understand how these three elite athletes each experienced normative transitions they went through in preparation of the 2000 Olympic Games. A second way consists, of course, of delving further into the scientific literature, including the 2004 *Psychology of Sport and Exercise* special issue on career transitions (Wylleman *et al.*, 2004) as well as Alfermann and Stambulova's *Career Transitions and Career Termination* (2007; Wiley) – both of which provide good overviews of research and conceptualizations.

NOTES

1 See Wylleman and Lavallee (2004) for a more detailed description of this model, including relevant references.
2 Flanders is the northern, Dutch-speaking part of Belgium. Since sport in Belgium is the responsibility of the regions (Flanders, Wallonia and German-speaking communities), each with their own ministries of sport and budgets, there is no national sport policy.

BIBLIOGRAPHY

Alfermann, D. and Stambulova, N. (2007). Career transitions and career termination. In G. Tenenbaum and R. C. Eklund (Eds.), *Handbook of sport psychology* (3rd edn, pp. 712–733). New York: Wiley.

Australian Institute of Sport (2011). Talent transfer. Available at www.ausport.gov.au/sportcoachmag/development_and_maturation2/talent_transfer, accessed 6 June 2011.

Australian Sports Commission (2003). *How do elite athletes develop? A look through the 'rear-view mirror'. A preliminary report from the National Athlete Development Survey (NADS).* Canberra, Australia: Australian Sports Commission.

Baker, J. (2012). Do genes predict potential? Genetic factors and athletic success. In J. Baker, S. Cobley and J. Schorer (Eds), *Talent identification and development in sport* (pp. 13–24). London: Routledge.

Bloom, B. S. (Ed.). (1985). *Developing talent in young people.* New York: Ballantine.

Bolchover, D. and Brady, C. (2002). *The 90-minute manager. Business lessons from the dugout.* London: Pearson Education.

Bouchetal Pellegri, F., Leseur, V. and Debois, N. (2006). *Carrière sportive. Projet de vie.* Paris: INSEP-Publications.

Bruner, M. W., Munroe-Chandler, K. J. and Spink, K. S. (2008). Entry into elite sport: A preliminary investigation into the transition experiences of rookie athletes. *Journal of Applied Sport Psychology, 20,* 236–252.

Bussmann G. and Alfermann D. (1994). Drop-out and the female athlete: A study with track-and-field athletes. In D. Hackforth (Ed.), *Psycho-social issues and interventions in elite sport* (pp. 89–128). Frankfurt: Lang.

Danish, S. J., Petitpas, A. J. and Hale, B. D. (1993). Life development intervention for athletes: Life skills through sports. *The Counseling Psychologist, 21,* 352–385.

De Bosscher, V., De Knop, P. and van Botterburg, M. (2008). *Vlaanderen sport, ook aan de top.* Nieuwegein, the Netherlands: Arko Sports Media.

De Bosscher, V., De Knop, P., van Bottenburg, M., Shibli, S. and Bingham, J. (2009). Explaining international sporting success. An international comparison of elite sport systems and policies in six nations. *Sport Management Review, 12,* 113–136.

De Knop, P., Wylleman, P., Van Hoecke, J. and Bollaert, L. (1999). Sports management – A European approach to the management of the combination of academics and elite-level sport. In S. Bailey (Ed.), *Perspectives – The interdisciplinary series of physical education and sport science* (pp. 49–62). *School Sport and Competition (Vol. 1).* Oxford: Meyer & Meyer Sport.

Donnelly, P. (1993). Problems associated with youth involvement in high-performance sport. In B. R. Cahill and A. J. Pearl (Eds), *Intensive participation in children's sports* (pp. 95–126). Champaign, IL: Human Kinetics.

Erikson, E. H. (1963). *Childhood and society.* New York: Stonton.

Finch, L. M. and Gould, D. (1996). Understanding and intervening with the student-athlete-to-be. In E. F. Etzel, A. P. Ferrante and J. W. Pinkney (Eds), *Counseling college student-athletes: Issues and interventions* (pp. 223–245). Morgantown, WV: FIT.

Fry, M. D. and Duda, J. L. (1997). A developmental examination of children's understanding of effort and ability in the physical and academic domains. *Research Quarterly for Exercise and Sport, 68,* 331–344.

Gould, D., Dieffenbach, K. and Moffett, A. (2002). Psychological characteristics and their development in Olympic Champions. *Journal of Applied Sport Psychology, 14,* 172–204.

Grijsbach, M. (2010). *Vancouver 2010: de mislukte Spelen van Sven Kramer.* Available at www.rnw.nl/nederlands/article/vancouver-2010-de-mislukte-spelen-van-sven-kramer.

Haerle, R. K. (1975). Career patterns and career contingencies of professional baseball players: An occupational analysis. In D. W. Ball and J. W. Loy (Eds), *Sport and social order* (pp. 461–519). Reading, MA: Addison-Wesley.

Holbeche, L. (2005). *The high performance organization. Creating dynamic stability and sustainable success.* Amsterdam: Elsevier Butterworth-Heinemann.

Jowett, S. and Meek, G. A. (2000). The coach-athlete relationship in married couples: An exploratory content analysis. *The Sport Psychologist, 14,* 157–175.

Kerr, G. and Dacyshyn, A. (2000). The retirement experiences of elite, female gymnasts. *Journal of Applied Sport Psychology, 12,* 115–133.

Koukouris, K. (1991). Disengagement of advanced and elite Greek male athletes from organized competitive sport. *International Review for the Sociology of Sport, 26,* 289–306.

Lavallee, D., Gorely, T., Lavallee, R. M. and Wylleman, P. (2001). Career development programs for athletes. In W. Patton and M. McMahon (Eds), *Career development programs: Preparation for life long career decision making* (pp. 125–133). Camberwell, VIC: Australian Council for Educational Research Press.

Leonard II, W. M. (1996). The odds of transiting from one level of sports participation to another. *Sociology of Sport Journal, 13,* 288–299.

van der Meulen, M. and Menkehorst, H. (1992). *Intensieve sportbeoefening in ontwikkelings-psychologischperspectief* [*Intensive sports participation in developmental psychological perspective*]. In M. van der Meulen, H. Menkehorst and F. C. Bakker (Eds), *Jeugdig sporttalent: Psychologische aspecten van intensieve sportbeoefening* (pp. 93–114). Amsterdam: Vereniging Sportpsychologie Nederland.

Mihovilovic, M. (1968). The status of former sportsmen. *International Review of Sport Sociology, 3,* 73–93.

Naul, R. (1994). The elite athlete career: Sport pedagogy must counsel social and professional problems in life development. In D. Hackfort (Ed.), *Psycho-social issues and interventions in elite sport* (pp. 237–258). Frankfurt: Lang.

North, J. and Lavallee, D. (2004). An investigation of potential users of career transition services in the United Kingdom. *Psychology of Sport and Exercise, 5,* 77–84.

Petitpas, A. J., Champagne, D., Chartrand, J., Danish, S. and Murphy, S. (1997). *Athlete's guide to career planning. Keys to success from the playing field to professional life.* Champaign, IL: Human Kinetics.

Pummell, B., Harwood, C. and Lavallee, D. (2008). Jumping to the next level: A qualitative examination of within-career transition in adolescent event riders. *Psychology of Sport and Exercise, 9,* 427–447.

Redgrave, S. and Townsend, N. (2001). *A golden age.* London: BBC Books.

Reints, A. and Wylleman, P. (2009). *Athletic and post-athletic career support services: Evaluation of supply and user satisfaction using a mixed-method study.* Paper presented at the 12th World Congress of Sport Psychology. Marrakesh, Morocco: ISSP, 17-21.06.

Reints, A., Wylleman, P. and Dom, L. (2008). *Kwalitatief onderzoek naar relatie tussen beroepsgerichte na-carrièreplanning en huidige beroepssituatie van Vlaamse ex-topjudoka's* [*Qualitative research into the relationship between profession-oriented past-career planning and current professional situation of Flemish former elite judokas*]. During the Congres VSPN 'Van wetenschap naar praktijk'. Amsterdam, the Netherlands: Vereniging Sportpsychologie Nederland – VUAmsterdam.

Robertson-Wilson, J. and Côté, J. (2002). *The role of parents in children's hockey participation* (p. 46). Report for the Canadian Hockey Association.

Salmela, J. H. (1994). Phases and transitions across sports career. In D. Hackfort (Ed.), *Psycho-social issues and interventions in elite sport* (pp. 11–28). Frankfurt: Lang.

Sampras, P. (2008). *A champion's mind: Lessons from a life in tennis*. New York: Crown Publishers.

Schlossberg, N. K. (1981). A model for analyzing human adaptation. *The Counseling Psychologist*, 9, 2–18.

Schlossberg, N. K. (1984). *Counselling adults in transition*. New York: Springer.

Sinclair, D. A. and Orlick, T. (1994). The effects of transition on high performance sport. In D. Hackfort (Ed.), *Psycho-social issues and interventions in elite sports* (pp. 29–55). Frankfurt: Lang.

Smith, A. L. (2003). Perceptions of peer relationships in physical activity contexts: A road less travelled in youth sport and exercise psychology research. *Psychology of Sport and Exercise*, 4, 25–39.

Stambulova, N. (1994). Developmental sports career investigations in Russia: A post-Perestroika analysis. *The Sports Psychologist*, 8, 221–237.

Stambulova, N. B. (2000). Athlete's crises: A developmental perspective. *International Journal of Sport Psychology*, 31, 584–601.

Stephan, Y., Torregrosa, M. and Sanchez, X. (2007). The body matters: Psychophysical impact of retiring from elite sport. *Psychology of Sport and Exercise*, 8, 73–83.

Torres, D. (2009). *Age is just a number*. New York, NY: Broadway Books.

Van Aken, I., Wylleman, P., Taelman, K., De Knop, P. and Clonen, J. (2008). *Het recht van een getalenteerd kind om al dan niet sportkampioen te worden* [*The right of the young talented athlete to (not) become a champion*]. *Tijdschrift Jeugd- en Kinderrechten*, 2, 101–109.

Wilkinson, J. (2006). *Jonny Wilkinson: My world*. London: Headline Publishing.

Wylleman, P. (2004). Athletic career development and the relevance of lifestyle management to elite athletes. In *Proceedings European Forum on Lifestyle Management for Elite Athletes* (cd-rom). London: UK Sport.

Wylleman, P. (2005). *Career and lifestyle management for talented, elite and former elite athletes*. During the National Conference 'Topsport in Sweden'. Örebro, Sweden: Regionalt Elitidrottscentrum, 17 March.

Wylleman, P. (2008). *From talented to elite to retired athlete: A holistic perspective on career development and transitions*. During the Personal Lifestyle Conference 2008 'The Contribution of Performance Lifestyle to Athlete Legacy'. London: UK Sport, 14 May.

Wylleman, P. (2009). *From talented to elite player*. During the seminar Elite Team Sport Coaches. Magglingen, Switzerland: Bundesamt für Sport BASPO, Eidgenössische Hochschule für Sport EHSM, Ressort Leistungssport, 23 November.

Wylleman, P. (2011). *Dual careers in elite sport: Recommendations for European policy, cooperation and service provision*. During the EPP Hearing on Sport. Brussels, Belgium: European Parliament, 30 March.

Wylleman, P. and Debois, N. (2007). *Lifestyle and career management*. During the FAST Professional workshop. Halkidiki, Greece: Forum for Applied Sport psychologists in Topsport, 4 September.

Wylleman, P. and Debois, N. (2009). *Lifestyle and career management*. During the coaches' seminar of the Games of the Small Nations. Larnacca, Cyprus: Cyprus Olympic Committee, 30 May.

Wylleman, P. and Lavallee, D. (2004). A developmental perspective on transitions faced by athletes. In M. Weiss (Ed.), *Developmental sport and exercise psychology: A lifespan perspective* (pp. 507–527). Morgantown, WV: FIT.

Wylleman, P. and Parker, R. (2004). Lifestyle management for elite athletes: A European perspective. In E. D. Boever (Ed.) *Book of abstracts of the 12th European Congress on Sport Management* (p. 263). Ghent University, Belgium: European Network of Academic Services, 9 November.

Wylleman, P. and Taelman, K. (2007). *Carrièrebegeleiding en de combinatie van studie en topsport* [*Career management and the combination of study and elite sport*]. During the 10th ENAS Conference 'Securing the Future of University Sport'. Ghent, Belgium: European Network of Academic Sport Services – Ghent University, 9 November.

Wylleman, P. and Waser, J. (2007). *Services to athletes*. During the IOC Athletes' Commission meeting. Lausanne, Switzerland: IOC, 6 February.

Wylleman, P., Alfermann, D. and Lavallee, D. (2004). Career transitions in perspective. *Psychology of Sport and Exercise*, 5, 7–20.

Wylleman, P., De Knop, P. and Schouterden, N. (2001). Managing elite athletes: A career transitions perspective. In *Proceedings of the 9th European Congress on Sport Management* (pp. 287–288). Vitoria-Gasteiz, Spain: European Association for Sport Management.

Wylleman, P., De Knop, P., Menkehorst, H., Theeboom, M. and Annerel, J. (1993). Career termination and social integration among elite athletes. In S. Serpa, J. Alves, V. Ferreira and A. Paula-Brito (Eds), *Proceedings of the VIII World Congress of Sport Psychology* (pp. 902–906). Lisbon, Portugal: International Society of Sport Psychology.

Wylleman, P., De Knop, P., Verdet, M-C. and Cecić-Erpič, S. (2006). Parenting and career transitions of elite athletes. In S. Jowett and D. Lavallee (Eds), *Social psychology of sport* (pp. 233–247). Champaign, IL: Human Kinetics.

Wylleman, P., Harwood, C., Elbe, A-M., Reints, A. and de Caluwé, D. (2009). A perspective on education and professional development in applied sport psychology. *Psychology of Sport and Exercise*, 10, 435–446.

Wylleman, P., Lavallee, D. and Alfermann, D. (Eds). (1999). *FEPSAC Monograph Series. Career transitions in competitive sports*. Lund, Sweden: European Federation of Sport Psychology FEPSAC.

Zaichkowsky, L., Lipton, G., & Tucci, G. (1997). Factors affecting transition from intercollegiate sport. In R. Lidor, & M. Bar-Eli (Eds.), *Innovations in sport psychology: linking theory and practice* (pp. 782–784). Netanya, Israel: The Wingate Institute of P.E. and Sport.

182

Chapter 10

Support services in athletic development
Good practices from the field

Peter Fricker
Australian Institute of Sport

LEARNING OUTCOMES

Upon completion of this chapter the reader should be able to:

1   understand the nature of sports science, sports medicine and the counselling services that can be provided to athletes and coaches in a high performance environment;
2   understand the contribution these services can make to high performance;
3   understand the relationship between service provision and high performance coordination; and
4   understand the role of the coach and the high performance manager in a high performance environment.

OVERVIEW

This chapter describes the different disciplines in the areas of sport science, sports medicine and counselling which may be used to contribute to athlete development in a high performance environment. These disciplines include sport and exercise medicine, physiotherapy, soft tissue therapy, strength and conditioning, recovery, nutrition and dietetics, physiology, biomechanics, performance analysis, skill acquisition and decision making, psychology, vocational guidance and support, and information management and data mining.

For each discipline this chapter provides a description that includes the professional training and qualification required in current practice, and refers to the applications of research which may emanate from within the discipline. The importance of applied research in high performance sport is emphasised and the relationship between service providers, coaches and high performance managers is described. This provides a framework for reference when considering the structure of the operations of a high performance team. The athlete remains central to this framework.

SPORT AND EXERCISE MEDICINE

Sport and exercise medicine is now recognised as a medical specialty in Australia, New Zealand, the United Kingdom and many countries in continental Europe. The professional training required for specialist qualifications requires some years of experience in general medicine followed by specialised training in appropriate clinical centres of expertise. These may include sports medicine clinics in private practice or hospital settings, or rotations for experience in orthopaedic surgery, cardiology, podiatry and similar relevant disciplines. Qualifications depend upon successful performances at structured examinations (often written and oral). In Australia and New Zealand, for example, fellowship in the Australasian College of Sports Physicians takes approximately six years of appropriate postgraduate training in sport and exercise medicine (Fricker, 2000). Research and participation in specialist conferences is a prerequisite for fellowship, and a rigorous post-fellowship programme of maintenance of professional skills (appropriately documented) is compulsory. The range of skills required includes traumatology and musculoskeletal medicine, internal medicine, psychology and nutrition, among others.

The practitioner consults with patients in a traditional doctor–patient setting, and provides advice and case management for the range of illnesses and injuries that athletes encounter. This doctor and patient setting also applies when doctors travel with teams and must not be neglected even while the doctor may pick up other duties while touring – such as assisting team management or providing other services such as nutrition, recovery, rehabilitation or psychological counselling.

It is particularly important that the practitioner understands the implications of doping – especially inadvertent doping – so that appropriate medications can be prescribed and exemptions are sought for therapeutic use of otherwise proscribed substances. Familiarity with the World Antidoping Agency (WADA) Code is essential. Concerns around doping also apply to any advice on nutrition and the use of supplements being offered.

The practitioner may refer athletes to other specialists including orthopaedic surgeons, cardiologists, respiratory physicians and gynaecologists. Musculoskeletal imaging is particularly important, and while the practitioners expected to be expert in this area, radiologists and ultrasound diagnosticians can often be involved.

Protecting the privacy of the athlete as a patient underpins the interactions of the practitioner with all others involved in the athlete's daily training environment.

Information on the ability of the athlete to perform must often be provided to a third party such as a coach or high performance manager. In this situation (and on every occasion) it is important that the athlete agrees to personal information being made available to the third party, noting that it is in the interests of the athlete to do so. Only that information which is necessary for appropriate management can be provided (Holm *et al.*, 2011). This consideration must also be given to other health service providers including physiotherapists, psychologists and nutritionists/dieticians.

PHYSIOTHERAPY

A physiotherapist involved in the care of high performance athletes is a university graduate who, after graduating, has undertaken some years of clinical experience and training in the care of athletes. There are now qualifications available that recognise training and experience and/or that require formal examination. Many physiotherapists have masters' degrees or appropriate diplomas in the sports physiotherapy field, and there are increasing numbers of physiotherapists who have successfully obtained doctoral degrees through clinical practice and research.

Physiotherapists' primary role is to advise, and to prescribe and monitor programmes for the rehabilitation of injury. In order to achieve this, they work closely with medical practitioners in the day-to-day care of athletes, and mutual respect prevails given the particular skills and knowledge provided by each. Sports physiotherapists can diagnose and manage athletes' musculoskeletal conditions, and often perform relevant diagnostic investigations such as ultrasound studies. Physiotherapists employ a number of modalities in practice – including ultrasound, laser, transcutaneous electric nerve stimulation, shock waves (sound), interferential therapy, shortwave diathermy and related electrotherapies together with manual techniques such as massage, stretching, resistance exercise, and joint and soft tissue mobilisation.

Physiotherapists also have a key role in the development and implementation of programmes for the prevention of injury, and in this capacity they work with professionals in the areas of strength and conditioning, rehabilitation medicine, and sport and exercise medicine. The physiotherapist is often at the centre of the support system for the athlete and has a responsibility to ensure an effective, coordinated programme of care. This makes the role of a physiotherapist invaluable when they travel with teams or athletes.

In special cases, physiotherapists administer medications from a limited range of analgesics and anti-inflammatory drugs, but in principle the author recommends that this practice be carefully considered and managed, as the prescription and supply of medications is traditionally in the domain of qualified medical practitioners.

SOFT TISSUE THERAPY

Soft tissue therapy includes massage, myotherapy, acupressure, myofascial and trigger point therapies, and may include (as it does in Australia) acupuncture and dry needling. Soft tissue therapists in the high performance environment are usually professionally trained in clinical sciences, particularly anatomy, physiology, neurology and psychophysiology, and have established academic qualifications and documentation of appropriate experience to safeguard and promote this practice as a profession. Most professionals have at least an undergraduate degree or equivalent supported by three to five years' recognised training and experience. There is also an increasing database of good research that underpins their practice. Current areas of research include the effects of massage on muscle soreness after exercise, injuries, and biochemical markers of exercise (Brummit, 2008).

The use of needles in the management of soft tissue conditions (e.g. muscle soreness, muscle tightness, cramps) is still under debate in terms of documented efficacy. Dry needling is the term used to describe the insertion of sterile needles to varying depths in soft tissue (up to

185

5 cm is common). The needle acts as an irritant and is not used to deposit any pharmaceutical (or other) agent – hence 'dry'. The irritant effect is believed to initiate a desired response such as relief of muscle spasm and associated pain. The mechanism for this is unclear, although much has been made of acupuncture techniques in this regard, and the link to endorphin release in response to needling at an acupuncture point or trigger point is often cited (Zhao, 2008).

A qualified, competent soft tissue therapist can diagnose and manage a range of soft tissue complaints, but any concerns that a soft tissue therapist has must be referred to a qualified medical or physiotherapy practitioner.

STRENGTH AND CONDITIONING

This discipline is a fundamental service for maintaining the health and fitness of athletes in high performance environments. Strength and conditioning coaches are typically professionals qualified in exercise science and/or physical education with experience in a high performance competition environment. There are numerous national accreditation programmes and the reader is referred to the literature (available on the Internet) for further information. There is an emphasis on research underpinning practice and there are now numerous publications and a growing body of work in the research literature that focuses on advances in the understanding of this science (Hibbs et al., 2008; Myer et al., 2008).

This service is based on principles of physiology and a thorough understanding of musculoskeletal mechanics and development. The service may be described in various ways, including physical preparation or physical conditioning, and is linked with clinical services (medicine, rehabilitation, physiotherapy) and with recovery and recuperation. It also integrates closely with coaching for high performance.

Strength and conditioning programmes are tailored to individual athletes. An assessment is made of the athlete's particular strengths and weaknesses, and a specific programme of exercises is designed, implemented and supervised to ensure the development of appropriate muscles, muscle groups and performance-related techniques. Measurement of progress is necessary and for an athlete in high performance, attendance at the gym for strength training and conditioning may occur several times a week, for an hour or two at a time.

A strength and conditioning programme may be very complex, with particular elements of the programme devoted to aspects of performance such as speed, power, agility, proprioception (and balance), core strength for skeletal support during activities, and exercises for throwing, jumping and pulling. As an athlete progresses through his/her season, exercises vary in content and intensity to allow for development, recovery or maintenance of skills as required.

Strength and conditioning coaches use a range of equipment including cable-linked weight machines, weight machines in which the ranges of movement of exercising joints are fixed, treadmills, steppers, climbers, stationary cycles, grinders, free weights, benches and bars, and Swiss balls for specific exercises (focusing on spine and trunk in particular).

RECOVERY

This discipline focuses on recuperation, and the management of fatigue and the adaptations to training.

A recovery specialist has an academic qualification in an exercise-related science discipline such as exercise physiology and has experience in a high performance setting. At the highest level the recovery specialist has a doctoral degree and is highly familiar with related disciplines in recovery – including the clinical disciplines previously mentioned and the broader group of science disciplines.

The science of recovery is an offshoot of exercise physiology but there are elements of psychology, rehabilitation, nutrition and physical therapy involved. While recovery practices involve routine procedures performed after training sessions – such as cold water immersion, hot and cold contrast baths or showers, the use of high-powered water jets in spas, stretching and massage – there is also the strategic application of techniques to manage jet lag, sleep deprivation and performance decrements. Sleep is a key area of interest and research has been conducted into sleep architecture and its variations under different training conditions (Netzer et al., 2001). Similarly, research has been conducted on the management of training-related muscle soreness, fatigue and the relative benefits of the various modalities of recovery such as cold therapies (Halson, 2011; Pournot et al., 2011; Vaile et al., 2008).

The ability of a recovery specialist to work with a coach and with athletes is imperative as recovery is a highly applied service.

NUTRITION AND DIETETICS

Sports dieticians (or sports nutritionists) 'promote healthy eating to enhance performance . . . whatever their level of physical activity'. The practice is centred on sound science (nutrition) as a foundation for prescribing healthy eating habits (dietetics). Qualifications required include an undergraduate degree (typically over four years) in science and nutrition (or dietetics), plus postgraduate qualifications such as a masters degree or doctorate in a relevant field of science. To practise as a sports dietician then often requires postgraduate experience in a high performance setting over a number of months or years.

Areas of research include the appropriate use of nutritional supplements for performance enhancement, appropriate dietary strategies for training, competition and recovery, and managing body mass in high performance sport. The reader is referred to an excellent text, *Nutrition in Sport* (ed. Ron Maughan, 2000, Wiley, UK), for further reading.

Information provided ranges from advice on nutrition for healthy weight management (especially for athletes in weight-controlled sports such as boxing and rowing) to the appropriate use of ergonomic aids and dietary supplements. High performance athletes rely on sports dieticians to provide current information on food and fluids for performance (exercise) and recovery.

Sports dieticians often travel with athletes and provide all meals, or prescribe all food and fluid intake, throughout a period of training and competition.

There is a strong crossover with other disciplines including medical practitioners and psychologists. Clinical problems such as eating disorders and anxiety-related conditions are

187

seen among high performing athletes – as much as they are seen in the broader community – and a 'clinical team' approach is taken to manage such conditions appropriately.

Sports dieticians bear the same level of responsibility with respect to athlete/client/patient privacy and confidentiality as medical practitioners and physiotherapists. Informed consent for the release of any personal information to a third party is an absolute 'must', and the athlete involved must understand if information is provided to a third party it is in the best interests of the athlete (and often the athlete's team). Sports dieticians may be confronted with doping practices, for example, and the legal and ethical provisions that apply must be considered before appropriate action is taken.

Sport dieticians must be familiar with WADA's Anti-Doping Code and must understand the process of therapeutic use exemptions and notifications. For example, a dietician looking after a diabetic athlete must know about the use of insulin in a high performance environment where athletes are subject to random dope testing.

PHYSIOLOGY

The modern physiologist in a high performance environment holds a postgraduate qualification (usually a doctorate) in sport and exercise physiology, and has extensive experience in a physiology testing laboratory or closely related facility. The most useful criterion in selecting a physiologist in this context is demonstrated successful experience working with high performance coaches and athletes – and this should extend over five years at least. The possession of a doctorate demonstrates an ability to understand research and it is often the task of a sports physiologist to conduct cost-effective studies with high performing athletes to answer a particular question from a coach. Physiology is focused on the chemistry of exercise (or work) and, as a subdiscipline, sport and exercise physiology is an area of immense effort today in research and in its application. There is an enormous and rapidly expanding body of knowledge in the research literature on the effects of training represented in physiological terms – oxygen consumption, lactic acid (lactate) production, heart rates, body temperature, fluid balance to name a few (*Journal of Applied Physiology*, 2011). Estimates of muscle mass, body fat and measures of height and limb length all contribute to an understanding of the impact of exercise and the accumulated effects of training (Veale *et al.*, 2010). Studies of adaptation to altitude, and to hot and cold environments are all a part of the sports physiologist's repertoire. All this work provides an evidence base for recommending to a coach how an athlete's programme might best be structured, and perhaps where an athlete may be over-reaching in training and deteriorating in performance. Monitoring and advice are key functions for the physiologist.

Newer areas of interest in the discipline include the effects of exercise on gene expression (which provides an understanding of exercise physiology at a molecular level and, incidentally, contributes to an understanding of doping in sport as an important outcome) as well as the effects of exercise on immune system health (recognising that athletes who train intensely sustain an increased risk of illness and infection).

An effective sports scientist must be familiar with the athlete and coach environment, and must be able to communicate effectively (and not necessarily in scientific terms) with the athlete and coach. It must be remembered, for example, that the high performance athlete has a different physiological profile from that which might be expected as a result of reading the 'standard' exercise physiology literature. Hence there is a need for frequent individualised monitoring and testing in as controlled a setting as possible in order to understand each and every athlete. In this the physiologist may find that they spend most of their working day on a pool deck, on a football field or in a laboratory.

Physiologists often travel with athletes and teams, and must adapt their knowledge and their practice to a 'field' setting. They relate with nutritionist/dieticians, strength and conditioning coaches, recovery experts and the clinicians who may accompany the athletes or teams. Respect for confidentiality and privacy is paramount (as it is for all disciplines) and having regard to the Anti-doping Code is also central, given that physiologists may be asked about supplements and performance-enhancing agents.

BIOMECHANICS

Biomechanics has a strong foundation in basic science and reflects the physics of human movement training/qualifications. A biomechanist in high performance would be expected to hold a degree in science, sport science, engineering or computer science, with postgraduate qualifications – usually a doctorate – in biomechanics in sport or in a related field such as performance analysis or skill acquisition. Together with tertiary qualifications extensive experience (over five years or more) in the collection, analysis and reporting of performance and biomechanical data is a prerequisite. Areas of research at the forefront of biomechanics in high performance sport include reduction of hydrodynamic drag (e.g. in swimmers) and aerodynamic drag (e.g. in cyclists) (Defraeye et al., 2010).

The basic tools of a biomechanist include force plates for the measurement of the forces involved in jumping, landing and pushing (off a wall during a turn in swimming, for example), cameras for understanding the path of motion of particular segments of the body during performance, sensors for detecting movement so velocity and acceleration can be measured, and sophisticated software to allow for the synthesis of data and presentation to a coach and athlete in a usable timely manner. Modern technology allows one to see a range of performance characteristics, such as throwing, in three-dimensional displays with opportunities to focus on minute details or to manipulate the data to allow for any increments in time (slowing down a movement, for example).

The biomechanist uses this technology to monitor or profile movement, and then calculates forces, vectors and speed characteristics from the data collected. In this role, the biomechanist is working in a day-to-day environment of applied science – part researcher and part scientist (in the academic sense) – and in a high performance setting, which is often laboratory based, with a skill set that allows for on-field, on-water or in-water testing. The use of portable technologies that provide useful data during performance, enabled by radio transmission that permits data collection at a distance and in real-time, is a major advance.

With an emphasis on testing, good laboratory skills are essential and the ability to communicate with the coach and athlete is a must. Conveying information simply and clearly with an emphasis on practicability is vital. Service providers from all disciplines must remember they are there to change practice for the better.

Biomechanists necessarily interact with other disciplines and cooperate on injury prevention programmes, decision-making analysis and competition analysis.

PERFORMANCE ANALYSIS

Performance analysis provides a focus for the use of information and communication technology by coaches and athletes in a daily training environment and leading up to competition. Performance analysis improves athlete performance by changing techniques or tactics. The performance analyst is typically trained in science and has a background of experience, and often research, in a sport-related field such as biomechanics, motor learning, physical education and/or coaching. Often the performance analyst is a member of the coaching staff or support staff who travels with the athlete or the team. As such, the analyst is necessarily integrated into the high performance team and must be familiar with the disciplines of the clinical practitioners and other service providers such as strength and conditioning staff, dieticians, psychologists and physiologists, for example.

As stated by the Australian Institute of Sport:

> those interested in developing the application of performance analysis in training and competition environments share the following characteristics. They:

- make a permanent record of performance
- observe in a systematic way
- record and then analyse selected aspects of performance
- provide quantitative and qualitative information

(www.ausport.gov.au/ais/sssm/ais_movement_science, 2011, p. 1)

The technology embraces digital video and software to record motion and images, and then allows for analysis of selected segments of the information collected. Various software packages provide tailored programmes for player analysis, competition analysis and performance parameters in terms of skill, accuracy, decision making and tracking relevant changes over time.

To see the work behind the scenes for a tennis player at a major tournament is to appreciate the value this discipline can provide to an athlete. Analysis of the position of the player and his/her opponent(s) during play, of the movement of the ball from serving, service returns and during rallies, linked with results in terms of points won or lost, is most illustrative. It provides the player and coach with real-time information to assist in improving performance as well as providing a bank of data for reflection and development of better techniques for the player and coach.

Areas of research in performance analysis are wide and varied. Much work is being done on competition analysis – linking player movement characteristics with the risk of injury, for example, and on aspects of physical performance to better understand the needs of individual training ('to be fit for purpose'). In Australia, the Research Board of the Australian Football League puts significant resources into research like this. Rules of competition have been changed in response to the findings of well-structured research and player safety is being monitored to ensure that rule changes are achieving their objectives.

190

SKILL ACQUISITION AND DECISION MAKING

Only recently has the application of research in these areas been seen as a viable investment for and by high performing clubs and sporting bodies. From a strong academic base in motor development and learning and in applied psychology, we are seeing practitioners literally 'in the field' with specific input into coaching practice and athlete training. At the Australian Institute of Sport skill acquisition experts work in applied research and in day-to-day applications to assess how athletes combine their sensory awareness and motor skills to perform in their sport, and they assist coaches to apply the latest developments in applied learning research. Much of the day-to-day practice is around interactive visual simulation (and stimulation!). The underlying philosophy is that of understanding how athletes develop particular skills and how they are retained, refined and executed under pressure during competition. Skill is one aspect of performance but skills cannot be executed effectively unless good decisions are made at the appropriate times. Skill acquisition is thus a complex area and requires much work with athletes (and coaches) to ensure the effective use of training and practice time by athletes.

Modalities used in skill acquisition and decision making include simulated situations using video technology to challenge a player and force decision making and the execution of a particular skill. An example is a simulated play of a basketballer (or two) that is seen during a particular passage of play in a competition situation. Images are projected on to a wall (or walls) to provide a 'virtual' game and at critical times the video is stopped and the player on the 'virtual court' must make a decision about how to respond to the situation. Feedback is then provided on what the consequences of that decision could be. Similarly, a football goalkeeper may be equipped with goggles that shut out all vision at an instant. Vision of footballers taking penalty shots is then provided in a real life scenario and just as the kick is about to be taken, the goalkeeper is temporarily blinded and must dive to save the ball. Decisions based on reading the play and predicting where the ball will be kicked are practised and feedback is provided for the goalkeeper to learn by his/her 'successes' and 'mistakes'.

Psychology has a role in considering the various factors at play when athletes are attending to the activities involved in motor skill acquisition. Athletes respond in different ways to coaching. Some may respond best to a sense of feel (kinesthetics), others to visual cues and others to auditory cues. Some athletes can focus on their own internal processes; others are more aware of external processes during training or competition.

The role of memory and retention and their relationship to skill execution and decision making are also factors in performance enhancement, as is understanding the transition from executing simple movements to more complex and coordinated ones. In addition to this range of considerations skill acquisition specialists need to understand functional anatomy and biomechanics, against a background of a broader understanding of strength and conditioning, psychology and physiology, for example.

PSYCHOLOGY

Psychology in sport is fundamental to successful performance. Most professional teams and many professional athletes have dedicated specialised sport psychologists. Modern sports psychologists involved in high performance usually have doctoral degrees in psychology, with many years of experience in sport. Current practice in sport psychology can be divided into two broad areas that overlap considerably.

The first is performance enhancement and it focuses on techniques such as mental imagery and mental routines to promote confidence, settle anxiety in competition, eliminate distractions, control emotions and minimise fatigue.

The second area has more to do with the clinical aspects of psychology that deal with such issues as injury, disordered eating, illness, stress and anxiety not necessarily related to performance, social issues with friends or family, work–life balance and time management.

There is the need for a holistic approach to the care of an athlete's mental well-being, and this care extends into the care of the athlete's physical well-being. We cannot and should not separate the mind from the body. The sport psychologist must therefore be very well trained in all aspects of sport and clinical psychology, and be very comfortable working in a team environment with medical practitioners, physiotherapists, soft tissue therapists, physiologists, and strength and conditioning staff who may all play a part in the daily training environment of the athlete. Most importantly, the sport psychologist must be comfortable working with the coach and a high performance manager if there is one. There are very strong ties between the psychologist and his/her athlete as client, and often issues arise around coaching style, discipline and confidentiality. It is important to remember that the support staff all work in the athlete's best interests but under the overall direction of the coach. It is the coach, after all, who carries responsibility for the success or otherwise of the athlete or the team.

The difficulty for the psychologist – as for a medical practitioner or physiotherapist – is to maintain the trust of the athlete while working under the direction of the coach. Often conflict arises over withholding personal information about an athlete from the coach, who believes it is the coach's right to know. It is imperative that the athlete understands that their consent at the beginning of their association with the coach is needed so the psychologist knows how much personal information they can make available to the coach. Consent from the athlete is paramount, and if a discussion around consent is not held early, the resulting conflict can become quite problematic. Chapter review questions on an issue involving conflict like this is provided at the end of this chapter.

Psychologists often travel with teams and must be resilient and flexible as demands on their time from athletes and coaching staff can be exhausting. Dealing with emotional issues such as a death in an athlete's family while overseas, or an injury suddenly eliminating an athlete from a major competition (like the Olympic Games) can occur more frequently than may be expected.

Psychology in sport has a strong research base and much work is being done to validate the benefits of techniques such as mental imagery to improve performance (Callow and Roberts, 2010) or to address mental toughness in order to minimise distractions at critical times in performance (Crust, 2007). Similarly, research in the clinical areas of psychological practice is being translated into the care of athletes (Gustafsson *et al.*, 2011).

VOCATIONAL GUIDANCE AND SUPPORT

The life of every athlete must have balance. Balancing training and competition with recovery from the physical and mental effort involved is one thing, but balancing sporting endeavours with the other demands of life is another challenge. On top of this is the need to balance aspirations in life – from short-term aspirations that may revolve around success in sport, to longer term aspirations that may focus more on a career outside of (or beyond) sport, family and social activities.

For an athlete in a high performance environment balancing all these goals takes planning, creativity and compromise. Finding ways to integrate the various elements in an athlete's life requires:

■ identifying and planning around the priorities in life;
■ setting goals to help establish direction; and
■ good time management.

Once these basic strategies become established and put into practice, attention can be paid to the detail around meeting each and every goal, short term and long term. To help with this, high performance training centres around the world use the services of professionals who assist athletes in the development of plans, and reviewing and refining these in the course of the athlete's career.

A key aspect of the professional servicing of the athlete's needs in this respect is taking a tailored approach to each individual. At the Australian Institute of Sport, for example, professionals in the Athlete Career and Education (ACE) Programme offer assistance with:

■ career counselling and planning;
■ personal development training (through training in public speaking, media, time management, financial planning and interview skills, for example);
■ educational guidance (assisting with university study options and liaison with universities, vocational training opportunities and assistance with meeting demands of high school education, as appropriate);
■ employment preparation (writing résumés, applications for employment and assistance with job searching);
■ career referral networks (using established online resources to assist athletes in remote areas or internationally based athletes);
■ referrals (to services for counselling, psychological support, financial advice, for example); and
■ lifestyle management (finding the balance between sporting demands and non-sporting demands).

(www.ausport.gov.au/participating/career_and_education, 2011, p. 1)

The Australian Institute of Sport's ACE advisers are professionals who have qualified as teachers, counsellors or psychologists, and have a skill set that is often a mix of these. Each adviser meets with his or her athletes regularly and, after an assessment of their needs, maps out a programme of activities and reviews, and provides a monitoring service that allows for early intervention on issues which need action. They also encourage and support the athlete as he or she takes on the challenges of sport and life.

There are opportunities for professional development of ACE advisers, and in Australia and in the United Kingdom qualifications in this area can be obtained from recognised tertiary

193

institutions. Research has also become important, particularly to establish whether the interactions between advisers and athletes are effective and, if necessary, to change behaviour for the better so that educational and vocational objectives are met. Early work in this area is certainly reassuring and further evaluation will assist in refining the practice of advisers.

INFORMATION MANAGEMENT AND DATA MINING

The challenge for high performance sport today is using all relevant information to shape decision making and achieve success. The area of high performance sport has seen a real shift over recent years away from traditional practices in sport to practice based on evidence that particular elements or activities have been successful.

The phenomenal growth in information technology and in its applications across communication has seen new ways of operating emerge in the day-to-day relationships between athletes, coaches and their support staff (clinicians, scientists, managers and administrators). Huge amounts of data are being gathered and assembled, and then passed between the coach and the athlete to provide feedback and instruction. The use of video and of selected data presented as graphs and images has greatly enhanced the ability of coaches to coach and athletes to learn. The athlete of today is comfortable with social media and this has facilitated both the input of data by athletes into their training logs (or databases), and the retrieval of personalised information by their coaches.

Information technology experts can tap into a huge resource available on the Internet as open source software and they can use aggregated capacity such as cloud computing to process the data being captured and stored by athletes and coaches.

Data mining is now being employed to explore the data held on athlete performance and to seek out possible contributors to success (as well as to identify possible detractors from success). Data mining can be defined as 'the process of analysing data to find hidden patterns using automatic methodologies' (MacLennan et al., 2009, p. 1). In practice, data mining reveals hidden patterns rather than cause and effect, and one must be careful to remember this. A pattern may not necessarily indicate a direct cause-and-effect relationship and any possible cause-and-effect relationship must be tested appropriately before one proposes any change to coaching practice (or to any other elements of an athlete's training environment).

Data mining generally draws conclusions based on widely accepted mathematical techniques for pattern matching. Typically, these advanced techniques come from mathematicians, and data mining is an active area of university research (Tabladillo, 2010). Data mining, in other words, produces models and these can be presented as equations or formulae, with statistical parameters applied.

For example, Schroeder et al. (2011) produced a paper on the use of data mining methodologies to determine patterns in tennis rallies that can be used in a real competition. Their paper introduces the concept of connections of events that are then layered over time to indicate potentially significant associations – some deemed long-term patterns (and permanent patterns) and others short-term patterns. In the authors' terms, cells (of associated events) that are stimulated (by frequency) grow stronger, while cells that do not receive sufficient input are weakened and 'may die'.

Tennis is examined in terms of its specific actions during a rally (e.g. the ball touches the ground in the right back corner of the court). Patterns of association are then determined through the course of the game/set/match and then those patterns with the highest frequency of association are determined (e.g. the stroke played where the ball touches the ground to the left front of Player B is most often associated with the stroke played where the ball goes out on Player A's side). Thus there is an indication of a need to change tactics and perhaps for a refinement of skill.

Data mining and analytics is necessarily linked with performance analysis, information and communication technology and high performance coaching. The advances this will lead to have the potential to take sport to a new level.

CASE STUDY 10.1

TRAVELLING AND THE IMPACTS OF ATHLETE NUTRITION ON HIGH PERFORMANCE MANAGEMENT

Louise M. Burke

Australian Sports Commission

The training and competition requirements of elite sport include busy travel schedules, often involving long journeys across multiple time zones or relocation to challenging environments. The achievement of the athletes requires an understanding of specific needs arising from the phase of their periodised programme as well as special features of the environment (heat, humidity, altitude, etc.). The athlete may need to achieve these goals in an environment where foods are different, or where appropriate foods are difficult to obtain. Challenges include a different catering style (e.g. all you can eat buffets), the absence of habitually consumed foods in a foreign country and exposure to an increased risk of gastrointestinal infections because of differences in food and drink hygiene. With careful organisation, the athlete and their support staff can implement a travel nutrition plan to overcome these challenges. The Beijing Olympic Games provides an interesting example where such a plan was implemented.

Participation in an Olympic Games is likely to be the highlight of an athlete's career. However, the challenges involved in team travel can make it difficult for athletes to perform at their best. The Beijing Olympic Games in 2008 offered a significant number of areas for concern. Instead of seeing this as a problem, however, members of the Australian Olympic team were encouraged to see it as an opportunity to develop creative solutions that would give them an advantage over the other competitors. A range of plans was developed to tackle the identified problems; these were implemented at levels ranging from whole team policies and organisation, to protocols practised by a specific sporting team through to self-management by the athlete. A summary of the challenges identified at the Beijing Olympic Games and the strategies used to address them is provided in Table 10.1.

Table 10.1 Challenges and solution for the travelling athlete

Challenges of travelling	General strategies to cope with the challenges of travelling	Specific strategies used at the Beijing Olympic Games (BOG)
• Disruptions to the normal training routine and lifestyle while the athlete is en route • Changes in climate and environment that create different nutritional needs (e. g. altitude or heat) • Jet lag • Changes to food availability including absence of important and familiar foods • Reliance on hotels, restaurants and takeaways instead of home cooking • Exposure to new foods and eating cultures • Temptations of an 'all you can eat' dining hall in an Athletes Village • Risk of gastrointestinal illnesses due to exposure to food and water with poor hygiene standards • Excitement and distraction of a new environment	**1 Planning ahead** • The athlete should investigate food issues at their destination and on travel routes (e.g. airlines) before leaving home. Caterers and food organisers should be contacted well ahead of the trip to let them know meal timing and menu needs. **2 Supplies to supplement the local fare** • A supply of portable and non-perishable foods should be taken or sent to the destination to replace important items that missing. • The athlete should be aware that many catering plans only cover meals. Since the athlete's nutrition goals are likely to include well-timed and well-chosen snacks, supplies should be taken to supplement meals en route and at the destination	• Test events held in Beijing a year before the Olympics provided an opportunity for Australian athletes and teams to experience the challenges. These experiences, including problems and any strategies used to prevent problems, were collated to allow the Olympic team managers and medical team to formulate a plan for the Games • The BOG Organizing Committee was contacted to find out information about catering in the Village Dining Hall and competition venues • Newsletters and forums were used to disseminate information to the sporting teams within the Australian Olympic Team (AOT) • Containers were sent by ship six months before the Games. Supplies included a range of non-perishable sports foods and snack foods that were commonly used by Australian athletes, especially to meet sports nutrition goals around training sessions and events. Even though some of these products would be available via the BOG catering, we wanted to ensure that supplies were adequate in quantity and type to meet the usual practices of our athletes

3 Eating and drinking well en route

- Many athletes will turn to 'boredom eating' when confined. Instead they should eat according to their real needs, taking into account the forced rest while travelling

- When moving to a new time zone, the athlete should adopt eating patterns that suit their destination as soon as the trip starts. This will help the body clock to adapt

- Unseen fluid losses in air-conditioned vehicles and pressurised plane cabins should be recognised and a drinking plan should be organised to keep the athlete well hydrated

4 Taking care with food/water hygiene

- It is important to find out whether the local water supply is safe to drink. Otherwise, the athlete should stick to drinks from sealed bottles, or hot drinks made from well-boiled water. Ice added to drinks is often made from tap water and may be a problem

- In high-risk environments, the athlete should eat only at good hotels or well-known restaurants. Food from local stalls and markets should be avoided, however tempting it is to have an 'authentic cultural experience'

- Food that has been well cooked is the safest; it is best to avoid salads or unpeeled fruit that has been in contact with water or soil

- A fact sheet on simple travel advice was developed with tips for travelling teams

- Since Beijing is in a similar time zone and a relatively short fight time (~10 h) from Australia, travel advice only needed to cover tips on hydration, avoiding boredom eating, and suggestions for extra food supplies for athletes with high energy requirements

- Australian athletes who were travelling to Beijing from other locations (e.g. competition in Europe or North America) received additional advice about long-haul flights and jet lag

- All athletes and teams were advised to eat only in the Village Dining Hall, official catering at competition venues and official ceremonies in large hotels until the completion of their events

- An overall Team Hygiene plan was developed and provided to all athletes and sporting teams within the AOT. Individual sporting groups within the AOT included added strategies that were specific to their sport and its extra challenges (e.g. contact with water in lakes/ocean). Strategies included the development of kits for team members to prevent gastrointestinal illnesses (e.g. antiseptic wipes) or treat them (e.g. oral rehydration solutions)

- The official guidelines regarding food in the Village (e.g. safety of salad and uncooked fruits/vegetables) were made only after the Team medical staff met with BOG catering staff and did an inspection of the kitchen in the Dining Hall. In general, the hygiene standards were deemed to be of very high quality and few restrictions, other than the use of bottled and hot drinks rather than tap water, were recommended

5. **Adjusting eating and drinking to suit current nutrition needs**

- The athlete should be aware of their actual energy and nutritional requirements arising from the periodisation of their training or competition preparation. These may be different from other parts of the year

- The athlete may need to adjust their intake to suit special needs imposed by the environment (e.g. fluid needs in hot weather)

6. **Adhering to the food plan**

- The athlete should choose the best of the local cuisine to meet their nutritional needs, supplementing with their own supplies where needed

- The athlete should be assertive in asking for what they need at catering outlets – e.g. low fat cooking styles or an extra carbohydrate choice

- The challenges of 'all you can eat dining' should be recognised. The athlete should resist the temptation to eat 'what is there' or 'what everyone else is eating' in favour of their own meal plan

- Sports scientists within the medical team of the AOT and its individual sporting groups developed special plans to cope with exercise in the heat and humidity of Beijing. This included:

  - strategies to monitor hydration levels and hydrate appropriately during and after exercise

  - use of pre-cooling techniques, including the combination of external (ice towels and ice vests) and internal (consumption of ice slurries) cooling strategies

- On arrival at the Beijing Olympic Village, Australian sporting teams were provided by the AOT dietitian with information on the Village Dining Hall, and the opportunity for a guided tour. Key messages of these educational opportunites included:

  - strategies to gain access to special food needs

  - understanding nutritional information available in the Dining Hall

  - strategies to stay focused on competition nutritional goals

CASE STUDY 10.2

BEST PRACTICE IN BIOMECHANICS AND HOW IT CAN BE USED IN HIGH PERFORMANCE SPORT: THE LONGITUDINAL FOLLOW-UP DURING COMPETITION OF AN ELITE HIGH-JUMP ATHLETE

Philippe Malcolm and Dirk De Clercq

University of Ghent

Biomechanical analyses typically require sophisticated laboratory methods. However, peak performances in elite sports are difficult to reproduce in a laboratory environment (e.g. Semin *et al.*, 2008) and should therefore be recorded during competition where possible. This and other problems pose specific challenges to the biomechanical analysis of elite performances that are different from the requirements of the scientific research context. In this chapter we propose a set of guidelines for biomechanical analyses of high performance sports and illustrate them based on the case of the scientific support we provided for an elite high-jumping athlete. The analyses consisted of 3D kinematics recorded with high-speed cameras in six international level competitions during the two-year build-up prior to the 2008 Beijing Olympics (Malcolm *et al.*, 2009). From these measurements different parameters were derived such as approach run speed, joint angles, and so on, and correlations with performance parameters were examined in order to advise the athlete.

As stated in the introduction, we believe that measurement should be preferably done in competition. The high-jumping athlete who was analysed had personal bests of 2.05 m in competition but 'only' 1.92 m in training. If the analyses would have been done in training only the lower range of the competition heights would have been reproduced. In this situation it would have been unclear whether the trends observed in these training jumps could be extrapolated to draw conclusions that were applicable to the athlete's higher competition jumps. There are, however, several obstacles when doing measurements in competition. There can be no interaction with the athlete, so advanced automatic motion capture cameras that require markers on the athlete could not be used and the athlete's movement had to be manually tracked frame-by-frame from video images. Furthermore, the proceedings of the competition could not be disturbed so the set-up had to be approved by the organisers, officials, TV-crew and others (e.g. for the camera shown in Figure 10.1 a position had to be adapted that did not hinder the officials who had to have a clear lateral view of the bar).

The methods used should be adapted for each athlete. In the case of high jumping, each athlete usually has a morphology that is very different from the available segmental mass distribution models in the literature (Dapena, 2000). In this case study a custom segmental mass distribution model was used that was based on estimated segmental volumes from frontal and sagittal pictures. The trajectory from the whole-body centre of mass during the flight over the bar based on the custom segmental mass model had a correlation of 0.999 ± 0.001 with the trajectory that could be expected based on the known gravitational constant, which confirms that the custom model yielded realistic results. Figure 10.2 shows the apex heights of forty-five flight paths that were calculated in this way versus approach run speed.

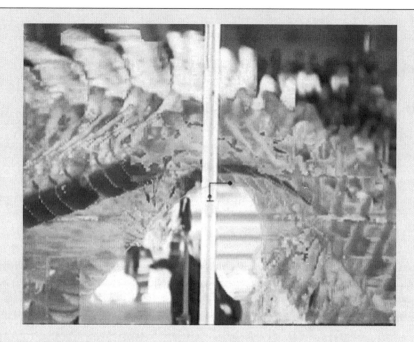

Figure 10.1 *Overlay of sagittal images of the bar-crossing phase*

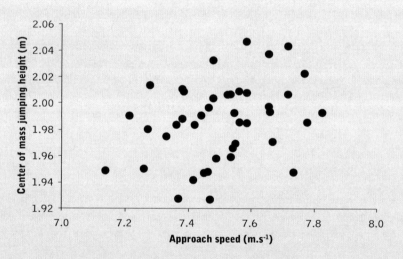

Figure 10.2 *Jump height measured from the centre of mass trajectory versus approach run speeds from forty-five analysed jumps*

The accuracy should be maximised in order to detect differences between trials because elite athletes often move in a very consistent way. For example, the standard deviation of the approach speed in the charts in Figure 10.1 is only 0.15 m.s^{-1} or 2 per cent of the mean speed. Within the jumps of one competition this range is even smaller. In order to find trends the data should be carefully processed and improved if possible. The calculation of the apex height of the flight path was, for example, improved by smoothing the centre of mass trajectory with a function based on the gravitational constant.

Measurements should be repeatable in order to allow comparing different measurement sessions and to advise accordingly. The technique of 3D reconstruction required that the camera's images were calibrated with a cubical frame with known dimensions. This frame was always placed in the same way. In order to check the reconstruction error we compared the reconstructed bar height from our video images with the actual bar height that was set and determined by the officials. The mean absolute error was 8+/–7 mm, which was acceptable for a measurement volume of several square meters.

The results should be rapidly but carefully communicated. The athlete needs the information as quickly as possible in order to adapt their training. While the focus of our measurements was 3D kinematics, we always did some extra 2D analyses that required less processing time and could therefore be delivered within days. We took care to always communicate our results to the coach instead of discussing them directly with the athlete. Biomechanical analyses can give a lot of information (around fifty parameters per trial were calculated). The athlete is better off not thinking of all this information so the coach is best placed to selectively communicate the results at the appropriate time in the training process.

Probably the biggest challenge is to present the results in a format that can be easily understood and applied by the athlete in training and competition. For example, it is better to talk in terms of less or more push off than in terms of running speed or to talk of foot positioning instead of horizontal radius of the approach run trajectory. While the apex height of the centre of mass trajectory gives the best indication of the mechanical performance of a jump, what counts in high jumping is whether the bar is touched or not. This type of practically relevant output was given from a specific 2D analysis of the bar-crossing phase (Figure 10.1). Aside from the height at bar crossing, this type of output could also predict the optimal take-off distance and the bar-crossing height if the athlete takes off from this optimal distance.

Although it can be challenging to adhere to the given guidelines, the potential rewards are high in technique-oriented sports, especially since the margin between winning and losing in high performance sports can be small. The athlete for whom we provided scientific support won an Olympic gold medal with the smallest possible margin. That is, she completed the same height as the silver medalist but with one less attempt. The silver medalist had undergone similar biomechanical analyses (Atekolovic et al., 2006) so it could even be argued that biomechanical analyses are becoming a necessity for competing at the top level in high jumping. We believe that with the advent of fully automated and markerless systems, in a few decades most technical obstacles will have disappeared and biomechanical analyses will become part of any high performance athlete's support programme. While the methods will evolve, the guidelines described here will probably remain mostly valid.

SUMMARY

There are many support services in the world of high performance sport. It is important to remember that the focus is always on developing the athlete to create the best possible chance of success, and all services must be strategically aligned, coordinated and delivered with a maximum of efficiency. Issues around confidentiality and privacy must be resolved prior to any service being provided. Accountability is paramount and it is thus important that each service provider knows what it is that is being delivered and what the measurable outcome will be. If it cannot be measured, it cannot be managed! The high performance manager must be the coordinator of services and work under the direction of the coach. Service provision in this environment is dynamic and challenging. It demands flexibility and agility in thinking and the highest standards of ethics and professionalism in delivery.

DISCUSSION QUESTIONS

You are the psychologist working with a team of footballers and the high performance manager of the team informs you that he is aware that one of the footballers is experimenting with illegal substances. He asks you to manage this and provide a report to him on what needs to be done as he must recommend appropriate action to the owner of the team.

1 Discuss the issues involved in this study and in particular your duty of care and professional responsibilities to the player, the coach and the team.
2 How would you approach the player about this situation?

KEY TERMS

■ High performance
■ Sports science
■ Clinical sciences
■ Confidentiality

GUIDED READING

These texts are recommended by the heads of the servicing and research disciplines at the Australian Institute of Sport.

Physiology

Tanner, R. (Ed.). (2012). Physiological tests for elite athletes (2nd edn). Champaign, IL: Human Kinetics.

202

Nutrition

Burke, L. (2007). Practical sports nutrition. Champaign, IL: Human Kinetics.
Burke, L. and Deakin, V. (2010). Clinical sports nutrition (4th edn). Sydney: McGraw-Hill.

Biomechanics

Ackland, T., Elliott, B. and Bloomfield, J. (2009). Applied anatomy and biomechanics in sport (2nd edn). Champaign, IL: Human Kinetics.
Zatsiorsky, V. (2000). Biomechanics in sport: Performance enhancement and injury prevention. Oxford: Wiley-Blackwell Scientific.

Performance analysis

Lyons, K. (2005). Performance analysis in applied contexts. *International Journal of Performance Analysis in Sport*, 5(3), 155–162.
O'Donohue, W. (2009). Research methods for sport performance analysis. London: Routledge.

Skill acquisition

Williams, A. M. and Hodges, N. J. (2004). Skill acquisition in sport: Research, theory and practice. London: Routledge.

Strength and conditioning

Baechle, T. and Earle, R. (2003). In P. V. Komi (Ed.). Strength and power in sport (2nd edn). Oxford: Blackwell Scientific.
Baechle, T. R. and Earle R. W. (Eds). (2008). Essentials of strength and conditioning. Champaign, IL: Human Kinetics.

Case study 10.1

Reilly, T., Waterhouse, J., Burke, L M., Alonso, J. M., International Association of Athletics Federations. (2007). Nutrition for travel. *Journal of Sports Science*, 25(Suppl. 1), S125–S134.
Young, M. and Fricker, P. (2010). Medical and nutritional issues for the travelling athlete. In L. Burke and V. Deakin (Eds), Clinical sports nutrition (4th edn, pp. 651–658). Sydney: McGraw-Hill.

Recommended websites

Australian Institute of Sport (www.ausport.gov.au/ais)
Journal of Applied Physiology (http://jap.physiology.org)
Sports Dieticians Australia, 2011 (www.sportsdietitians.com.au/content/312/whatwedo/)
World Antidoping Agency (WADA) (www.wada-ama.org)

BIBLIOGRAPHY

Brummitt, J. (2008). The role of massage in sports performance and rehabilitation: Current evidence and future direction. *National American Journal of Sports Physical Therapy*, 3(1), 7–21.
Callow, N. and Roberts, R. (2010). Imagery research: An investigation of three issues. *Psychology of Sport and Exercise*, 11, 325–329.

Crust L. (2007). Mental toughness in sport: A review. *International Journal of Sport and Exercise Psychology*, 5, 270–290.

Dapena, J. (2000). The high jump. In V. Zatsiorsky (Ed.), *Biomechanics in sport* (pp. 283–311). Oxford: Blackwell Science.

Defraeye, T., Blocken, B., Koninckx, E., Hespel, P. and Carmeliet, J. (2010). Computational fluid dynamics analysis of cyclist aerodynamics: Performance of different turbulence-modelling and boundary-layer modelling approaches. *Journal of Biomechanics*, 43(12), 2281–2287. Epub. 21 May.

Fricker, P. (2000). Sports medicine education in Australia. *British Journal of Sports Medicine*, 34, 240–241.

Gustafsson, H., Goran, K. and Hassmen, P. (2011). Athlete burnout: An integrated model and future research directions. *International Review of Sport and Exercise Psychology*, 4(1), 3–24.

Halson, S. (2011). Does the time frame between exercise influence the effectiveness of hydrotherapy for recovery? *International Journal of Sports Physiology and Performance*, 6(2), 147–159.

Hibbs, A. E., Thompson, K. G., French, D., Wrigley, A., Spears, I. (2008). Optimizing performance by improving core stability and core strength. *Sports Medicine*, 38(12), 995–1008, doi:10.2165/00007256-200838120-00004.

Holm, S., McNamee, M. J. and Pigozzi, F. (2011). Ethical practice and sports physician protection: A proposal. *British Journal of Sports Medicine*, doi:10.1136/bjsm.2011.086124.

MacLennan, J., Tang, Z. and Crivat, B. (2009). Data mining with SQL Server 2008. Indianapolis, IN: Wiley Publishing.

Malcolm, P., De Clercq, D. and Van Lancker, W. (2009) Regression analysis on longitudinal kinematical data from one elite high jump athlete in competition. Paper presented at the XXII Congress of the International Society of Biomechanics, Cape Town.

Myer, G. D., Paterno, M. V., Ford, K. R. and Hewett, T. E. (2008). Neuromuscular training techniques to target deficits before return to sport after anterior cruciate ligament reconstruction. *Journal of Strength and Conditioning Research*, 22(3), 987–1014.

Netzer, N. C., Kristo, D., Steinle, H., Lehmann, M. and Strohl, K. P. (2001). REM sleep and catecholamine excretion: A case study in elite athletes. *European Journal of Applied Physiology*, 84(6), 521–526.

Pournot, H., Bieuzen, F., Duffield, R., Lepretre, P. M., Cozzolino, C. and Hausswirth, C. (2011). Short term effects of various water immersions on recovery from exhaustive intermittent exercise. *European Journal of Applied Physiology*, 111(7), 1287–1295. Epub 4 December 2010.

Schroeder, B., Hansen, F. and Schommer, C. (2011). A methodology for pattern discovery in tennis rallys (*sic*) using the adaptive framework ANIMA. Available at www.liaad.up.pt/jgama/IWKDDS/Papers/p11.pdf.

Semin, K., Stahlnecker, A. C., Heelan, A., Brown, G. A., Shaw, B. S. and Shaw, I. (2008). Discrepancy between training, competition and laboratory measures of maximum heart rate in NCAA division 2 distance runners. *Journal of Sports Science and Medicine*, 7, 455–460.

Tabladillo, M. (2010). Why use Data Mining? *The Solidq Journal*, 40–45. Available at www.solidq.com/sq.

Vaile, J. P., Halson, S., Gill, N. and Dawson, B. (2008). Effect of hydrotherapy on the signs and symptoms of delayed onset muscle soreness. *European Journal of Applied Physiology*, 102, 447–455, doi 10.1007/s00421-007-0605-6.

Veale, J. P., Pearce, A. J., Buttifant, D. and Carlson, J. S. (2010). Anthropometric profiling of elite junior and senior Australian Football players. *International Journal of Sports Physiology and Performance*, 5(4), 509–520.

Zhao, Z. Q. (2008). Neural mechanisms underlying acupuncture analgesia. *Proceedings in Neurobiology*, 85(4), 355–375. Epub 5 June.

Chapter 11

Coaching high performance athletes and the high performance team

Dave Collins, John Trower and Andrew Cruickshank

University of Central Lancashire

LEARNING OUTCOMES

Upon completion of this chapter the reader should be able to:

1. describe, recognise and understand what it takes to be a successful high performance (HP) coach;
2. understand the basics of how HP coaches can best be supported by staff, systems and structures to bring out the best in their performers;
3. recognise what may change in coaching systems at different stages of the athlete's and coach's career;
4. understand the role of performance directors/managers in HP;
5. describe and understand the construct of 'nested thinking' and how can it be used as a basis for optimising HP outcomes; and
6. recognise the importance of 'culture' in HP and how it may best be manipulated.

OVERVIEW

There is always a big discussion on who can offer the best advice. Do you seek out the high performing individuals in your chosen environment, those who have worked with people trying to achieve greatness, or do you consult academics who can offer an evidence-based explanation of how greatness may best be achieved? In colloquial terms, 'those who can, do; those who can't, teach; those who can't teach, research teaching!' This is a common dilemma that is solved by different people in very different ways. For example, the media will typically support the appointment of 'those who can', favouring ex-performers, often at the expense of well-qualified and clearly committed professionals. Businesses will seek out specialist trainers while governments prefer those with academic qualifications. Our point in this preamble is that each choice has its own strengths and weaknesses. Those who 'did' know what works practically but only for one individual – namely, themselves. Those who teach can come up with very elegant and easily understandable solutions, which may belie the complexity of the real challenge. The scientist can describe things with (apparently) amazing accuracy and rigour but miss the nuances, the 'art' of how things are done, which is at least as important and much more commonly used. In choosing between these three, there are some important extra considerations. For example, HP environments change quickly and this means that any advice may soon be out of date. This is true whether the advice comes from academics or from those with practical experience. As a consequence, future proofing is an essential, satisfied in this case by ensuring a constant search for the next edge.

In this regard, sport is an unforgiving challenge. Stand still and you go backwards; run fast and you can maintain parity; run extra fast, or find a short cut, and you might well get ahead for a moment. Accordingly, the answer is to combine the best features of all three approaches listed above: always focus on the practical, train while encouraging challenge and research at leisure while generating new, 'cutting-edge' ideas against logic but not proof. In similar fashion, no HP coach comes from just one of these three approaches. We all have experiences and approaches from at least two and often all three of these essential components of knowledge and practice in elite sport. Accordingly, as we present our ideas, we ask you to apply the practical (Will it work?), process (How could you develop people to do it?) and scientific (Is there a sound basis to the idea?) trinity which, we suggest, is essential but often lacking in elite sport management practice.

Our ideas are structured as follows: first, we examine the HP environment and the characteristics necessary to work in them. After some thought on how these characteristics may best be modelled or recruited, we offer some recent developments (e.g. nested thinking) on how HP coaches need to work. Next, we consider ways in which the HP demands may change with age, both for the performers and the coaches. Finally, after some examination of the importance of culture change and relationship management, we look at management structures that may help to optimise the HP system. Our conclusion offers a summary of key points about HP coaches and support workers that have evolved through the chapter, before offering some key questions that readers might like to consider.

CONTEXT: WHAT MAKES THE HP ENVIRONMENT?

An important first distinction is to point out the difference between a high perform-*ance* environment and high perform*ing* environment. There are a lot of high performance environments. They are identifiable by the level of peer challenge, the financial and other rewards available, and the stakes in the competitive setting. High performing environments are much rarer – they display all the first set of characteristics but crucially, they also show an extra set of qualities such as effective two-way communication, well-managed and positive conflict, a strong and mutually supportive team ethos, and a longer record of success and, in many cases, consistency of personnel. It is a common but silly mistake to think that, just because you are looking at, say, a Premier League club, that means that all their systems are premier! This is a consideration that is similar to the need to distinguish between the quality of the coach and his/her processes and the success of the athlete (Abraham and Collins, 2011). Good performances *may* be associated with good coaches but there are other possible explanations for success – for example, an upwardly mobile coach may, like a drowning person, cling to an extreme talent as the key to personal survival. As such, and reflecting our comments in the introduction, you should apply the practical/process/science triangulation test to what you experience or read about.

CHARACTERISTICS: HOW DO THINGS WORK BEST IN AN HP ENVIRONMENT (AND FOR WHOM)?

Assuming that from now on we take HP to mean high performing rather than just high performance, what will such an elusive construct look like? Well our earlier statements on this are supported by a variety of empirical evidence and authoritative writing in the area. Central to our conceptualisation is an awareness that *enduring* success cannot be achieved through well-intended top-down directives alone. Indeed, recognising that peak performance is a culmination of outputs from appropriately focused and highly motivated coaches, other support staff and performers, any system dependent upon a sole command centre is highly susceptible to collapse or insurrection. Of course, such a structure may be effective if the environment is made up of particularly naive/trusting/fearful top-level performers and staff. However, as the likelihood of this scenario is minimal, particularly in contemporary HP settings, a more holistic and integrated approach is therefore required.

Although effective leadership has a long history in performance optimisation (Case, 1987; Chelladurai and Saleh, 1978), current theories are limited in accounting for the programme-shaping power of leaders of HP environment team members, both performers and staff. For example, acknowledging that performers are usually extremely committed (Krane and Williams, 2006), highly ego-orientated (and task-orientated: Kingston and Hardy, 1997) and exceptionally well paid (Harris, 2011), management/coaching practice that fails to identify then shape the perceptions of those delivering the product is a strategic, political and tactical faux pax! In short, there must be an explicit focus on getting the team on board, with compatible goals and expectations, rather than just 'buying the best available', then lumping them together. Similarly, because they can either invigorate or derail a programme, support staff also need to be on the same page (Bloom *et al.*, 2003). Consequently, because HP settings involve multiple and variably motivated individuals interacting in highly change-able conditions, they require individuals who can do much more than just apply *general* competencies to *general* challenges (Jones and Wallace, 2005). We explore this idea in greater depth in the next section.

Certainly, with power distributed both across and within key employee groups (i.e. boards of directors, performance management, coaches, other support staff, performers), programme delivery is a highly interpersonal *and* contested activity; that is, lots of interaction but also lots of conflict (Côté *et al.*, 1995; Jones *et al.*, 2004; Potrac and Jones, 2009). Accordingly, with all actors able to reinforce or restrict the actions and reactions of others (albeit to varying extents), research and practice based upon linear assumptions (if I do *this* then *this* will happen . . . and so on) just doesn't cut it (cf. Bowes and Jones, 2006). Indeed, without tools and techniques to continually monitor and reconcile differing perceptions,

207

scenarios may arise in which performers do not try their hardest, coaches and other staff fight to achieve selfish goals and those 'above' deny the resources needed to improve performance or even to keep it at the current level. To flourish, performance managers and coaches must therefore be aware that superiors and subordinates will *always* have opinions on how things should be done and so continually seek out, manage and adapt to such 'decentred' influences (cf. Bevir and Rhodes, 2003; Bevir and Richards, 2009a, 2009b).

Grounded in political network literature, the 'decentred' perspective encourages a focus on the socially constructed nature of individual beliefs, extending to an acceptance that hierarchical structures often fail, or at least have less impact, in situations of distributed power. Hence, in practical situations, embracing a multitude of views (e.g. via 360-degree feedback: Cope *et al.*, 2007) will promote novel and integrated solutions 'owned' by the group in question (Lee *et al.*, 2009). But on the other hand, taking account of a multitude of views is time-consuming and may result in a loss of focus and thrust. This is especially the case when these views are prone to the performance-irrelevant, self-interested undercurrents that often blight elite settings. Accordingly, and recognising that success requires flexibility but never compromise, HP coaches need to be sensitive to the 'to and fro' nature of decision making *and* who are able to guide this process – i.e. who is really in charge. Of course, this is not to say that effective leadership is not important. In fact, the optimal blend for success is an astute amalgamation of open, critical discussion (as provided by the preceding conditions) with a clear understanding of who makes the final call.

Indeed, conferring control (or at least a sense of it: Fletcher and Arnold, 2011; Potrac and Jones, 2009) upon qualified others is not only beneficial but *necessary* for sustaining an HP environment. The knowledge, skills and active involvement of different professions (including head coach, specialist coach, doctor, physiotherapist, strength and conditioning coach, sport psychologist) are required when moving from one phase of training to another. This applies whether the situation involves a performer returning from injury or a team progressing from a conditioning to a tactical focus during pre-season training.

However, remembering that power will remain 'decentred' regardless of involvement level (where you stand in the pecking order), establishing a clear agreement about who is to coordinate particular stages of training is vital for ensuring that the whole team remains focused and united on the processes most likely to facilitate peak performance (Collins and Collins, 2011). Accordingly, negotiated and commonly understood (and adhered to) lines of demarcation are required, so that everyone knows who is 'in charge' of a particular phase and directs all comments through them. Imagine an injured athlete confused by advice on exercise from the doctor and suggestions of drugs or tests from the physiotherapist and you will have a perfect example of this process *not* working. This is not to say that various specialists won't have differing opinions about what is going on; indeed, as we will examine later, constructive disagreement is a crucial characteristic of an HP environment. In *properly* high perform*ing* settings, however, such disagreement and debate will go on away from performers (unless they specifically need to be involved) and staff will present a united front so that the athlete remains confident in the quality of the service they are receiving.

Certainly, without clearly demarcated lines of responsibility, disagreements will tend to roll on and on, often building to team-busting proportions. If managed well, however, this model of shared expertise will offer unrivalled solutions to many performance-related issues as many heads are almost always better than one (so long as they don't all talk at once). Accordingly, HP organisations/teams will therefore do well to recruit, develop and retain coaches who can provide a cutting-edge contribution from this 'bigger picture' perspective that both embraces and adjusts to the complexity in the environment. Only in moments of high drama, often occurring in the 'heat of competition', will 'command' decisions and decisive leadership represent the best option.

Modelling the skills required: competency versus expertise

When selecting and training their staff many businesses now make use of competency frameworks to describe, and then obtain, what they want from their employees in any particular role. Coaching and elite performance management are no different, and a number of set-ups around the world are developing their own competency-based models, usually in conjunction with recruitment, coaching or other business-related firms. For an example of this in coaching, refer to the website for High Performance Sport, New Zealand, which describes the model they have developed.

Such approaches are seductive, apparently simple and straightforward, offering a clear and concise picture of what is required. At one level this is true; role clarity is a commonly noted feature of high performing environments (Collins and Collins, 2011) so anything that details expected good practice is bound to have an effect. Thus, in the New Zealand example you will note items like 'High Speed Learning – seeks learning activities – or Getting the Best Out of Others – uses various approaches to ensure athlete learning' (High Performance Sport, New Zealand, 2011). Such lists of laudable aims and qualities are almost face valid in that no one could really disagree with them. As such, competency matrices are rather like good job descriptions, focusing the mind and seeking commonality in the way people work.

But let's take a slightly deeper look at the competency examples shown above. The big issue with the 'simple' competency description is that it is just too simple – it doesn't take account of the complexities that are involved in almost everything to do with humans (cf. Schippmann et al., 2000; Lievens et al., 2004). Thus, for example, what sort of learning activities should the ideal coach seek? When should they seek them, for what purpose and under what conditions? In similar fashion, how would the HP coach choose which approach to use with which athlete and at what time? There are rich research literatures to inform all these decisions but, crucially, the coach has to be on at least nodding terms with this knowledge if s/he is to make the optimum decisions. The coach will need to make many such decisions, since each of the exemplar areas are multifactorial (like most things in elite performance). The situation gets more challenging since elite performance almost invariably means coming up with novel answers to novel questions which take the performer to new heights. And the factors usually have an interactive effect so that a change in just one will impact on other factors in different ways at different times with different individuals. This combination of complexity[1] with interaction between individualisation and underpinning science and with overarching originality means that coaching is, in many ways, an exercise in making optimum decisions.

Accordingly, much of the authors' research and applied work in performance support has focused on understanding and improving the provider's decision-making skills as a fundamental

209

feature of their professional expertise. Clearly built on an essential knowledge base (which can be *somewhat* defined by approaches such as Applied Cognitive Task Analysis – ACTA; Militello and Hutton, 1998), this ability represents true expertise in the chosen field. So, for example, performance psychologists focus on why a certain approach should be used, as well as on knowing what might be useful (Martindale and Collins, 2010). In similar fashion, performance coaches design individual practices, sessions or entire programmes to attain an 'optimum blend' that involves a trade-off of a wide variety of possible actions (Abraham and Collins, 2011). The important message is that expertise, especially in high performance environments, is heavily dependent on decision-making skills and the possession of a knowledge base to underpin them. Unfortunately, this is something about which researchers and applied practitioners have an insufficient knowledge (cf. Yates and Tschirhart, 2006), making it a genuine area for growth.

As a consequence, evaluating and, most importantly, enhancing expertise in high performance practitioners is based on improving two factors: the quality and correctness of these decisions. First the quality: there is an expanding literature about the process of making good decisions and the interested reader is directed to articles by Klein and colleagues (e.g. Phillips *et al.*, 2004) on Naturalistic Decision Making or NDM. NDM highlights the successes of expert intuition as opposed to the more traditional heuristics and biases approach, which has commonly found intuitive judgement to be flawed. Since experts (as opposed to expertise) are often characterised by such 'intuitive', snap and gut-feel judgements, understanding and improving the process can bring about improved outcomes (see also Kahneman and Klein, 2009; Kiely, 2011). We return to this aspect in the later section on performance management.

The second issue is the correctness criteria that are applied to the decisions, whether they are initially taken by the performance director, the performance manager, the coach, the support practitioner or the athlete. Science is based on experimentation – try things out to get a sense of what will work. This approach also works in elite performance, although the 'experimentation' is at a less formal level. Thus, many coaches have training groups in which lower level performers act as 'tryouts' for new ideas. Such 'experimentation' is an important if neglected aspect of critical thinking, which is pushed as a key construct for elite practitioners across a variety of fields (Abraham and Collins, 2011; Schön, 1987). In the absence of such experimentation, and even in parallel to it, the criteria against which the decision is judged become very important. In elite performance, where new ideas are the lifeblood of success, best guesstimates are both common and important, and are best based on a really deep and detailed understanding of the underpinning principles of the activity. This 'declarative knowledge' (Abraham and Collins, 1998) is sometimes neglected but forms an essential part of the elite performance provider's armoury, enabling the discovery/invention process we describe here and also facilitating learning from others through ideas such as the 'community of practice' (Schön, 1987).

Nested thinking and the essentials of a 'multiple personality'

The inherent complexity of performance, together with the added, often unnecessary but perhaps inevitable complications of politics, personality and multiple stakeholders, mean that the HP manager and coach must develop the skills of decision making highlighted above but also the ability to pursue a number of agendas at once. Perhaps the best way of conceptualising and operating this multiple agenda is provided by the construct of nested thinking. Developed for sport psychology by Martindale and Collins (in press) and subsequently applied to coaching by Abraham and Collins (2011), the model looks at the way in which shorter term (micro/weekly) agendas are subsumed/embedded within meso/season and macro/annual or quadrennial plans. This is shown in Figure 11.1.

As Figure 11.1 shows, the coach (or any other support provider) focuses on the aims of the session for that week (micro) but also keeps the longer (meso and macro) term aims in mind. This sort of approach is typical at all stages of the performance pathway. In the earlier stages of the pathway, this is because training is generally aimed at longer term developmental agendas while in the later stages this is because the typical models of periodisation mean that the weekly schedule is but part of a bigger picture.

Reflecting ideas on decision making explored earlier, the right-hand column in Figure 11.1 shows the balance of Naturalistic Decision Making versus Classical Decision Making which

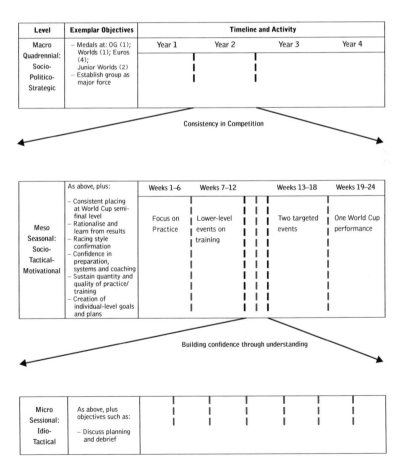

Figure 11.1 Nested thinking: an exemplar from short track speed skating

Adapted from Abraham & Collins, 2012

will characterise the thinking styles applied (see Abraham and Collins 2011 for a more detailed consideration of these factors). Day-to-day decisions tend to be more 'seat of the pants', while major planning across a year or years involves a more considered approach. The risks of short-term decision making, however, have already been explored (cf. Kahneman and Klein, 2009) and it is certain that, unless a weather eye is kept on the longer term, which is made explicit by nested thinking, decision making will not meet the criteria for the HP challenge.

CHALLENGE: HOW DO THE CHALLENGES, AND THEREFORE CHARACTERISTICS, CHANGE WITH AGE?

Put simply, the performer needs different things as s/he gets older and more mature. As the athlete gets older, both training age and performance challenges increase. In parallel, the coach also undergoes an important, but less acknowledged, maturation process that determines how s/he can work. Consider, for example, the differences in management style between Sir Alex Ferguson (the manager of Manchester United football team, who has over thirty years of HP experience) and a new young manager in their first football club. Differences are both logical and inevitable. So what does the progressions look like for both performer and coach?

What does a maturing athlete need at different stages of their career?

High performance maturity in a young athlete is evidence that they are able to compete at the top level. Crucially, however, this does not necessarily mean that they are *actually* mature physically or mentally. Due to this common contradiction, and the inherent complexity of the development process itself, guarantees of continued high level performance can never be made even if generic training environments are provided as the athlete matures. Accordingly, potent and bespoke mixes of a variety of elements have to be employed if the athlete is to avoid joining the pile of discards and some of the ingredients of these mixes are considered below.

First, the athlete has to develop a respectful and committed partnership with the right coach. The partnership has to have a clear training philosophy and an environment based on a good work ethic. Parental influence and input would have been crucial up to this point and continues, particularly with regard to compliant support, throughout these formative years. In parallel, an assessment of 'physical robustness' with clear evaluation measures has to be created, conducted and monitored. Physical development of the athlete has to be geared to the specific event that is being pursued *but also* has to be based on a clearly developed 'fundamental functional movement' skills process enabling the formation of a 'bedrock' of movement skills and physical/structural resilience. Drill-based and innovative, such programmes have to be learned, practised and increased in intensity for physical progression in 'robustness' to be made.

Second, for all but the simplest sports, the design and development of a simple but effective technical model, individualised within certain parameters, is essential. The technical model should be based on available expertise and benchmarked against known comparisons (e.g. current world-class performers of similar stature/characteristics) with a high input from the coach.

In pursuit of both these agendas, 'short-circuiting' within the training environment will take place based entirely on the declarative knowledge of the coach – in other words, on the basis of the coach's ability to reason out alternatives based on knowledge and experience (cf. our earlier ideas on decision making). There are no short cuts in high level performance but coaching knowledge and experience will ensure that time is not wasted on superfluous exercises and fads that can sometimes interfere with the development process.

Finally, and reflecting the need to develop an independent performer capable of surpassing the coach's skill level and past experience, the overall style must build autonomy. After all, world-class performers must achieve things that no one has achieved before; hence the need for independence of thought. As a general rule (bearing in mind that general rules have limited validity), simple instruction based on a clear cause-and-effect dialogue with a questioning style of delivery is a productive coaching method. This method works with all levels of maturity and encourages the athlete to take responsibility for their actions as early as it is possible to do so.

How does coaching style (and consequent management) change with age and achievement?

As highlighted above, empowering the performer to think and work for themselves must be a fundamental and essential element of the training environment if they are to develop and compete effectively in the HP environment. This has to start from day one. Furthermore, aside from the technical, physical and tactical evolution of the performer, there are a series of psychological characteristics that must be developed to both facilitate the development process towards elite status *and* to succeed at the top level (cf. MacNamara *et al.*, 2010a, 2010b). Being highly motivated and having a strong self-belief are very important for becoming an elite performer. Mental toughness under pressure is vital at the highest levels. Training and practice routines have to reflect these traits, day in and day out, for them to become naturally available without conscious thought in the heat of battle. Developing oneself and productive self-reflection have to be passed on to developing athletes, almost without them knowing that they are being armed with incredible weapons for the wars/challenges that lie ahead of them in the high performance arena.

Ultimately the aim of the high performance coach is to achieve redundancy in the high performance arena – the athlete performing intrinsically, unconsciously at the gold medal performance level all by themselves! However, even after this stage is reached, the coach is also available to cajole, direct or advise appropriately at any time or, better still, just enjoy that medal winning performance.

So, against these varied and varying demands, is there a pattern of *coach* development that can inform optimum management style? The best clue we have seen to this is based around a quote from Aldous Huxley: 'experience is not what happens to a man, it is what he does with what happens to him'. In the current context the implication is that, just because a coach has 'been around' does not mean that the coach/manager (Head Coach, Performance Director, etc.) can assume internalised knowledge and a better behavioural repertoire. In fact, just as with the performer, coaches will have varying levels of ability to learn from experience, as discussed earlier in this chapter. Crucially, a successful coach will also have an 'openness

213

to new ways' that also seems to be a reasonably measurable trait (Collins *et al.*, in press). Finally, as a general (but not automatic) rule, coaches with longer service and/or better records tend to be more overtly confident and clear in their direction, especially when dealing with less well-performed or less experienced athletes. Reflecting all these individual differences, the sensible coach/athlete manager will keep her/his style as individualised and non-systematic as possible while also, as a longer term agenda, setting up various developmental experiences, mentoring relationships and practice opportunities for coaches to maximise the 'internal learning and behaviour change' that results from what they have experienced. As with performers, maturity *does not* equal chronological age.

CULTURE: HOW DO YOU BEST ESTABLISH AND MANAGE A HIGH PERFORMANCE ENVIRONMENT?

Culture, simplistically described as 'how things are around here', is a key driver of HP. For example, as a major focus for his/her role, HP managers and coaches should work hard to establish a 'way of thinking, working and interacting' that focuses on effective processes. If they do this, the culture, and the terminology associated with it, permeates all aspects of the environment, with performers and coaches able to recognise and acknowledge, or recognise and question, examples of positive and negative behaviour.

As a crucial 'setting condition' for the culture, management structure and roles within it are an important consideration. Central to such structures, we suggest, is the part played by the HP manager. This comparatively new profession is increasingly acknowledged as an essential component of the HP system, supplementing rather than supplanting the coach by taking control of the increasingly complex team of support staff who characterise today's HP environment.

In the past (and still for some countries/sports), management systems in HP were characterised by the schematic in Figure 11.2.

Characterised by the slogan of the day, 'athlete centred – coach led', this system saw all control in the hands of the coach. Indeed, in the times before national sports institutes were the norm, a coach's status was often determined in part by her/his network of contacts, which could enable rapid and bespoke support to address a problem (cf. Moore *et al.*, 1997). The problem was that, in the absence of such a 'network', the coach was left high and dry in terms of where to turn for help. As another challenge, even if the network included all the requisite

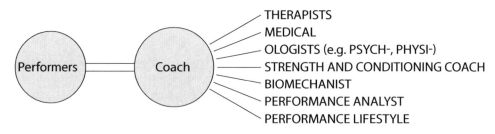

Figure 11.2 *The 'coach-led' HP system*

Adapted from Abraham & Collins, 2011

contacts, the coach was now often side-tracked from his/her primary role to deploy and manage the informal support team (which by its nature was not very team-like). Finally, coaches with world-class skills as technical coaches, sport science/medicine authorities *and* top-class managers were somewhat rare.

Figure 11.3 represents a more common picture today, with the manager role taken on by someone variously called a manager (e.g. football), performance director (e.g. cycling) or, sensibly, performance manager.

For a variety of reasons, this system is most common in operations based at a single venue, such as professional team sports clubs/academies or centralised training venues for elite squads. Here, the role of the manager is to allocate and deploy the various talents in an optimum blend that can be varied, even day by day, to keep things working as well as possible. Clearly, the manager needs to know enough about the potential contributions of each discipline so that the blend is kept as optimum as possible. In addition, they need a good sense of 'how to manage', which is not necessarily a universal characteristic of good coaches. In short, it may well be useful to consider this as a new discipline in itself, with specific training preparing the individual for this specialist role.

By contrast, Figure 11.4 shows a variant that is more appropriate when performers are geographically spread, each with their own coach or when there are a number of dispersed training squads. This is more appropriate as the close daily contact between coach and athlete is acknowledged and catered for. Such a system currently characterises several sports, such

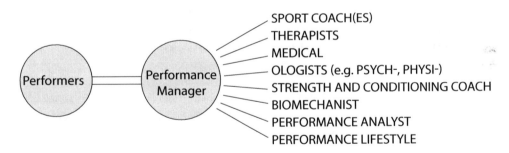

Figure 11.3 *The performance-centred approach in a single site setting*

Adapted from Abraham & Collins, 2011

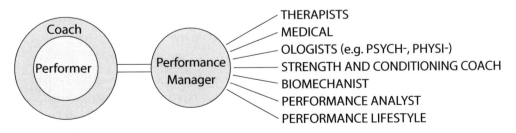

Figure 11.4 *The performance manager system in distributed HP settings*

Adapted from Abraham & Collins, 2011

as athletics and some martial arts. In fact, this approach may also offer a better fit with the social mores of the sport; for example, the relationship between athlete and coach is very close in many sports. In such cases, treating the coach and athlete as a performance dyad is a practical best-fit solution.

Certainly, in all cases the performance manager (in whichever guise) can serve as a useful sounding board/devil's advocate/challenger of ideas. Given experts' penchant for 'gut-feel' decisions, some challenge is an essential feature of the HP environment.

Optimising coach relationships and interactions with 'the management'

Finally, we must consider how the relationships between coaches and managers can be tuned for the best performance impact. We have already alluded to the micro-politics that characterise any high intensity human relationships (Potrac and Jones, 2009). Indeed, despite the commonly expressed aversion to politics publicly espoused by coaches, there is no doubt that many gain advancement by a level of Machiavellian skill that would not disgrace a professional politician. In fact, catering for the political dimension of elite coaching should not be a taboo subject; rather, it is an inevitable feature of any human interaction and must be addressed, just not overdone or seen as the sole focus as is the case with a few coaches.

Butcher and Clarke (2008) contend that 'rational' development is not enough in today's environment. However logical and worthy an agenda is, its implementation must be accompanied by a well thought through and consistently executed, political intervention. Buy-in and overt support from senior management is an essential feature of this change process, a fact that is demonstrated by the first author's recent experiences in HP sport. Consequently, 'managing upwards' (cf. our earlier comments of the decentred approach), literally having an explicit focus on managing perceptions, expectations and opinion of those above you in the hierarchy, remains an important aspect of work for coaches and managers involved in HP.

As another aspect of senior management/HP worker interaction, the working environment must be considered. The work environment should facilitate and encourage interactions that question aspects of practice (Collins, 2003). Genuinely challenging and yet supportive environments are hard to generate. However, we would contend that such 'shared expertise', flat structure collations of specialists represent the most effective coaching and support teams in the United Kingdom at present. British Cycling, Leicester Tigers Rugby and Team Bromley (the support structure to skeleton bob sliders Shelley Rudman and Kristen Bromley) are three good examples. Such constant-challenge, low external threat environments require careful development and constant, soft-touch maintenance. They are based on mutual respect and clear task delineation (cf. Collins and Collins, 2011) but, once established, will continue to generate both immediate (through performance outcomes, for example) and longer term rewards (by constant enhancement of process).

All these qualities are a good deal more likely to be present in an HP team where everyone is confident in the contribution s/he is making, where each contribution is acknowledged and valued, and where each person's opinion is valid and important. Several studies in HP (e.g. Moore and Collins, 1996), attest to the destructive impact of role conflict in sports teams. By contrast, positive and well-managed conflict is an essential characteristic. Accordingly, making sure everyone knows (and respects) the contribution that each person is making is an important management function for all environments. This is perhaps harder to achieve in HP settings as 'hangers on' are almost inevitable. However, the complexity of the recipe for the performance pie makes it pointless to attempt to disaggregate the contributions of individuals and/or disciplines to the overall performance. Such a reductionist approach, commonly but unfortunately applied by bean counters in many funding agencies, can destroy all but the strongest 'teamwork' HP support environments. So, know why and value individuals, or get rid if you don't think they are needed, and take the praise (and the stick) as a group!

SUMMARY

Given this book's focus on management, it seems pertinent to conclude by offering some summary points on what the ideal HP worker is like and how they may best be applied. Of course, like any job description, there will be essential and desirable characteristics, although in some cases, these may well be 'either/or'. In doing so, we take as read the empathy and commitment to HP, the high level product knowledge in the particular sport/support discipline, plus the essential luck of the draw in having a talented performer/the opportunity to work at this level and the chance to get through the early mistakes that almost all make; a tolerant/understanding boss is a big advantage here.

So these 'givens' notwithstanding, what are the characteristics that make for success in HP? One of the most significant is the approach to innovation. As we suggested earlier in the chapter, there are some HP coaches/workers who know what they know and stick with it. Generally experienced and charismatic, with high street cred due to previous successes, these individuals (we have termed them 'vampires'; Collins et al., 2012) are most effective in HP with almost fully developed performers. Their success is generally most dependent on their autocratic, 'I know best', interpersonal manner, which generates compliance and confidence in the performer. By contrast, the open-minded coach/worker, hungry for new ideas and always looking for the next edge (we call them 'wolves'), will be the major innovator and is often associated with a performer over longer periods, bringing them through to success and keeping them there for a while. These two extremes are often orthogonal (either/or) and will clearly require different styles of management and leadership to bring out the best. Working with both types on your team (very much the norm) adds to the challenge. The chapter should have offered you some insights and systems that will help.

Related to this factor is the ability to work with and fully exploit fellow experts. As standards continue to rise, HP success is often related to making the best use of available expertise, indeed searching it out where it is most needed (cf. our earlier comments on networks). Of course, effective management of the team is essential to make the most of what you have. So, having management ability (or knowing you haven't and passing this role to someone else) is also important.

Finally, regular review, reinvention and nested action are central to HP success in modern sport. Once again, look at the personal ideals and philosophy of the coach/worker and how these fit with what they do and how they work (epistemological chaining: see Grecic and Collins, in press). We would encourage readers to take these characteristics and to consider how the various concepts in the chapter may best be applied.

217

DISCUSSION QUESTIONS

1   What are the pros and cons of a competency-based approach to the recruitment and professional development of HP management?
2   How might a manager employ ideas from decentred theory in setting and managing the culture and environment in the HP setting?
3   How would you expect a manager's approach to change with age and time in the job?
4   What factors may determine the best placement in a staffing schematic for the performance manager role?
5   Discuss the importance of decision making for HP coaches.

GUIDED READING

Collins, D., Button, A. and Richards, H. (Eds) (2011). *Performance psychology: A practitioner's guide*. Oxford: Churchill Livingstone.
   This text offers a strong overview of the HP environment and several levels, considering applications from performance and organisational psychology to enhance both effectiveness and outcome.
Jones, R. L., Armour, K. M. and Potrac, P. (2004). *Sports coaching cultures: From practice to theory*. London: Routledge.
   This book presents reflections on practice from elite coaches across football, rugby, athletics, swimming and netball, paying particular attention to the personal and social complexity of the coaching challenge.
Reid, C., Stewart, E. and Thorne, G. (2004). Multidisciplinary sport science teams in elite sport: Comprehensive servicing or conflict and confusion? *The Sport Psychologist*, 18, 204–217.
   This paper provides a first-hand insight into developing and working in an elite sport multidisciplinary sports science team, considering the complex interpersonal needs and challenges of optimal functioning and performance.

NOTE

1   Readers might like to refer to ideas on complex systems to improve understanding of the implications here (e.g., Bowes and Jones, 2006; Cilliers, 2000).

BIBLIOGRAPHY

Abraham, A. and Collins, D. J. (1998). Examining and extending research in coach development. *Quest*, 50, 59–79.
Abraham, A. and Collins, D. (2011). Taking the next step: Ways forward for coaching science. *Quest*, 63, 366–384.

Bevir, M. and Rhodes, R. A. W. (2003). *Interpreting British governance*. London: Routledge.

Bevir, M. and Richards, D. (2009a). Decentring policy networks: A theoretical agenda. *Public Administration*, 87(1), 3–14.

Bevir, M. and Richards, D. (2009b). Decentring policy networks: Lessons and prospects. *Public Administration*, 87(1), 132–141.

Bloom, G. A., Stevens, D. E. and Wickwire, T. L. (2003). Expert coaches' perceptions of team building. *Journal of Applied Sport Psychology*, 15, 129–143.

Bowes, I. and Jones, R. L. (2006). Working at the edge of chaos: Understanding head coaching as a complex, interpersonal system. *The Sport Psychologist*, 20(2), 235–245.

Butcher, D. and Clarke, M. (2008). Politics and worthy management agendas. *Management Online Review*, available at www.morexpertise.com, ISSN 1996-3300.

Case, B. (1987). Leadership behaviour in sport: A field test of the situational leadership theory. *International Journal of Sport Psychology*, 18(4), 256–268.

Chelladurai, P. and Saleh, S. D. (1978). Preferred leadership in sport. *Canadian Journal of Applied Sport Sciences*, 3, 85–92.

Cilliers, P. (2000). What can we learn from a theory of complexity? *Emergence*, 2(1), 23–33.

Collins, D. J. (2003). *Developing high performance personnel in an institute environment*. Invited presentation at the International Forum on Elite Sport, Loughborough, 14 September.

Collins, D. and Collins, J. (2011). Putting them together: Skill packages to optimize team/group performance. In D. Collins, A. Button and H. Richards (Eds), *Performance psychology: A practitioner's guide* (pp. 361–380). Oxford: Elsevier.

Collins, D., Abraham, A. and Collins, R. (2012). On vampires and wolves – Exposing and exploring reasons for the differential impact of coach education. *International Journal of Sport and Exercise Psychology*, 43, 255–271.

Cope, C. J., Eys, M. A., Schinke, R. J. and Bosselut, G. (2007). Coaches' perspectives of a negative informal role: The 'cancer' within sport teams. *Journal of Applied Sport Psychology*, 22, 420–436.

Côté, J., Salmela, J., Trudel, P., Baria, A. and Russell, S. (1995). The coaching model: A grounded assessment of expert gymnastic coaches' knowledge. *Journal of Sport and Exercise Psychology*, 17, 1–17.

Fletcher, D. and Arnold, R. (2011). A qualitative study of performance leadership and management in elite sport. *Journal of Applied Sport Psychology*, 23(2), 223–242.

Grecic, D and Collins, D. (in press). The epistemological chain: Application in sport. *Quest*.

Harris, N. (2011). *Global Sports Salaries Survey 2011*. Available at http://sports.espn.go.com/espn/news/story?id=6354899.

High Performance Sport, New Zealand (2011). Available at www.sparc.org.nz/en-nz/high-performance/Coaches/High-Performance-Coaches/Coach-Accelerator/.

Jones, R. L., Armour, K. and Potrac, P. (2004). *Sports coaching cultures: From practice to theory*. London: Routledge.

Jones, R. L. and Wallace, M. (2005). Another bad day at the training ground: Coping with ambiguity in the coaching context. *Sport, Education and Society*, 10(1), 119–134.

Kahneman, D. and Klein, G.(2009). Conditions for intuitive expertise: A failure to disagree. *American Psychologist*, 64(6), 515–526.

Kiely, J. (2011). Planning for physical performance: The individual perspective. In D. Collins, A. Button and H. Richards (Eds), *Performance psychology: A practitioner's guide*. Oxford: Elsevier.

Kingston, K. M. and Hardy, L. (1997). Effects of different types of goals on processes that support performance. *The Sport Psychologist*, 11, 277–293.

Krane, V. and Williams, J. M. (2006). Psychological characteristics of peak performance. In J. M. Williams (Ed.), *Applied sport psychology: Personal growth to peak performance* (pp. 207–227). New York: McGraw-Hill.

Lee, S., Shaw, D. J. and Chesterfield, G. (2009). Reflections from a world champion: An interview with Sir Clive Woodward, director of Olympic performance, the British Olympic Association. *Reflective Practice*, 10(3), 295–310.

Lievens, F., Sanchez, J. I. and De Corte, W. (2004). Easing the inferential leap in competency modelling: The effects of task-related information and subject matter expertise. *Personnel Psychology*, 57, 881–904.

MacNamara, Á., Button, A. and Collins, D. (2010a). The role of psychological characteristics in facilitating the pathway to elite performance. Part 1: Identifying mental skills and behaviours. *The Sport Psychologist*, 24, 52–73.

MacNamara, Á., Button, A. and Collins, D. (2010b). The role of psychological characteristics in facilitating the pathway to elite performance. Part 2: Examining environmental and stage related differences in skills and behaviours. *The Sport Psychologist*, 24, 74–96.

Martindale, A. and Collins, D. (2010). But *why* does what works work? A response to Fifer, Henschen, Gould and Ravizza. *The Sport Psychologist*, 24, 113–116.

Martindale, A. and Collins, D. (in press). A professional judgment and decision making case study: Reflection-in-action research. *The Sport Psychologist*.

Militello, L. G. and Hutton, R. J. B. (1998). Applied cognitive task analysis (ACTA): A practitioner's toolkit for understanding cognitive task demands. *Ergonomics*, 41(11), 1618–1641.

Moore, P. and Collins, D. (1996). Role conflict in team sports settings. In H. Steinberg and J. Annett (Eds), *Workshop report on teamwork* (pp. 112–130). Leicester: British Psychological Society.

Moore, P., Collins, D. and Burwitz, L. (1997). *The development of sporting talent*. Technical Report, English Sports Council.

Phillips, J. K., Klein, G. and Sieck. W. R. (2004). Expertise in judgment and decision making: A case for training intuitive decision skills. In D. K. Koehler and N. Harvey (Eds), *Blackwell handbook of judgment and decision making*. Oxford: Wiley-Blackwell.

Potrac, P. and Jones, R. (2009). Power, conflict and cooperation: Toward a micropolitics of head coaching. *Quest*, 61, 223–236.

Schön, D. (1987). *Educating the reflective practitioner*. San Francisco, CA: Jossey-Bass.

Schippmann, J. S., Ash, R. A., Battista, M., Carr, L., Eyde, L. D., Hesketh, B., Kehoe, J., Pearlman, K. and Prien, E. P. (2000). The practice of competency modelling. *Personnel Psychology*, 53, 703–740.

Yates, J. F., and Tschirhart, M. D. (2006). Decision-Making Expertise. In K. A. Ericsson, N. Charness, R. R. Hoffman and P. J. Foltovich (Eds), *The Cambridge handbook of expertise and expert performance*. Cambridge: Cambridge University Press.

Chapter 12

Managing athletes' post-athletic careers

Anke Reints and Paul Wylleman

Vrije Universiteit Brussel

LEARNING OUTCOMES

Upon completion of this chapter the reader should be able to:

1   identify reasons for athletic retirement and recognize its influence on the transition out of elite sport;
2   define and identify multilevel challenges related to the transition out of elite sport;
3   identify factors that facilitate adjustment to the post-athletic career;
4   recognize the importance of an idiosyncratic, holistic and lifespan approach when providing career support services to support athletes preparing to retire and those who have retired; and
5   identify available career support services provided to senior, retiring and retired athletes.

OVERVIEW

In view of the significance of athletes' transition out of elite sport into a post-athletic career life, this chapter provides information and research data on the relevance of athletic retirement and the provision of athlete career support services to retiring and retired athletes. In particular, this chapter provides an outline of the service provisions of twenty-seven career development projects worldwide regarding education management, career management and life skills training. This analysis resulted in the conclusion that athlete service providers need to create or develop services targeting the social development of athletes, the detraining after retirement and the identity development of retiring and retired athletes. Finally, specific recommendations are formulated for stakeholders to recognize the significance of athletic retirement and the challenges retired athletes face via an awareness-creating campaign and by doing so they not only manage and minimize possible negative influences on athletic performance, but also optimize the retirement from elite sport.

THE SIGNIFICANCE OF ATHLETIC RETIREMENT

International athletic performances and success are only possible when personal resources (e.g. time, energy, money) are invested to such a degree that competing in elite sport becomes equal to a professional occupation (Conzelmann and Nagel, 2003). As a consequence, athletes are left with little time to engage in the self-development and self-exploration needed to make responsible and effective life choices outside the sport milieu (Gordon and Lavallee, 2004). As a result, athletes may not be prepared for athletic retirement (Murphy, 1995; Scanlan *et al.*, 1989; Taylor and Ogilvie, 2001) and experience distressful reactions upon athletic retirement (Lally, 2007; Lavallee and Robinson, 2007) including a heightened sense of hopelessness (Gardner and Moore, 2006), identity crisis (Brewer *et al.*, 1993; Ogilvie and Howe, 1982), emotional difficulties (Allison and Meyer, 1988) and decreased self-confidence and life satisfaction (Werthner and Orlick, 1986).

Taking into account its significance, the aim of this chapter is to provide in the first instance more insight into the possible causes and consequences of athletic retirement. Second, using survey data of services provided by twenty-seven career development projects worldwide, the importance of providing three types of career support (i.e. education management, career management, life skills training) to (retiring) senior and retired athletes will be highlighted. In conclusion, recommendations will be formulated not only on the need to provide specific career support services (i.e. social development, detraining, identity development), but also on the way stakeholders can recognize the significance of athletic retirement and the challenges retired athletes face via an awareness-creating campaign in order to optimize retirement from elite sport.

CAUSES AND CONSEQUENCES OF ATHLETIC RETIREMENT

Four major reasons for athletic retirement have been delineated (Ogilvie and Taylor 1993; Taylor and Ogilvie, 2001). A first major reason is injury. As athletes are rarely prepared for a sudden end to their careers, this involuntary retirement is not only particularly difficult to cope with (Werthner and Orlick, 1986) but has also been shown to lead to more dissatisfaction with their entire career among retired athletes (Alfermann and Stambulova, 2007). A second reason is ageing that, due to, for example, loss of strength, vision sharpness and coordination (Nevid and Rathus, 2005; Whitbourne, 1996), will lead athletes to perceive their athletic skills and prowess to wither and thus may cause them to retire. In fact, few professional athletes remain at the top of their sport after their mid-30s (Kail and Cavanaugh, 2008). A third major reason is deselection that takes place when athletes, on the basis of the decision of the team coach or sports federation, are excluded from a team or a sport programme or when they do not get a new professional contract. Finally, athletes will, of course, also retire from elite sport by free choice (Alfermann, 1995; Taylor and Ogilvie, 2001).

Whether forced (i.e. injury, age, deselection) into or chosen freely, retirement remains a critical life event. Notwithstanding its possible criticality, Coakley (1983) suggests that athletic retirement can also be seen as a form of 'social rebirth', that is, an opportunity to change one's lifestyle and to welcome a new career with an open mind. In fact, retired athletes recognized several positive aspects to their athletic retirement, including the possibility of changing their lifestyle, being able to spend time on other aspects of their lives and being able to have a more serene life (Fernandez et al., 2006). Therefore, while athletic retirement brings with it several (critical) challenges, the quality of the retirement itself and of the following post-athletic career will depend on different factors.

Athletic identity is one of the factors that can interfere with the way in which athletes cope with athletic retirement, particularly when an athlete's self-identity is derived primarily from his or her role as an athlete (Brewer et al., 1993). After having dedicated close to 100 per cent of their resources and time to the pursuit of their athletic goals, athletes may experience identity foreclosure – a process in which athletes strongly commit to the athlete role while not exploring other social roles (Brewer et al., 1993) and thus not developing coping strategies necessary to deal with a new life and a new lifestyle. Therefore, athletes who undergo athletic retirement may experience disruption to, as well as loss of their identity (Pearson and Petitpas, 1990).

In addition to loss of identity, poor performances, not having enough assistance (e.g. a lack of support from family, friends and coaches), a lack of coping strategies, a lack of career options and financial difficulties (Sinclair and Hackfort, 2000) may also contribute to a more difficult retirement. Finally, Werthner and Orlick (1986) add to this list several other factors, including unaccomplished goals, encountering daily reminders of missed opportunities and coaching and management disputes.

Certainly not all athletes experience athletic retirement as traumatic. While earlier studies reported 70–80 per cent of athletes to have experienced a traumatic retirement, more recent studies suggest this percentage to be in-between 13 and 15 per cent (Alfermann, 1995; Wylleman et al., 1993). Athletes' perceptions of the control they had in deciding whether or not to retire has been found to impact the quality of their athletic retirement. In this way, voluntary retirement was shown to be strongly correlated to heightened feelings of self-efficacy, which is important for behavioural change and adjustment (Alfermann et al., 2004; Bandura, 1997; Cecić Erpič et al., 2004; Taylor and Ogilvie, 2001). It should be noted, however, that ending an athletic career voluntarily does not necessarily preclude athletes from having transition difficulties (Kerr and Dacyshyn, 2000).

Athletes also tend to adjust better if they have made plans for their career after retirement. This process of pre-retirement career planning has been described as a cognitive process of structuring the future whereby the social environment as well as individual circumstances of an athlete's life are taken into account (Alfermann et al., 2004). Athletes who value, or who have an occupational plan, show not only significantly more satisfaction with life at the time of retirement in comparison to those who do not have such a plan (Perna et al., 1999) but are also found to adjust better to, and experience more satisfaction with their new lifestyle (Hawkins and Blann, 1996).

Finally, the degree to which athletes consider alternative role possibilities is also an indicator of successful athletic retirement (Blinde and Greendorfer, 1985). Having a strong athletic identity has been found to negatively impact the transition process, but when athletes pursue other interests and activities during their careers, the transition is less disruptive (Sinclair and Orlick, 1993). Athletes who maintain a balance in their life are more ready to explore other roles and challenges into which they can channel their energy (Werthner and Orlick, 1986).

Taking into account the challenges and demands of athletic retirement, the question remains: what kind of support is and should be provided to retiring and retired athletes?

SUPPORT PROVISION FOR RETIRING/RETIRED ELITE ATHLETES

Worldwide several career development programmes were established to support athletes' personal growth, balance their lifestyles and to optimize life after retirement (Lavallee *et al.*, 2001; Wylleman *et al.*, 2004).

The Olympic Job Opportunities Program (OJOP) was initiated in 1996 in Australia, South Africa and the United States to create job opportunities for potential Olympians, by identifying job positions and providing a professional network, career analysis services, personal aptitude tests and interview skills training (Gordon, 1995). The Canadian Olympic Athlete Career Centre (OACC) was launched in 1985 to assist Canadian athletes through retirement by offering them career and education planning. Some concrete services offered by the OACC included pre-retirement planning, clarification of career planning needs, life skills training and transition workshops. The Athlete Career and Educational Program (ACE) was initiated to provide career and education services to Australia's elite athletes, and included individual athlete assessments to map their needs, educational flexibilities, career and education planning and a transition programme.

In Belgium, the Vrije Universiteit Brussel provides since 1988 through its Study and Talent Education Program support to its elite student-athletes in order to enable them to achieve academic and athletic excellence and thus prepare for their future athletic retirement (De Knop and Wylleman, 2008). The Vrije Universiteit Brussel also initiated and developed in 2007 the career development programme 'Carrièrebegeleiding Topsport Vlaanderen'. This programme, which since 2011 is administered by the Flemish sports administrative body BLOSO, provides via two career counsellors career support services (e.g. advice on career and lifestyle management) to Flemish elite athletes to enable them to combine elite sports with an academic career or with employment as preparation for their post-athletic careers.

While each has its specificities, these career development programmes have in common that they cover services in three major areas, namely career management, education management and life skills training. These three areas of career development services will now be discussed in more detail using data from a major survey of twenty-seven career development programmes worldwide (for more details see Reints, 2011).

SERVICE PROVISIONS OF ATHLETE CAREER DEVELOPMENT PROGRAMMES

Education management

Several studies have shown the positive influence of educational status on the quality of athletic retirement and post-athletic careers. For example, Cecić Erpič *et al.* (2004) demonstrated that a higher educational status contributed to retired athletes' vocational opportunities during their post-athletic career. Taking into account the positive influence of athletes' educational status on the post-athletic career, European institutions of higher education have been found to increase their efforts to cater for the demands of 'dual' careers (i.e. combination of an athletic and academic career) (De Knop et al., 1999). Services aimed at facilitating a dual career generally include distance learning, providing tutors, a flexible exam and study schedule, and elite sport schools.

Results from a survey of services provided by twenty-seven career development programmes (Reints, 2011) showed that distance learning and a flexible exam schedule are generally provided to athletes in higher education. About three-quarters of these programmes provide flexible study schedules for athletes in secondary and higher education.

By providing support services enabling the combination of an elite athletic and academic career, elite athletes are able to prepare for a post-athletic career dominated by a labour market where more and more companies want employees – including retired elite athletes – with high education grades (Stambulova et al., 2007).

Career management

Career management involves career support services aimed at meeting athletes' requirements for their transition to the labour market. Sturges et al. (2002) identified two types of career management: the first is aimed at furthering the athlete's career within an organization, while the second type is focused on furthering their career outside the organization. Athletes who want to develop a career within their sport organization (e.g. as coach) may benefit from the opportunity to acquire a coaching certificate and from networking with decision-makers. For athletes who aim at pursuing a professional career outside the sport system, job placement strategies may help them to find a job matching their knowledge and skills.

Career management strategies cannot only facilitate retirement from elite sport (Hawkins and Blann, 1996; Zaichkowsky et al., 1997) but also decrease the amount of anxiety athletes may have about their post-athletic life (Hinkle, 1994; Murphy, 1995). Career management has thus become an integral part of career development programmes designed to address athletes' long-term career development needs.

A majority of the twenty-seven surveyed career development programmes provided career management services to senior and retired athletes: for senior athletes, programmes assisted in the development of job application skills (82 per cent), job placement strategies (78 per cent) and networking skills (67 per cent); for retired athletes, services included development of job application skills (67 per cent), job placement strategies (74 per cent) and networking skills (56 per cent) (Reints, 2011).

Life skills training

Life skills are skills transferable to other fields or careers, regardless of where they were initially developed (Bolles, 1996). Examples include problem-solving skills, organizing skills, goal-setting skills, self-motivation skills and the ability to perform under pressure. As shown by Petitpas et al. (1992) teaching athletes to develop life skills not only increased their level of

225

confidence about skill transfer to non-athletic settings, but challenged also their doubts about their retirement and post-athletic careers. Life skills training have thus become an integral part of athlete career development programmes (Hesketh, 1997).

The survey of the twenty-seven career development programmes revealed that while more than three programmes in four (78 per cent) helped senior athletes in developing life skills (e.g. goal setting skills, time management training, media training), few programmes actually provided a similar support to retired athletes (Reints, 2011). Services most frequently provided included teaching skills directly related to the transition out of elite sport (74 per cent), goal setting training sessions (44 per cent) and relationship training (26 per cent).

It can be concluded that most career development programmes take a proactive stance towards athletic retirement by teaching not only retired athletes but also senior athletes life skills that increase their resources to cope with the demands of retirement and post-athletic life (Danish *et al.*, 1993; Petitpas *et al.*, 1992). This approach aligns with research showing that, as successful experience with a previous transition is predictive of later transition success, programmes are best implemented when athletes start developing into elite athletes (Schlossberg *et al.*, 1995). Career development should therefore concentrate not exclusively on retirement and post-retirement interventions, but also on the pre-retirement phase (Lavallee *et al.*, 2001).

CASE STUDY 12.1
SPORT CAREER TRANSITION: THE CASE OF ELITE INDIGENOUS AUSTRALIAN BOXERS

Megan Stronach

University of Technology, Sydney

Australian sport has provided career opportunities for a few talented Indigenous professional athletes, but their transition to life after sport has tended to be difficult. The sport of boxing has attracted many Indigenous competitors, both in professional and amateur ranks. Research into the retirement experiences of fourteen Indigenous boxers has enabled an understanding of their post-sport career decision making. Boxers are understandably reliant on their physicality, which limits career alternatives, particularly if their physical condition deteriorates abruptly. The sample of Indigenous boxers had some engagement with educational and vocational training, yet their post-boxing career aspirations focused on occupations that complemented their physicality, such as personal training. Indigenous boxers also viewed retirement as linking with their belief in the virtues of physical culture, Indigenous values of kinship and both family and community obligations.

Indigenous Australian peoples have for many years had the highest rates of unemployment, the lowest rates of education and the greatest health problems among all socio-economic groups in Australia. For a few talented Indigenous athletes, sport has provided career opportunities. The sport of boxing has attracted many Indigenous competitors, both in professional and amateur ranks, offering glamour, status, financial reward and a means of overcoming racism. Indigenous boxers have won silver and bronze medals at Olympic Games and have won numerous professional world titles. In spite of this proud history, little is known about the adjustment to life after sport of Indigenous boxers. Research into the retirement experiences of fourteen Indigenous Australian boxers, as part of a broader Ph.D. study, provides an understanding of their post-sport career decision making. Data is derived from interviews, and is supplemented by the 10-point Athletic Identity Measurement Scale (AIMS) (Brewer *et al.*, 1993).

The AIMS is a short questionnaire measuring Athletic Identity (AI). AI is 'the degree of importance, strength, and exclusivity attached to the athlete role that is maintained by the athletes and influenced by environment' (Li, 2006, p. 22). Many researchers (Brewer *et al.*, 1993; Lavallee *et al.*, 1995, 1997) have acknowledged advantages associated with a strong AI, in particular a determination to achieve athletic excellence. However, there are also risks associated with high levels of AI, many of which are associated with sport career transition. Athletes who place too much emphasis on sport to the exclusion of other identity factors are more likely to experience social and psychological difficulties during sport cessation or transition periods, such as being cut from a team, experiencing an injury, or retirement from sport (Brewer *et al.*, 1993; Lavallee and Grove, 1997; Li, 2006).

Identified issues

The data from interviews of the fourteen boxers, and from their responses to the 10-point AIMS scale, reveal the following issues:

(a) Sporting acumen has long been a source of pride for many Indigenous Australian people. However, there is a widespread and longstanding stereotypical belief (and self-belief) about 'natural' sporting talent. While there is no scientific evidence to support such a belief (Adair and Stronach, 2011; Tatz and Adair, 2009), it can have the effect of causing Indigenous athletes to focus on sport rather than more intellectual occupations as their most promising career paths (Godwell, 1997).

(b) As a corollary, boxers considered they were not 'naturally' suited to positions of responsibility or decision making outside of sport performance. Although they resented the lack of Indigenous personnel in administration, coaching and management, none of them indicated a desire to assume a senior role in their sport.

(c) Boxers held a special set of personal values: pride in their Indigenous heritage, unique kinship and community obligations and a commitment to support disadvantaged Indigenous people, in a formal or informal capacity. The obligation to 'give back' to family and community was regarded as the 'natural order' of Indigenous men. Several boxers described their own difficult, even dysfunctional family backgrounds, assuming that these experiences imbued them with the skills to provide expert assistance to others in similar situations.

Problems in sport career transition

Stereotypical beliefs and the unique values outlined above influenced the boxers' career decision-making. A narrow range of career choices emerged, and along with them came certain challenges and constraints. On the whole, the post-boxing career aspirations of the group were limited to occupations that complemented either their physicality or their Indigenous cultural values. The challenges they faced when seeking a post-boxing career include:

(a) There is a strong belief in 'natural' athleticism, as boxers identified strongly with the athlete role and recorded comparatively high levels of AI. Becoming a Personal Trainer was the most popular career or career choice, with seven of the fourteen boxers stating that they worked in the occupation or would like to do so. The required qualification is the Vocational and Educational Training (VET) Certificate III in Fitness, which 'prepare(s) you to work in any capacity on the gymnasium floor with confidence' (Fitness Institute Australia, 2009). A career as a personal trainer thus promises a continued involvement with the sport and a reasonable livelihood. Yet only one of the fourteen interviewees had completed the required training. Furthermore, boxers described serious ongoing physical health problems related to their sport careers that were likely to restrict their capacity to 'work on the gymnasium floor' for any length of time.[1]

(b) Many of the interviewees mentioned they wanted to work in remote and dysfunctional Indigenous communities. This is certainly a noble intention, but attempts to turn such activity into a career are fraught with difficulties, and may be to the detriment of the economic well-being of the ex-athletes themselves. Few such community support roles generate much (or indeed any) income, and they offer little prospect or further opportunities for professional development.

(c) Boxers who had been part of the Australian Institute of Sport (AIS) elite boxing squad had received support and career counselling from the Athlete Career and Education (ACE) programme personnel, and had also encountered VET programmes. Indeed, several had commenced the training for their chosen vocation (most often the Certificate III in Fitness or Youth support work) while on scholarship at the AIS, yet only two had actually completed the training requirements. Like many elite athletes, the boxers' intense involvement with sport had placed significant restrictions on opportunities for educational attainment. As a result, several had left school early or quit education programmes. They felt justified in choosing sport over education, albeit with some regret at having no real academic qualifications at the end of their sport career.

Strategies to overcome these problems

Elite Indigenous boxers are highly competent and focused individuals. They have the potential to be role models whose interests and talents extend beyond the sporting field, and, given the right conditions, they have the ability to move into other occupational spheres once their sport careers are over. But to do this they need appropriate support and career counselling throughout their athletic careers. The support which had, at times, been provided to the boxers in this study had come from non-Indigenous people. The boxers require culturally appropriate support, and they believed that this support should ideally come from other Indigenous people. While it may not be feasible, logistically, for all Indigenous boxers around Australia to have access to a counsellor with Indigenous heritage, a base-line position ought to be that personnel involved in Indigenous development and transition programmes undergo education in culturally appropriate ways to engage with athletes of varying cultural backgrounds. Areas of need are:

(a) Encouragement and support from coaches and managers to actually complete VET and other academic programmes.

(b) Support to access a broader range of career pathways, which also complement Indigenous values of 'giving back' to community, such as teaching, health, police work and so on.

(c) For many of the former boxers, community support work will likely remain philanthropic and purely voluntary. However, if Indigenous athletes are provided with appropriate leadership and mentoring skills, such as those provided by the National Aboriginal Sporting Chance Academy (NASCA), the National Rugby League's (NRL) 'One Community' or the Australian Football League's (AFL) 'Flying Boomerang' programmes, it can also be socio-culturally significant and 'life-changing', for both the mentor and the mentee. Leadership training provided in these programmes is valuable and worthy preparation, with many potential transferable applications, and similar programmes could be developed by boxing organizations.

(d) As elite athletes, these boxers have much to contribute to their sports organizations. A normal progression is often from athlete to coach or manager, but this pathway seems not to be pursued by Indigenous boxers. It appears that the cause is nothing to do with potential or ability, but simply to the widely held belief (and self-belief) that while Indigenous boxers may perform well in the ring, they are not suitable to lead, manage or coach. Therefore a concerted effort is needed from those in positions of authority to refute this stereotypical belief and bring about a shift in attitudes, policies and practices.

Case study questions

1   AI is mentioned as a major predictor of quality of sport career transition. Discuss other factors that might also influence this process.

2   The world-renowned ACE Programme is run through the AIS and its affiliated state and territory academies and institutes. What are some strengths and weaknesses of this programme?

3   Australia is generally regarded as a multicultural nation. With this in mind, discuss how National Sporting Organizations (NSOs) in Australia can better support and nurture elite athletes as they approach the end of their sport careers.

4   In his book *Darwin's Athletes* John Hoberman challenges the notion of the 'natural black athlete'. Discuss this notion in light of the statistical 'over-representation' of Indigenous athletes in high-profile Australian sports such as AFL, NRL and boxing.

SUMMARY

While research reveals that the most common difficulties encountered by athletes upon retirement are psychosocial in nature (Cecić Erpič et al., 2004), very few support services for retired athletes target this type need. A first recommendation for athlete service providers consists therefore of creating or developing more services (e.g. relationship training, networking, social skills training) targeting the social development of athletes (e.g. Rees and Hardy, 2000; Wylleman et al., 2006). This can also be accomplished by having athletes explore ways of broadening their social identity and by encouraging them to expand their social support system to people outside of the sports context. Furthermore, as support from family, friends, peers (e.g. other former elite athletes) may assist retired athletes to adjust to athletic retirement (Botterill, 1981; Sinclair and Orlick, 1993; Werthner and Orlick, 1986), it is also recommended that these significant others are made aware of the significance of athletic retirement and of the ways they can contribute to the quality of the post-athletic career.

As athletic retirement typically involves a significant decrease in athletic participation, former athletes are also confronted with a significant decrease in the hours they spend practising and competing, which often induces substantial bodily changes (e.g. weight gain, muscle loss). In order to prepare for, and cope with these changes, retiring and retired athletes should be encouraged to gradually 'detrain', that is, decrease their physical training, rather than abruptly end their athletic career. Besides preventing them from unpleasant physical retirement, a gradual decrease in engaging in elite sport may also protect retired athletes from experiencing the diminished self-worth and loss of identity that can be caused by abrupt physical transformations (Stephan et al., 2003). A second recommendation therefore is that, while most career development programmes enable athletes to get physical and medical support, they should also raise awareness among the to-be retired athletes of the importance of detraining and provide them with specific support and facilities to detrain.

A third aspect related to retirement from elite sport is athletes' feeling that they are no longer famous and suddenly 'like everyone else', causing changes in self-worth (Stephan et al., 2003). Concerns about not being exceptional any more are most likely to occur among athletes who made an exclusive commitment to their athletic career (Brewer et al., 1993). Cecić Erpič et al. (2004) found that a strong athletic identity was related to more severe and frequent psychological difficulties at retirement, suggesting that it is important to provide retiring elite athletes with support aimed at reducing the degree of exclusivity of athletic identity (Shachar et al., 2004). Furthermore, athlete service providers are also encouraged to teach retiring and retired athletes life skills that may directly help them to achieve success outside of the sporting domain (Petitpas and Schwartz, 1989) and thus provide them the possibility to develop other identities.

Finally, stakeholders (e.g. national Olympic Committees, international sports federations, universities) are encouraged to take leadership in acknowledging the significance of athletic retirement and the challenges faced by retiring and retired athletes. This could be done via an awareness-creating campaign, aimed at athletes and coaches, and involving all other stakeholders (e.g. parents, lifetime partners, businesses, actors on the labour market). Such a campaign should in the first instance address a concern frequently expressed by athlete service providers, namely their inability to fully and effectively reach and inform all athletes, coaches and athletes' families and friends about the significance of the athletic retirement and the need for career support services.

Second, the focus of his campaign should at all times be on the development of self-regulating and self-reliant athletes. Athletes should be kept aware of the impact and consequences of retirement from sport, and they should be encouraged to engage in career and pre-retirement planning.

Third, this campaign should also promote and encourage providers of career development programmes to optimize the currently available career support services by focusing on an idiosyncratic, holistic and lifespan approach as advocated in the developmental model of Wylleman and Lavallee (2004) (see Chapter 9 for more details). By taking into account the reciprocal and interactive nature of the four different developmental contexts (i.e. athletic, psychological, psychosocial, academic/vocational), the impact of athletic retirement can be understood more easily. For example, as the model illustrates, retirement from elite sport is accompanied by the transition into a professional occupation. When this is the case, entering the labour market also brings about, on top of other transition demands (e.g. change in identity, bodily changes), specific demands that 'athletes-in-transition' need to cope with (e.g. the need to learn new professional competences, adaptation to new daily routines, new professional responsibilities).

Finally, this campaign should underline the need to provide career support services before retirement, that is, during the athletic career itself. Career development programmes should have not only a problem-focused approach (e.g. support is provided when the retired athlete reports a problem) but also an educational (i.e. proactive) approach. In this way, athletes' readiness for athletic retirement could be enhanced by increasing their sense of control over changes related to their retirement and post-athletic career and by enabling them to develop resources for managing these changes (e.g. increased self-efficacy to cope with psychological challenges, improved financial management skills).

DISCUSSION QUESTIONS

1   In what ways can career planning facilitate retirement from elite sport?
    Career planning facilitates retirement from elite sport in several ways. First, it prepares athletes for their post-athletic career by providing future career options, setting career goals and identifying employment opportunities. The development of various individual life skills as a result of career planning instils an attitude that promotes a recognition of the positive opportunities offered by retirement rather than a purely loss-oriented attitude (i.e. 'social rebirth' rather than 'social death'). Career counsellors can assist athletes in developing these individual life skills by understanding the career process and identifying personal career needs.

In addition, having a retirement plan increases the likelihood of a voluntary retirement. Ending the athletic career by free choice has been found to be the most desirable option, because the decision resides within the athletes' control (Taylor and Ogilvie, 2001). This subjective feeling of control over retirement plays a key role in the quality of the transition process, as voluntary retirement is strongly correlated to heightened feelings of self-efficacy, which is important for behavioural change and adjustment (Bandura, 1997).

2   What are multilevel challenges related to the transition out of elite sport?
Retirement challenges may be related to several contexts, including demands faced at the psychological, psychosocial and academic/vocational levels (Wylleman and Lavallee, 2004). For example, at the psychological level, retiring athletes may have to deal with the loss of an identity that is dominated by their role as an elite athlete. For many athletes, athletic identity is central, as they have dedicated 100 per cent of their resources and time to the pursuit of their sporting goals. As a result, athletes may experience identity foreclosure in which athletes strongly commit to the athlete role while not exploring other social roles (Brewer *et al.*, 1993) and which inhibits their personal development, as they may not have developed the coping strategies necessary to deal with a new life and a new lifestyle.

One psychosocial challenge faced by retiring athletes is a changing social environment as athletes may lose contact with individuals who were significant to them during their athletic career. Research has shown that athletes who experience a difficult retirement transition often mention the loss of their support system as a number one reason for a difficult transition (Cecič Erpič *et al.*, 2004).

At the academic/vocational level, athletes may be confronted with demands related to their entry into the labour market. For example, due to time constraints and a strong commitment to sport, many athletes have not had the opportunity that many of their peers have had to gain experience by doing summer jobs or internships. As a consequence, these athletes may, in comparison to their non-athletic peers, lack the relevant professional competences required to succeed in their post-athletic careers. Experiencing this 'occupational delay' (Naul, 1994) may be a particular problem for athletes as research shows that employers often value job-related experience and skills over qualifications (Spilsbury and Lane, 2000).

3   What role can stakeholders play in optimizing the transition of athletes out of elite sport?
Stakeholders, including national Olympic Committees and international sports federations, may take the lead in acknowledging the significance of the ending of athletes' careers and the challenges they face after they retire from elite sports. This could be done via an awareness-raising campaign that supports athletes in achieving a well-balanced and holistic career development. This campaign should also promote and encourage athlete service providers to optimize the currently available provision of career support services by focusing on an idiosyncratic, holistic and lifespan approach. These career support services should be available during the athletic career itself.

KEY TERMS

- Athletic retirement
- Post-athletic career
- Athlete career support services
- Career development programmes
- Indigenous
- Athletic identity
- Vocational education
- Culture

NOTE

1 Injuries identified by interviewees included fractures, resulting deformities and arthritis, particularly of the hands, osteo-articulatory stress, scratched or detached retina, severe cardiovascular dysfunction, renal dysfunction and cognitive impairment.

BIBLIOGRAPHY

Adair, D. and Stronach, M. (2011). Natural born athletes? Australian Aboriginal people and the double-edged lure of professional sport. In J. Long and K. Spracklen (Eds), *Sport and challenges to racism* (pp. 117–134). London: Palgrave Macmillan.

Alfermann, D. (1995). Career transitions of elite athletes: Drop-out and retirement. In R. Vanfraechem-Raway and Y. Vanden Auweele (Eds), *Proceedings of the ninth European congress of sport psychology* (pp. 828–833). Brussels, Belgium: European Federation of Sports Psychology FEPSAC.

Alfermann, D. and Stambulova, N. B. (2007). Career transitions and career termination. In G. Tenenbaum and R. C. Eklund (Eds), *Handbook of sport psychology* (3rd edn, pp. 712–736). New York: Wiley.

Alfermann, D., Stambulova, N. and Zemaityte, A. (2004). Reactions to sport career termination: a cross-national comparison of German, Lithuanian, and Russian athletes. *Psychology of Sport and Exercise*, 5, 61–75.

Allison, M. T. and Meyer, C. (1988). Career problems and retirement among elite athletes: The female tennis professional. *Sociology of Sport Journal*, 5, 212–222.

Australian Institute of Sport. (2004). The National Athlete Career and Education Program (ACE): A balanced approach to sporting excellence. Available at http://ausport.gov.au/ais/ace/about.

Bandura, A. (1997). *Self-efficacy: The exercise of control*. New York: W.H. Freeman.

Blinde, E. M. and Greendorfer, S. L. (1985). A reconceptualization of the process of leaving the role of elite athlete. *International Review for Sociology of Sport*, 20, 87–93.

Bolles, R. N. (1996). *What color is your parachute? A practical manual for job-hunters and career-changers*. Berkeley, CA: Ten Speed Press.

Botterill, C. (1981). What 'endings' tell us about 'beginnings'. In T. Orlick, J. Partington and J. Salmela (Eds), *Mental training for coaches and athletes* (pp. 164–165). Ottawa, ON: Coaching Association of Canada and Sport in Perspective.

Brewer, B. W., Van Raalte, J. L. and Linder, D. E. (1993). Athletic identity: Hercules' muscles or Achilles heel? *International Journal of Sport Psychology*, 24, 237–254.

Cecić-Erpič, S., Wylleman, P. and Zupančič, M. (2004). The effect of athletic and non-athletic factors on the sports career termination process. *Psychology of Sport and Exercise*, 5, 45–59.

Coakley, J. (1983). Leaving competitive sport: retirement or rebirth? *Quest*, 35, 1–11.

Conzelmann, A. and Nagel, S. (2003). Professional careers of the German Olympic athletes. *International Review for the Sociology of Sport*, 38, 259–280.

Danish, S. J., Petitpas, A. J. and Hale, B. D. (1993). Life development intervention for athletes: Life skills through sports. *The Counseling Psychologist*, 21, 352–385.

De Knop, P. and Wylleman, P. (2008). 20 jaar Topsport en Studie in publicaties en presentaties (20 years elite sport and study in publications and presentations), unpublished raw data.

De Knop, P., Wylleman, P., Van Houcke, J. and Bollaert, L. (1999). Sports management – A European approach to the management of the combination of academics and elite-level sport. In S. Bailey (Ed.), *Perspectives: The interdisciplinary series of Physical Education and Sport Science* (pp. 49–62). School Sport and Competition (Vol. 1). Oxford: Meyer & Meyer Sport.

Fernandez, A., Stephan, Y. and Fouquereau, E. (2006). Assessing reasons for sports career termination: Development of the athletes' retirement decision inventory (ARDI). *Psychology of Sport and Exercise*, 7, 407–421.

Fitness Institute Australia (2009). Available at www.fia.com.au/FIAcourses/programs_fr.html, accessed 7 December 2009.

Gardner, F. and Moore, Z. (2006). *Clinical sport psychology*. Champaign, IL: Human Kinetics.

Godwell, D. (1997). Aboriginality and rugby league in Australia: An exploratory study of identity construction and professional sport. Dept of Kinesiology, University of Windsor.

Gordon, S. (1995). Career transitions in competitive sport. In T. Morris and J. Summers (Eds), *Sport psychology: Theory, applications and issues* (pp. 474–501). Brisbane, Australia: Wiley.

Gordon, S. and Lavallee, D. (2004). Career transitions in competitive sport. In T. Morris and J. Summer (Eds), *Sport psychology: Theory, applications and issues* (2nd edn, pp. 584–610). Brisbane, Australia: Wiley.

Hawkins, K. and Blann, F. W. (1993). *Athlete/coach career development and transition*. Canberra, Australia: Australian Sports Commission.

Hesketh, B. (1997). Dilemmas in training for transfer and retention. *Applied Psychology*, 46, 317–386.

Hinkle, J. S. (1994). Integrating sport psychology and sports counseling: Developmental programming, education, and research. *Journal of Sport Behavior*, 17, 52–59.

Kail, R. V. and Cavanaugh, J. C. (2008). *Human development: A life-span view* (5th edn). Belmont, CA: Wadsworth Publishing.

Kerr, G. and Dacyshyn, A. (2000). The retirement experiences of elite, female gymnasts. *Journal of Applied Sport Psychology*, 12, 115–133.

Lally, A. (2007). Identity and athletic retirement: A prospective study. *Psychology of Sport and Exercise*, 8, 85–99.

Lavallee, D., Gorely, T., Lavallee, R. M. and Wylleman, P. (2001). Career development programs for athletes. In W. Patton and M. McMahon (Eds), Career development programs: Preparation for life long career decision making (pp. 125–133). Camberwell, Australia: Australian Council for Educational Research Press.

Lavallee, D. and Robinson, H. K (2007). In pursuit of an identity: A qualitative exploration of retirement from women's artistic gymnastics. *Psychology of Sport and Exercise*, 8, 119–141.

234

Lavallee, D., Gordon, S. and Grove, J. R. (1995). *Athletic identity as a predictor of zeteophobia among retired athletes.* Paper presented at the 12th Annual Conference of Counseling Athletes, Springfield, MA.

Lavallee, D., Gordon, S. and Grove, J. R. (1997). Retirement from sport and the loss of athletic identity. *Journal of Personal and Interpersonal Loss*, 2, 129–147.

Li, H. Y. (2006). *Validation of the athletic identity measurement scale with a Hong Kong sample.* Melbourne: Victoria University.

Murphy, S. (1995). Transitions in competitive sport: Maximizing individual potential. In S. M. Murphy (Ed.), *Sport psychology interventions* (pp. 331–346). Champaign, IL: Human Kinetics.

Naul, R. (1994). The elite athlete career: Sport pedagogy must counsel social and professional problems in life development. In D. Hackfort (Ed.), *Psycho-social issues and interventions in elite sport* (pp. 237–258). Frankfurt: Lang.

Nevid, J. S. and Rathus, S. A. (2005). *Psychology and the challenges of life: Adjustment in the new millennium* (9th edn). Hoboken, NJ: Wiley.

Ogilvie, B. C. and Howe, M. (1982). Career crisis in sport. In T. Orlick, J. T. Partington and J. H. Salmela (Eds.), *Proceedings of the fifth world congress of sport psychology* (pp. 176–183). Ottawa: Coaching Association of Canada.

Ogilvie, B. C. and Taylor, J. (1993). Career termination issues among elite athletes. In R. N. Singer, M. Murphey and L. K. Tennant (Eds), *Handbook of research on sport psychology* (pp. 761–775). New York: Macmillan.

Pearson, R. E. and Petitpas, A. J. (1990). Transitions of athletes: Developmental and preventive perspectives. *Journal of Counseling and Development*, 69, 7–10.

Perna, F. M., Ahlgren, R. L. and Zaichkowsky, L. (1999). The influence of career planning, race, and athletic injury on life satisfaction among recently retired collegiate male athletes. *The Sport Psychologist*, 13, 144–156.

Petitpas, A. J. and Schwartz, H. (1989). Assisting student athletes in understanding and identifying transferable skills. *The Academic Athletic Journal*, 6, 37–42.

Petitpas, A. J., Danish, S., McKelvain, R. and Murphy, S. (1992). A career assistance program for elite athletes. *Journal of Counseling Development*, 70, 383–386.

Rees, T. and Hardy, L. (2000). An investigation of the social support experiences of high-level sports performers. *The Sport Psychologist*, 14, 391–409.

Reints, A. (2011). *Development and validation of a model of career transition and the identification of variables of influence on ending the career among elite athletes.* Brussel: VUB Press.

Scanlan, T. K., Stein, G. L. and Ravizza, K. (1989). An in-depth study of former elite figure skaters: 1. Introduction to the project. *Journal of Sport and Exercise Psychology*, 11, 54–64.

Schlossberg, N., Waters, E. B. and Goodman, J. (1995). *Counseling adults in transition: Linking practice with theory.* New York: Springer.

Shachar, B., Brewer, B., Cornelius, A. E. and Petitpas, A. J. (2004). Career decision-making and adjustment difficulties among retired Athletes: A comparison between coaches and noncoaches. *Kinesiologia Slovenica*, 10, 71–85.

Sinclair, D. A. and Orlick, T. (1993). Positive transitions from high-performance sport. *The Sport Psychologist*, 7, 138–150.

Sinclair, D. A. and Hackfort, D. (2000). The role of the sport organisation in the career transition process. In D. Lavallee and P. Wylleman (Eds), *Career transitions in sport: International perspectives* (pp. 131–142). Morgantown, WV: Fitness Information Technology.

Spilsbury, M. and Lane, K. (2000). *Skills needs and recruitment practices in central London.* London: Focus Central London.

Stambulova, N. B., Stephan, Y. and Jäphag, U. (2007). Athletic retirement: A cross-national comparison of elite French and Swedish athletes. *Psychology of Sport and Exercise*, 8, 101–118.

Stephan, Y., Bilard, J., Ninot, G. and Delignières, D. (2003). Repercussions of transition out of elite sport on subjective well-being: A one-year study. *Journal of Applied Sport Psychology*, 15, 354–371.

235

Sturges, J., Guest, D., Conway, N. and Davey, K. M. (2002). A longitudinal study of the relationship between career management and organizational commitment among graduates in the first ten years at work. *Journal of Organizational Behavior*, 23, 731–748.

Tatz, C. and Adair, D. (2009). Darkness and a little light: 'Race' and sport in Australia. *Australian Aboriginal Studies*, 2, 1–14.

Taylor, J. and Ogilvie, B. C. (2001). Career termination among athletes. In: R. N. Singer, H. E. Hausenblas and C. M. Janelle (Eds), *Handbook of sport psychology* (pp. 45–58). New York: Wiley.

Werthner, P. and Orlick, T. (1986). Retirement experiences of successful Olympic athletes. *International Journal of Sport Psychology*, 17, 337–363.

Whitbourne, S. K. (1996). *The aging individual: Physical and psychological perspectives.* New York: Springer.

Wylleman, P., De Knop, P., Menkehorst, H., Theeboom, M. and Annerel, J. (1993). Career termination and social integration among elite athletes. In S. Serpa, J. Alves, V. Ferreira and A. Paula-Brito (Eds), *Proceedings of the eighth world congress of sport psychology* (pp. 902–906). Lisbon: International Society of Sport Psychology.

Wylleman, P. and Lavallee, D. (2004). A developmental perspective on transitions faced by athletes. In M. Weiss (Ed.), *Developmental sport and exercise psychology: A lifespan perspective* (pp. 507–527). Morgantown, WV: Fitness Information Technology.

Wylleman, P., Alfermann, D. and Lavallee, D. (2004). Career transitions in perspective. *Psychology of Sport and Exercise*, 5, 7–20.

Wylleman, P., De Knop, P., Verdet, M-C. and Cecić-Erpič, S. (2006). Parenting and career transitions of elite athletes. In S. Jowett and D. Lavallee (Eds), *Social psychology of sport* (pp. 233–247). Champaign, IL: Human Kinetics.

Zaichkowsky, L., Lipton, G. and Tucci, G. (1997). Factors affecting transition from intercollegiate sport. In R. Lidor and M. Bar-Eli (Eds), *Innovations in sport psychology: Linking theory and practice* (pp. 782–784). Netanya, Israel: The Wingate Institute of P.E. and Sport.

Part C

Issues in the management of high performance sport

Chapter 13

The influence of commercialisation and globalisation on high performance sport

Hans Westerbeek

Institute of Sport, Exercise and Active Living (ISEAL), Victoria University

Allan Hahn

Australian Institute of Sport and Institute of Sport, Exercise and Active Living (ISEAL), Victoria University

LEARNING OUTCOMES

Upon completion of this chapter the reader should be able to:

1   describe what the main trends have been with regard to the globalisation of sport;
2   identify the sport products for which high performance sport (HPS) is the central and critical element;
3   explain why the commercialisation of sport, and of HPS in particular, has led to the emergence of a sub-industry of high performance experts and facilitators such as agents, coaches and consultants;
4   explain how the pressure to perform applies not only to the athlete but to others involved in HPS as well; and
5   provide an overview of how sport business, sport governing bodies and sport high performance institutes are required to carefully consider and balance each others' interests and objectives.

OVERVIEW

This chapter shows that the explosive development of HPS is driven by its economic value. Sport has become a global industry and global sport properties achieve enormous market penetration through the mass media. Athletes and their international support teams are increasingly exposed to problems and temptations due to the financial rewards they can acquire. We show how general management and marketing models are now applied to HPS and in the concluding case study we provide an insight into the day-to-day functions of an international HPS operation – with a specific focus on the commercialisation of sport science research that is being conducted to allow for world-beating performances. This chapter is about the globalisation of sport and how the resulting increase in its economic value can affect HPS. It is important to realise that HPS is simply sport at the highest level of performance possible – just as it was 100 years ago. What has changed and continues to change is the HPS context and the rules by which HPS is being played. The context and the rules continue to be rewritten because of the commercial interests that are invading the HPS landscape.

THE EMERGENCE OF A GLOBAL SPORT INDUSTRY

Various authors have commented on the emergence of sport as an industry and a field of business (Trentberth and Hassan, 2011; Westerbeek and Smith, 2003). The mechanisation of production during the Industrial Revolution in England was instrumental in the evolution of sport. Games changed from being unstructured play into codified and structured competitions between individuals or teams. The latter, of course, is broadly defined as sport. It can be argued that the Industrial Revolution signalled the start of the development of sport

Table 13.1 *Sport globalisation trends*

1   Proliferation of sports on television and other media/entertainment mechanisms (radio, print, internet, pay television).

2   Ongoing increase in value of genuinely global sport properties, including athletes.

3   Blurring of what is sport and what is entertainment.

4   Vertical and horizontal integration of sport enterprises by entertainment and media companies.

5   Integration and consolidation of sport, leisure, recreation, television, film and tourism industries into elements of the entertainment industry.

6   Growth in the economic effects and impacts of sport.

7   Increase in venture capital and investment in transnational sports and sport properties.

8   Defragmentation of sport governance.

9   Simultaneous professionalisation and marginalisation of smaller sports and leagues (they will professionalise their management and marketing, but the gap between the sport enterprises that are globally successful and those that remain only domestically viable, will enlarge).

10 Convergence of economic power in sport ownership. Fewer and fewer will own more and more of sport.

11 Development and utilisation of technologies that enhance the entertainment value and radically improve the diffusion and distribution of sport to new markets.

12 Increase in world acceptance of capitalism as the pre-eminent economic philosophy and of sport as an effective vehicle for achieving wealth.

13 Increase in 'Americanisation' and 'Westernisation' of sport.

Source: Westerbeek and Smith (2003: 48–49)

as an industry. In many ways the Industrial Revolution was also the start of globalisation – in other words, of the integration of economies around the world, underpinned by trade and financial interaction. An important part of globalisation is the movement of people or labour, and knowledge or technology, across borders. In high performance sport, this mainly involves the movement of athletes, coaches, scientists and managers. An interesting aspect of HPS is that customers (spectators) also frequently move across borders to watch the sporting spectacle 'live' onsite. Table 13.1 shows thirteen trends identified by Westerbeek and Smith (2003) that summarise how and why sport has become a globalised field of business.

It is beyond the scope of this chapter to discuss each of the thirteen trends in detail. Suffice to say that the economic development of the sport industry, facilitated by the rapidly expanding influence of information and multimedia technologies, has led to a global sport industry that continues to grow in size, scope and opportunities. According to PricewaterhouseCoopers or PwC (2011) we can divide market share for elite sporting events across four regions – North America (41 per cent), Europe/Middle East/Africa or EMEA (35 per cent), Asia Pacific (19 per cent) and Latin America (5 per cent). Global revenues related to elite sporting events amounted to US$121 billion in 2010. PwC predict that global revenues will grow to US$145 billion in 2015 and that Latin America will achieve the biggest growth rate at 4.9 per cent per annum, followed by North America (4 per cent), Asia Pacific (3.9 per cent) and EMEA (2.9 per cent). It can be derived from these figures that even during times of global economic hardship the sport industry has shown surprising resilience. Elite sporting events seem to be a 'safe' marketing option for organisations that continue to seek a public platform for the promotion of their products and services. HPS in that regard provides a refreshingly simple proposition – wanting to be the best and always striving to win. It is in this context of hyper-commercialisation of sport that HPS is further considered in this chapter.

GLOBAL SPORT PROPERTIES – MASS MEDIA MARKETS – ATHLETES AS ENTERTAINERS

It could be argued that all thirteen sport business globalisation trends presented in Table 13.1 apply specifically to elite sport. Although elite sport and mass participation sport are often considered to be part of the same continuum, few would dispute that HPS is in many respects very different from grassroots sport. HPS has characteristics that make it commercially highly attractive. In many ways, the defining characteristics of sport, such as being competitive and having an uncertain outcome, are amplified at the elite level. The 'us versus them' scenario, combined with not knowing who is going to win, seems to captivate and magically attract billions of sport spectators. Of course, to be popular a sport needs to be 'easy on the eye' and reasonably simple to understand for people of all ages and cultural backgrounds. In the competition for a share of the global sport spectator market it also is a major advantage to be among the sports that entered the market first. Football (soccer), for example, was one of the first sports to be exported. In the mid-1800s it spread from England to other countries and continents and has become the sport of the masses. This has given football (soccer) a hard-to-beat lead in the global popularity stakes.

The most conclusive evidence that we can present to show that the economic value of HPS has been further multiplied by the application of media technology is presented in

Figure 13.1. It shows the ever-increasing value of media rights to two of the most global sports properties – the Olympic Winter and Summer Games. We have taken the 1980 monetary values of media rights to Moscow (Summer Games at US$88 million) and Lake Placid (Winter Games at US$21 million) as our baseline data. These amounts represent the standardized (= 1) scores in 1980. The graph shows the relative increase in value of media rights compared to the 1980 figures. In other words, the Winter Games' value in 2006 is 40 times that of the 1980 value. It can be seen that although the absolute value of the Summer Games (19 times $88 million) is almost twice that of the Winter Games (40 times $21 million), the snow-covered Olympic event has increased its value for media partners significantly more than the Summer Games.

Both these events have a truly global reach. Cumulative audiences amount to billions of spectators, and as such, offer mind-boggling commercial exposure opportunities through the mass media. Due to the gigantic economic value of sport events, the owners of the mass media and their sponsors place sky-high expectations on the athletes and their support staff. And let us not forget the expectations of those who ultimately pay the bills for everything – the sport fans.

THE PRESSURE TO PERFORM

Grassroots sport participants play sport primarily for fun and maybe personal performance objectives rather than money. The professional athlete, on the other hand, is driven by economic interests to develop into the best athlete he or she can possibly be, and is exposed to a number of risks that are unique to HPS. Because HPS careers are often short, and because few athletes reach the level of performance that will make them independently wealthy during their careers, athletes inevitably push physical, mental and, increasingly, ethical boundaries in order to earn as much as they can while they can.

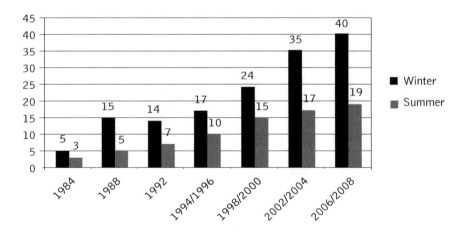

Figure 13.1 The standardised monetary value of media rights to Winter and Summer Olympic Games, 1980–2008

Source: www.olympic.org

HPS risks include a number of temptations to which some athletes may succumb as a result of intense performance pressure and the lure of large sums of money. The most pressing temptations involve performance enhancing drugs and increasingly, gambling. Athletes may be pressed to provide information on match conditions or even to influence the course of a match. Further pressure is exerted by the societal expectation that elite athletes have a responsibility to act as role models for the younger generation. Any misbehaviour, or failure to behave as expected, may have immediate and dire consequences regarding the commercial value of the athlete. And with regard to the commercial value of athletes, it is important to note that growth in the global market for HPS is primarily driven by the growth of sport sponsorship (PwC, 2011). In other words, most of the additional money is coming from commercial investors in sport, and not the sport spectators (income from gate revenues is predicted to plateau). The commercial entities will demand a (performance) return on their investment.

As a direct result of the increasing complexity of the high performance environment, a whole sub-industry of coaches, agents, managers, advisers, consultants and trainers has developed. In the demanding world of HPS, professionals are required to help athletes perform at their peak. The difference between public glory and financial wealth on the one hand, and good but not good enough on the other, is measured in thousandths of seconds. In this sub-industry, the professionals that are supposed to support the athletes are also subjected to performance pressure. Player agents in football have been known to trade young African talents between clubs as often as possible as they receive a cut of the fee for each transfer. High performance coaches or sport medicine doctors have often been accused of providing their athletes with supplements on the banned substances list. It is therefore clear that not only the athletes themselves but also those supporting them are exposed more and more to the lure of making money by illicit means.

Even within the bounds of completely fair play, there is enormous pressure to achieve on-field success in order to reap the available financial rewards. This pressure provides a stimulus for innovations such as new approaches to training and the development of new sporting equipment that can yield performance gains. The introduction of a winged keel to the Australian 12-m racing yacht that captured the 1983 America's Cup was an early example of the latter, with more recent cases involving refinements to design of bicycles, swimming costumes and skeleton helmets. Questions have been raised as to whether such innovations constitute 'techno-doping' and many sporting organisations are now finding it necessary to mandate that any new equipment must be accessible to all competitors for a specified period before major events. Commercial technology companies are frequently willing to invest in the development of new equipment for use at major sporting events in the knowledge that massive exposure is likely to create a wider market.

The financial incentives associated with the HPS sector are also stimulating the emergence of highly professional and systematic approaches to the preparation of athletes and teams. These approaches entail the adoption of general management and marketing principles, and closely resemble the product development and innovation processes existing in other competitive industries, as outlined in the section below.

FROM PRODUCT DEVELOPMENT/INNOVATION TO ATHLETE DEVELOPMENT INNOVATION

In many industries, success depends on the development and marketing of 'winning' products. The process typically occurs in accordance with a model such as that illustrated in Figure 13.2. A vital first step is the identification of the necessary product characteristics. This often requires considerable insight into contemporary population trends and a substantial amount of market research. The next steps involve establishing a blueprint for an ideal product and the planning and costing of manufacture. The blueprint then needs to be assessed in relation to the availability of funds and other resources, and modifications may have to be made. Once the design and planning phases have been completed, the necessary components or 'raw materials' must be acquired, and a production team with appropriate expertise and task commitment assembled. This is followed by the implementation of production and the testing and refinement of the product for purposes of quality assurance. Eventually, the product is released on to the market and actively promoted. The outcome is carefully monitored, and the information is used to guide changes to the product or the design of entirely new products as part of an iterative feedback loop.

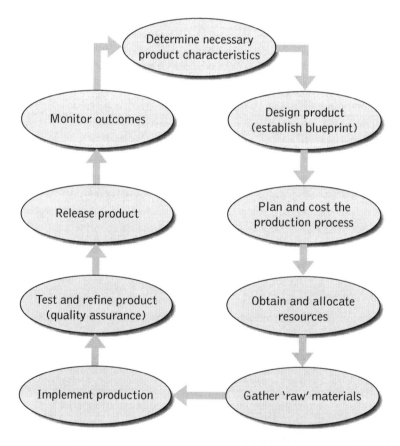

Figure 13.2 *An overview of the standard industrial product development process*

The above model for product development and innovation has become operative also in HPS as part of the quest for the rewards on offer. It is pursued in a number of different contexts within a multifaceted HPS network that includes numerous sports, all incorporating international, national, regional and club-level organisations that operate in highly competitive environments.

National sporting organisations may be seen as 'factories' or 'warehouses' that aim to produce world-beating athletes. To consistently achieve this aim, they need to have a clear understanding of the attributes that will be required to win at peak competitions such as world championships and Olympic Games. The development of that understanding requires knowledge of the characteristics of current champions together with an analysis of performance trends. It might also incorporate ideas thought to have potential for transformational effects on performance. The understanding enables the formulation of a blueprint for an internationally successful athlete or team. Attention must then be given to the feasibility of realising the blueprint. This entails detailed planning and costing of the developmental process, and in some cases changing the plan to reflect budgetary realities. A highly expert support team consisting of coaches, managers, scientists and medical staff then has to be put in place. 'Raw materials' – consisting of athletes regarded as having the potential to conform with the blueprint – must then be recruited into what is in essence a systematic production cycle. Once production has been initiated, the quality of its output is continually evaluated by involving the athletes in competitions of progressively increasing standard and in some cases conducting regular sports science testing. In time, the athlete products of the system are released into the highly competitive markets associated with peak global sporting events and their performances are closely observed. The results help to guide product design and development procedures for the ensuing years. The parallels with the models employed in the innovative manufacturing industries are obvious.

The rules of the global marketplace also extend their reach to HP sport. Standard economic principles now apply to the product development activities of national sporting organisations. The activities require the availability of capital which, at least in Australia, generally comes from three main sources – membership fees, government grants and corporate sponsorship. Since level of expenditure influences competitive outcomes (Bloomfield, 2003; De Bosscher et al., 2008; Forrest and Simmons, 2000; Pahls 2006), more often than not those national sporting organisations able to attract the greatest amount of revenue from these sources, and spend a significant part of that money on their elite development programmes, tend to be the most successful in producing internationally successful products. The success tends to reinforce their position, but they need to be constantly vigilant to ensure ongoing alignment with the major financial and social agendas of their supporters.

For globalised manufacturing industries, many governments have 'incubator' programmes in which they invest funds to assist and accelerate the development of products considered capable of yielding significant returns to the nation. In Australia and a number of other countries, such programmes have arisen also in the HPS industry as part of the more professional approach that has been driven by the globalisation and commercialisation of sport. The Australian Institute of Sport (AIS) and the state sports institutes and academies are effectively industry incubators that greatly assist selected national sporting organisations in the area of product realisation. They achieve this by running intensive training programmes for elite and emerging athletes, providing outstanding training facilities, employing leading coaches, enabling high-level scientific and medical support, and increasing the access of athletes to appropriate competitions. A crucial point concerning the incubators is that the extent of their engagement with national sporting organisations depends on the ability of the athletes to definitively demonstrate their potential to develop into products that are exceptional by global standards. Some of the incubators have themselves attracted corporate support because of their media profiles and popular association with success, and have begun taking on the characteristics of public–private partnerships.

A further similarity between manufacturing and HPS concerns the role of specialised groups in getting products to major markets and vigorously promoting them. National Olympic and Paralympic Committees are comparable to the product distributors and retailers of other fields, since they play a key role in 'packaging' and 'branding' of the athlete products, gaining endorsements, introducing the products into the most publicly visible international 'markets', advocating for them, ensuring optimal conditions in the marketplace, informing relevant authorities of outcomes and recommending follow-up actions. Of course, these committees are themselves driven by economic forces since their ability to generate income to maintain and expand their activities depends on product performance. They therefore have a vested interest in the entire product development process.

Manufacturing facilities are generally subject to scrutiny from industry regulatory bodies charged with guarding against illicit product development processes that might provide a competitive advantage but could cause human harm. Here, too, there are equivalents in the HPS industry in the form of the World Anti-Doping Agency (WADA) and corresponding national organisations. As the globalisation and commercialisation of sport have increased the rewards that can be gained through competitive success, and the temptation to seek advantage through improper practices has accordingly grown, the role of the regulatory bodies has become more important and there has been a need for more investment in their activities. The WADA budget, which consists of contributions from national governments and matching from the International Olympic Committee, has risen from US$15.2 million when the organisation was established in 2002, to almost US$27 million in 2011 (www.wada-ama.org/en/About-WADA/Funding/).

Competitiveness in the HPS domain is becoming ever more intense, as evidenced by the fact that the number of nations competing in the Olympic Games has risen from seventy-two in 1956 (Melbourne) to 204 in 2008 (Beijing). Nations wishing to achieve and/or retain international prominence in HPS are finding it necessary to continually improve the efficiency, effectiveness and overall quality of their product development systems. Greater breadth and depth of expertise is being brought to bear on the systems, often through partnerships with other industry sectors. The influence of an increasingly global and commercial HPS sector on the professionalisation of the infrastructure and methodologies supporting the preparation of athletes has been profound.

While the above is focused on the application of product development processes at the national level as a framework for the production of world-class athletes, the concept is relevant at virtually all levels of the HPS network. Just as the national sporting organisations of different countries compete against one another for international success, so do regional sporting organisations compete for national success. As available rewards grow and competitive pressures mount, the need for the adoption and constant refinement of a systematic approach increases, and formal product development approaches tend to emerge.

Even the international organisations responsible for administering particular sports on a global level operate in a very competitive setting and must continually respond to economic imperatives. They compete for market share, which is related to public interest and inclusion in major events such as the Olympic Games and other prominent sporting competitions. In each case, their whole sport is essentially a product that must be made as attractive as possible to existing and potential supporters, and particularly to the media. In recent years, numerous sports have pursued initiatives aimed at enhancing their appeal. The initiatives have included changes of rules; modifications to competitive environments to reduce performance variability (e.g. installation of synthetic playing surfaces, building of indoor facilities); the introduction of new technologies to aid judging; the construction of competition venues designed to maximise spectator comfort and engagement; the implementation of stringent anti-doping policies; and the presentation of a 'green and clean' image. These actions can be construed as resulting from largely unconscious attention to product development concepts that by their iterative nature have much in common with the traditional scientific method.

The traditional sport participation pyramid, in which the most talented amateur sport participants naturally progress to become elite performers, has lost its intuitive logic. HPS has developed into such a specialised industry that it can be argued it has become totally detached from grassroots sport. Indeed, in some professional sporting competitions, such as the National Basketball Association in the United States or the Australian Football League (AFL), the development of talented young players is totally separated from the running of professional teams. 'Raw materials' are being produced elsewhere, in clubs, colleges, schools or grassroots competitions and are only tapped into when they are developed enough to fit the basic requirements of HPS. In both the United States and Australia, draft camps or talent identification events are organised to select the most talented athletes from those organisations or clubs that have developed and nurtured them. In other words, success can be manufactured and as such, be bought.

BUYING SUCCESS – PUBLIC AND PRIVATE SPONSORSHIP AND OWNERSHIP OF TEAMS AND ATHLETES

The hard core marketing approach to developing talent described above is also present in the way that government and commercial organisations look at HPS. The marketing of cities through the promotion of sport has seen a massive growth in the past decade. Cities around the globe use sporting events to promote their attractiveness as tourist destinations to the rest of the world. For example, the city government of Melbourne and the State government of Victoria joined to pay Tiger Woods millions of dollars to play in a professional golf tournament. Organisations such as the International Management Group (IMG) own a raft of sporting events that they use to achieve various commercial objectives. Not only do these privately owned sporting events serve as platforms for the athletes that they have under management to perform, but IMG and other such companies also self-produce media and broadcast products, sponsorship products and even advisory and consultancy products. Also much advertised are the acquisitions of European football clubs by billionaire Americans,

Russians or Arabs. Some are commercial investments but most are ego-driven ventures that primarily promote the 'brand' of the owners themselves. Rather than 'sponsoring' an athlete or a team in the traditional way – paying for the privilege of association – organisations are increasingly trying to control more comprehensively the marketing messages that are sent in relation to athletes or teams. In the Netherlands, where speed skating is one of the most popular sports, commercial organisations such as the transportation insurance company TVM do not 'sponsor' a skating team – they have actually offered long-term employment contracts to all athletes, coaches and support staff. By doing this, they guarantee that all marketing communication in relation to competitive performance, and also events such as training camps and product launches, can be carefully prepared, scripted and controlled (Hoye *et al.*, 2012).

CASE STUDY 13.1

HPS CYCLING RESEARCH AT VICTORIA UNIVERSITY'S INSTITUTE OF SPORT, EXERCISE AND ACTIVE LIVING (ISEAL)

David Rouffet

Victoria University

When the Institute of Sport, Exercise and Active Living (ISEAL) at Victoria University in Melbourne, Australia, was launched in 2010 with the statement that *ISEAL is the future of sport and science*, a new era in embedded HPS research was entered in Australia. ISEAL is located in a four-storey US$70 million purpose-built research facility that includes twenty-nine custom-designed sport science laboratories. ISEAL has developed a strategic partnership with the Australian Sports Commission (ASC) and the world-renowned Australian Institute of Sport (AIS). The partnership seeks to capitalise on 'on demand' access to elite athletes and elite sport scientists. In today's ultra competitive HPS landscape this more integrated way of bringing sport science to practising high performance athletes and their coaches is an important example of the ways in which Australia's sport managers are seeking to continue a top five ranking as an Olympic nation. Scientists from ISEAL and the AIS are collaborating on a range of interdisciplinary projects and there are an increasing number of joint professorial and research staff appointments. The organisations are committed to sharing their sport science laboratories. ISEAL partners also with organisations such as the local professional (Australian) football club (the Western Bulldogs), the Victorian Institute of Sport (VIS), the AFL, Tennis Australia (TA), the 16-country SPLISS consortium (sport policy factors leading to international sporting success) and world football governing body FIFA, focusing on research that provides the 'winning edge' for elite sport programmes.

High performance cycling research at ISEAL is focused on three main objectives: (1) to measure the impact of a wide range of human (e.g. anthropometric characteristics, physiological abilities), material (e.g. bicycle components, geometry) and environmental (temperature, altitude, humidity) variables on the performances produced by elite and sub-elite cyclists during specific races and within various disciplines (road, track, BMX); (2) to model the effect of these variables on different aspects of performance of cycling using a multidisciplinary approach developed by researchers with established expertise in the fields of biomechanics, neurosciences, physiology and engineering; and (3) to create new technologies and use state-of-the-art methodologies to quantify and explain variations of performance directly measured during training sessions and competitions. The ultimate goal of high performance cycling research at ISEAL is to create scientific knowledge, unique technologies and innovative methodologies that can provide cyclists with a winning edge. To maximise their chances of success in races such as the Tour de France and at events such as the Rio de Janeiro 2016 Summer Olympic Games, Australian track sprint cyclists and BMX cyclists are currently involved in a scientific project developed by ISEAL and supported with data input by the AIS. For this project, the best Australian athletes will use a unique technology allowing the key biomechanical determinants of performance to be measured during the lead-up to the Olympics. This new approach has been designed to obtain the most accurate biomechanical measures in the field without altering the capacity of the cyclists to produce maximal performances. It is anticipated that the technology developed within ISEAL will provide new insights into the performance readiness of the cyclists for the different cycling events. More generally, ISEAL's philosophy in high performance cycling research has been defined from previous findings showing that the analysis of cycling performances suffers from many limitations when it is only based on data collected in a laboratory environment. Consequently, high performance cycling research at ISEAL will take sport science where it should be: where the cyclists and their bicycles interact with the environmental conditions specific to the competition. By taking this approach, ISEAL will maximise its chances to provide cyclists with a competitive advantage.

CASE STUDY 13.2
ISSUES REGARDING THE MANAGEMENT OF INTERNATIONAL COMMERCIAL SUCCESS IN HPS: THE EXAMPLE OF CYCLING AUSTRALIA

Allan Hahn

Australian Institute of Sport

Cycling is one sport that now operates in a global environment. There are currently eighteen Pro Tour road cycling teams that make up what is effectively a major international league. The teams are backed by substantial commercial sponsorships. They have annual budgets of up to €20 million and recruit outstanding talent from around the world. The top riders can earn more than €2 million per year. Historically, most of the teams have been headquartered in mainland Europe, but this has begun to change over the past few years and there are now teams that have their financial bases in the United States, England and Australia. At present, about thirty Australians are contracted by overseas Pro Tour teams, and spend the great majority of their time living, training and competing away from home. This creates major challenges for Cycling Australia, the national organisation responsible for the sport. One of the primary goals of Cycling Australia is the achievement of success at such events as the Olympic Games, world championships and Commonwealth Games. In pursuing this goal, Cycling Australia depends very heavily on the Australian Pro Tour athletes, but compared to the payments of the Pro Tour teams, the financial incentives it is able to offer are small.

The National Performance Director for Cycling Australia, Kevin Tabotta, and an Australian Pro Tour cyclist, Matthew Hayman, recently outlined some of the complexities associated with the above situation. Cycling Australia has very limited immediate access to most of its leading athletes and, in order to be effective, needs to establish strong working relationships with Pro Tour teams. This requires the negotiation of mutually beneficial arrangements that reflect sensitivity on the part of Cycling Australia to the levels of investment made by the teams and to their needs, obligations and sponsorship arrangements. For the teams, competitive success can be vital to the retention of the sponsorships on which their survival depends, so they are sometimes reluctant to release athletes to attend national camps or even to represent Australia at competitions other than the Olympic Games and world championships. Organising national team calendars to avoid clashes with prominent Pro Tour events is critical, but providing promotional value to the Pro Tour teams, through such steps as displaying their names and logos on national team equipment and apparel, can also help to secure favourable responses.

Because the Pro Tour teams operate in a commercial environment, they change continually with some teams disappearing and new ones emerging (e.g. only seven of the 2012 teams existed under their current names in 2008). As a result, Cycling Australia is regularly in the position of having to forge new international relationships. The process is made easier when Australians are employed in coaching or management positions by the new teams.

Maintaining an awareness of the factors influencing the progress of the Pro Tour athletes, including their injury status, requires a focus on communicating regularly with athletes based in different locations, and Cycling Australia has a staff member dedicated specifically to that task. The communication has to be handled carefully because of the confidentiality demands of all the parties involved. It has been necessary to develop extensive networks to ensure that athletes requiring sports science and medicine support additional to that available from their Pro Tour teams can be provided without the cyclists having to travel long distances. Cycling Australia makes extensive use of a specialised European Training Centre that the Australian Institute of Sport has established in Italy to facilitate support for Australian athletes based overseas.

The recent formation of an Australian-owned Pro Tour team, GreenEdge, is itself a reflection of the globalisation of the sport, but is likely to lessen the difficulties faced by Cycling Australia in communicating with and supporting potential members of national teams, particularly as the initial GreenEdge team consists predominantly of Australians.

While interactions with Pro Tour teams can be complicated, the experience and conditioning that athletes gain through being part of those teams can considerably enhance their chances of eventually achieving high-level success as representatives of their nations. It is therefore in the interests of Cycling Australia to have its athletes recruited by Pro Tour teams. To maximise the chances of such recruitment, Cycling Australia has a programme that involves taking talented young cyclists to Europe for substantial periods each year, and exposing them to lower-level tour racing. This enables them to become familiar with the lifestyle, conditions and demands that they could eventually encounter as Pro Tour riders. It also increases their visibility to recruiters and gives them an opportunity to make connections that could be valuable in the future. The young cyclists are supported by Cycling Australia coaches and other specialist staff who travel extensively with them.

The globalisation of cycling has also affected approaches to the research activities conducted to yield new knowledge of value to Cycling Australia. A number of large-scale research projects have been carried out in overseas locations, and have often entailed collaboration with scientists from other nations, requiring the formulation of agreements about how the resultant intellectual property should be handled. Australian researchers sometimes need to spend several months of each year in Europe to obtain data. Occasionally, arrangements have been made for scientists originating from and living permanently in Europe to pursue research activities on behalf of Cycling Australia.

The commercialisation of cycling, and the associated increases in the amounts of money on offer, might have increased the temptation to use illicit substances to gain a competitive advantage. This could create a problem for national federations such as Cycling Australia, since the loss of athletes due to doping penalties could greatly affect outcomes achieved at events such as Olympic Games and world championships, and damage Australia's international reputation. However, history shows that Pro Tour teams have much to lose if their athletes are found to have engaged in doping practices. Withdrawal of sponsorships in the aftermath of doping scandals has led to the forced closure or revamping of some teams (e.g. in 2007 the German telecommunications company Deutsche Telekom AG withdrew its sponsorship of a Pro Tour team as a result of a doping incident involving a team member). As can be seen from this brief overview, the pressures resulting from globalisation and commercialisation have gradually but fundamentally changed the operating environment of organisations such as Cycling Australia, and an ability to adapt has been essential to ongoing success.

SUMMARY

Having observed and discussed the recent revolutionary commercialisation of sport and its products, one may be lured into thinking that all HPS is doomed to become subservient to the commercial objectives of its owners. Fortunately this holds true only for a minority of ultra-commercial global sporting ventures such as the football (soccer) World Cup, the Olympic Games and for teams in professional leagues like the English Premier League (soccer), the Indian Premier League (cricket), and in the United States, the National Basketball Association, the National Football League and Major League Baseball. Much HPS remains simply what the name implies – sport that is driven by the goal of performing at the highest possible level. Many athletes are, first and foremost, drawn into sport because they love to play, and love to explore the boundaries of their own or their team's performance. However, it is not the athletes who are the main drivers of change in the industry. Agents, advisers and consultants, particularly those who use the athletes to ensure an income for themselves, are motivated more by the lure of financial gain than by the desire to achieve uncertain sporting outcomes. It is also new businesses such as online and real time sport gambling that are invading the HPS space and are threatening sport's integrity. The purpose of this chapter was to provide a broad overview of the influence of commercialisation and globalisation on HPS. This influence is undoubtedly significant and is increasing rapidly, but with a better understanding of it comes the ability for sport managers to prepare for it, and to take corrective action where needed and where possible. In the end, the increasing commercial value of sport also offers great opportunities for many people around the world to turn their passion into a career, and that is worth something surely!

DISCUSSION QUESTIONS

1   In Table 13.1 thirteen sport globalisation trends are presented. Which three trends would you argue provide sport organisations with the greatest opportunities with regard to HPS? Which three trends represent the greatest threats to the integrity of HPS? Justify your answers.

2   Elite athletes have always been under pressure to perform. The sources of this pressure are shifting under the influence of commercialisation and globalisation. Discuss with two or three fellow students what you consider to be the top five performance pressures faced by modern-day athletes.

3   In this chapter, a generic product development process (a marketing activity) was applied to HPS. In your opinion, is sport and the sport industry similar enough to other industries for such generic models to be applicable? Justify your answer. If you feel that the sport industry cannot be compared to other industries, what, in your opinion makes sport so different?

4   You are a beginning sport agent in the football industry. You get a wonderful chance to set up your international business as a result of a tip you received about a talented Brazilian teenage player who has been convinced to sign with you. You already have two European clubs that are interested in his services. You can maximise your profit by setting up a short-term contract with one club and then quickly trading the player to the other next year. What do you do? (Discuss in groups of three or four.)

5   In the case study about HPS research at ISEAL, it was outlined that 'new technology' was being developed that could deliver cyclists distinct performance advantages. In the context of commercialising such technology, what are the dilemmas that university-based research institutes are faced with when presented with such opportunities?

KEY TERMS

- Globalisation of sport
- Commercialisation of sport
- HPS product development
- Performance pressure
- Management of high performance success

GUIDED READING

Hoye, R., Smith, A., Nicholson, M., Stewart, B. and Westerbeek, H. M. (2012). *Sport management: Principles and applications* (3rd edn). London: Routledge.

Provides a broad and comprehensive introduction to the different sectors in the sport industry and how sport management can influence these sectors. Case studies from all over the world are further used to enhance understanding.

Rosner, S. R. and Shropshire, K. L. (2011). *The business of sports* (2nd edn). London: Jones & Bartlett Learning.

Provides an interesting overview of sectors in the sport industry that specifically deal with the business of elite sport. Next to generic insights into the structure of leagues and issues such as competitive balance, the book provides information on one of the world's most highly developed sport business economies – the United States.

Recommended websites

www.olympic.org
www.pwc.com/sportsoutlook
www.imgworld.com
www.vu.edu.au/iseal
www.greenedgecycling.com

BIBLIOGRAPHY

Bloomfield, J. (2003). *Australia's sporting success: The inside story*. Sydney: UNSW Press.

De Bosscher, V., Bingham, J., Shibli, S., Van Bottenburg, M., De Knop, P. (2008). The global sporting arms race: An international comparative study of sports policy factors leading to international sporting success. Oxford: Meyer & Meyer Sport.

Forrest, D. and Simmons, R. (2002). Team salaries and playing success in sports: A comparative perspective. *Zeitschrift fur Betriebswirtschaft*, Special Issue on Real Option Valuation, 72(4).

Hoye, R., Smith, A., Nicholson, M., Stewart, B. and Westerbeek, H. M. (2012). *Sport management: Principles and applications* (3rd edn). London: Routledge.

Pahls, M. C. (2006). Athletics success and program expense in NCAA sports. Doctoral dissertation, University of Kansas, Lawrence, KS.

PricewaterhouseCoopers (2011). Changing the game: Outlook for the global sports market to 2015. Available at www.pwc.com/sportsoutlook/, accessed 21 December 2011.

Trentberth, L. and Hassan, D. (2011). *Managing sport business: An introduction.* New York: Routledge.

Westerbeek, H. M. and Smith, A. (2003). *Sport business in the global marketplace.* London: Palgrave.

Chapter 14

A holistic approach to risk management
A participant perspective

Dag Vidar Hanstad
Norwegian School of Sport Sciences

Svein S. Andersen
Norwegian Business School and Norwegian School of Sport Sciences

LEARNING OUTCOMES

Upon completion of this chapter the reader should be able to:

1   understand the nature of high performance management within the context of sporting events from the perspective of participating teams and athletes;
2   define and identify the nature of key elements relating to risk management during/before major events;
3   clarify boundaries between organizers' responsibilities and concerns, and risks that participating teams must accept; and
4   detail aspects of key issues relating to living conditions, transport, illness and injuries, mental stress, coaching, leadership, and relationships with the media.

OVERVIEW

This chapter explores the management of a major sporting event from the perspective of a participating team. More specifically, the chapter examines how a national team before and during the 2010 Olympic Winter Games (OWG) in Vancouver (i) identified the risk management issues and (ii) handled risk strategies. The qualitative case study utilized previous research on risk management and strategic management in order to analyse participating teams' preparation and implementation. A framework for dealing with risk management issues experienced by participating teams at sporting events is provided.

PARTICIPATING TEAMS IN SPORTING EVENTS

Participating and competing in the Olympic Games is an experience for the very few and may happen just once in a lifetime. Athletes and coaches work diligently on physical, technical and mental factors that can add an extra edge to the performance level during these games. However, in any sporting event, from local competitions to mega-events such as the Olympic Games, risk is pervasive, both in the preparation and performance during the event. Chappelet (2001) states that '[d]ue to its duration, cost and complexity, a major project [or sporting event] is inevitably subject to unforeseen events, to setbacks, and to numerous, major areas of uncertainty that are inevitable because of so many risks that exist' (p. 7). A key to success is how event managers and leaders/coaches in participating teams deal with these risks.

Topics that have been covered on risks in sporting events include the effects of terrorism (Atkinson and Young, 2002; Giulianotti and Klauser, 2010; Taylor and Toohey, 2006, 2007; Toohey, 2008; Toohey et al., 2003), security (Giulianotti and Klauser, 2010), crowd control (Appenzeller, 2005), security for sporting facilities (Ammon et al., 2004; Preuss, 2004; Walker and Stotlar, 1997), actual losses associated with the event (Chang and Singh, 1990), incidents (Fuller and Myerscough, 2001), injuries (Fuller and Drawer, 2004) and the overall impact on stakeholders of these risks, and the related risk management issues (Leopkey and Parent, 2009a) and strategies (Leopkey and Parent, 2009b).

Even though delegations/participants have been treated as stakeholders in some of these studies (e.g. Fuller and Drawer, 2004, Leopkey and Parent 2009a, 2009b) little research has been carried out on how the participating teams manage risks in events. Such efforts must be considered in the context of what organizers have achieved. To some extent organizers and participating teams have separate responsibilities, but this is not the case in every situation. Participants must simply trust that competition facilities are in accordance with international standards and requirements. However, in the areas of housing, transport and health, participating teams have an independent responsibility to ensure that everything works for their athletes.

The purposes of this chapter are (i) to identify the risk management issues in a large-scale sporting event from the perspective of a participating national Olympic team (Norway) and (ii) analyse how the team handled risk strategies before and during the event, which was the 2010 OWG in Vancouver, Canada.

The chapter is organized as follows. First, some general issues for participating teams are presented, followed by a section on settings and methodology. Findings are then discussed. Finally, concluding remarks and avenues for future research are explored.

Many issues may disrupt the preparation and participation of teams and individuals competing in sporting events. There may be great variations with respect to challenges related to locality, climate, infrastructure and culture. For some leaders and coaches, and particularly athletes, attending a major international event is a new experience. The management of Olympic participation focuses on minimizing the chances of negative events occurring, and dealing with them if they do occur, but it also involves focusing on optimal performance. The challenge is that almost any negative factor can undermine a participant's capacity for optimal performance. In many events the margins between the best performers are very small. This means that preparation must take account of all possible contingencies and those responsible must pay attention to small details that in many other settings would be considered insignificant.

Risk management must be a proactive process (Getz, 2005; Wideman, 1992). This involves 'assessing all possible risks to the event and its stakeholders by strategically anticipating, preventing, minimizing, and planning responses to eliminate or mitigate those identified risks' (Leopkey and Parent, 2009b, p. 1999). However, as Perminova *et al.* (2008, p. 77) point out, traditional planning and risk analysis cannot take account of all possible contingencies. They argue that the key to successful risk management is reflective learning and sensemaking that enables flexible responses.

Some risk factors may be almost completely eliminated through careful preparation. Practical problems related to logistics and living conditions may be largely controlled. The risk of illness can be reduced, but cannot be completely eliminated. If illness occurs, it may be difficult to manage. Isolation and heightened awareness about such risks can even have negative psychological effects on athletes. This means that corrective measures may introduce new risks. Also, serious accidents in or outside competition may undermine concentration. The effects of such negative events are likely to be reinforced by media coverage (Andersen and Hanstad, 2013).

To summarize: in Olympic participation small negative events, and the way they are handled, may have a significant impact on results. Both preparation and participation require skilled and careful attention from athletes and leaders. It seems likely that a national team's ability to manage such challenges depends on the quality of both everyday development work and the specific preparations for the Olympics.

SETTING AND METHODOLOGY

The 2010 OWG were held from the 12th to the 28th of February in Vancouver, Canada. More than 2,600 athletes representing 82 countries participated. The Games were covered by 10,000 media representatives and 3 billion television viewers worldwide followed the event. In addition to competitions in the host city of Vancouver, other venues were in Richmond and Whistler. The Games were a great success. The President of the International Olympic Committee (IOC), Jacques Rogge, said at the closing ceremony that 'this extraordinary embrace by the entire city is something unique and has given a great atmosphere for these Games' (BBC, 2010b, p. xxx). The United States of America had the highest number of medals (thirty-seven) while the host Canada, with its 'Own the Podium' programme, won the most gold medals (fourteen) (Barnes, 2010; BBC, 2010a).

Norway was number four in medals ranking (nine gold medals and twenty-three medals in total) and received considerable attention in the international press. The *Wall Street Journal* wrote about 'the Mystery of Norway' (Futterman and Helliker, 2010) and said that the performance was hard to fathom because Norway has only 4.7 million people. The Norwegian team for the 2010 Vancouver OWG included 99 athletes (25 women, 74 men), participating in 11 sports. A total of 22 of the athletes (9 women, 13 men) had also competed in the 2006 Turin OWG. Most of the athletes and their support personnel stayed in the two Olympic Villages in Whistler Mountains and Vancouver but two teams (the alpine skiing and biathlon teams) were located in private houses rented by the Norwegian Olympic Top Sports Program – hereafter called *Olympiatoppen*.

A total of sixteen key actors in the *Olympiatoppen* and two national sport federations were interviewed in order to identify key opportunities and concerns, measures taken and related outcomes during the OWG. These key actors included the head of *Olympiatoppen*, who was Chef de Mission in the OWG, the heads of Norwegian contingents in different camp sites, the head of logistics, press services representatives, medical support personnel, nutritionists, psychological support personnel, coaches responsible for overall coordination, support personnel in different localities and athletes.

CRITICAL ISSUES FOR THE NORWEGIAN OLYMPIC TEAM

From a Norwegian point of view, an overall impression was that results of the Turin OWG were a disappointment. Some informants argued that it was just bad luck, and that this is bound to happen from time to time. However, others suggested that something in the planning and preparation had failed to meet the strict quality standards required. One of the main organizers of the 2006 team said about the Turin experience:

> Almost everything that could go wrong went wrong. Results did not materialize, illness developed partly because living conditions were not good enough, we had negative press coverage, members of the ski preparation team were involved in fist fights and some athletes were partying. In one sport, there were cooperation problems. However, all negative experiences have been used to improve preparations and relationships between the Olympic Top Sports program and the sport teams.

While this may be a considered by some to be an overstatement, it seems clear that the debate about what happened in the Turin OWG was an important input in the Norwegian planning and preparations for the Vancouver Olympics. Such experiences became a focal point for learning and improvement, but lessons were interpreted in the wider context of experiences from other important competitions and the ongoing development work in between the two Winter Olympics. Some of the organizational improvements had already been implemented for the Beijing Summer Games in 2008. Below we discuss how challenges were perceived and dealt with from the perspective of knowledge transfer.

From the interviews fourteen specific risk issues were identified: living conditions, transport, illness, injuries, nutrition, accidents, goal setting, pressure of expectations, mental factors, coaching, collective sentiments, relationships, media access and media coverage. We grouped the risk issues in five focus areas for risk reduction:

1 practical aspects, including living conditions and transport;
2 health, including illness, injuries, nutrition and accidents;
3 mental factors, including goal-setting process and high expectations;
4 coaching and leadership, including collective sentiments and relationships in the whole team; and
5 media, including access to athletes and media coverage.

Below we will discuss how challenges were perceived and dealt with from the perspective of knowledge transfer.

Practical aspects, including living conditions and transport

In Turin, the team was spread over several different locations outside the Olympic Village. However, in the wake of several negative events, including illness among some athletes, this special accommodation came to be viewed as a negative factor, adding to the misery caused by illness. In Vancouver, risks related to living conditions, food and hygiene were reduced by simply taking advantage of the facilities in the Olympic Villages. In addition to the usual inspection visits, the *Olympiatoppen* also had a representative living in the area for one year prior to the games (2007–2008) and this person later became the Assistant Chef de Mission and head of the Norwegian Olympic Village in Whistler. This provided her with a unique opportunity to follow preparations closely. I also served as a liaison for all visiting groups from Norway, including sports directors and coaches. Good facilities and *Olympiatoppen's* preparations paid off. According to our informants, results at the Games were not affected by any problems related to living conditions.

Health, including illness, injuries, nutrition and accidents

In Turin some of the best athletes became ill, and the resulting preoccupation with illness during the games had a negative psychological effect on the whole team (Hanstad and Engebretsen, 2007). There were also problems related to food and nutrition for those located outside the Olympic Village.

> In Vancouver routines were improved, but the main difference was how they were implemented in the teams. Better access to teams during general training and preparations and increased attention to athletes with special needs created a different situation. We could also build on positive experiences from the Beijing Olympics in 2008 (research interview, 6 January 2010).

The incidence of illness and injury at the Vancouver Games were the lowest on record. Routines for handling contingencies were in place (Hanstad *et al.*, 2011). Athletes with signs of illness were sent away. Experts on nutrition had been embedded in team preparations.

Mental factors, including goal-setting process and high expectations

In Turin, overly ambitious public goals were not realized. Failure to reach such goals contributed to uncertainty and pessimism. Before Vancouver there was a conscious policy of keeping leaders, coaches and athletes from creating high expectations that could add to the pressure that everyone feels in such situations. In each sport processes were implemented to ensure that objectives were realistic. The capacity for support and mental training had been expanded and embedded in the team. The team was prepared for a bad start, to reduce negative psychological effects. 'I have been involved in several Olympics to provide mental support. It is clear that disappointing performances from team mates during the first days can have a strong influence on others' (research interview, 2 February 2010). Despite some disappointments during the first days of the Games, reports indicate that this did not undermine the team's confidence. 'I was sure that the medals would materialize and this was communicated to everyone in the team' (research interview, Chef de Mission, 22 April 2010).

Coaching and leadership, including collective sentiments and relationships in the team

The role of leaders and coaches is to coordinate and support team coaches and athletes. In Turin the experience was that roles were not sufficiently clear, and practices and communications differed. 'One of the coaches from the *Olympiatoppen* I had never met before we were in Turin. We did not know each other well enough and this complicated cooperation in situations of vital importance' (research interview, 8 January 2010). There was a lack of strong team sprit across sports and some conflicts arose. Before Vancouver, the development of the competences and roles of coaches had been a priority, as it had been in the preparation for the 2008 Summer Olympics in Beijing. During the Games this represented new leadership capacities for the team. 'Positive personal relationships among coaches and leaders in different sports created a sense of security' (research interview, 29 April 2010). The fact that more athletes were placed in the same location added to the overall team feeling.

Media, including access to athletes and media coverage

The relationship between the Norwegian team and the media was subject to a detailed set of rules set down in an agreement. Despite this, in Turin, relationships with the media were stressful. The Norwegian media chose to highlight the team's failure to achieve the results that had been expected of it. Illness in the team also became a key issue. 'Negative news coverage was the first thing that met team members when they opened Norwegian newspapers' (research interview, 2 February 2010). Medical personnel got too much media space. In the years preceding Vancouver, new routines were developed for coordinated contacts between media and team representatives and athletes. In addition, athletes were trained to handle the media. During the Games, both journalists (Hanstad and Skille, 2010) and the press attachés (group interview, 22 April 2010) found the collaboration to go more smoothly than expected. However, the athletes still felt the media as a stress factor because of the tendency to devote excessive attention to some events (Kristiansen *et al.*, 2011).

In Leopkey and Parent's (2009a) study the various stakeholder groups (including delegations/participating teams) identified fifteen risk issue categories. Some of these categories coincide with the ones identified in the interviews discussed in this chapter: infrastructure, media, relationship, human resources ('coaching' in this study), interdependence and of course sport because this study is about the participating team. The other nine categories identified in Leopkey and Parent's work (environment, financial, legacy, operations, organizing, participation, political, relationships, threats and visibility) are either not relevant or are part of a broader view of planning such a project.

The five different risk issues discussed above were not ranked by our informants. However, they all pointed to illness as the biggest risk for the Norwegian Olympic team. In the next section we use the area of illness prevention to illustrate different risk management strategies.

STRATEGIES FOR RISK MANAGEMENT: DEALING WITH ILLNESS IN THE TEAM

It is of paramount importance for the athletes to avoid illnesses and injuries during these critical weeks leading up to the Games. Illnesses and health-related factors were considered to be a major reason for the underperformance of the Norwegian team in general in Turin (Hanstad, 2006; Hanstad and Engebretsen, 2007). Because of the experience in Turin, the *Olympiatoppen* had a strategy for reducing illnesses among the athletes in the period leading up to and during the OWG in Vancouver 2010 (Rønsen, 2010).

Leopkey and Parent (2009b) emphasized the need to create strategies or tactics to deal with risks. They identified seven strategies for coping with risks viewed from an organizer's perspective: reduction, avoidance, reallocation, diffusion, prevention, legal buffering and relationship-based mediation. From the point of view of the interviewees, all of whom participated in organizing the Vancouver team, we found that three of these strategies were relevant: reduction, avoidance and relationships.

Reduction: Olympiatoppen had a clear organizational goal regarding the health of athletes at the Vancouver project: that Norwegian athletes should have access to the best expertise in sports medicine, sports nutrition and sports psychology. As a consequence, a medical team with the highest level of competence and an optimal composition, including expertise in sports medicine, nutrition and psychology was selected (staffing). The increased focus on a strategy to reduce illness was also reflected in the fact that the leader of the healthcare team was a specialist in preventive medicine, while the head of the Turin project had been an orthopaedic surgeon.

The Chief Medical Officer (CMO) implemented guidelines through education of the medical team members and carried out information campaigns with all the sport-specific teams (Rønsen, 2010). Based on the experience of failure at Turin, special considerations relating to living conditions, single room occupancy and general hygiene, including food safety, were implemented at the pre-Games camps and during the Games. In the Olympic Village in Whistler there was a need to make more specific rules and consistently remind athletes and coaches about the importance of the strict compliance with these rules to avoid illnesses. The post-Games interviews confirmed the effective implementation of the routines.

One of the staff in the health team described simple routines that contributed to illness prevention:

> Instant intake of drinks and food right after competitions and training were a success factor. This was good recovery and prevented illness for athletes. The support personnel also provided dry clothes immediately after training and competitions because the immune system is vulnerable at that moment.

Vaccination (e.g. H1N1 and seasonal flu shots) was available for all the athletes. During the autumn of 2009 there was an intense focus on avoiding swine influenza, in the Norwegian society and within the Olympic team, which made athletes extra careful. This resulted in the widespread use of disinfectant hand gels and wipes, and information on illness prevention measures in the teams. All candidates for the Vancouver Olympic team were screened and athletes with respiratory problems were followed up (controlling). A system was established for immediate isolation if signs of infection were detected in a team member (including coaches and support staff). During the Games any coaches and athletes who became ill or showed signs of illness were moved out of the Olympic village.

Avoidance: Olympiatoppen provided high quality expertise for the assessment and treatment of illnesses and injuries, as well as for nutritional and psychological issues related to performance. Based on research and evaluation, measures were implemented during the preparation for the Vancouver OWG, and during the Games themselves, to avoid illness. These measures included screening for asthma and allergies with follow-up of athletes with respiratory problems and the use of single rooms for illness-prone athletes. Individual event assessments consisted of identifying individual needs for the prevention of specific illnesses and injuries, and implementing practical measures to achieve optimal health and performance in each athlete. These procedures continued during the event.

Relationships: The medical personnel from *Olympiatoppen* worked together with medical teams of each sport federation and each national team to minimize the occurrence of illness and injury (embedded cooperation). Trust and harmonious relationships between the health team and sports teams were established. This seems to be a core element in successful team preparation and illness prevention. Before Turin, health staff from the *Olympiatoppen* included in some of the teams were seen as newcomers or 'strangers'. They failed to develop the necessary relationships with athletes and trainers. Preparations for Vancouver emphasized the importance of better relations between the health team and the performance groups. Doctors, nutritionists and sports psychologists were to a greater extent included in teams over a minimum period of 16 months. The team most affected by illness in Turin was the cross-country skiing team, and so they received special attention in Vancouver. Here, *Olympiatoppen* decided to use the mean CMO as the leader of the health team.

The strong focus on relationships and building up confidence between the athletes and the medical team was demonstrated when one of the skiers decided not to participate in a competition even though he was among the favourites because he had signs of illness (Kvamme, 2010).

Through closer and more enduring relationships with the cross-country skiing team, as well as other teams, the *Olympiatoppen* medical team was able to ensure that measures were actually implemented. A new strategy regarding communication relating to illness was also implemented in Vancouver. In Turin, illness in the team was exacerbated by the fact that some of the health personnel were very visible in the media. In meetings with the media, doctors in some sports presented 'today's medical bulletin'. Before the Vancouver OWG the visibility of health staff was discussed in both the health and press team of the *Olympiatoppen*. Openness was important, but it was made clear that it needed to be balanced by the need to avoid too much attention on health issues.

MANAGING FOR OPTIMAL PERFORMANCE

In elite sport competitions the margins between success and failure are small, and minor advantages can be the key to major successes. Details that in many other settings would be considered insignificant can have a major impact on results. Risks can be regarded as negative outcomes of uncertainties. No activity is risk-free and the process of risk management cannot realistically expect to reduce levels of risk to zero (Fuller, 2007). However, the people involved in the planning did not use the word 'risk'. Even though there was a focus on what they called fears or threats the terms 'risk' and 'risk management' were a part of their everyday vocabulary.

During a group interview one of the leaders in *Olympiatoppen* stated that he found the use of the term 'risk management' strange:

> We never use the word risk in our work. Risk is something defensive and it gives a wrong impression to what we are doing at *Olympiatoppen*. In my view our approach focuses on opportunities to gain advantages over others. Before the Winter Games in Vancouver I never thought about risks. It was about opportunities, opportunities and opportunities.

Others in the leader group modified the statement, but they supported the idea that *Olympiatoppen's* planning and preparation was about opportunities. For an Olympic team that is looking to gain an advantage over other nations, opportunity should be as central a theme as risk. However, in our interviews, the focus on opportunities was downplayed, compared with risk management. This may be due to the negative experiences from Turin, which were to be avoided at all cost.

In a similar vein, the project literature pays most attention to risks, and less to how opportunities can be exploited (Olsson, 2007). Hopkin (2010) states that organizations should continue to look for opportunities and, from time to time, acknowledge 'that there is a good opportunity that looks very risky' (p. 331). This understanding is in line with previous research. Risk management may uncover opportunities (Bowdin *et al.*, 2006).

However, minimizing risk can also cause one to miss out on the opportunities associated with risk taking (Besley and Maitreesh, 2005). Awareness about such trade-offs are important for a team preparing for an event such as the Olympic Games.

CASE STUDY 14.1

JUDGING SPORT WITH TECHNOLOGY: MANAGING THE INTEGRATION OF PERFORMANCE ASSESSMENT TECHNOLOGY INTO ELITE-LEVEL HALF-PIPE SNOWBOARDING

Jason Harding
Griffith University

Half-pipe snowboarding is not a traditional Olympic sporting discipline. Competitors are required to perform aerial acrobatic routines on a half-pipe made of snow (Figure 14.1) and performances are assessed with a purely subjective measure termed 'overall impression'. The sport is focused upon the aesthetic (Best, 1978) and the method by which athletes execute the required manoeuvres is of the utmost importance (Wertz, 1979). Snowboarding, like other board-riding activities, exists simultaneously as a lifestyle, an art and a sport. Upon acceptance into the Olympic Games in 1998, the sport of snowboarding began as an emergent activity in relation to the other more traditional events and has become established as an Olympic sport on a par with more traditional events (Popovic, 2006). At first, snowboarding displayed numerous intricacies of the subculture that were vastly different from already existing Olympic sporting disciplines. The sport, however, has begun to shift to more traditional patterns with formalized rules, organizational control, and guidelines regarding what are acceptable behaviours (Popovic, 2006). This process has continued until the present and even though prowess within the snowboarding community continues to be defined by core members and although the sport retains an underlying anarchist, non-conformist and punk rock ideology (Harding *et al.*, 2008b), snowboarding has become an accepted Olympic sport.

It is important that the Olympic movement embraces sports that are popular among young people in order to maintain relevance. Many of these types of sports, however, all enter the Olympic arena with a history of having assessed performance in a subjective manner. From an Olympic perspective, subjective performance assessment protocols have uncertain accuracy and reliability and are open to manipulation and corruption. Furthermore, the Olympics has had problems in the past with controversial competition results arising from subjectively judged results (such as in boxing, gymnastics and ice skating). In light of these past problems, processes need to be put into place that allow for the successful integration of innovative judging protocols when they are made available by technology or other means. Consequently the methodology underpinning how coaches assess athletic progression and how judges score half-pipe snowboard competition performance is open to debate and discussion (as is the case with all sports that rely on subjective judging criteria). Discussing and understanding the consequences of the potential rule changes that are made possible by new technology or

Figure 14.1 *US professional snowboarder competing at Burton Open Australian Half-Pipe Championships, Perisher*

Source: Heidi Barbay, 2008

other innovations is an extremely important, and frequently overlooked, aspect of this integration process. Furthermore, it is believed that the practice community (in this case, those who are directly involved with the sport) should be provided with the opportunity not only to express their opinions in forums that influence decision makers, but also to have some element of control over how consultation about new rules takes place.

Since 2006 there has been an increase in research-related and industry-related activity focused specifically on objectifying specific components of snowboarding performance. For example, although half-pipe snowboarding is judged by purely subjective measures, it has been shown that there are strong, positive correlations between the objective key performance indicators of average air time (AAT) and average degree of rotation (ADR), and subjectively judged competition scores. Air time is measured in seconds and reflects the amount of time an athlete spends in the air during an aerial acrobatic manoeuvre, while degree of rotation is measured in degrees and reflects the number of rotations an athlete completes during the period of air time. An analysis of both men's and women's performances at the Burton Open Australian Half-Pipe Championships over a three-year period (2006, 2007, 2008) shows that when combined, AAT and ADR could explain 71–79 per cent of the men's subjective competition scores and 80–94 per cent of the women's scores. Moreover, there were significant differences in AAT and ADR between athletes achieving top three (podium) final rankings and those achieving final rankings outside the top three (Harding and James, 2010a). Based on these results, this type of objective information has been put forward as a possible component of an improved judging protocol for elite-level half-pipe snowboard competitions. The study, however, used video and video analysis software to calculate the data. The capture and post-run processing of video data is not automatic; it is extremely labour intensive, and is associated with a long time delay in information feedback. This prevents any chance of video-based objective information being provided to judges quickly.

Recent technological advances (the use of micro-technology in combination with signal processing techniques), however, now make it possible to automatically calculate the same objective information (i.e. air time and degree of rotation). Two separate studies proved that micro-technology and signal processing techniques can automatically calculate air time and degree of rotation during elite-level half-pipe snowboarding (Harding et al., 2007, 2008a) thereby removing the limitations of time delay caused by using video-based generation of the same information. This successful tailoring of technology is one example of providing the sport with an increased ability to remove the potential for controversial results, to enhance the accuracy and reliability associated with the current subjective judging protocols, and to provide judges, at the very least, with an additional tool to utilize. Nevertheless, the major concern of many sporting communities is that improvements in sport science and technology can remove the stylistic components from a sporting discipline and thereby reduce the magic of a performance to a series of mathematical equations (Brodie, 2008; Miah, 2000; Morgan, 1994; Tenner, 1996). Perhaps the most significant aspect of proposed changes like this in sport, however, is that once such changes are introduced, reversing them is very difficult (Miah, 1998, 2000). Hence, athletes, coaches, competition judges and the sport's governing bodies are often reluctant to adopt new equipment and performance assessment technologies (Chi et al., 2005).

In many cases, the rules associated with particular sports must be changed in order to accommodate new technology and innovative concepts. Furthermore, athletes, coaches and competition judges often need to be convinced that their cooperation is essential for increasing mainstream interest and performance assessment accountability in their particular discipline (Fuss, 2008). This issue is compounded by further complexities in half-pipe snowboarding, a sport with an underlying anarchistic and anti-authoritarian ideology, a habitual focus on athletic individuality and freedom of expression, and a community with strong views on how performance should be valued and assessed. As such, the introduction of technology (whether focused on performance assessment in training or competition) into half-pipe snowboarding will no doubt provide implementers and those affected with challenges (Harding *et al.*, 2009). As argued by Miah and Mitchum (2005), changes, technological or otherwise, should be preceded with substantial discussion about what future is sought for a specific sport and thus, where limits might be drawn on the changes. Defining who should determine the nature of a sport ought not to be a difficult issue. It seems imperative that implementers consider and respect the personal concerns of those affected and ensure that practising communities are allowed to articulate their interests in forums that have the ability to influence decision makers (Morgan, 1994). Furthermore, practice communities should be provided an element of control over the integration of any innovative concepts into their sport (Fuss, 2008, Miah, 1998; Miah and Mitchum, 2005; Morgan, 1994).

It is largely unknown if competitive half-pipe snowboarding can indefinitely maintain its subjective style of performance assessment in an era when there are calls for more objectivity in judging Olympic sports. With this in mind, a number of researchers set out to seek the views of a wide international community of elite-level half-pipe snowboard competition judges on the potential of technology to improve the current half-pipe snowboard judging protocol. This research focused on initiating and maintaining a relationship with the practice community and in doing so maintained a balanced approach sympathetic to the sporting discipline's underlying cultural ethos. Furthermore, this research afforded elite-level competition judges a forum to communicate their perceptions of the potential impact and future management of a proposed technological change within their sport. At the time this case study is being written, this research is an ongoing project, but a number of dominant themes are emerging. There was a strong resistance to any automated judging if it were based on objective information alone. One judge said that 'This would be the death of half-pipe snowboard competition' and this was a typical response. The strength of the general response to this proposition may be related to the vested interest of the population sampled, as judges may feel their careers will be compromised if they can be replaced by an automated system of assessment. It is more likely, however, that this response is related to a vested interest in maintaining snowboarding's cultural ethos and what is valued within the sport by the practice community. One judge warned:

> We must be very careful as we continue down the road of amalgamating snowboard competition and technology. If misused, it has the potential to ruin the pureness we find in the sport today.

The option of integrating technology with the current subjective judging protocol was, however, viewed more positively as long as the amalgamation continued to allow athletic freedom of expression in elite competition. One judge said:

I see great potential for continued advancement and implementation of technology into snowboard competition to produce more accurate outcomes [but] only if the athletes' ability to perform in an independent and creative manner is not compromised.

Most importantly, competition judges are not opposed to the idea but there is a widespread view that further development should be conducted in close collaboration with the community and that the integration process should be controlled from within the sport.

SUMMARY

This chapter has identified challenges facing national teams participating in major sporting events. Our case study examined how Norway's national team prepared for the 2010 OWG in Vancouver, identified risk management issues and handled risk strategies. The experiences from the 2006 Turin OWG became a focal point for learning and improvement. Risks were identified and measures were taken to successfully prevent negative events.

The study contributes to the literature on risk management in three ways.

Most of the literature has an organizer's perspective. This involves 'assessing all possible risks to the events and its stakeholders by strategically anticipating, preventing, minimizing, and planning responses to eliminate or mitigate those identified risks' (Leopkey and Parent, 2009b, p. 1999). The participants' perspective provides complementary perspective on risk management. From a participant's perspective, risk management is not only a proactive process. Building capacities for managing situational contingencies is essential.

However, as Perminova *et al.* (2008, p. 77) point out, traditional planning and risk analysis cannot fully grasp all future contingencies. They argue that the key to successful risk management is reflective learning and sensemaking that enables flexible responses. This study has emphasized the importance of organizational characteristics that support such processes. Particular attention is paid to the nature of personal relationships. An Olympic team consists of many people, groups and sport-specific teams that are under pressure during such an event. A key factor for effective risk management in all the defined risk issues was good personal relationships, based on mutual trust and knowledge about each others' competences and capacities.

Finally, while this study has focused on risk prevention, a theme that emerged during the study was the ability to exploit opportunities embedded in the uncertainties that face a participant team. It was not possible to pursue here, but it points to an additional strategic dimension. This topic is also under-researched in the general project management literature.

DISCUSSION QUESTIONS

1 Imagine you are the head of a team participating in a national or international competition. What would you consider as key risks?

2 Identify the risk management issues in an event you are familiar with. Put yourself in a position as the head of the organizing committee. What are possible risk management strategies?

3 How can such strategies influence opportunities or introduce new risks?

4 Discuss other sporting disciplines where rule changes have had either positive or negative impact on the game itself, competition results or the manner in which spectators engage with the sport.

5 Provide an example of a sport where the integration of technology or a rule change has had a *positive effect* on the sport itself, on competition results or on spectator engagement, and discuss why you believe this change had a positive effect.

6 Provide an example of a sport where the integration of technology or a rule change has had a *negative effect* on the sport itself, on competition results or on spectator engagement, and discuss why you believe this change had a negative effect.

KEY TERMS

- Risk
- Risk management
- Sporting event
- *Olympiatoppen*

GUIDED READING

Appenzeller, H. (2005). *Risk management in sport: Issues and strategies* (2nd edn). Durham, NC: Carolina Academic Press.
Herb Appenzeller provides a good introduction to risk management issues and strategies in sport.

BIBLIOGRAPHY

Ammon, R. Jr., Southall, R. M. and Blair, D. A. (2004). *Sport facility management: Organizing events and mitigating risks.* Morgantown: Fitness Information Technology.
Andersen, S. S. and Hanstad, D. V. (2013). Project-based learning in a mindful organization.
Appenzeller, H. (2005). *Risk management in sport. Issues and strategies* (2nd edn). Durham, NC: Carolina Academic Press.

Atkinson, M. and Young, K. (2002). Terror games: Media treatment of security issues at the 2002 Winter Olympic Games. *Olympika, XI*, 53–78.

Barnes, S. (2010). Well done, Canada, you Own The Podium. *The Times*. Available at www.timesonline.co.uk/tol/sport/columnists/simon_barnes/article7041547.ece, accessed 20 September 2010.

BBC (2010a). Canada revel in record gold medal haul. *BBC*. Available at http://news.bbc.co.uk/sport2/hi/olympic_games/vancouver_2010/8539912.stm, accessed 10 June 2010.

BBC (2010b). Vancouver bids Olympics farewell. *BBC*. Available at http://news.bbc.co.uk/sport2/hi/olympic_games/vancouver_2010/8542068.stm, accessed 20 June 2010.

Besley, T. and Maitreesh, G. (2005). Incentives, risk and accountability in organizations. In B. Hutter and M. Power (Eds), *Organizational encounters with risk* (pp. 149–166). Cambridge: Cambridge University Press.

Bowdin, G., Allen, J., O'Toole, W., Harris, R. and McDonnell, I. (2006). *Event management* (2nd edn) Amsterdam: Elsevier.

Brodie, M., Walmsley, A. and Page, W. (2008). Fusion motion capture: A prototype system using inertial measurement units and GPS for the biomechanical analysis of ski racing. *Sports Technology*, 1(1), 17–28.

Chang, P. C. and Singh, K. K. (1990). Risk management for mega-events. The 1988 Olympic Winter Games. *Tourism Management*, 11(1), 45–52.

Chappelet, J.-L. (2001). Risk management for large-scale events: The case of the Olympic Winter Games. *European Journal for Sport Management*, 8(Special Issue), 6–21.

Chi, E. H., Borriello, G., Hunt, G. and Davies, N. (2005). Pervasive computing in sports technologies. *IEEE Pervasive Computing*, 4(3), 22–25, July/September.

Fuller, C. W. (2007). Managing the risk of injury in sport. *Clinical Journal of Sport Medicine*, 17(3), 182–187.

Fuller, C. W. and Drawer, S. (2004). The application of risk management in sport. *Sports Medicine*, 34(6), 349–356.

Fuller, C. W. and Myerscough, F. E. (2001). Stakeholder perceptions of risk in motor sport. *Journal of Safety Research*, 32(3), 345–358.

Fuss, F. K. (2008). Instrumentation of athletes and equipment during competitions. *Sports Technology*, 1(6), 235–236.

Futterman, M. and Helliker, K. (2010). The mystery of Norway. *The Wall Street Journal*. Available at http://online.wsj.com/article/SB10001424052748704188104575084093472505542.html?mod=WSJ_olympics_LeftTopHeadlineHighlights, accessed 10 May 2010.

Getz, D. (2005). *Event management & event tourism* (2nd edn). New York: Cognizant Communication Corporation.

Giulianotti, R. and Klauser, F. (2010). Security governance and sport mega-events: Toward an interdisciplinary research agenda. *Journal of Sport and Social Issues*, 34(1), 49–61.

Hanstad, D. V. (2006). *Olympiatoppens planlegging og gjennomføring av vinterlekene i Torino 2006 [Olympiatoppen's planning and implementation of the 2006 Olympic Winter Games in Turin]*. Oslo: Norwegian School of Sport Sciences.

Hanstad, D. V. and Engebretsen, L. (2007). *Sykdom i OL-troppen i Torino 2006 [Illness in the Olympic Team in the 2006 Olympic Winter Games in Turin]*. Tidsskrift for Norsk Lægeforening, 127(5), 614–616.

Hanstad, D. V., Rønsen, O., Andersen, S. S., Steffen, K. and Engebretsen, L. (2011). Fit for fight? Illnesses in the Norwegian team in the Vancouver Olympic Games. *British Journal of Sports Medicine*, 45(7), 571–575.

Hanstad, D. V. and Skille, E. (2010). *Journalisters syn på samarbeidet med den norske OL-troppen under vinterlekene i Vancouver 2010 [Journalists' views on the collaboration with the Norwegian Olympic Team during the 2010 Olympic Winter Games in Vancouver]*. Norsk medietidsskift, 17(4), 348–363.

269

Harding, J. W. and James, D. A. (2010). Performance analysis during three years of The Burton Open Australian Half-Pipe Championships. *International Journal of Performance Analysis in Sport,* 10(1), 47–53.

Harding, J. W., Mackintosh, C. G., Martin, D. T., Hahn, A. G. and James, D. A. (2009). Automated scoring for elite half-pipe snowboard competition – Important sporting development or techno distraction? *Sports Technology,* 1(6), 277–290.

Harding, J. W, Mackintosh, C. G., Hahn, A. G. and James, D. A. (2008). Classification of aerial acrobatics in elite half-pipe snowboarding using body mounted inertial sensors. In M. Estivalet and P. Brisson (Eds), *The Engineering of Sport 7,* Vol. 2 (pp. 447–456). Springer-Verlag, France.

Harding, J. W., Toohey, K., Martin, D. T., Hahn, A. G. and James, D. A. (2008). Technology and half-pipe snowboard competition – Insight from elite-level judges. In M. Estivalet and P. Brisson (Eds), *The Engineering of Sport 7,* Vol. 2 (pp. 467–476). Springer-Verlag, France.

Harding, J. W., Small, J. W. and James, D. A. (2007). Feature extraction of performance variables in elite half-pipe snowboarding using body mounted inertial sensors. In D. V. Nicolau, D. Abbott, K. Kalantar-Zadeh, T. Di Matteo and S. M. Bezrukov (Eds), *BioMEMS and Nanotechnology III, Proceedings of SPIE* (Vol. 6799). Bellingham, WA: SPIE, 679917.

Hopkin, P. (2010). *Fundamentals of risk management.* London: Kogan Page.

Kristiansen, E., Hanstad, D. V. and Roberts, G. C. (2011). Coping with the media at the Vancouver winter Olympics: 'We all make a living out of this'. *Journal of Applied Sport Psychology,* 23(4), 443–458.

Kvamme, S. (2010). *Hattestad grât da han ga fra seg plassen* [*Hattestad cried when he resigned not available to the competition*]. *Dagbladet.* Available at www.dagbladet.no/2010/02/23/sport/ol_i_vancouver/ol_2010/10548234/, accessed 20 November 2010.

Leopkey, B. and Parent, M. M. (2009a). Risk management issues in large-scale sporting events: A stakeholder perspective. *European Sport Management Quarterly,* 9(2), 187–208.

Leopkey, B. and Parent, M. M. (2009b). Risk management strategies by stakeholders in Canadian major sporting events. *Event Management,* 13(3), 153–170.

Miah, A. (2000). New balls please: Tennis, technology, and the changing game. In S. Haake and O. A. Coe (Eds), *Tennis science and technology* (pp. 285–292). London: Blackwell Science.

Miah, A. and Mitchum, C. (2005). Sport technology: History, philosophy and policy. *Journal of the Philosophy of Sport,* 32, 223–226.

Morgan W. J. (1994). *Leftist theories of sport: A critique and reconstruction.* Urbana, IL: University of Illinois Press.

Olsson, R. (2007). In search of opportunity management: Is the risk management process enough? *International Journal of Project management,* 25(8), 745–752.

Perminova, O., Gustafsson, M. and Wikström, K. (2008). Defining uncertainty in projects – A new perspective. *International Journal of Project Management,* 26(1), 73–79.

Popovic, M. (2006). From Terje to the flying red tomato: Snowboarding's incorporation into the Olympic Games. In *Proceedings of the 8th International Symposium for Olympic Research,* The International Centre for Olympic Studies, The University of Western Ontario London, Ontario, Canada, 19–21 October (pp. 273–278).

Preuss, H. (2004). *The economics of staging the Olympics: A comparison of the games 1972–2008.* Cheltenham: Edward Elgar.

Rønsen, O. (2010). *The CMO's strategic plan on health care for the Norwegian Olympic Team.* Oslo: Olympiatoppen.

Taylor, T. and Toohey, K. (2006). Impacts of terrorism-related safety and security measures at a major sport even. *Event Management,* 9(4), 199–209.

Taylor, T. and Toohey, K. (2007). Perceptions of terrorism threats at the 2004 Olympic Games: Implications for sport events. *Journal of Sport & Tourism,* 12(2), 99–114.

Tenner, E. (1996). *Why things bite back: Predicting the problems of progress.* London: Fourth Estate.

Toohey, K. (2008). Terrorism, sport and public policy in the risk society. *Sport in Society*, 11(4), 429–442.

Toohey, K., Taylor, T. and Choong-Ki, L. (2003). The FIFA World Cup 2002: The effects of terrorism on sport tourists. *Journal of Sport & Tourism*, 8(3), 167–185.

Walker, M. L. and Stotlar, D. K. (1997). *Sport facility management*. Sudbury, MA: Jones & Bartlett Publishers.

Wertz S. K. (1979). Are sports art forms? *Journal of Aesthetic Education*, 13(1), 107–109.

Wideman, M. R. (1992). *Project and program risk management: A guide to managing project risks and opportunities*. Newton Square, PA: Project Management Institute.

Chapter 15

The management of performance-enhancing drugs in high performance sport

Jason Mazanov

University of New South Wales

LEARNING OUTCOMES

Upon completion of this chapter the reader should be able to:

1   explain the prevalence of performance-enhancing drug (PED) use in sport;
2   discuss different models explaining athletes' PED use and their implications for managers of high performance sports;
3   describe the policy context for managing PED in sport; and
4   discuss management implications arising from the World Anti-Doping Code.

OVERVIEW

This chapter aims to provide high performance sport managers with the necessary background to make policy and operational decisions around the role of PEDs in their programmes. The chapter locates managers as actors in the policy space, who influence the broader world of high performance sport as well as their own programmes. It examines how prevalent PED use is and offers some explanations for why athletes use PED. The management implications arising from the World Anti-Doping Code (WADC) are also discussed. Issues covered include the moral basis for anti-doping, the impacts of out-of-competition testing on human rights, variable evidentiary requirements across the appeals process, the conflict between WADC reporting obligations and health professional duty of care to patients, and policy alternatives to anti-doping.

PERFORMANCE-ENHANCING DRUGS

An essential part of producing modern high performance athletes is the deployment of performance-enhancing technologies, from talent identification to training techniques to equipment. While most performance-enhancing technologies are celebrated (e.g. *Australia II*'s winged keel) others are deemed to have a negative impact on competition and are banned (e.g. 'shark skin' swimsuits). One class of performance-enhancing technology managed very differently in high performance sport is drugs; some PEDs are permitted (e.g. caffeine) while others are prohibited (e.g. anabolic androgenic steroids). This means that elite athletes' use of PEDs has to be managed to ensure they access those that are legitimate and avoid those that are prohibited.

PEDs can be used in three ways. The first is to treat a healthy athlete with a drug in an attempt to improve performance against a benchmark, such as a personal best. For example, using erythropoietin to enhance endurance in cross-country skiing. The second is to treat a healthy athlete with a drug as a preventative measure, to boost their immune system or to prevent injury. The third is to treat an unhealthy athlete with the aim of returning their performance to a benchmark. This may be in response to an injury (e.g. anabolic steroids), pain management (e.g. local anaesthetic injections) or a chronic condition (e.g. using beta-blockers to control performance anxiety).

PREVALENCE RATES

The pharmacological arms race in sport means that high performance athletes who fail to augment their performance with some kind of substance are likely to be competing at a disadvantage. This makes the use of PEDs an essential part of the sports science supporting the athlete. As a result, the use of substances to enhance sporting performance is widespread. To get some insight into the prevalence of legitimate performance-enhancing substance use, around 75 per cent of Olympic athletes passing through doping control at the Sydney (Corrigan and Kazlauskas, 2003) and Athens games (Tsitsimpikou *et al.*, 2009) self-reported using at least one supplement or medication. The bias inherent in self-reported studies such as these suggests that the actual population prevalence rate is above 75 per cent. To put this in perspective, in any given sprint line-up at least six of the eight athletes have taken a supplement or legal medication to enhance their performance. This puts the one or two athletes competing without enhancement at a potential disadvantage that could have significant implications for the return on the investments (such as financial support from governments or sponsors) made on those athletes.

As therapeutic medications, a number of PEDs can be used safely under medical supervision. For example, Harmer (2010) asserts that the medically supervised use of anabolic androgenic steroids (AAS) has led to few or no reported negative side effects. The problem emerges with regard to drug use outside qualified supervision. For example, athletes may be given drugs by well-intentioned coaches who lack an understanding of the drugs' effects other than that they enhance performance. This creates the potential for drug abuse (e.g. prescribing dosages on the principle that if some is good, more is better). While one would hope this practice has been stamped out in high performance sport as a result of anti-doping (see 'The Evolution

273

of Drug-Free Sport' below), managers of high performance sport still need to be vigilant around this issue.

The potential for abuse increases if athletes seek to use substances without supervision. Some athletes using drugs without supervision are conscientious and engage in extensive research in relation to the drugs they use, becoming 'pharmacologically literate' (Stewart and Smith, 2010). Others take a variety of drugs without being conscientious. This ignorant use of drugs creates a very real danger of abuse. The abuse of PEDs can lead to significant health effects. While Harmer (2010) notes the supervised use of AAS is relatively safe, the negative health consequences of abuse are well documented (George and Mottram, 2011) and could develop into a dependence disorder (Kanayama et al., 2009).

Most of the drugs likely to lead to significant harm as a result of abuse, such as AAS, have been prohibited under the World Anti-Doping Code (WADC) (see 'An Overview of the WADC' below). The rates of use or abuse of prohibited substances are basically unknown. The problem lies in establishing a reliable epidemiology of prohibited drug use in sport (Kayser et al., 2007; Quirk, 2009). The official rates of prohibited drug use based on the ratio of positive results to drug tests tend to be very low. The international benchmark reported by Mottram (2011) is that 1.6–2.0 per cent of tests yield positive results, while in some countries, like Australia that has a 0.2 per cent rate (ASADA, 2010), the proportion is much lower.

However, the capacity of drug testing to establish the prevalence rate has been questioned (Mazanov and Connor, 2010; Striegel et al., 2010), especially in the context of anecdotal evidence indicating much higher rates of drug use. For example, Lazarus et al. (2010) report that Greek athletes who have 'ever used' prohibited PEDs estimate that 74.3 per cent of their fellow athletes have used illegal PEDs and those who have 'never used' prohibited PEDs estimate that 52.1 per cent of their fellow athletes have used illegal PEDs. This compares with a self-reported 'ever use' rate of 9.9 per cent and a self-reported 'systematic use' rate of 2.0 per cent in Lazarus et al.'s study. The latter results accord with official rates, and suggest that testing may pick up the systematic use of prohibited drugs but is less likely to pick up other use patterns. Significant effort has gone into developing methods to establish more reliable indicators of prevalence (e.g. Berglund et al., 2007; Simon et al., 2006; Uvascek et al., 2011), although there is, as yet, no clear convergence. It is likely that the prevalence of prohibited drug use is higher than the official estimates and lower than people believe it to be.

PRESSURE TO USE DRUGS

It is simplistic to say that high performance athletes and their support personnel move towards PED use 'to win' (Mazanov and McDermott, 2009). The reasons behind such drug use are more nuanced. There is a range of psychological and sociological variables that provide insight into the pressure to use PEDs. This section describes the models of PED use and then explores the managerial implications arising from those models, summarized in Table 15.1. Notably, these models primarily explore the use of prohibited drugs, which means they may fail to translate to the use of legitimate drugs. It also means that the models struggle to explain the use of legitimate PEDs.

Table 15.1 *Summary of management lessons from models of drug use*

Model	Lessons
SDCM	• Describes compliance with drug management system • Management of drugs affordable/available can influence use
DSDM	• Manage how athletes see cost/benefit of drug use to promote abstinence/legitimate use
MM	• Programmes emphasizing intrinsic motivation drug resistant • Programmes emphasizing extrinsic motivation promote drug use
LCM	• Look for function of drug use in athlete's goals • Use goal cycle to define intervention points • Programme social structures influence way drugs are used (see MM)
SM	• Be aware of internal and external structural influences on drug use • Create social structures that promote desired behaviour • Influence the external structural constraints (e.g. lobbying)
GM	• Modify performance-reward link (e.g. superannuation) • Develop athlete pharmacological literacy • Make athletes aware of management support around legal defence • Combine formal and informal sanctions to promote desired behaviour

Sports Drug Control Model (SDCM)

Donovan *et al.* (2002) articulate the first explanation of athlete PED use, the Sports Drug Control Model (SDCM). The SDCM establishes six factors influencing attitudes and intentions regarding PED use: threat appraisal (e.g. health), benefit appraisal (e.g. performance improvement), personal morality, perceived legitimacy of the enforcement framework, reference group opinion (e.g. senior athletes) and personality. The attitudes and intentions translate into compliance or non-compliance with the rules about the use of prohibited substances. Compliance is also influenced by affordability and availability. Gucciardi *et al.* (2011) report the SDCM explained that 30 per cent of attitudes towards drug use, and 11 per cent of susceptibility to use in a sample of elite Australian athletes. This leaves 70 per cent of attitudes and 89 per cent of susceptibility unexplained.

The value of the SDCM for managers is that it deals with the factors that influence whether or not athletes decide to comply with a drugs management system, rather than with what their drug use is. This is an important distinction given that what is prohibited can and does change. Another key aspect of this model useful to managers is the notion of affordability and availability. Managers can make some drugs more available or affordable than others and by doing so they can control what kinds of drugs athletes use (or consider using). This may be a useful strategy for protecting the return on investment by avoiding sanction.

Drugs in Sport Deterrence Model (DSDM)

Strelan and Boeckmann (2003) articulate a model based in deterrence theory's efforts to understand compliance with the law (p. 177). Strelan and Boekmann confine their model to a cost-benefit analysis. Deterrents (costs) include legal, social sanctions (e.g. ostracism), self-imposed sanctions (e.g. guilt) and health concerns. These are balanced against benefits that include material gains (e.g. prize money), social acclaim and achievement satisfaction. This trade-off is moderated by situational factors, including athlete perceptions of prevalence (social normative), competitiveness in their event, perceived legitimacy of authorities enforcing regulations and the type of drug. The moderated cost-benefit analysis leads to the decision.

A test of the DSDM saw athletes indicate their percentage likelihood of use in response to a set of hypothetical scenarios (Strelan and Boekmann, 2006). Two variables explained 48 per cent of the variations in self-reported likelihood to use, moral beliefs and health concerns. This suggests the legal deterrents upon which the DSDM is predicated fail to influence the decision to use, and the model as a whole may be flawed. However, it still points to a range of variables that are amenable to managerial control. The focus on the cost-benefit analysis indicates that the ways in which the athletes construct these variables influence their decisions. The DSDM suggests managers can influence the way athletes see the costs and benefits to promote abstinence or legal substance use over illegal substance use.

Motivational Model (MM)

Donahue *et al.* (2006) describe an empirically derived model based on the premise why athletes engage in sport influences how they engage with sport and what they are willing to do with regard to PED use. Three variables, intrinsic and extrinsic motivation and sportspersonship orientation (e.g. respect for formal and informal rules or sport, officials and opponents), were correlated with self-reported use of thirty different performance-enhancing substances (fifteen legitimate and fifteen prohibited) using a sample of Canadian national athletes (aged 10–20 years). The results indicate that both internal and external motivation factors influenced how much importance athletes attached to fair play. Intrinsic motivations had a positive relationship with orientation and extrinsic motivations had a weak negative relationship. Orientation then had a negative relationship with drug use, showing that lower scores predicted an increased likelihood of reporting any PED or prohibited substance use.

The Motivational Model is a highly constrained approach, exploring the effect of only three variables (intrinsic and extrinsic motivation, and sportspersonship orientation). It is therefore likely to overlook the influence of other factors (e.g. those considered in the SDCM). The results suggest that intrinsically motivated athletes (e.g. those motivated by the joy of their sport) were more likely to respect the formal and informal rules of sport and were therefore less likely to use PEDs. Conversely, more instrumentally (extrinsically) motivated athletes are less likely to respect the rules of sport and are more likely to use PEDs. From the manager's point of view, these results suggest that programmes emphasizing intrinsic motivations and the importance of engaging with the 'spirit' of sport, as much as the importance of working within the rules, are likely to result in less PED use. Programmes that emphasize material gains and dogmatic adherence to rules may result in wider PED use.

Life-Cycle Model of performance enhancement (LCM)

Petroczi and Aidman (2008) offer a model based in sport psychology. At its core, this model considers how personality and systemic and situational factors influence the use of prohibited drugs in the context of working towards sports-related goals. The reason for situating drug use within goal attainment is an assumed functionality of drug use. That is, the LCM assumes that athletes use PEDs to achieve a performance goal, rather than for experimental or recreational reasons or because they are dependent on the drugs. The model uses three factors to explain drug use through a staged-goal attainment cycle (e.g. entry, choice, goal commitment, execution, feedback, goal evaluation and adjustment, to exit or back to entry) that moves this model from describing influential variables (content) to articulating how the behaviour occurs (process) (cf. Huybers and Mazanov, in press). Intervention that focuses on these factors can then occur at different stages of the cycle. For example, one stage is goal commitment. This stage sees athletes asking themselves 'how badly do you want it?' The answer to this question changes depending on personality and systemic and situational factors. For example, some athletes might have a 'whatever it takes' approach while others may be highly moralistic about naturalness and authenticity in performance. There has been no empirical test of this model.

Petroczi and Aidman's (2008) model offers three key improvements on the previous models. First, describing drug use as being functional towards achieving a goal suggests managers need to consider the different functions PED use might have in their programme. For example, athletes could be looking to use a PED to prolong their careers. Alternatively, support personnel may be seeking to protect a contract contingent on achieving certain performance goals; promoting drug use among athletes may be less attractive to support personnel if certain performance outcomes are removed from employment contracts.

Second, locating the model in the different stages of the goal achievement life cycle provides managers with a way to understand the stage athletes are at with regard to PED use. For example, if an athlete is at the choice stage managers can influence the choice by offering a range of performance-enhancing alternatives. The LCM is also based on the understanding that the way in which support personnel develop and execute goal-driven performance programmes with athletes changes their relationship to PEDs.

Third, this model attaches more importance to psychological factors such as motivational climate and programme culture. For example, Petroczi and Aidman (2008) posit that focusing a programme on developing a mastery climate that encourages a task orientation to sport-related goals may make PED use non-normative and therefore less likely to occur within a programme (cf. MM).

Sociological Model (SM)

Stewart and Smith (2008) propose a sociologically influenced model. They view PED use as the consequence of three 'rings' of structural constraints to drug use behaviour: system, interpersonal and intrapersonal. The first ring of constraints (the sporting system) provides the context for drug use, including government funding based on 'gold medal potential' (e.g. facilities and development programmes), nationalism and commercial pressure for on-field success. These structural constraints define the second ring of interpersonal constraints (social issues), such as the sports culture (e.g. win at all costs) and social sanctions for deviant behaviour. With this background of systemic and social constraints, the third ring represents the intrapersonal constraints of the individual actor (psychological issues) defined by previous models (e.g. personality, threat appraisals and morality). Qualitative evidence supportive of the SM is reported by Stewart and Smith (2010).

This model posits that managers need to manage the relationship with organizational units outside their programme (e.g. government bodies, national sporting organizations or sponsors) as much as those in their programme (e.g. their athletes and support personnel). The previous models focus heavily on managing individuals or collections of individuals within a programme. However, managers also need to look at how their programme interacts with other programmes, and also with society more broadly. For example, managers of high performance sport can lobby for or against certain PEDs appearing on the prohibited list in order to benefit their programme (by enhancing the performance of their programme through the use of a particular drug, or by removing a drug from a competing programme). Equally, managers could look to invest in the development of legitimate PEDs. Alternatively, managers might look to restructure commercial relationships to mitigate some of the pressures for on-field success. (This last point is for the argument; the pragmatics of doing so is a different issue.) The key implication for managers of high performance sport is that while external influences impact on their programme, managers can shape those external influences by politicizing the process (e.g. by lobbying for policy amendments).

Grounded Model (GM)

Mazanov and Huybers (2010) provide a model of PED use, developed using the grounded theory method based from a sample of Australian elite athletes and support personnel. According to Mazanov and Huybers the decision to use a drug is driven by four clusters of variables: (i) objective of drug use (performance outcomes, financial gain and contractual obligations); (ii) context of drug use (social influence, source of information and health effects); (iii) the deterrence system (likelihood of detection and, separately, prosecution); and (iv) consequences if prosecuted (fines, public humiliation). This empirical model correlates strongly with the factors identified in previous models.

The management implications arising from the first cluster suggest the need for a close examination of the links between performance and reward. For example, to mitigate the lure of big prize money it has been suggested that athletes should receive a base wage, with additional earnings sequestered in superannuation or other investment accounts (Mazanov et al., 2011). Changing the link between performance and the reward may reduce the consideration to use PED.

The second cluster suggests that the ways in which athletes get information about drugs, especially about their health effects, influence their decisions about whether to use them. Managers may do well to ensure athletes are literate about the performance-enhancing and health effects of drugs, especially about the relative risks of drugs (see Gillespie, 2011). This might start with teaching athletes how to understand the relative risks of side effects as described in pharmaceutical product disclosure statements (Huybers and Mazanov, 2012).

The third cluster suggests that the integrity of the system governing prohibited drug use matters. Athletes are aware that even if they are caught using illicit drugs, there is a chance to 'roll the legal dice'. It may be worthwhile communicating to athletes the level of legal support they can expect from their sporting programme should they be detected using prohibited drugs. For example, high performance athletes may use illicit drugs on the assumption their programme will use a chunk of its budget to protect the investment in that athlete; telling athletes otherwise may dissuade some from using illicit drugs.

Finally, athletes need to know that there are consequences to being caught that extend beyond sanctions. For example, in addition to formal sanctions (bans), managers may wish to implement a system of fines and social sanctions from within the club. This may include making public disclosure of PED use more credible by getting the athlete to explain themselves to members of their squad, fans or school children.

THE EVOLUTION OF DRUG-FREE SPORT

The ways in which drugs in sport have been managed have been driven by the social ideal of 'drug-free sport'. Despite being a part of some sports from their very inception (e.g. cycling; Waddington and Smith, 2009), the debate around the role of drugs in sport emerged in the 1920s and 1930s (Mazanov and McDermott, 2009). While stimulants were used to enhance the combat performances of soldiers in the Second World War (Gahlinger, 2004; Houlihan, 2002), the critical developments in the use of PEDs came as a result of advances in pharmacology and pharmaceuticals and television technology. The televising of Olympic events saw scandals erupt around allegedly PED-related deaths (see Moller, 2010). Intertwined with this was the Cold War, where communist-bloc scientists (especially those in the German Democratic Republic) pioneered systematic doping (Spitzer, 2004). The negative reaction to the use of PEDs in high performance sport was increased by the negative health consequences arising from their abuse. The combination of threats to athlete health and to broadcast revenue along with the political climate led to the development of the drug-free sport ideology.

The ideology of drug-free sport is expressed in the World Anti-Doping Code (WADC) that is administered by the World Anti-Doping Agency (WADA) (WADA, 2009a). WADA has been working towards achieving 'policy harmonization' so that the WADC can be consistently applied across sports and countries (Houlihan, 1999). Policy harmonization was needed due to the variations in approaches to managing drugs in sport that emerged in the pre-WADA era. For example, the policy in athletics was different from that in cycling and the policy in France was different from that in Norway. Under policy harmonization, governments and the governing bodies of sports are required to engage in a range of activities that promote the drug-free sport ideology, including in- and out-of-competition testing, education and sanctions. Importantly, these activities extend to non-Olympic sports, and government support for sports can be contingent on compliance with WADC regulations (WADA, 2009a).

AN OVERVIEW OF THE WADC

The policy context of the WADC is provided here as it represents the starting point for how PEDs should be managed in high performance sport. Importantly, the WADC makes clear that it is the responsibility of those involved in sport to be familiar with their obligations, effectively removing ignorance as a defence for violations. While this overview provides the basics, high performance sport managers should have a copy of the WADC handy to ensure that they and their staff understand the obligations and consequences of working towards drug-free sport.

The WADC seeks to protect athletes' rights to participate in doping-free sport as a way of promoting health, fairness and equality in competition, by focusing on detection, deterrence and prevention of doping (WADC, 2009a, p. 11). The rationale for the WADC is given as the 'Spirit of Sport' statement, which identifies eleven values that represent the essence of the Olympic ideal (see Table 15.2). There is no guidance in the WADC on what is meant by these values. Doping is defined as being fundamentally contrary to the Spirit of Sport (WADC, 2009a, p. 14).

Article 2 of the WADC identifies eight ways an athlete or support person can commit an Anti-Doping Rule Violation (ADRV) (see Table 15.3). Notably, Articles 2.4–2.8 have implications for support personnel. For example, support personnel could be sanctioned for possessing a banned PED at an event (Article 2.6). It is unclear whether support personnel need to seek therapeutic use exemptions in the same way that athletes do (Mazanov *et al.*, 2008). Equally, if it can be proven that someone was aware of the use of banned PEDs and failed to report the infringement, they can be sanctioned. Both the athletes and the programme support personnel need training about their responsibilities.

Table 15.2 *The Spirit of Sport values*

Ethics, fair play and honesty	Dedication and commitment
Health	Respect for rules and laws
Excellence in performance	Respect for self and other participants
Character and education	Courage
Fun and joy	Community and solidarity
Teamwork	

Adapted from the World Anti-Doping Code

Table 15.3 *WADC Article 2 Anti-Doping Rule Violations*

Article	Anti-Doping Rule Violations
2.1	violations arising from a positive drug test
2.2	use or attempted use by an athlete (and strict liability)
2.3	athlete refusal, failure or evading sample collection
2.4	out-of-competition testing
2.5	protects doping control from tampering or attempted tampering
2.6	possession of prohibited substances or methods
2.7	trafficking of prohibited substances or methods
2.8	sanctions administration, attempted administration, assisting, encouraging, aiding, abetting, covering up or any other type of complicity involving an attempted or actual anti-doping rule violation

Adapted from the World Anti-Doping Code

Articles 3–8 provide details on the testing process. Articles 9–12 deal with the consequences of an ADRV. These articles deal with sanctions as they relate to disqualification of results (including medals, points and prizes) (Article 9), sanctions on individuals (Article 10), consequences to teams (Article 11) and sanctions against sporting bodies (Article 12). The appeal process is articulated in Article 13 and the confidentiality and reporting of results is outlined in Article 14. Articles 18 and 19 establish the roles of education and research.

Of more interest to high performance sports managers are Articles 20–22, which establish the roles and responsibilities of different actors within the policy space. Article 20 outlines the basics of what signatories are required to do with regard to making anti-doping work, from the IOC to international federations to major event organizations to WADA. That is, Article 20 articulates what each organization has agreed to do (and not to do). This provides insights into where information may be sourced, either formally or informally. Article 21 outlines the roles and responsibilities of athletes and support personnel. While the roles and responsibilities of the athlete are straightforward (i.e. they are required to comply with the system), there are additional responsibilities confronting support personnel that managers need to be aware of. The discussion of these responsibilities is developed below. Article 22 defines the UNESCO Convention as the instrument that ties the WADC together internationally, and outlines the consequences of any failure to comply (e.g. nations become ineligible to bid for the right to host the Olympics).

POLICY IMPLICATIONS AND IMPLEMENTATION OF THE WADC

The administrative system devised to manage performance-enhancing drugs in sport (the WADC and UNESCO Convention) has created new problems (anti-doping could therefore be characterized as a 'wicked problem'; Rittel, 1972). These new problems and the implications that arise from both the policy as it stands and its implementation are discussed in this section as they apply to managers of high performance sport. Note that discussing responses from the perspective of high performance sport is different from how the issue might be discussed from other perspectives (e.g. community sport or drug control).

Moral basis for the WADC

As noted above, the moral basis for anti-doping is established as the right to participate in dope-free sport, and the promotion of health, fairness and equality for athletes worldwide (WADA, 2009a, p. 11). This moral basis can be challenged at every step. The first challenge is whether athletes can ever participate in dope-free sports given that some PEDs are permitted. The only difference between doping and legitimate PED use is an administrative decision. This is demonstrated by the variability of substances that are prohibited; some substances that have been banned in the past have subsequently been permitted despite having scientifically demonstrated performance-enhancing effects (e.g. caffeine). The second challenge is that the risks to athlete health from PED use are actually less than participation in elite sport (e.g. chronic injury) (Waddington, 2000). For example, long-term brain injury associated with contact sport is an ongoing problem (Daneshvar et al., 2011; Omalu et al., 2010). The third challenge is whether sport can be considered fair given that sport is designed to promote the search for innovations unavailable to competitors, such as the Fosbury Flop high jump technique. Finally, athletes are treated inequitably. For example, elite fencing athletes receive very different support from professional tennis players (e.g. government grants and prize money). The contradiction that undermines the moral basis for the WADC is that the threats posed by doping are already compromised by the nature of sport.

The failure to establish a compelling moral basis for anti-doping can lead athletes and support personnel to search for alternative moral justifications for opposing the use of PEDs (Mazanov and Connor, 2010). The first alternative justification is usually an appeal to the Spirit of Sport as organizational citizenship behaviour; athletes are expected to do the 'right' thing in sport by engaging in behaviours that protect the integrity of sport above their own interests (e.g. only use PEDs within the rules). Appealing to athletes to put the integrity of sport first can be very different from what is right for athletes to do, especially when most athletes face a brutally short career with uncertain financial returns (Mazanov and Connor, 2010). Consequently, the alternative moral justification of being a good sports citizen has to compete with high performance athletes acting rationally by putting their own interests ahead of sport as a whole.

The second alternative is to argue that without an agreement to abide by the rules there is no sport (Suits, 1973). The problem is that a clear source of competitive advantage comes from taking advantage of loopholes in the rules governing sport.

The third alternative is that athletes and support personnel develop their own morality around PED use. As indicated by the models of PED use, managers can have a significant effect on the norms around drug use in their programmes. Equally, managers may need to influence governing bodies (e.g. WADA, government bodies and sporting federations) towards establishing a moral framework for the use of PED use that is more consistent with the 'lived experience' of people involved in high performance sport (Stewart and Smith, 2010).

Out-of-competition testing

Some ADRVs relate to actual drug use while others relate to administrative mechanisms designed to protect the anti-doping system, such as out-of-competition testing (OOC). The OOC system was developed as some drugs are metabolized and leave the body quickly while the ergogenic effect remains. The OOC testing system requires athletes to nominate, three months in advance, a time and place at which they guarantee to be available for testing (WADA, 2009b). Some countries require athletes to be available any day of the year (including public and religious holidays). These requirements have raised questions about the ethics of reducing athlete rights and welfare in order to protect an administrative system (Hanstad and Loland, 2009; Houlihan, 2004; Waddington, 2010). The debate centres on whether athletes enjoy the same rights to privacy, autonomy and self-determination that other citizens have (Malloy and Zuckus, 2002). WADA justifies the reduction in rights as the price elite that athletes have to pay for clean sport (Hanstad and Loland, 2009, p. 6). The broader question is whether athletes *should* have to pay this price.

Managerially, one might argue that athletes sign away these rights as part of the conditions of private employment, similar to signing away certain rights upon joining the armed services. However, signing away one's rights so that one can defend one's homeland is very different to signing away one's rights so that one can be part of a profit-making venture in the entertainment industry. In the Industrial Revolution, employee exploitation of this sort led to unionization and labour laws that prescribe the minimum working conditions. The architecture protecting these rights has been established by the Universal Declaration of Human Rights (UN, 1948), and is elaborated by subsequent declarations of human rights in other jurisdictions. The danger for managers is that sanctions relating to compliance with OOC testing may lead to costly legal action, as has been the case for Belgian tennis players Wickmayer and Malisse. These players challenged their sanctions for failing to file OOC testing information, which were subsequently overturned on appeal. Despite the immediate success, the ramifications of this case continue with challenges to the legality of the OOC testing system in the European Commission and the European Court of Human Rights.

Evidence and Anti-Doping Rule Violation (ADRV) appeals

Managers need to be aware of the different standards of evidence that exist with regard to ADRV. Coleman and Levine (2011) argue that the myriad of standards of evidence creates costly legal problems when athletes challenge positive test results, or analytic positives. For example, sporting federations simply define testing as infallible, which contradicts the growing literature that demonstrates it is not (e.g. Berry, 2008; Mazanov and Connor, 2010). If the test is positive the athlete has doped, and it is up to the athlete to demonstrate otherwise on appeal. If an athlete appeals to the sports federation or the Court of Arbitration for Sport (CAS), the athlete has to either demonstrate the fallibility of a test administratively defined as infallible or find another reason for the positive result, such as a kiss (CAS, 2009). If an athlete appeals to a court of law rather than CAS (which is an arbiter rather than a legally binding court), a different standard of evidence applies. In the United States, the standard of evidence that applies in duly constituted courts makes it easier to rebut a doping charge (Coleman and Levine, 2011, p. 42). If an athlete tests positive, the standards of evidence required clearly have an impact on the level of support a programme can give and they have an impact on the strategies that may be deployed in defending the case. For example, the programme may decide it has a better chance of success outside the sports arbitration system.

Coleman and Levine's focus on analytic positives opens the question of how standards of evidence apply to non-analytic positives, which rely on circumstantial evidence to imply an athlete has committed an ADRV (McClaren, 2006). What may happen with regard to support personnel prosecuted is also open to speculation.

This issue is part of the background that managers and their programmes need to be aware of in relation to the management of PED use. It also points to another issue that managers can lobby to change. For example, it may be argued that being bound by agreements to use CAS can be changed by pointing out the efficiencies to be had through the normal court system.

Policy disharmony: health professionals and reporting obligations

There is growing concern about the way that the obligations of health support personnel (e.g. physicians, physiotherapists or psychologists) to report ADRVs to national anti-doping organizations (NADO) interact with their professional obligations. For example, if an athlete discloses PED use to a physician to avoid contraindications, the physician is obliged to report that PED use to their NADO or risk being banned from sport. McNamee and Phillips (2011) outline the duties of healthcare professionals with regard to the bodies that oversee their profession, whether governmental (e.g. register for a licence to practice) or professional (e.g. the relevant medical association). These duties include confidentiality of disclosure and acting in the best interests of clients. McNamee and Phillips argue that, in serving the best interests of the athlete-patient, physicians risk being open to a charge of aiding and abetting doping (an ADRV) or being struck off the medical practice register for disclosure. This is even more concerning given the apparent ignorance about WADC obligations among physicians (Backhouse and McKenna, 2011).

Article 20 of the WADC places the obligations related to anti-doping education (interpreted in this instance as training compliance with the WADC) on the national Olympic and Paralympic committees, international federations, national anti-doping organizations and event organizers. Given that knowledge about the issues involved is inadequate among physicians, one can only speculate as to the level of education among allied health professionals (e.g. physiotherapists and psychologists) and non-health support personnel (e.g. sports trainers). There are three implications for managers. The first is the need to avoid sanctions that may mean that the cost of education has to be paid by the programmes they run. The consequences of doing otherwise may be the inadvertent sanctioning of athletes or support personnel. The second implication is that there is a risk that sanctions could be appealed on the basis of a lack of knowledge of obligations under the WADC. The WADC is clear that it is the responsibility of support personnel to understand their obligations. What is less clear is how the validity of this requirement would stand up to scrutiny by external bodies, such as health professional organizations or duly constituted courts of law. The third implication is that managers may need to lobby the relevant institutions to provide the required education.

Athlete health and welfare

The WADC appears to protect the integrity of sport at the expense of athletes' health and welfare (Waddington, 2000). For example, the administrative mechanisms in the WADC protect the integrity of anti-doping while diminishing athletes' rights. Some writers argue that the case for anti-doping should attach a high priority to athlete health and welfare. This is known as the health-based harm-minimization approach (Kayser et al., 2007; Mazanov, 2011; Smith and Stewart, 2008). Harm minimization is best practice evidence-based treatment drawn from drug management literature, and is the drug-control model advocated by health practitioners (e.g. BMA, 2002). This approach to managing the role of drugs in sport has been criticized for condoning drug use. However, the WADC itself condones PED use by allowing some of them to be used.

There is effectively a continuum of harm minimization approaches, from permission through to prohibition (Mazanov, 2008). The problems of unregulated permissiveness are the same as those revealed in prohibition: medically unsupervised use of PEDs can expose athletes to drug abuse, blood-borne infections (through needle sharing) and pharmaceutically impure drugs. This implies that medical supervision of PED use may be preferable. An alternative approach under harm minimization would follow the 'blood passport' ideology, where athletes demonstrating a biological profile known to threaten their health (e.g. haematocrit above a prescribed level) are withdrawn from competition until their profile returns to a level deemed safe (Savulescu *et al.*, 2004). These approaches are permissive in nature, enabling athletes to use PEDs.

A mixed approach (combining permissiveness and prohibition) is the drug diary (Bird and Wagner, 1997) where athletes are sanctioned if they test positive for any substance missing from their diarized record of substances taken over a specified period. That is, athletes are sanctioned if there are unknown or unrecorded substances in their bodies. This places the onus on athletes and support personnel rather than administrators.

A prohibition form of harm minimization is to suspend athletes who test positive for drug use from competition until they demonstrate they are unlikely to reoffend. This assumes that drug use is an abnormal (pathological) behaviour to be fixed by treating an athlete until they engage in the desired behaviour. Unfortunately, this approach may fail to interact with the current system based on the WADC given the variability in what is prohibited (see 'Moral Basis for the WADC' above). Under this model athletes who used caffeine while it was banned would be deemed abnormal the day before it came off the list and treated. The same athlete would be considered normal the day it came off the list and receive no treatment. Following the 'wicked' nature of drug control in sport, each of these policy paradigm alternatives introduce new problems.

Managers of high performance sport need to be aware of harm minimization and other policy alternatives. First, awareness of these alternatives enables managers to be part of the broader conversation about how they want PEDs in sport to be managed. Second, managers who can explain why they support an anti-doping policy rather than alternative policy approaches can help athletes find their own reasons for supporting one approach or another. This is likely to be a more convincing basis for establishing a normative approach to PED within the programme. Third, understanding the policy alternatives enables managers to strategize about responses to any potential changes in policy (however unlikely they seem at present).

CASE STUDY 15.1
DISPUTE RESOLUTION IN HIGH PERFORMANCE SPORT AND HOW IT INFLUENCES ELITE ATHLETES' CAREERS

Johnny Maeschalck

Van Landuyt & Partners

Sports legislation is not particularly extensive in Flanders. Taking the federal Sports Act of 24 February 1978 on labour agreements for professional athletes and the Decrees of 24 July 1996 on the establishment of the status of non-professional (amateur) athletes and of 13 July 2007 on medically and ethically sound sports practices into consideration, sports legislation is *sensu strictu* limited.

Nevertheless, both Belgium and Flanders show 'eagerness' in terms of the application and interpretation of sports law. Both court and appeal court judgement sometimes look beyond the sacred cows. The judgement of the European Court of Justice of 15 December 1995 on Jean-Marc Bosman is a good example of this.

The courts may, can and must supervise compliance with rules, regulations and procedures. However, on the basis of their 'marginal judicial review' they cannot review the expediency but only the legality of cases and the courts eagerly embarked on this path.

Increasingly, however, attempts are being made to sideline judges using rules and regulations, which, in my view, contradict long-established legal principles and do not qualify as such. Nevertheless, athletes must have and find the courage to question these rules and regulations that seem to be issued non-stop, and they must get back on their feet and continue to fight.

Take, for example, matters concerning (performance-enhancing) drugs. The 'Belgian' Act of 2 April 1965 already existed. For various reasons it was hardly applied. It was, for example, very difficult to prove the moral aspect, and, more importantly, it was not a priority for the prosecution services.

Following state reforms and the transfer of competences (public health) to the Communities, Flanders was quick to adopt the Decree of 27 March 1991. Flanders intended to grant greater responsibilities to sports associations and to decriminalize the assessment of these cases, taking the competence away from criminal courts. This is how it was stipulated in the Decree and both the legal doctrine and the highest ranking members of the prosecution services always adhered to this interpretation.

Then there was the case of (the cyclist) Frank Vandenbroucke. If ever a case study was needed, this case and the fourteen legal proceedings initiated on behalf of Frank fit the bill. On 27 February 2002 Mr Bernard Sainz was stopped by the roadside, referring to an agreement with Vandenbroucke, following which the cyclist's house was searched.

Three (expired) ampoules of epo, an unopened box of Clenbuterol and three doses of morphine were found.

The investigating magistrate ordered his arrest. In order to make sure there would be television footage, the officers carrying out the arrest paraded the cyclist a number of times before the TV cameras. These images are still regularly shown.

Although the investigation was far from complete, the UCI forced Mr Vandenbroucke to appear before the Disciplinary Committee of the Cycling Association, which suspended him for six months with immediate effect on 21 March 2002.

Since this committee was neither competent, nor recognized by the Flemish Authorities (a condition imposed by the Decree), the defence lawyers filed an appeal before the Tribunal Arbitral du Sport (TAS). The decision of the Royal Belgian Cycling Association (KBWB) was annulled in Lausanne on 24 June 2002. Frank Vandenbroucke was off the hook.

However, following this initial treatment of the case by a sports association, the Flemish Community took over proceedings. Mr Vandenbroucke was called before the Disciplinary Committee of the Flemish Community. On 4 July 2002, he was suspended for a period of eighteen months, of which six months represented the actual suspension.

Appeal proceedings against the decision of the Disciplinary Committee were held before *the* Disciplinary Committee of The Flemish Community on 13 August 2002. The decision was confirmed, albeit on different grounds. The KBWB decided to (geographically) limit this sanction to Flanders.

Suddenly, however, the prosecution services intervened and brought the case before the Chambre du Conseil (the court sitting in chambers). Given the provisions imposed by the Decree and the intention to decriminalize drugs-related issues, these court proceedings were obviously questioned.

Mr Vandenbroucke was referred to the Criminal Court and proceedings were continued before the court's indictment division, the latter confirming the referral to the Criminal Court in Dendermonde that sentenced the cyclist to 200 hours community service on 6 December 2004.

This judgement – given the same reasons cited by Mr Vandenbroucke with regard to decriminalization and therefore incompetence of the court – was appealed before the Court of Appeal in Ghent. On the basis of a 'creative' judgement of 20 April 2005, Mr Vandenbroucke was sentenced to pay a fine of €250,000.

A logical consequence of all this was, of course, that the defence initiated proceedings before the Court of Cassation (the Supreme Court of Belgium). With the judgement of 14 February 2006 the Court of Cassation annulled the judgement by the Court of Appeal in Ghent and referred the case – with the same issues being unresolved – to the Court of Appeal in Brussels. This court acquitted Mr Vandenbroucke on 12 December 2006.

This did not suffice for the prosecution services and new proceedings before the Court of Cassation were initiated. The Court of Cassation passed a judgement whereby – pending a final judgement – a question concerning Article 44 of the Decree of 27 March 1991 was referred to the Constitutional Court.

The Constitutional Court passed its judgement during a public session on 10 April 2008 and referred it back. The Court of Cassation, after having received a reply from the Constitutional Court, referred the case to the Court of Appeal in Antwerp, where the case was reopened and pleas were submitted.

Exactly three days prior to the judgement of the Court of Appeal in Antwerp, on 12 October 2009, Frank decided that all proceedings should be stopped. However, this case makes the desire to restrain the use of (performance-enhancing) drugs abundantly clear.

As early as the proceedings before the Criminal Court in Dendermonde, it was suggested that a question be referred to the (then) Court of Arbitration. This suggestion was not followed up and the prosecution services always objected to referring a question to superior courts. Only in the last instance and on the occasion of the second appearance before the Court of Cassation did the prosecution service of the Court of Cassation request that the question be referred to the Constitutional Court.

Mr Vandenbroucke was not responsible for these extremely long proceedings. The cure is sometimes worse than the illness. Moreover, this issue lingers since proceedings have meanwhile been revised but many questions remain unanswered. There is no other legal matter in which (1) a third party, a party who is not concerned, (2) can appeal – not merely file a protest against – a decision, (3) using a specially created and longer appeal period than the parties concerned, (4) in another language and (5) in another country. All of this in (6) arbitration proceedings with (7) (previously appointed) arbitrators selected by the organization, whereby (8) the two parties involved in the first proceedings must jointly appoint one arbitrator.

And the soap opera continues, since starting with the appeal proceedings initiated by WADA only (9) the TAS rules apply and *en cours de route,* (10) Swiss law applies with the only possibility for review being the . . . Federal Court of Switzerland.

Perhaps sport is not the most important thing in life, but what about the rights of athletes?

CASE STUDY 15.2
EXPANSION OF ANTI-DOPING ORGANIZATIONS

Dag Vidar Hanstad

Norwegian School of Sport Sciences

Since the 1990s anti-doping activity has gone through comprehensive changes. The scandal during the 1998 Tour de France has been described as a watershed (Houlihan, 2002) because it showed that (i) doping was widespread in a number of sports, (ii) the sport movement was not able to clean up its own house and (iii) governments in the Western world decided actively to intervene. In 1999 the World Anti-Doping Agency (WADA) was established with the Olympic movement and governments as equal stakeholders. WADA is one among many 'newcomers' in the field of anti-doping during the last decade. Other units, at national, international and global level, have changed their approach from a passive role to a more active involvement. The aim of this case study is to explore how the number of organizations in the 'anti-doping industry' has increased and become increasingly interconnected since the establishment of the WADA.

Before the establishment of WADA, in the 1980s and 1990s, just a few units were involved in anti-doping activity and many of those involved (e.g. the IOC) lacked credibility. Others were represented only by small numbers; for example, the great majority of governments were not involved in anti-doping, while some were actually involved in state-sponsored doping (Houlihan, 2002). Further, relatively few national Olympic Committees and international federations were involved in anti-doping. For example, a great majority of sports organizations had *not* established adjudication and appeals committees, or a special commission to deal with anti-doping.

Certainly some credible initiatives were taken in the 1990s, for example, when Western countries signed the Memorandum and formed the International Anti-Doping Arrangement (IADA) to pursue international harmonization through the development and implementation of best practice in national anti-doping programmes. This includes just around ten governments. Another unit with credibility in the fight against doping was the Council of

Europe (CoE) that initiated anti-doping work in the 1960s and created an Anti-Doping Convention in 1989. A monitoring group was established in the same year (Houlihan, 2002).

The 1999 World Conference on Doping in Sport in Lausanne, held in the aftermath of two scandals in 1998 (the Tour the France and the bribery scandal in Salt Lake City) is seen as a watershed because it initiated the establishment PED of WADA later the same year. In the following years the number of units involved in anti-doping has greatly increased. Sports organizations, governments, (inter)governmental organizations and other units (such as sponsors, broadcasters and journalists) have all become more aware of and involved in this issue.

With so many units it is necessary to limit the focus here to some key actors and the relationships between them: governments and the sports organizations. Within the sport movement more than 650 sports organizations (including government-funded organizations such as NADOs) have accepted the World Anti-Doping Code (WADA, 2011), the core document that provides the framework for harmonized anti-doping policies, rules and regulations within sport organizations and among public authorities (WADA, 2009a). Acceptance of regulations is not more than an indication of improvement but WADA's own evaluation on compliance and implementation has shown progress (WADA, 2008a). Another indication of change is the increase in the number of doping controls. The number of tests ('A samples') analysed in the accredited laboratories was 105,250 in 1998 and 118,259 in 1999 (Mottram, 2005), compared to 277,928 in 2009 (WADA, 2010).

A key change has been the increasing involvement of public authorities. Governments, in contrast to the period prior to 1998 when just a few were involved, have taken a much more active position in anti-doping work. In addition to their WADA involvement, they have transformed a common policy into the International Convention against Doping in Sport that provides a legal framework in which all governments can address the use of drugs (UNESCO, 2005). More than 150 governments have ratified the Convention (UNESCO, 2011). Operations by governmental units, such as police and customs, have unmasked drug use, for example BALCO in the United States and Operación Puerto in Spain. This seems to have taken anti-doping work in a new direction. Public authorities and WADA have established a power platform with other sport organizations in a new and less powerful position. This has led to intensifying anti-doping work.

SUMMARY

PEDs have a role in high performance sport, demonstrated by their widespread use. It is up to managers to ensure that their programmes navigate that role without transgressing the established system. The models explaining PED use point to the very important role that high performance sport managers play in creating, sustaining and modifying the established system. The established system of dealing with PEDs raises a range of other issues that could easily absorb significant amounts of time and other resources.

The fundamental question is whether the current system is appropriate or whether it needs to be changed. There is evidence that the WADC is amenable to change. Recognition that support personnel are usually complicit in athlete doping resulted in changes to the WADC (WADA, 2009a) that mean support personnel can now be sanctioned. This demonstrates that the WADC is a living policy that managers can influence. Managers of high performance sport and their governing bodies have the capacity to shape the management of PED. Moreover, managers of high performance sport and their governing bodies *should* be shaping the management of PED in sport. The next step is working out how to do it.

DISCUSSION QUESTIONS

1   What role, if any, should managers of high performance sport have in setting policies that govern the role of PED at national and international levels?
2   Is the current mixed model (in which some PEDs are allowed, and some are not) a critical weakness in the way PEDs are managed?
3   Is the integrity of sport more or less important than the welfare of an individual athlete?
4   Should the WADC be made to harmonize with standards established outside high performance sport (e.g. legal evidence and disclosure), or should high performance sport be considered a 'special case' where societal norms no longer apply?
5   What would a system of fines and social sanctions for PED use look like and how would it work?

KEY TERMS

■   Anti-doping
■   Doping
■   Drug control
■   Harm minimization
■   Performance-enhancing drug
■   World Anti-Doping Code

GUIDED READING

Waddington, I. and Smith, A. (2009). *An introduction to drugs in sport: Addicted to winning.* Abingdon, UK: Routledge.
   This book is an essential introduction to the sociology of drugs in sport. It provides a comprehensive discussion of the issues involved for anyone seeking to engage with the role of drugs in sport at a deeper level.
Mottram, D. R. (2011). Prevalence of drug misuse in sport. In D. R. Mottram (Ed.), *Drugs in sport* (5th edn). Abingdon, UK: Routledge.

This book deals with the science behind how PEDs work. It summarizes the necessary information on what PEDs are, their expected effects and their unexpected effects.

Mazanov, J. (Ed.). (2011). *Towards a social science of drugs in sport.* Abingdon, UK: Routledge. This book provides an overview of the different ways that social science informs the role of drugs in sport. Key authors have written on the ways in which philosophical, sociological, legal, economic and psychological analyses of the issue inform the debate.

Recommended websites

www.wada-ama.org
The best place to go for information is the primary source. The WADA site provides all the official information you need to engage with this topic.

www.doping.au.dk
This is the website for the *International Network for Humanistic Doping Research*. It presents a diversity of views about performance-enhancing drug use in sport, and in society more broadly. The editorial series are thought-provoking pieces by experts in the field.

BIBLIOGRAPHY

ASADA (2010). *ASADA Annual Report 2009–2010.* ASADA, Canberra, Australia.

Backhouse, S. and McKenna, J. (2011). Doping in sport: A review of medical practitioners' knowledge, attitudes and beliefs. *International Journal of Drug Policy*, 22, 198–202.

Berglund, B., Ekblom, B., Ekblom, E., Berglund, L., Kallner, A., Reinebo, P. and Lindeberg, S. (2007). The Swedish Blood Pass Project. *Scandinavian Journal of Medicine and Science in Sports*, 17, 292–297.

Berry, D. A. (2008). The science of doping. *Nature*, 454, 692–693.

Bird, E. J. and Wagner, G. G. (1997). Sport as a common property resource. A solution to the dilemmas of doping. *Journal of Conflict Resolution*, 41(6), 749–766.

British Medical Association (2002). *Drugs in sport: The pressure to perform.* London: BMJ Publishing Group.

CAS (2009). CAS 2009/A/1926 *International Tennis Federation v Richard Gasquet*, CAS 2009/A/1930 *WADA v ITF & Richard Gasquet* at [2.17]. Available at www.tas-cas.org.

Coleman, J. E. and Levine J. M. (2011). The burden of proof in endogenous substance cases: A masking agent for junk science. In M. McNamee and V. Moller (Eds), *Doping and anti-doping policy in sport* (pp. 27–49). London: Routledge.

Corrigan, B. and Kazlauskas, R. (2003). Medication use in athletes selected for doping control at the Sydney Olympics (2000). *Clinical Journal of Sports Medicine*, 13, 33–40.

Daneshvar, D. H., Nowinski, C. J., McKee, A. C. and Cantu, R. C. (2011). The epidemiology of sport-related concussion. *Clinics in Sports Medicine*, 30(1), 1–17.

Donahue, E. G., Miquelon, P., Valois, P., Goulet, C., Buist, A. and Vallerand, R. J. (2006). A motivational model of performance-enhancing substance use in elite athletes. *Journal of Sport and Exercise Psychology*, 28, 511–520.

Donovan, R. J., Egger, G., Kapernick, V. and Mendoza, J. (2002). A conceptual framework for achieving performance-enhancing drug compliance in sport. *Sports Medicine*, 32(4), 269–284.

Gahlinger, P. (2004). *Illegal drugs: A complete guide to their history, chemistry, use and abuse.* New York: Plume.

George, A. J. and Mottram, D. R. (2011). Anabolic agents. In D. R. Mottram (Ed.), *Drugs in sport* (5th edn, pp. 49–81). Abingdon, UK: Routledge.

Gucciardi, D. F., Jalleh, G. and Donovan, R. J. (2011). An examination of the Sport Drug Control Model with elite Australian athletes. *Journal of Science and Medicine in Sport*, doi: 10.1016/j.jsams.2011.03.009.

Hanstad, D. V. and Loland, S. (2009). Elite athletes' duty to provide information on their whereabouts: Justifiable anti-doping work or an indefensible surveillance regime? *European Journal of Sports Science*, 9(1), 3–10.

Harmer, P. A. (2010). Anabolic-androgenic steroid use among young male and female athletes: Is the game to blame? *British Journal of Sports Medicine*, 44, 26–31.

Houlihan, B. (1999). Policy harmonisation: The example of global anti-doping policy. *Journal of Sport Management*, 13, 197–215.

Houlihan, B. (2002). *Dying to win. Doping in sport and the development of anti-doping policy* (2nd edn). Strasbourg: Council of Europe Publishing.

Houlihan, B. (2004). Civil rights, doping control and the World Anti-Doping Code. *Sport in Society*, 7(3), 420–437.

Huybers, T. and Mazanov, J. (2012). What would Kim do: A choice study of projected athlete doping considerations. *Journal of Sport Management*.

Kanayama, G., Brower, K. J., Wood, R. I., Hudson, J. I. and Pope, H. G. (2009). Anabolic-androgenic steroid dependence: An emerging disorder. *Addiction*, 104, 1966–1974.

Kayser, B., Mauron, A. and Miah, A. (2007). Current anti-doping policy: A critical appraisal. *BMC Medical Ethics*, 8(2), doi: 10.1186/1472-6939-8-2.

Lazarus, L., Barkoulis, V., Rodafinos, A. and Tzortbatzoukis, H. (2010). Predictors of doping intentions in elite-level athletes: A social cognition approach. *Journal of Sport and Exercise Psychology*, 32, 694–710.

Malloy, D. C. and Zakus, D. H. (2002). Ethics of drug testing in sport – An invasion of privacy justified? *Sport, Education and Society*, 7(2), 203–218.

Mazanov, J. (2008). The death knell of the anti-doping policy. *Bulletin of Sport and Culture*, 29, 5–6.

Mazanov, J. (Ed.) (2011). *Towards a social science of drugs in sport*. Abingdon, UK: Routledge.

Mazanov, J. and Connor, J. (2010). Rethinking the management of drugs in sport. *International Journal of Sport Policy*, 2(1), 49–63.

Mazanov, J. and Huybers, T. (2010). An empirical model of athlete decisions to use performance-enhancing drugs: Qualitative evidence. *Qualitative Research in Sport and Exercise*, 2(3), 385–402.

Mazanov, J. and McDermott, V. (2009). The case for a social science of drugs in sport. *Sport in Society*, 12(3), 276–295.

Mazanov, J., Hemphill, D. and Connor, J. (2008). Fearless research and frank advice on anti-doping policy. *Sport Health*, 26(1), 8–10, 15.

Mazanov, J., Huybers, T. and Connor, J. (2011). Qualitative evidence of a primary intervention point for elite athlete doping. *Journal of Science and Medicine in Sport*, 14(2), 106–110.

McClaren, R. H. (2006). An overview of non-analytic positive and circumstantial evidence cases in sports. *Marquette Sports Law Review*, 16(2), 194–212.

McNamee, M. and Phillips, N. (2011). Confidentiality, disclosure and doping in sports medicine. *British Journal of Sports Medicine*, 45, 174–177.

Moller, V. (2010). *The ethics of doping and anti-doping: Redeeming the soul of sport?* Abingdon, UK: Routledge.

Mottram, D. R. (2011). Prevalence of drug misuse in sport. In D. R. Mottram (Ed.), *Drugs in sport* (5th edn, pp. 373–385). Abingdon, UK: Routledge.

Mottram, D. R. (2005). Prevalence of drug use in sport. In D. R. Mottram (Ed.), *Drugs in sport* (4th edn, pp. 357–380). London: Routledge.

Omalu, B., Bailes, J., Hammers, J. L. and Fitzsimmons, R. P. (2010). Chronic traumatic encephalopathy, suicides and parasuicides in professional American athletes: The role of the forensic pathologist. *American Journal of Forensic Medicine and Pathology*, 31(2), 130–132.

292

Petroczi, A. and Aidman, E. (2008). Psychological drivers of doping: The life-cycle model of performance enhancement. *Substances Abuse Treatment, Prevention and Policy*, 3(7).

Quirk, F. (2009). Health psychology and drugs in sport. *Sport in Society*, 12(3), 375–393.

Rittel, H. (1972). On the planning crisis: Systems analysis of the 'first and second generations'. *Bedrifts Okonomen*, 8, 390–396.

Savulescu, J., Foddy, B. and Clayton, M. (2004). Why we should allow performance-enhancing drugs in sport. *British Journal of Sports Medicine*, 38, 666–670.

Simon, P., Strigel, H., Aust, F., Dietz, K. and Ulrich, R. (2006). Doping in fitness sports: Estimated number of unreported cases and individual probability of doping. *Addiction*, 101, 1640–1644.

Smith, A. C. T. and Stewart, B. (2008). Drug policy in sport: Hidden assumptions and inherent contradictions. *Drug and Alcohol Review*, 27, 123–129.

Spitzer, G. (2004). A Leninist monster: Compulsory doping and public policy in the GDR and the lessons for today. In J. Hoberman and V. Møller (Eds), *Doping and public policy* (pp. 133–144). Odense, Denmark: University Press of Southern Denmark.

Stewart, B. and Smith, A. C. T. (2008). Drug use in sport: Implications for public policy. *Journal of Sport and Social Issues*, 32(3), 278–298.

Stewart, B. and Smith, A. (2010). Player and athlete attitudes to drugs in Australian sport: Implications for policy development. *International Journal for Sport Policy*, 2(1), 65–84.

Strelan, P. and Boeckmann, R. J. (2003). A new model for understanding performance-enhancing drug use by elite athletes. *Journal of Applied Sport Psychology*, 15, 176–183.

Strelan, P. and Boeckmann, R. J. (2006). Why drug testing in elite sport does not work: Perceptual deterrence theory and the role of personal moral beliefs. *Journal of Applied Social Psychology*, 36(12), 2909–2934.

Striegel, H., Ulrich, R. and Simon, P. (2010). Randomized response estimates for doping and illicit drug use in elite athletes. *Drug and Alcohol Dependence*, 106(2–3), 230–232.

Suits, B. (1973). The elements of sport. In R. Osterhoudt (Ed.), *The philosophy of sport*. Springfield, IL: C. C. Thomas Publisher.

Tsitsimpikou, C., Tsiokanos, A., Tsarouhas, K., Schamasch, P., Fitch, J., Valasiadis, D. and Jamurtas, A. (2009). Medication use by athletes at the Athens 2004 Summer Olympic Games. *Clinical Journal of Sport Medicine*, 19(1), 33–38.

UN (1948). *The Universal Declaration of Human Rights*. Available at www.un.org/en/documents/udhr/.

UNESCO (2005). *International Convention against Doping in Sport*. UNESCO. Paris: United Nations Educational, Scientific and Cultural Organization.

UNESCO (2010). Milestone reached with Anti-Doping Convention. UNESCO. Available at www.unesco.org/new/en/social-and-human-sciences/themes/sport/anti-doping/sv15/news/fiji_becomes_150th_state_to_tackle_doping_in_sport/, accessed 25 June 2011.

Uvascek, M., Nepusz, T., Mazanov, J., Naughton, D., Ranky, M. and Petroczi, A. (2011). Self-admitted behaviour and perceived use of performance-enhancing versus psychoactive drugs among competitive athletes. *Scandinavian Journal of Medicine & Science in Sports*, 21(2), 224–234.

WADA. (2008a). Matter for WADA Executive Committee/Foundation Board. Code Compliance and Implementation Report. Montreal, Canada: World Anti-Doping Agency.

WADA (2008b). *World Anti-Doping Code, 2009*. Montreal, Canada: World Anti-Doping Agency.

WADA (2009a). *The World Anti-Doping Code*. Montreal, Canada: World Anti-Doping Agency.

WADA (2009b). *The International Standard for Testing*. Montreal, Canada: World Anti-Doping Agency.

WADA (2010). *Adverse analytical findings and atypical findings*. World Anti-Doping Agency. Available at www.wada-ama.org/Documents/Science_Medicine/Anti-Doping_Laboratories/Lab_Statistics/WADA_2009_LaboratoryStatisticsReport_Final.pdf, accessed 25 June 2011.

WADA (2011). *Code acceptance*. World Anti-Doping Agency. Available at www.wada-ama.org/en/World-Anti-Doping-Program/Sports-and-Anti-Doping-Organizations/The-Code/Code-Acceptance/, accessed 10 November 2009.

Waddington, I. (2000). *Sport, health and drugs*. London: E & FN Spon.

Waddington, I. (2010). Surveillance and control in sport: A sociologist looks at the WADA whereabouts system. *International Journal of Sport Policy*, 2(3), 255–274.

Waddington, I. and Smith, A. (2009). *An introduction to drugs in sport: Addicted to winning*. Abingdon, UK: Routledge.

Afterword on managing high performance sport

David Lavallee

University of Stirling

The afterword to a book presents an opportunity to reflect, to look back on what has been achieved and, perhaps, what else could have been written. Normally this reflection is restricted to the contents of the book itself. However, on this occasion I thought it may be interesting to initially widen the scope of the endeavour and use this opportunity to consider where this book currently stands in relation to the broad expanse of work described under the label of high performance sport.

As an identifiable field of scholarship, high performance sport is in its relative infancy. However, the literature in the area is developing rapidly. Earlier books have been successful in reviewing material available at that time but in highly specific areas (e.g. sport policy and governance, elite sport development, risk management in sport). Having spent time reflecting on the contributions to *Managing High Performance Sport* set against earlier efforts, I believe that the years have been more than kind. Not only have earlier expectations of progress been met, they have been exceeded in a way that would have seemed improbable even ten years ago. As one unexpected consequence, I think it is now a much more daunting task to try to summarize the extant literature on high performance sport in one volume, but this book has gone a long way towards achieving that goal.

The reader of this volume cannot fail to be impressed by the wide range of topics, methods and disciplinary matrices being brought to bear on high performance sport. If nothing else this recent burgeoning of interest in the subject speaks to bold pioneering efforts of the editors of, and contributors to, this book. But this same diversity also raises the question of whether this is a bridge too far. I do not believe it is because the high performance sport 'bridge' is still at the construction stage and needs a lot of thought and work before it will be sturdy. Many foundational ideas and useful research approaches are displayed here, but the array of topic reflected in the book, while representative, is still incomplete in its coverage of issues. However, the editors have fostered scholarly exchange among investigators who would otherwise be isolated in their respective specializations, whether management, organizations, etc. The synergy of such an exchange is explicit in several of the chapters, and in a more general sense, characterizes the book as a whole. One could argue that this openness to cross-fertilization among distinct fields is essential to the full understanding of high performance sport.

The book has global appeal, drawing upon work from North America, United Kingdom, Europe, Australia, New Zealand, Middle East and Asia. It fills a niche and growing market, and will help further promote interest in the field. The book's accessibility is a strength, as it will be of interest to high performance managers, academics, researchers, students, policymakers and practitioners in high performance sport. In offering a holistic understanding of the management processes that allow high performance in sport to take place, this book will appeal to readers beyond sport interest in high performance in a range of contexts and settings.

In reference to a topic from the current volume – transitions in sport – transitions are considered, in relation to elite athletes, as *an event or non-event that results in a change in assumptions about oneself and the world and thus requires a corresponding change in one's behaviour and relationships.* It is probably fair to say that the field of high performance sport is in a period of rapid and extensive transition. There has not been a specific event that has led to this transition, but the field is making new assumptions about itself as it evolves. As a result, it requires change in the way it behaves as a field and also its relationships with other fields. It is my view that high performance managers, coaches, sport scientists and other relevant high performance sport organizations and agencies need to continue to work together to address current and future challenges.

I would like to conclude by returning to the funnel of high performance sport management introduced by the Editors in the book's Preface. The funnel shows how the three levels that provide the structure of the book (high performance management of elite sport, managing high performance athletes and the environment of high performance) interact. My view is that the knowledge presented in each of these three parts across the book naturally flow into research, pedagogy and practice (see Figure B).

In terms of research, cutting-edge studies across various topics associated with managing high performance are weaved through the book. For research to move forward in the area, researchers need to take into account what is known and explore the unknown with the aim to advance knowledge. This book makes a contribution towards shaping theoretical constructs and feeding that to researchers interested in the field when reviewing the literature and in identifying research gaps. With regard to pedagogy, there is a need for continuing education for individuals working in the high performance profession along with those with an ambition to do so. Universities have an important role to play in designing courses, particularly at the postgraduate level.

Finally, in terms of practice, despite the abundance of resources in the areas of coaching, training, sport science and sport medicine, there has been a lack of emphasis on the role of management in successful athletes and team. This book collates information for practitioners in a way that relates to an increasing important aspect of elite success, that is, managing high performance sport. In some chapters more than others, practice takes centre stage but this does not detract from but actually enhances the significant research and pedagogy contributions that the chapters are able to make. As such, I view this volume as a 'sourcebook' in the management of high performance sport because it will stimulate ideas and research across the field. It is designed to collect in a single book the writings of a set of distinguished scholars to address their ideas on high performance sport. The chapters and authors in this volume were chosen so as to represent some of the most interesting current work in high performance sport across a wide range of disciplines. I do not believe that any current volume reveals as much breadth on the topic, covered by scholars with active research programmes, as is provided in *Managing High Performance Sport*.

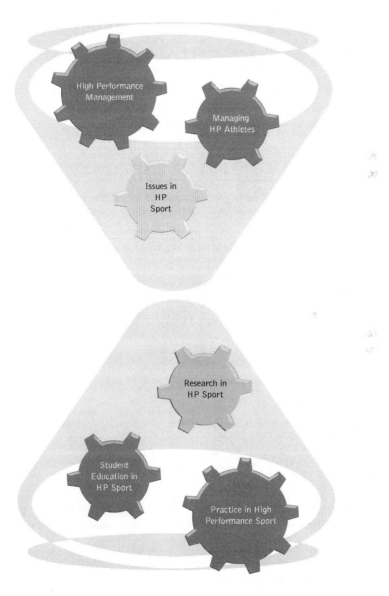

Figure B *The influences of broadening our perspectives on managing high performance sport*

List of critical success factors, used in the SPLISS study 2011, at national overall sports level*

PILLAR 1: FINANCIAL SUPPORT FOR SPORT AND ELITE SPORT

There is sufficient national level financial support for sport

CSF1.1 Total national expenditure on sport (cash terms) (including elite sport) national lotteries, central government and Olympic Committee (overall and per head of population)

CSF1.2 Total national government expenditure on sport as a proportion of total national government expenditure

CSF1.3 Increase/decrease in national expenditure on sport during the last 12 years (3 Olympic cycles)

CSF1.4 Total government expenditure on sport at the regional and local level: provinces and municipalities**

There is sufficient national level financial support for elite sport

CSF1.5 Total national expenditure on elite sport (cash terms) from national lotteries and central government (overall and per head of population)

CSF1.6 National expenditure on elite sport as a proportion of total national expenditure on sport

CSF1.7 Increase/decrease in total national elite sport expenditures during the last 12 years (3 Olympic cycles) from national lotteries and central government

CSF1.8 Total government expenditure on elite sport, if there are any of major importance, at the regional and local level: provinces, cities and municipalities**

CSF1.9 Total national expenditure on elite sport by sponsors**

CSF1.10 Total national expenditure on elite sport by the media**

---

* Reprinted with permission from VUBPRESS, De Bosscher, De Knop and Van Bottenburg, 2007, p. 227.

** CSF that mainly need to be measured at other levels than in this research.

There is sufficient financial support per sport from national collective sources (i.e. national lotteries, central government and NOC), through National Governing Bodies (NGBs) and/or sport clubs

CSF1.11 Total funding per sport from national lotteries, central government and NOC (cash terms): for NGBs, and/or sport clubs (overall and per head of population; and per governing body/or per recognised sport)

There is sufficient financial support from national lotteries/central government and the National Olympic Committee for specific elite sport (disciplines) through National Governing Bodies (NGBs) and/or sport clubs

CSF1.12 Total funding/financial support per elite sport from national lotteries/central government and the National Olympic Committee: for NGBs, and/or sport clubs (cash terms)

CSF1.12B Average funding from collective sources for elite sport (see 1.12) per recognized elite sport (discipline)

CSF1.13 Total funding/financial support per elite sport as a proportion of total financial support for sport

PILLAR 2: THE GOVERNANCE, ORGANISATION AND STRUCTURE OF ELITE SPORT. AN INTEGRATED APPROACH TO POLICY DEVELOPMENT

There is strong coordination of all agencies involved in elite sport, with clear task descriptions and no overlap of different tasks

CSF 2.1 Coordination of financial inputs (horizontal direction) and activities: expenditure and activities on elite sport at the national level are recorded and coordinated centrally, so that no overlap takes place

CSF 2.2 Coordination of financial inputs (vertical direction) and activities: allocation of funding and management of activities with regard to elite sport at regional/district level: if there is any significant financial input of this type it is recorded and coordinated nationally

CSF 2.3 There is only one organisation at the national level that is exclusively responsible for elite sport (and not for sport for all/mass sport participation)

CSF 2.4 Elite sport is recognised as a valuable component of a politician's portfolio of responsibilities

There is evidence of long-term planning for elite sport development with the commitment of subsidies for elite sport and professional elite sport development

CSF 2.5 Long-term policy plans are developed (at least on a 4-8 year period) specifically for elite sport and are communicated in public, regularly evaluated and supported with financial resourcing

CSF 2.6 Policy is regularly evaluated with athletes, coaches, performance directors who are formally invited to be involved in the evaluation process

CSF 2.7 NGBs are subsidised for (at least) a four-year cycle

CSF 2.8 The government/NSA has implemented a series of programmes and organisational requirements on the NGBs/clubs/sports regarding the development of elite sport

CSF2.9 Long-term policy plans are required for governing bodies in order to receive funding

CSF2.10 Athletes and coaches are represented within National Governing Bodies

CSF2.11 The board of NGBs is composed of professionals who make decisions on elite sport

CSF2.12 There is a formal objective measurement instrument to evaluate the NGB funding criteria, undertaken by an independent organisation

Resources are targeted at relatively few sports through identifying those that have a real chance of success at world level

CSF2.13 Number of NGBs that are funded for elite sport purposes

A full-time management staff member in the NSA is responsible for the elite sport development process

CSF2.14 A full-time management staff member in the NSA is responsible for the specific purpose of the development and support of elite coaches, elite athletes, sport science, NGBs, marketing and communication

Effective communication: there is an unbroken line up through all levels of sport agencies

CSF2.15 There is an efficient, punctual decision-making structure regarding elite sport policies at all levels

CSF2.16 The board is composed of professionals who make decisions on elite sport, with relatively small management committees in the NOCs or national sport organisations so that quick decisions can be made

CSF2.17 Athletes and coaches are represented in the decision-making process of the NSA

CSF2.18 NGBs receive information and support services (other than financial) on different aspects of elite sport development

CSF2.19 Athletes and coaches are well informed about national policies, support services and other aspects

There is a structured cooperation and communication strategy with other countries, commercial partners and the media

CSF2.20 There is a structured cooperation and communication strategy with commercial partners

CSF2.21 There is a structured cooperation and communication strategy with the media

CSF2.22 There is a structured international cooperation strategy with regard to the training of athletes and the use of facilities on a regular basis

PILLAR 3: SPORT PARTICIPATION

Children have opportunities to participate in sport at school, during physical education (PE) or extra curricular activities

CSF3.1 There is a national statutory minimum amount of time for PE in nursery education

CSF 3.2 There is a national statutory minimum amount of time for PE in primary education

CSF 3.3 There is a national statutory minimum amount of time for PE in secondary education

CSF 3.4 There is a sufficiently high weekly average amount of time for PE in nursery education (in minutes per week, at least 100 minutes)

CSF 3.5 There is a sufficiently high weekly average amount of time for PE in primary education (in minutes per week, at least 100 minutes)

CSF 3.6 There is a sufficiently high weekly average amount of time for PE in secondary education (in minutes per week, at least 100 minutes)

CSF 3.7 Physical education lessons are delivered by a certified PE teacher in all grades

CSF 3.8 There are regular extra-curricular school (extra mural) sport competitions in primary education (at least 2 times/month)

CSF3.9 There are regular extracurricular (extramural) school sport competitions in secondary education (at least 2 times/month)

CSF3.10 There is an organisation/staff responsible for regular organisation and coordination of extra curricular school sport competitions

CSF3.11 School is finished early so that children get opportunities to sport during the day (or sport after school is included in the school curriculum)

There is a high general sport participation rate

CSF3.12 There is a high percentage of people who participate in sport (on a non-organised or organised basis)

CSF3.13 There is a high number of (registered) sports club members (=participation on an organised basis) (overall and per inhabitant)

CSF3.14 There is a high number of sports clubs, sufficiently spread around the country

CSF3.15 There is a high number of people who participate in sport competition

There is a national policy towards promoting the implementation of the principles of (total) quality management in sports clubs, at the level of mass participation and talent development

CSF3.16 There is a national policy implemented by the government and/or NOC, NSA towards the improvement of quality in sport clubs.

CSF3.17 There is a measurement tool to evaluate quality of clubs for youth sport.

CSF3.18 NGBs can receive funding for increased quality management projects in sport clubs

CSF3.19 There is a national policy towards improving the quality of talent development in sport clubs

CSF3.20 There is a measurement tool to evaluate the quality of talent development in sports clubs

CSF3.21 NGBs can receive funding for increased quality management linked to talent development in sports clubs

PILLAR 4: TALENT IDENTIFICATION AND DEVELOPMENT SYSTEMS

There is an effective system for the identification of young talented athletes, so that the maximum number of potential top level athletes are reached at the right time (age)

CSF4.1 There is a systematic talent selection process, which aims to identify potential elite athletes from outside a sport's participant base (non-sport specific, e.g. through schools) or by talent transfer (through other sports)

CSF4.2 NGBs can receive funding specifically for the identification (recognition and scouting) of young talented athletes and can also receive support services to plan and structure the organisation of talent spotting in their sport (e.g. staff)

CSF4.3 There is comprehensive planning for talent identification. NGBs have a written policy plan which describes a long-term planning for TID and a step-by-step how talents in their sport are recognised, identified and selected in order to receive funding

CSF4.4 The talent identification system is informed and covered by scientific research (including the socio-psychological development of children and the development of a stage-specific, individualised and balanced approach)

CSF4.5 NGBs receive sport-scientific support to develop a testing system (tests for the recognition of young talents) and monitoring system with clear criteria for the identification of young talents in each sport**

CSF4.6 NGBs have a testing battery to identify young talents and a monitoring system to follow them up, that is supported by scientific research**

CSF4.7 NGBs receive information, knowledge and support services on the development of talent identification programmes in their sport**

CSF4.8 The results of the talent-scouting process are filed in databases and are updated yearly (at least)**

CSF4.9 There is a national framework on how the talent identification and selection process has to look like (including, for example, early specialisation, diversification, maturation, relative age effect and the development of a stage-specific, individualised and balanced approach of talent identification and a long-term planning for TID)

There is nationally coordinated planning for NGBs in order to develop an effective system for the development of young talents in their sports

CSF4.10 NGBs and/or sports clubs can receive funding specifically for talent development

CSF4.11 There is a coordinated long-term and short-term planning for talent development. NGBs have a written policy plan describing step-by-step how talents in their sport are developed from club level to regional level to national level in order to receive funding

CSF4.12 National governing bodies or clubs receive information, knowledge and support services (other than financial) in order to develop their talent development programmes

CSF4.13 There is a national framework on how the talent development process has to look like (including, for example, deliberate practice, early specialisation, diversification, optimal training, . . .)

Young talents receive multidimensional support services appropriate to their age and level that are needed to develop them as young athletes at the highest level

CSF4.14 Young talents receive multidimensional support services at different levels, including training and competition support, medical/paramedical support and lifestyle support

CSF4.15 Young talents receive age-appropriate training and competition support, supervised by expert coaches with access to high standard facilities

Young talents receive nationally coordinated support for the combination of sports development and academic study during secondary education (12–16/18 years) and where relevant primary education (for early specialisation sports where such a system is required)

CSF4.16 There is a legal framework whereby young talents have their elite sport status recognised contractually by the ministry or national sports and education administration at the age that is appropriate to their sport

CSF4.17 There is a nationally coordinated system that facilitates the combination of elite sport and studies during secondary education (so that students/athletes are not dependent on variable locally implemented initiatives)

CSF4.18 There is a nationally coordinated system that facilitates the combination of elite sport and studies during primary education (so that students/athletes are not dependent on variable locally implemented initiatives for the (early specialisation) sports where such support is necessary

CSF4.19 Government or national sport agencies recognise the costs involved with this elite sport and study system in primary and secondary education, and provide the necessary financial and staff support to facilitate it

Young talents receive nationally coordinated support for the combination of sports development and academic study during higher education (university/college level)

CSF4.20 There is a legal framework whereby young talents have their elite sport status recognised contractually by either the ministry or national sports and education administration at higher education level

CSF4.21 There is a nationally coordinated system that facilitates the combination of elite sport and academic studies in higher education

CSF4.22 Government or national sport agencies recognise the costs involved with this elite sport and study system in higher education and provide the necessary financial and staff support to facilitate it

CSF4.23 The results on different tests (cognitive, anthropometry, sport abilities) that young talents have taken in elite sports schools (at secondary and higher education level) are filed in databases

PILLAR 5: ATHLETIC CAREER AND POST-CAREER SUPPORT

There is a nationally agreed definition of an elite athlete for all sports

CSF5.1 There is a standardised definition across all sports to define which athletes are eligible for support and perhaps direct funding

The individual living circumstances of athletes are sufficient so that they can concentrate on their sport full-time

CSF 5.2 Athletes' monthly income (total gross annual income) in general and income from their sport activities is sufficient

CSF 5.3 Employers are supportive towards athletes' careers

CSF 5.4 Elite sport is a full-time primary activity for elite athletes

CSF 5.5 Athletes can receive financial support that allows them to dedicate themselves sufficiently to their sport (sustain a living while preparing for and competing in elite sport)

There is a coordinated support programme for elite athletes

CSF 5.6 There is a coordinated support programme for elite athletes (apart from financial support) including career coaching, legal advice, media training, coaching support (specialist coaches), training and competition support (training facilities, training camps), sports science support (strength and conditioning, nutrition, mental coaching), sports medicine support (medical specialists, physiotherapists, etc.)

CSF 5.7 Specific personnel are appointed to guide and help athletes during their career

Athletes can receive post-career support and are adequately prepared for life after their sports career

CSF 5.8 Government/national sports bodies offer a post-career support programme to prepare and assist athletes for life after sports, such as: financial support (in the early stages) after their sports career, study support (for athletes who want to start studying or to finish their studies), job offers, advice and personal assistance (in the early stages) to find a suitable job after their sports career, lifestyle coaching, prepare for job applications, psychological support

CSF 5.9 The NSA has created specific partnerships (recruitment agency, employment agency, . . .) to guide and help athletes during and after their career

PILLAR 6: TRAINING FACILITIES

Nationally coordinated planning: sport facilities and elite sport facilities throughout the country are recorded and the needs of athletes and coaches are known and clearly mapped out

CSF 6.1 There is a database available of *sport for all*/grassroots sport facilities in the country and their characteristics regarding availability and quality (for elite sport use)

CSF 6.2 There is a database in the country of all *elite sports* facilities (infrastructure) and their characteristics regarding availability and quality

CSF 6.3 There is (research) data available on the needs of elite athletes and coaches with regard to training facilities

CSF 6.4 There is (research) data available on the travelling times of elite athletes and coaches to and from training facilities

CSF 6.5 Time spent on travelling for athletes and coaches is kept to a minimum

There is a network of high quality national/regional elite sports centre(s)/facilities, where athletes can train in appropriate conditions at any time of day

CSF 6.6 There is a sufficient number (no lack) of high quality sport facilities either exclusively for, or with prioritised use for elite sports

CSF 6.7 There is a network of high quality national/regional elite sports centre(s)/ facilities, including: an administrative headquarters; hotel facilities/overnight accommodation; a close link with sports medics; a close link with sports scientists/ cooperation with universities; and a close link with the education of younger athletes

CSF 6.8 Athletes can have full-time access to high level training facilities

CSF 6.9 There are specific national arrangements so that athletes can get priority access in certain regular sports facilities at any moment of the day

There is specific funding provided for the building and renovation of elite sport facilities

CSF 6.10 NGBs (or clubs) can receive funding for the renovation and building of sports facilities and elite sports facilities for their particular sport

PILLAR 7: COACH PROVISION AND COACH DEVELOPMENT

There is a sufficient number of well-trained and experienced elite coaches in the country

CSF 7.1 There is a database of coaches and elite coaches that is updated yearly, and contains details of qualifications and the date qualifications were achieved

CSF 7.2 There is a sufficient number of well-trained elite coaches in the country

A sufficient number of elite coaches are qualified: they have undertaken governing body training or other refresher training specifically in elite sport; and/or a training course at international level (this will partly be captured by the elite sport climate survey)

CSF 7.3 Coaches have experience at the elite level in their own career as an athlete

CSF 7.4 The NSA has a strategy for NGBs to attract the world's best coaches and external experts to train elite athletes and to improve the expertise of domestic coaches working at elite level

CSF 7.5 Athletes are satisfied on the level and expertise of their coaches during talent development and as an elite athlete

Coaches get sufficient opportunities to develop their coaching career to become a world-class elite coach

CSF 7.6 There is a nationally coordinating agency (often within the NSA) responsible for coaches' education in general and elite coach education in particular. This organisation aligns with the different levels of NGB courses and facilitates NGBs in the organisation of coach development and defines coaching profiles

CSF 7.7 There is a well-developed coach education system from the lowest level (courses for the recreational trainer/coach) to the highest level (education of elite coaches)

CSF 7.8 There are several services (such as regular refresher courses, information exchange opportunities) and resources supporting the continuous professional development of coaches

CSF 7.9 Coaches can receive specialist advice from other areas to help them improve the standard of their athletes (psychology, nutrition, physiology, biomechanics, data analysis)

CSF 7.10 Elite coaches are able to communicate and discuss their personal development as elite coaches and the development of elite athletes with other elite coaches (non-sport specific)

Coaches' individual living circumstances are sufficient for them to become professional coaches

CSF 7.11 Coaches' general monthly income (total gross annual income) plus income from their sport activities is sufficiently high to provide a good standard of living

CSF 7.12 Elite sport coaching is – or can be – a full-time primary activity for the best elite coaches. Coaches can receive direct financial support and there is a coordinated support programme for coaches that allows them to dedicate themselves sufficiently to their sport, and to spend sufficient time with their elite athletes and emerging young talents

CSF 7.13 Employers are supportive by taking into account the training needs of elite coaches

The status of coaches: the job of coaches is recognised as valuable throughout the country

CSF 7.14 The job of a coach is recognised in the country and the career prospects are high

CSF 7.15 Coaches have a written work contract for training activities; the job of a coach is contractually recognised and protected

CSF 7.16 There is a trade union for sports coaches and trainers

CSF 7.17 *Elite coaches receive a post-career support programme to prepare and assist for life after sport*

CSF 7.18 *A coaching qualification is mandatory to work in sport clubs and with young talents*

PILLAR 8: (INTER)NATIONAL COMPETITION

There is nationally coordinated planning to increase the number of international events that are organised in the country in a wide range of sports

CSF 8.1 There is a national coordination and long-term planning of event organisation and funding

CSF 8.2 NGBs and cities/municipalities or others are provided with assistance and advice on the organisation of major international sports events

CSF 8.3 NGBs and cities/municipalities or others receive funding for the bidding for, and the staging of, major international sports events

CSF 8.4 There is a high number of international events that have been organised in the country over the past five years in a (wide) range of sports for junior and senior athletes

Athletes can participate sufficiently in international (high level) events

CSF 8.5 There are sufficient opportunities for young talents to participate in international competitions, at the right age

CSF 8.6 There are sufficient opportunities for elite athletes to participate in international competitions

CSF 8.7 Young talents, athletes and coaches can receive reimbursement of their costs for participating in international competitions

The national competition has relatively high standards compared with the international standards

CSF 8.8 The national competition structure in each sport provides a competitive environment at an international top level at each age**

PILLAR 9: SCIENTIFIC RESEARCH AND INNOVATION

Scientific research is collected, coordinated and disseminated among coaches and NGBs

CSF 9.1 There is sufficient financial support for scientific research and innovation in elite sport

CSF 9.2 There is a national research centre that conducts applied elite sport research and coordinates research activities on elite sport nationally

CSF 9.3 Scientific support is provided in strong cooperation with universities and (sport) research centres

CSF 9.4 There is a specific responsibility within the NSA/national research centre for developing and coordinating innovative research projects in elite sport

CSF 9.5 There is a regularly updated database of scientific research that can be consulted by coaches and NGBs

CSF 9.6 There is a network to communicate and disseminate scientific information to the NGBs, clubs, elite athletes and coaches. Coaches receive scientific information from NGBs and other organisations and use applied sport science in their training activities

CSF 9.7 Coaches make use of sport-scientific information on elite sport, with regard to their sport

CSF9.8 Scientific research is embedded in coaches' education and coaches are taught how to search for scientific information and how to use research outcomes as part of their coaching

Sport-science support is provided at each level of elite sport development

CSF 9.9 Different areas of elite athlete development are supported by applied scientific research and innovation projects: talent identification, talent development, elite athletes (including their equipment, facilities etc.), sport policies and coaches

CSF 9.10 There are 'field laboratories' and/or embedded scientists that in situ develop, test and/or apply new technologies in cooperation with coaches and athletes at elite sport training centres

List of critical success factors used as part of talent detection and identification

TALENT DETECTION AND IDENTIFICATION

- CSF 4.1 The NGBA is able to manage and support the identification and development of potential elite athletes through a team of expert personnel and administrative support.
- CSF 4.2 There is comprehensive policy planning for talent identification and development.
- CSF 4.3 The NGBA generates financial and other support services specifically for talent identification and development of potential elite athletes.
- CSF 4.4 Clubs receive structural and financial support specifically for talent identification and development of potential elite athletes.
- CSF 4.5 Clubs are able to manage and support the talent development of potential elite athletes.
- CSF 4.6 There are different talent development plans for different disciplines.
- CSF 4.7 There are individual development pathways for potential elite athletes.
- CSF 4.8 Primary and secondary schools cooperate with local athletics club in the talent detection process of potential elite athletes.
- CSF 4.9 The NGBA cooperates with primary and secondary schools in the talent detection process by organising of school competitions.
- CSF 4.10 There are standardised test batteries used at different organisational levels.
- CSF 4.11 The identification of talented athletes is based on multidimensional characteristics during different test events.
- CSF 4.12 There is a national database on the test results of potential and successful athletes.
- CSF 4.13 There is a national scouting system for talent selection.

TALENT SELECTION AND DEVELOPMENT

■ CSF 4.14 Young potentials can make use of a discipline-specific support programme.

■ CSF 4.15 Young potentials receive age-appropriate training and competition support, supervised by expert coaches and with access to high standard facilities.

■ CSF 4.16 There are different regional and national talent pools for different age groups.

■ CSF 4.17 Selection criteria for the different regional and national talent pools are clearly expressed and communicated.

■ CSF 4.18 There is a nationally coordinated system in secondary and higher education so that athletes do not depend on individual school/college or university initiatives.

■ CSF 4.19 There are specific sport schools for athletics where young athletes can combine athletics and academic study develop during primary/secondary education.

■ CSF 4.20 Young talents in athletics receive age-appropriate training support in their educational institution.

■ CSF 4.21 Colleges and universities provide specific educational support services for young potentials.

■ CSF 4.22 Colleges and universities provide specific sport and athletic support services for young potentials.

■ CSF 4.23 Colleges and universities provide support services for the NGBA and clubs to develop young potentials.

■ CSF 4.24 Governments, the NSA and the NGBA recognise the costs for this elite sport and study system in higher education and provide the necessary financial or personnel support.

Index

Page numbers in *italics* refers to figures/tables

312